Lake Otsego

CHENANGO

NORTH BRANCH

0417

Elmira

Binghamton

CHEMUNG RIVER

Tioga River

Athens

DELAWARE RIVER

Towanda

NORTH BRANCH

Towanda Creek

LACKAWANNA RIVER

Loyalsock Creek

Lycoming Creek

Muncy Creek

Scranton

Jersey
Shore

Williamsport

Muncy

Wilkes-Barre

ntes
reek

Bloomsburg

Northumberland

Nescopeck Creek

Lewisburg

Shamokin Creek

UEHANNA
RIVER →

Sunbury

Swatara Creek

PENNSYLVANIA

doguinet Creek

Harrisburg

Conestoga
Creek

Breeches Creek

Conewago Creek

Marietta

Lancaster

Philadelphia

York

Columbia

Codorus Creek

Pequea Creek

Octoraro Creek

Delaware River

Port Deposit

NEW
JERSEY

Havre de Grace

Baltimore

Chesapeake
Bay

DELAWARE

Delaware
Bay

Susquehanna, River of Dreams

Susquehanna,

River of Dreams

Susan Q. Stranahan

The Johns Hopkins University Press

Baltimore and London

To Bill

The Johns Hopkins University Press
2715 North Charles Street
Baltimore, Maryland 21218-4319
The Johns Hopkins Press Ltd., London

Illustrations for title page and chapter openings by Barbara Seymour.
Endpaper map and map on page 10 by Kirk Montgomery.

Library of Congress Cataloging-in-Publication Data

Stranahan, Susan Q.
    Susquehanna, river of dreams / Susan Q. Stranahan.
        p.   cm.
    Includes bibliographical references and index.
    ISBN 0-8018-4602-1 (alk. paper)
    1. Susquehanna River.   2. Susquehanna River Valley.   3. Environmental protection—
Susquehanna River.   4. Natural history—Susquehanna River.   5. Water quality—
Susquehanna River.   I. Title.
    F157.S8S75   1993
    974.8—dc20   92-45039

A catalog record for this book is available from the British Library.

And when I asked the name of the river from the brakeman, and heard that it was called the Susquehanna, the beauty of the name seemed to be part and parcel of the beauty of the land . . . That was the name, as no other could be, for that shining river and desirable valley.

— *Robert Louis Stevenson*

Contents

Preface

Almost all my life has been spent in Pennsylvania, first as a youngster growing up in the western part of the state and later as a resident of Philadelphia—about as far in the opposite direction as you can go and still remain in the state I love.

Until recently, however, what I knew about the Susquehanna River was simple: It is pretty; it is big; it floods regularly; and it flows into the Chesapeake Bay.

Over the course of two decades of newspaper reporting, events along the river would draw me to places such as Wilkes-Barre, Harrisburg, Three Mile Island, or some other destination. But on those occasions the Susquehanna was little more than a backdrop for something else. Each time I returned to the river, I vowed to learn more, to explore. But like so many resolutions, this one went unfulfilled.

A few years ago, the opportunity arose to write a book, and the Susquehanna seemed a perfect subject. As I progressed with the project, the river never ceased to amaze me; nor did the people who have called it home over the centuries. The stories of the Susquehanna are mesmerizing, and they reflect the role the river has played in the nation's history from the earliest European settlements through today's decisions affecting the world we live in.

Anyone who sets out on such a voyage of exploration needs good guides, and I have been extremely fortunate. The number of people who provided information and advice is enormous. Their generosity in terms of time contributed to my quest is a measure of how much they care for the river.

My introduction to many of the people in this book was no more than: "I'm writing a book on the Susquehanna." In response, they would share a piece of their lives and reveal details and perceptions of the river and surrounding countryside that I never would have seen or understood on my own.

Others occupying these pages are old acquaintances whose knowledge of the Susquehanna's history and resources is deep. Little did they know when they volunteered to help that I would be back again and again.

There is a third group of people who graciously provided time and expertise behind the scenes, reading drafts of chapters, tracking down information, or sharing insights. Some, but by no means all, include Larry Schweiger, Fred Cropp, Maurice Hole, Tom Horton, Reds Wolman, Cheryl Riley, Bekki Guilyard, Wendy Plowman, Bill Marrazzo, and Lamont Garber.

New friend, or old, I hope that I have accurately recorded our conversations, thoroughly absorbed your instructions, and reflected in them the fascination, love, and hope we share for the Susquehanna.

One special person who taught me much about the river, and who exemplified the belief that a single person *can* make a difference even in issues as complex as protecting a watershed, sadly isn't around to see the finished product. When I began this book, the first person I sought out was Ralph Abele, and he reassured me I was embarking on a worthy mission. When Ralph died in 1990, the Susquehanna and all of Pennsylvania lost a tireless conservationist.

I began this book blithely planning on completing it in a year or so. It has taken longer than that, and I am indebted to the *Philadelphia Inquirer* for providing me two leaves of absence. Special thanks to former *Inquirer* executive editor Eugene L. Roberts who first sent me out to the Susquehanna to do extended reporting, and to his successor, Maxwell E. P. King. Both understand the value of giving daily journalists an opportunity to stretch their wings.

Thanks also are in order for the many librarians in Pennsylvania, Maryland, and New York, who never tired of looking for obscure bits of data to fill in some missing detail about the Susquehanna and its inhabitants. Leading the list is the staff at the *Inquirer* library, who assisted my rambles among the old clips and photographs. The librarians at the James V. Brown Library in Williamsport, the Ousterhout Free Library in Wilkes-Barre, the Enoch Pratt Library in Baltimore, the Mariam Coffin Canaday Library at Bryn Mawr College, the Pennsylvania State Archives, the Canal Museum of the Pennsylvania Canal Society in Easton, and at a dozen or more small libraries and historical societies along the Susquehanna also gave freely of their time.

Finally, special thanks are due a few individuals who played critical roles in this effort. Among them are my long-time friends and colleagues at the *Inquirer,* Donald L. Barlett and James B. Steele, who never once failed to drop what they were doing to offer invaluable help and encouragement.

Mary Lowe Kennedy, who read this manuscript with her keen eye, made scores of wonderfully thoughtful and helpful suggestions. And, then there is J. G. Goellner, director of the Johns Hopkins University Press and my editor, whose wise counsel and enthusiasm for this book were unmatched. To these four friends, I am sincerely grateful.

Susquehanna, River of Dreams

Prologue

Rivers offer the perfect framework for a storyteller. They provide a beginning and an end with an obvious flow from one to the other. They neatly link people and events in history. They serve as paths of discovery and arteries of commerce. Not only can rivers be counted on for moments of great drama, but they also invariably attract their share of eccentric characters. So it is with the Susquehanna.

The Susquehanna is not simply a framework on which to hang a story, but the story itself. This river possesses an uncanny ability to fire the imagination, to stir the senses, to inspire dreams. It is a living thing, quirky and independent. No matter how frequently you travel beside it, or how patient a vigil you maintain on its edge, the river is ever-changing, a source of constant surprise, revealing or concealing intriguing bits of information, drawing you along with its ceaseless movement, urging you to take up the journey. The Susquehanna is a writer's wellspring—generous, beckoning, majestic.

This, then, is the Susquehanna's story. It also is the story of people who struggled mightily to transform the river into something nature never intended, often at a terrible price. Indeed, the history of the Susquehanna is one of repeated assaults—by humans *and* by the river. The early race to control the riches of the Susquehanna extracted a toll. Canal builders diverted water and erected obstacles that impeded those who once traveled the river freely. Waves of loggers and miners laid bare the hillsides and opened veins of coal. The river retaliated with rampaging floods, but ultimately descended into squalor, choked with filth from the towns and industries that grew along its banks.

Today's problems appear more subtle, but nevertheless pose daunting challenges to the Susquehanna. Even such a seemingly benign neighbor as farming has inflicted serious harm. Experts are only beginning to understand the mysterious synergies that operate in the fragile ecosystem dominated by the Susquehanna. One thing has become obvious, however. The focus of responsibility has shifted. No longer is it a simple matter of pointing to someone else and affixing blame. Rather, the mundane daily decisions made by all who live within its vast watershed will determine the future of this beautiful river.

The Susquehanna is a study in contrasts, clean and healthy along much of its length, but in a few places so polluted that nothing can survive. It flows through some of the wildest country remaining in the Northeast, yet elsewhere a population boom jeopardizes its well-being. A century and more ago, poets, artists, and writers here and abroad celebrated small details of the Susquehanna; today, few Americans could even describe its route with certainty.

The Susquehanna is the longest nonnavigable river in North America. Although it was never important as an avenue of commerce, its vast drainage basin supplied the raw materials that fueled this nation's growth from a colony to a world power. Some of the richest coal deposits and most fertile farmland in the world lie along its banks. The finest timber on the planet once blanketed its hillsides. The struggle over who would profit from the riches of the Susquehanna influenced the political landscape of the young United States for more than a century. In the quest, blood was spilled and fortunes were made and depleted. And in the end, the Susquehanna was nearly destroyed.

Measured in numbers alone, the Susquehanna is an impressive resource. The river drains 27,500 square miles, an area larger than Vermont, New Jersey, Massachusetts, and Delaware combined, and just as disparate, with rugged mountain ridges, tidal marshlands, broad, fertile valleys, and high, rocky plateaus. The Susquehanna basin is so large it experiences marked variations in climate, with average annual temperatures differing by almost ten degrees. The river drains almost half of Pennsylvania and 13 percent of New York State.

The Susquehanna is shaped like a free-form Y, with a West Branch, a North Branch, and the main stem flowing from their union. The West Branch curves east-northeast for much of its 240-mile length before dropping southeast to a rendezvous with the North Branch at Northumberland, near the center of Pennsylvania. The North Branch meanders for about 324 miles in an S-shaped curve out of New York and back again before finally returning to Pennsylvania. Once united, the Susquehanna flows another 111 miles south, then southeast, entering Maryland for the final 12 miles of its journey before it joins the Chesapeake Bay.

Approximately 448 miles separate the river's northernmost point, at Lake Otsego in Cooperstown, New York, from its mouth at Havre de

Grace on the Chesapeake. The Susquehanna is the Chesapeake's largest tributary, providing 90 percent of the fresh water to the upper half of the bay, 50 percent of all the fresh water in the estuary. No other eastern U.S. river delivers more water to the Atlantic Ocean than the Susquehanna. On an average day, that amounts to 25 billion gallons—enough water to supply the needs of every household in the United States, with a billion gallons left over. In time of flood, the Susquehanna once sent 650 billion gallons roaring into the Chesapeake in a single day, nearly twice the amount consumed in twenty-four hours by every water user in the United States—industry, business, utility, household, and farm. But during days of extreme drought the river has delivered as little as 2 billion gallons of water to the huge estuary that depends on the Susquehanna for its very existence.

The Susquehanna has influenced the lives of all who have lived along its banks. The names chosen by European settlers reflect not only the characteristics of the river and its tributaries, but also the abundant resources along them. Seven creeks are named for the pine that once flourished. There are four Mill Creeks, four Roaring Creeks or some variation thereof, and six Muddy Creeks. Five creeks are named for elk and four each for buffalo and beaver. Five contain the name "Fishing" and two were named for trout.

In that regard, these newcomers to the Susquehanna were doing what Native Americans had done for centuries. Their choice of place names served as geographic reference points along the river's route. Lycoming means "sandy or gravelly creek"; Tioga, "the forks of a stream" or, perhaps, "the place where two rivers meet"; and Wyoming, a corruption of Indian names meaning "the river of extensive flats" or the valley of "extensive plains or meadows."

No one is certain about the origin of the Susquehanna's name, or even its precise meaning. Translations are often at odds, as are spellings. By all accounts, the suffix *-hanna* is Algonquin, meaning "stream" or "river," and can be attributed to the fact that the interpreters accompanying Capt. John Smith on his exploratory visit to the river in 1608 spoke Algonquin. Smith subsequently identified the natives who greeted him as Sasquesahannocks and Sasquesahanougs. The tribe eventually became known as Susquehannocks.

An eighteenth-century authority on Indian and place names claimed that *Susquehanna* was a corruption of the Susquehannock word *Queischachgekhanne*, meaning "the long reach river," a name then used to refer to the West Branch. Others speculate that the word means "long crooked river," and a few even favor "the place of the straight river," based on a translation of the Delaware word *saskwihanang*. A Moravian missionary who traveled extensively in the region declared the name *Susqueh* to mean "mud," and at least one historian speculated that a European visitor had overheard a native observe, "How muddy the stream is!" and took that to be the name.

The meaning of its name is just one of the mysteries about the Susquehanna that have perplexed those drawn to its banks for generations. Geologists still range along the river looking for explanations about the formation of the East Coast. Biologists study the puzzling habits of migratory fish in hopes of restoring premier species such as shad to this and other rivers. And scores of scientists are now striving to unlock the secrets of the river in a monumental effort to rescue the Chesapeake Bay.

In some instances, the Susquehanna has relinquished its secrets willingly. In others, however, it clings to them tenaciously. Those who claim to *know* the river are fooling themselves, as the Susquehanna has demonstrated time and again. There are things about the river that are meant to remain a mystery forever.

This is the story of the Susquehanna.

Chapter One

Geology

"Nature's handiwork on display"

Ask a resident of Cooperstown, New York, where the Susquehanna River begins and you get a quick answer: "Head down Main Street, turn left on River Street and walk as far as you can go." There, spilling from the toe of Lake Otsego, is the newborn North Branch, a small stream setting out on its long journey to the Chesapeake Bay. But ask a native of Carrolltown, Pennsylvania, where the river's West Branch starts and you'll very likely spark a debate. On maps, the thin blue vein that is the West Branch first appears just outside that small Cambria County coal-mining town. But exactly *where* is the source?

When the question is put to the mechanic at the Mobil station on Main Street, he apologizes for not knowing but volunteers to find the answer. "John," he calls to a customer just pulling up to the pump, "you know this area. Where does the Susquehanna begin?" Soon all gas sales and automotive repairs are forgotten as they discuss possibilities. The vicinity of Laurel Lick Run seems to be their favorite, but . . . The visitor moves on as the debate continues. Down the street, the attendant at Holtz's Sunoco shares none of the doubts that seized the Mobil folks. "It's off Route 219 near the Old Farm Inn," the young man says, wiping his hands on a red cloth. "Go out there and ask at the inn."

The Old Farm Inn sits at a curve in the road, and its few late-morning customers are drinking coffee or having an early lunch. "You're in the right place," says the bartender, putting away glasses. "Just walk around the bend, past the barn, and you'll see a dirt road off to the left. Walk down it. That's the beginning of the Susquehanna."

Like much else around this region, the barn and the field behind it have seen better days. If this *is* the place, then the West Branch of the Susquehanna—a river that has made people millionaires, devastated whole communities with stupendous floods, and rebounded from grievous depredations—springs from a rusty pipe sticking out of a hill in a rocky, badly eroded pasture inhabited by two tan draft horses. The Susquehanna spills into a battered white bathtub-turned-watering-trough and then splashes out on some weeds before beginning its arc-shaped journey to Northumberland, 240 miles away.

Additional confirmation seems in order. Perhaps at the Carrolltown Borough Hall? "If anybody should know the answer to your question," says the balding clerk there, "it's Frank Buck. He knows everything." Mr. Buck, the retired borough secretary, is located by phone. The question is put to him. "Well, it's always been a point of some contention among the people around here," he says cheerfully. "Everybody likes to think the Susquehanna begins on their property. I'd say the general view is it starts there behind the Old Farm Inn. The only other possibility is the farm just up the road." Hmm. The logical course of action seems to be to actually find the infant river somewhere downstream and trace it to its source.

The Susquehanna appears along Carrolltown Road as a littered gully in swampy woods. "That's the river, all right," says a passing motorist. Asked if he knows where it starts, he replies, "Oh sure. Up in an old railroad tunnel. Just drive back in along the abandoned rail bed and you'll come to it eventually." The tunnel, with water seeping down its stone façade, is not far from the rear of the Old Farm Inn, but it has nothing to do with the pipe in the pasture.

Which is the real source? Could there be even *another* contender? Certainly the nation's official mapmakers, the U.S. Geological Survey, should have the answer. Or the U.S. Army Corps of Engineers. "The source of the West Branch of the Susquehanna? I don't know if that question comes up too often," says a spokesman at the Geological Survey office in Harrisburg. "Talk to Bob Helm in our office. He'll know."

"I don't know," admits Helm. "Did you try the state? There's a chance that they have a handle on that. They publish a gazetteer of streams which lists every major stream in the state. Try that. You might also try the Susquehanna River Basin Commission; they certainly should know."

The *Pennsylvania Gazetteer of Streams* lists 571 streams, including 257 tributaries of the Susquehanna River, and details each one's source, drainage area, meander ratio, physiography, and course. However, the West Branch of the Susquehanna isn't among them. "That's because it's a river," explained a state official familiar with the gazetteer's preparation. "And we don't have a gazetteer of rivers."

As for the Army Corps of Engineers, which has made three surveys of the West Branch over the years . . . well, they can't even agree on the length of the river, let alone its starting point.[1]

1. The Corps's 1954 survey reported that the West Branch "rises in Cambria County, Pa." and flows 240 miles east. In 1930, the Corps said the river began in "the Allegheny Plateau"

Presumably the Susquehanna River Basin Commission, the government agency charged with managing the watershed, would know where its jurisdiction begins. The question is put to Richard Cairo, secretary of the commission. "*National Geographic* had an article some time ago about the Susquehanna and it had a map. I think we just use that." The *National Geographic* map is as vague as the state road map and the Rand McNally atlas.

Back at the U.S. Geological Survey, hydrogeologist Lloyd Reed offers to resolve the debate. "Oh, I can show you," he says. Tracing land contours on a topographic map of Carrolltown, he quickly works his way up the fine blue line that is the West Branch, eliminating tributaries as he goes. For a minute, he considers the local favorite, the Old Farm Inn site. Then he rejects it and instead chooses his own candidate: a tiny pond that empties into a creek north of Carrolltown Road. "That's it," Reed proclaims.

The question finally answered, his visitor turns to leave. "But I'm just guessing," he adds. "Why don't you just say it starts around Carrolltown."

The West Branch of the Susquehanna River starts around Carrolltown, in a bowl-shaped valley. For the next 240 miles, the West Branch reveals pieces of its history for those who take the time to look.

Rivers have always provided a particularly inviting place to study the evolution of the earth and its inhabitants. As natural trade routes, they lured the earliest civilized humans, who left fascinating traces along their banks. And as nature's bulldozers, rivers have exposed otherwise hidden secrets of the earth, enabling geologists to piece together the colossal histories of continents.

Even rivers as tiny as the West Branch in its first few miles of travel can contribute. One reason its source is so hard to trace is that the surrounding landscape has been carved by many such streams, giving it the texture of a wadded-up newspaper that has been spread flat again. In the crevices, many rivulets are still at work, eating through beds of sandstone, shale, limestone, and conglomerates that were laid down 280 to 325 million years ago—about the time the first reptiles appeared on Earth.

Other parts of the Susquehanna offer vastly different landscapes. In the north it flows through glacier country, marked by moraines, boulders, terraces, and, in one place, a large buried valley. Sometimes the river cuts through plateaus whose rock layers are as orderly as a stack of bond paper;

---

and flowed 228 miles. Back in 1890, the engineers had the river beginning in Clearfield County and its length 125 miles.

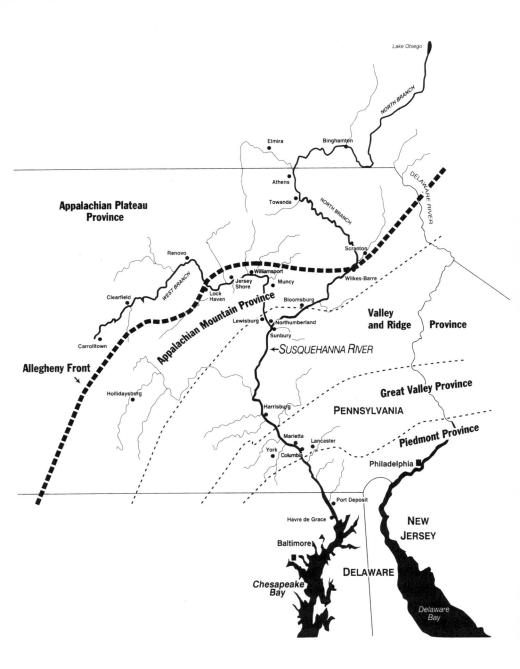

Geologic provinces of the Susquehanna River Basin.

in other places there is puzzling disorder, evidence that millions of years of geological history have somehow been erased. Along its lower end, the river lays bare rocks that give tortured witness to convulsive periods of mountain-building. In between lies the handiwork of erosion: distinctive ridges and canoe-shaped valleys.

But while the Susquehanna offers an unusually thorough record of the events that have shaped the Earth in the past billion years, it stubbornly withholds certain crucial details. The river presents a set of tantalizing mysteries that stir great debates among geologists and bring them back again and again: Why did the river cut through five sandstone ridges north of Harrisburg? And how? Why not go around them, like a normal lazy river? Did the river once flow north? If so, why did it reverse course? What carved the spoon-shaped "deeps" in the riverbed at the Susquehanna Gorge? And why do they occupy just one side of the river?

And the one that spawned the longest-running geologic debate in North America: What created the formations south of Columbia—a titanic upthrust along the edge of the continent, or is it merely a freak sequence of rocks?

Says William Sevon of the Pennsylvania Geological Survey, who has spent most of his professional life pondering the Susquehanna: "There are plenty of holes in the mystery story that we may never fill."

While the Susquehanna stubbornly guards its secrets, it also is a show-off, providing plenty of examples of the forcefulness and subtleties of nature. "Great raw theater" is how Ben Marsh describes the geology of the Susquehanna. Marsh, an assistant professor of geography at Bucknell University in Lewisburg, takes his classes on regular field trips along the river.

His course consists of basic geology with heavy doses of geography, environmentalism, and pop sociology. "It's my job not only to teach my students how geology affects our lives, but how humans affect the landscapes," explains Marsh, an energetic man with shaggy hair and bright blue eyes who began teaching at Bucknell in 1979. The two trips he had planned for his students this week would do just that. The destinations are an abandoned coal mine and a pretty limestone valley.

Once the bus heads into the countryside around Lewisburg, all the lectures the students have heard about uplift and erosion, sedimentary and metamorphic rocks, folding and faulting suddenly come alive outside the windows. "It never fails," says Marsh.

The best way to picture the geology of the Susquehanna watershed is to imagine a rumpled rug. This analogy was probably first used by George A. Ashley, who headed Pennsylvania's Geological Survey from 1919 to 1946. In his graceful literary style, he compared the state's landscape to "a pile of rugs spread out on the floor [and] pushed from one end"—the southeast. As the corner of the pile is pushed, tight wrinkles form, spreading out from the source of the pressure, and eventually becoming loose waves. Beyond the final upthrusts, the rugs lie smooth and undisturbed.

The terrain traversed by the Susquehanna is just like that, with gnarled rock structures near its mouth, rolling hills and valleys farther upstream, the parallel summits of the Appalachian Mountains behind them, and, finally, the flat highlands of western Pennsylvania and central New York, known as the Appalachian Plateau.

Ashley was unable to explain back in 1933 what had pushed the "rug." It would be another three decades before geologists generally agreed on the cause. They called it "plate tectonics," and it was a revolution in the science. Suddenly dozens of pieces in the worldwide geological jigsaw puzzle fit together, recalls Bill Sevon, who was just beginning his career with the state Geological Survey at the time.

Plate tectonics now is as fundamental to the science of geology as Darwin's theory of evolution is to biology. It says that the Earth's surface consists of continent-sized "plates" that continuously move and occasionally collide. Today, scientists believe that much of the Susquehanna's unique geology is the result of Africa's slamming into the side of North America (in geological slow motion, of course) about 250 to 300 million years ago. Indeed, satellite photographs of the ridges in southeastern Pennsylvania show that their bends fit exactly with the western coast of Africa. So strong was the impact off the present-day coast of New Jersey that a mountain range equal to the Himalayas was heaved upward, rocks inland were melted and transformed, and great sheets of rock were broken or thrust atop one another. To the northwest, flat rocks were bent into a rollercoaster topography.

In the Susquehanna watershed, the impact created a series of physiographic provinces, spreading concentrically from the point of impact. The Piedmont at the southern end, with its complex rock formations twisted and baked by enormous pressures, gives way to the Great Valley Province and then the Valley and Ridge Province. On the northwestern perimeter of the Valley and Ridge Province lie the Appalachian Mountains, and beyond them the sharp demarcation of the Allegheny Front. Finally, there is the relatively undisturbed Appalachian Plateau. Most of the Susquehanna's watershed lies in the Plateau and the Valley and Ridge provinces.

All this is deceptively simple, the stuff of grade-school science texts. And if that's all there was to the geology of the region, Bill Sevon and his colleagues wouldn't have spent nearly twenty years assembling the Pennsylvania Geological Survey's most recent map of the state, which identifies the rock structures underlying this mix of topography. Along the lower end of the Susquehanna, for example, more than sixty different rock formations are identified, zigging and zagging, surfacing and submerging in a colorful mosaic. That part of the map resembles a television set with a malfunctioning vertical hold.

The 1980 map, the latest addition to more than a century and a half of geologic research in Pennsylvania, represents the most current interpretation of an enormous amount of data. Even so, says Sevon with a sigh, "we may not understand what we see." Then, brightening, he adds, "But we know that eventually it will fit into the larger picture if we keep working on it."

The collision of the East Coast and Africa was what geologists call an orogeny, and it was the fourth to occur in the 2,000-mile-long belt stretching from Newfoundland to Alabama. In an orogeny, continental plates collide and the edge of one is pushed up over the other, creating mountains. Those then slowly erode, and the landscape becomes flatter and flatter until the next orogeny. On the East Coast of North America, the first orogeny occurred about a billion years ago, and the last, known as the Alleghenian Orogeny, about 200 to 300 million years ago. As with the other mountain-building episodes, erosion began immediately, with billions of tons of sediments eventually washing down the face of the mountains. Due to the prevailing slope of the land, drainage across much of the continent was to the north and west, and the ancestors of the Susquehanna dutifully transported sediments in that direction, cutting into the soft, nascent rock layers as they went.

As the mountains were worn down, their weight decreased, and the surface of the land rose, hastening the erosive processes and enabling the streams to cut more boldly through the rocks. Ultimately, sediments buried the rocks that the orogeny had pushed into folds, and the Susquehanna drainage basin became nearly level, its streams placidly meandering across the surface. They presumably still flowed to the northwest—but that is not certain. In fact, the exact course of the Susquehanna at this time (150 million years ago, or so) has been the subject of much controversy. The five ridges that cross the river north of Harrisburg are the reason.

Even the first European settlers who ventured upriver, people who knew nothing of geology, were struck by the anomaly of these ridges. They simply defy every rule of geology—*and* logic. Instead of avoiding the hard sandstone that forms these hills in its path, the Susquehanna attacked them frontally to win its freedom for the journey south. Experts still find the sight remarkable.

"Rivers basically are the laziest things on earth," said Frank Pazzaglia, a young geologist at Pennsylvania State University who had pulled his pickup truck off busy Route 322 to once again view the gaps in the mountains. "Why the Susquehanna did this, nobody can figure out."

And this is not the river's only peculiar stretch. It also cuts through a mountain on the North Branch near Wilkes-Barre. For geologists, these oddities raise two questions: Which was there first—the river or the mountains? And which way was the river flowing when its assaults on the mountains began? Geologists believe they know, but the answers were gleaned from information collected along the entire length of the Susquehanna. Even the first few miles of a river reveal a lot about what it will become.

The clear water spilling from Lake Otsego to form the North Branch of the Susquehanna will, under normal conditions, take six days to reach the Chesapeake, 448 miles away. Few of the throngs of visitors to Cooperstown trek to the pretty lakefront park to wish the river well on its journey. The crowds congregate elsewhere, paying homage to the town's other attraction, the dazzling monument to the heroes of baseball. That may be just as well, for at its origin here, just as on the West Branch, the Susquehanna seems as promising as an undersized, just-off-the-bus farm-team hopeful.

Ringed by forested hills, Otsego is long and narrow, the largest natural lake in the Susquehanna basin.[2] Like its nearby cousins, the Finger Lakes, Otsego was gouged out of rocks by glaciers. The retreating ice also left the region filled with bogs, springs, and swampy lakes that help feed the young river.

Within minutes of escaping the lake, the Susquehanna starts meandering southward through the gentle highlands of the Appalachian Plateau; half the river's 27,500-square-mile drainage basin lies within this physiographic province. Although the underlying rocks are like those on the West Branch—sandstone and shale—the countryside in New York is different because of the glaciers. The valleys on the North Branch are wider, more open, as a result of the grinding of the ice sheets, and the valley floors

---

2. Lake Otsego was "Glimmerglass" in the writing of native son James Fenimore Cooper.

are full of rocky debris. As it ventures out across these highlands, the Susquehanna passes dairy farms, trim houses, fields of corn, and meadows full of summer wildflowers, landscapes so pastoral and American they seem crafted by Norman Rockwell. The river is part of people's lives here, winding through towns and luring residents to its shady banks for fishing, a swim, or a nap.

Some geologists date the birth of the Susquehanna in New York to about 300 million years ago, when the surface of the state gradually began to emerge from a shallow sea that had formed to the west. Others say it is far younger, only about 60 million years old, born after the last great uplift of land. This uplift hastened the processes of erosion, reinvigorating streams grown sluggish during millions of years of flowing over plains. Across the Appalachian Plateau, the streams cut deep valleys through the soft rock, voraciously eating their way backwards like a gully in a downpour, capturing weaker waterways and growing larger with each conquest.

Glaciers, which made three passes over this region before their final retreat 10,000 years ago, obliterated certain clues to the river's northern origins. Some geologists believe that the Susquehanna began in the Adirondacks and flowed south, but was "captured" when the Mohawk River crossed its path and stole its waters. Others believe it avoided the Mohawk but flowed southeast, merging with the Delaware River. Only about ten miles separate the Susquehanna and the Delaware at their closest point in southern New York.

Either course was only temporary, geologically speaking, for the glaciers carved their own landscapes and again transformed the Susquehanna. As the ice receded, unsorted rocks—known as till—blocked many of the stream channels. The Susquehanna was one of the impounded rivers that engorged with glacial meltwater and eventually burst through the till to find their old courses or create entirely new ones.

The velocity of the water must have been extraordinary, unlike any deluge humans have experienced, even on the flood-prone Susquehanna. In Tioga County on Pennsylvania's northern border, a lake carved by glaciers suddenly broke through a ridge at its southern end, and the pent-up waters roared out, carving the 800- to 1,000-foot deep Pine Creek Gorge, which extends for fifty miles and today is known as the Grand Canyon of Pennsylvania.

The Susquehanna appears to be in no hurry to leave the gently rolling countryside of south-central New York, winding back and forth through the wooded hills like a tourist out for a Sunday drive. Then it seems to have a change of heart, veering into Pennsylvania and just as suddenly veering north again, creating a fifteen-mile detour known, aptly, as the Great Bend.

At Binghamton, the Susquehanna is joined by the Chenango, one of its major upstream tributaries. On it flows across heavily glaciated landscapes to the New York–Pennsylvania border, where the towns of Waverly, Sayre, and Athens intertwine.[3] Here, the beautiful Chemung, sweeping in a grand curve from the northwest, empties into the Susquehanna. By now, the Susquehanna has traveled 165 miles and bears faint resemblance to the quiet stream that departed Cooperstown. Its banks are broad cobble, its waters dark and swift-running. The few bridges that span it are built high and wide to give latitude to the temperamental Susquehanna during times of flooding.

It was at the junction of the Susquehanna and the Chemung that Indian travelers paused to camp and trade, for in addition to the stunning natural beauty and bounty of the place, the river valley served as a ready-made highway. The Chemung branches deep into rich fur country, and the Susquehanna gave access to the fertile northeast.

Between the river's edge and the rolling hills are high, broad terraces, the rocky residue of glacial ice. This feature prevails along much of the Susquehanna, for even though the glacial advance halted around Berwick on the North Branch and north of Williamsport on the West Branch, the tempestuous waters carried rocks large and small to the south. Today, these terraces provide a ready supply of raw materials for sand-and-gravel quarries.

Once in Pennsylvania for its second visit, the Susquehanna flows nearly due south until it reaches Towanda, where it begins a series of wide turns in a deep, narrow valley whose walls rise 500 feet above the water. This portion of the river intrigues geologists like Bill Sevon, who believe it is far newer than the rest, carved through the rock by ice-engorged meltwaters seeking an outlet. Whatever its origins, the river did a service for future inhabitants by cutting a passage through the rugged country. Indian trails followed its bank, eventually being replaced by narrow wagon tracks and, finally, the railroad and highway.

As the Susquehanna nears Wilkes-Barre, it leaves the soft rocks of the Appalachian Plateau and meets for the first time the more resistant sand-

---

3. One of the oddest remnants of the area's geological history exists here, and its presence intrigued early settlers and inspired local legends. Spanish Hill, a 200-foot-tall mound rising from the valley floor, was widely believed to have been a battlement for Susquehannock Indian warriors—or maybe Spaniards who, according to legend, explored the Susquehanna in the late sixteenth century. The hill is, in fact, nothing more than a monadnock—an outcropping of rock that somehow withstood the grinding action of the glaciers.

stone and conglomerate ridges of the Appalachian Mountains. And then, as it flows into the Wyoming Valley, 270 miles from Cooperstown, the Susquehanna suddenly comes of age.

Its upstream milieu of charming villages and attractive farms ends abruptly as the river breaks through Peterson Mountain at Exeter and makes a 90-degree turn into one of the most densely developed regions in the watershed. Humans extracted a terrible toll on the Susquehanna here, but the river has wreaked its own revenge—assisted in large measure by the odd geology of its seventeen-mile course through this part of the Wyoming Valley.

Geologists speculate that this dogleg turn into the valley developed after a young stream to the southwest—the main stem of the Susquehanna today—began advancing through a long bed of soft red shale, capturing small streams in its path, working its way northeast. In a final act of piracy, the hungry river tapped into the side of a stream flowing to the Delaware, diverting it from that basin and creating the mighty North Branch system that exists today.

Like many valleys in the region, the Wyoming is canoe-shaped. A sandstone mountain 600 feet high to the north and another nearly 1,500 feet high to the south shelter rich bottomlands that lured early settlers. These new arrivals eventually discovered that they were residing atop a colossal resource—billions of tons of anthracite coal.

The North Branch and a major tributary, the Lackawanna River, enter opposite each other about three-quarters of the way down the Wyoming Valley. The valley itself is sixty-five miles long, stretching northeast into the Pocono Mountains. Glacial activity here was intense. The rocky summit of Penobscot Mountain, which forms the valley's southern rim, is scratched by ice, and in places is barren of vegetation because glaciers stripped away the topsoil.

The Susquehanna portion of the Wyoming Valley is, in fact, much larger and deeper than it looks—a fact that has greatly complicated life here. Beneath the river lies a "buried valley." This hidden valley was formed when glacial ice became trapped between the mountains, prevented from moving on downstream by the ridge of hard rocks that forms the down-stream end of the valley at Nanticoke. As the ice melted, hydraulic forces increased, churning deeper and deeper into the rocks underneath, until the water carved a channel a mile wide and perhaps 300 feet below the current valley floor. The water was filled with rocks, which could not escape and remained in the valley. Streams flowing through the rubble into this deep channel created deltas, which remain as terraces.

The existence of this buried valley has long been known to those who mine coal, for it dramatically increases the risks of digging beneath the river. Normally, there would be a predictable layer of rocks above the coal seams; here, there often exists instead a jumbled assortment of loose boulders and sediments. Misjudgments about the strength of strata separating the river from a mine shaft have claimed dozens of lives.

Even before the first white settlers arrived, Indians used the Wyoming Valley as a favorite campsite, for its geology made access easily controllable; visitors came by river or they did not come at all, so impassable were the surrounding mountains. The valley did have one drawback: its propensity to flood. By the time the Susquehanna enters the Wyoming Valley, it is carrying the waters accumulated from more than 9,500 square miles of Pennsylvania and New York. When this drainage area is inundated by heavy rains and spring meltwater, the river swells into a torrent, sweeps down the valley—and then stalls when it encounters the gorge at Nanticoke, backing up rapidly just as the glacial water did. Land on the nearby hillsides (actually the terraces left behind by the glacial action) is in short supply, so most inhabitants of the 2½-mile-wide valley have built on the bottomlands—and await the next flood.

In its farewell to the Wyoming Valley, the river shows its muscle once again. It arrived by cutting through hard rock and it exits the same way, slicing through Lee and Penobscot mountains before reaching the broad valley and gravel-terraced banks that are home to Berwick and Bloomsburg. The Susquehanna has a free ride for the next sixty miles, through the softly rolling terrain of central Pennsylvania. Farms reappear and the countryside is reminiscent of that back in New York State.

As it heads southwest, the Susquehanna passes the Western Middle Anthracite Field, a separate field from that under the Wyoming Valley. This is Ben Marsh's destination for the day.

As the Bucknell bus rolls east along Shamokin Creek en route to anthracite country, the topography changes abruptly from hilly farmland to narrow valley. The towns grow increasingly small and impoverished—in striking contrast to the charming, prosperous university town of Lewisburg. Then, as the bus rounds a curve, looming through the windshield is what Ben Marsh calls "the world's largest pile of coal waste." Towering over the gap that Shamokin Creek had cut through a ridge, the sight of the black mountain of coal rubble, known as culm, silences the quiet chatter of students in the rear of the bus. For most, it is their first glimpse of the physical toll mining has taken on this region.

Soon the students are standing outside a long-closed mine whose boarded-up portal proclaims "Nov. 1934." Out from under the boards gushes brilliant rust-orange water that exudes the distinct odor of sulfur— the warning signs of a toxic brew. When water seeps into these old mines, sulfur in the rocks combines with iron and oxygen to produce the poisonous liquid, which pollutes streams, kills vegetation, and taints wells.

Drinking water for the local communities must be transported in from another valley, says Marsh, standing in front of the mine entrance leaning on the narrow spade he carries as a pointer, walking stick, and probe. "Last year somebody on this trip discovered a groundhog here, half in the water and half out," he says, gesturing downstream. "The top half had gone the way of all flesh. It was just a skeleton, but the bottom half in the water was pickled, like those things in bars in the jars."

The next stop is Bear Valley, legendary among geologists as one of the best places in the United States to see the powerful forces of nature. Trooping down a trail, Marsh leads the procession to an old open-pit anthracite mine. As the path turns, spreading before the hikers is an amazing display of sheer rock faces, tightly bent and twisted into the downward swoops called synclines and the upward folds known as anticlines.

A coal vein, visible on the east wall, is bent into a tight V. Scrambling over the crumbled shale that covers the ground, Marsh leads the students to the top of a rounded anticline known as Whaleback. So extreme were the twisting forces exerted on these rocks that an anticline abuts a syncline, a geologic anomaly.

Layers of coal once covered most of Pennsylvania—and at first they were nearly horizontal. They still are in the Appalachian Plateau, where the West Branch of the Susquehanna flows through sprawling deposits of soft, or bituminous, coal. Similar layers of coal once existed in the eastern portion of Pennsylvania, but the forces that created the Valley and Ridge Province had two consequences. One force was erosion, which washed most of the coal away—perhaps a hundred tons for every ton that remained. The only coal that survived was buried deep in the downward folds of the rocks. The second force was the gigantic pressure of the orogeny that created those folds. It also cooked the soft coal, converting it to the shiny hard anthracite that exists nowhere else in the United States. Approximately 7 billion tons of anthracite coal have been mined from these hills since the 1700s. An estimated 20 billion tons remain, but the difficulty and cost of extracting it from the contorted rocks have all but ensured it will stay underground.

The Susquehanna inspired dreams among all who saw it. Some visions wre rooted in reality. Others, such as this 1872 engraving from a series entitled "Picturesque America," are pure fantasy.

"River Rocks" by Lloyd Mifflin *(opposite, top)*. Born in 1846 in Columbia, Pa., Mifflin drew on the Susquehanna for his inspiration as an artist and poet. A descendant of the Wright family, which settled along the river in 1726, Mifflin was fascinated by the Susquehanna's "amethystine islands" and rugged rock formations. (The State Museum of Pennsylvania, Pennsylvania Historical and Museum Commission, with permission)

"The Invasion of the North—Destruction of the Bridge over the Susquehanna, at Columbia, Pa." *(opposite, bottom)*. Published in *Harper's Weekly,* July 18, 1863. Confederate troops, bound for Philadelphia, reached the bridge only to encounter local militia intent on blocking their advance. Vastly outnumbered, the locals first attempted to blow up the mile-long bridge. When that failed, they set it ablaze.

21

Ben Marsh's teaching duties done for the day, he and a friend venture out across the countryside around Lewisburg, concluding their tour at the promontory in Shikellamy State Park, which overlooks the union of the West Branch with the North. Peering down at the junction of the rivers in the late afternoon sunshine, Marsh observes, "This is the perfect place to have a town. The Indians knew that and the first settlers did, too."

Indeed, Northumberland, situated at the point formed by the two branches, was once an important river town. One of the largest Indian settlements on the Susquehanna was here. Joseph Priestley, the discoverer of oxygen, moved to Northumberland from England in 1794, and set up a small laboratory in the wilderness. Some of the world's finest timber, cut from hills upstream, floated past here en route to market. Thomas Edison found local investors willing to underwrite his experiments in electric lighting. Corporate empires were founded on the coal veins lying beneath these hills. Northumberland became a major rail hub, and nearby communities prosperous manufacturing centers.

But the miles of track and switching yards along the riverbanks are now nearly abandoned. The once-grand buildings of Sunbury, just downstream, are faded or empty. In recent years, the factories and mines have closed, jobs have gone elsewhere. Today, residents regard the Susquehanna only as a source of recreation and floods.

As they join, the two rivers tell the story of their travels. The West Branch has journeyed primarily through forests and is green and clear. The North Branch carries the murky brown scars of its 324-mile passage, the last leg of which passed through abandoned coal fields, drained by polluted streams. It will be many miles before these colors mix and disappear.

Geologically, the West Branch is a far simpler river than the North Branch. Glaciers occupied only its northernmost tributaries, and the rocks along its route were spared intensive folding. The dominant geologic event that occurred here is impossible to see: massive erosion of the layers of sandstone and shale that leveled land surfaces. As billions of tons of sediments were carried away, the entire region lifted and erosion began anew, forming deep valleys. The result: a series of uniform, flat-topped hills that rise 2,300 feet above sea level. Climb up one of the sheer valley sides to the crest of a hill and the view is one of identical plateaus, shrouded by trees, stretching to the horizon.

At their crests, these hills may be only a few yards wide, dropping off sharply on either side to narrow ravines far below, where tiny creeks sparkle through the trees. Bare patches on the hillsides reveal the horizontal rock strata, their patterns repeating from hill to hill. Like a broad red ribbon running through these rock layers is the thick band of Mauch Chunk shale, its vibrant color visible in practically every cliff and road-cut. Here it is horizontal; along the North Branch it is tilted on its side like the other rocks in the swooping formations of mountains and valleys.

The West Branch of the Susquehanna starts out its trip at an elevation of about 2,000 feet, gradually dropping more than 1,500 feet before reaching Northumberland. Like its sister North Branch, the river is in no hurry to depart its birthplace, meandering north from Carrolltown past countryside once so dense with pines and hemlocks that no light reached the ground. In the 1800s, the quality of those trees was known the world over. Today the hardwood timber that replaced them on the hillsides is coveted by lumber merchants here and abroad.

This is hardscrabble country. The economy is based on taking from the land, not cultivating it. First lumbering and then mining supported the small towns that string out along the river, and the price is still being paid. Along much of its early travels, the West Branch is rust-red, stained by mine runoff and heavy with sediments, its banks littered with coal waste and idled machinery. The river eventually becomes startlingly clear due to acidity levels so high that nothing can survive in the water.

The river is shallow as it curves toward Clearfield, growing slowly as streams flow in from nearby valleys. Throughout most of the year, the upper end of the West Branch barely covers the rocks that pierce and eddy its surface. But for a brief time each spring, when the dense snow on the high plateaus finally begins to melt, even the tiniest rivulet becomes a cascade, racing down the hillsides to the West Branch, which is transformed into a wide and impressive sight. Those who settled here came to count on these spring freshets, for they provided transportation to the outside world at a time when there was no other option. Logs tall enough to become ships' masts were borne on the floods to markets hundreds of miles to the south.

Today, coal-mining operations reach to within a few hundred yards of the West Branch. Mining is a tricky and environmentally risky business, for the rocks surrounding the bituminous coal contain the same chemicals—iron and sulfur—that created the poisonous streamlet Ben Marsh showed his students. Today's miners must take steps to prevent the poison from forming. Still, mining here is an easier task—and less costly—than in the anthracite fields. All that is required is to strip away the horizontal strata atop a coal seam and gouge.

Once past Clearfield, the Susquehanna enters the most remote country in its journey, twisting and turning eastward through a deep valley whose only hint of civilization is the railroad tracks that cling to a narrow ledge. Even dirt roads abandon the river here. Grouse inhabit the woods; wild turkeys call to each other, and elk stalk among the trees. Bears and bobcats prowl these rugged hills.

To the north, shaping their own landscapes through the plateau region, are several big tributaries of the West Branch. These streams—the Sinnemahoning, Kettle, Pine, Lycoming, and Loyalsock creeks—fan out in all directions, draining the heavily forested terrain of north-central Pennsylvania and southern New York. Less than a century ago, this land lay naked and barren, stripped of its most important economic resource by waves of loggers. Spring rainwaters then ran unimpeded into the Susquehanna and its tributaries, and the resulting torrents extracted nature's retribution.

Although human actions have contributed to the severe floods on the West Branch, the geology of the river compounds the problem. Upstream from Lock Haven, where the Susquehanna leaves the plateau country and drops down the Allegheny Front, there is a sudden change in topography. As the river approaches the western edge of the Appalachian Mountains, it slows to a gentle gradient, from 6.6 feet per mile to just 1.6 feet per mile.[4] At the same time, the narrow gorge through which the Susquehanna has flowed for much of its length opens into a broad valley, bounded on the south by Bald Eagle Mountain.

Just as in the Wyoming Valley, the geology here guarantees flooding—but for a different reason. In that valley, a narrow outlet causes the North Branch to back up. Here it is the wide-open spaces that create the problem. Ice moving down the West Branch stalls in the vicinity of Lock Haven as the river slows and levels out. The ice then acts as a dam, holding back additional water melting from the upstream heights, and soon the valley is underwater. No other river east of the Rockies is as prone to ice jams and subsequent flooding as the Susquehanna. Long-time residents joke that no one invests in a valuable that can't be carted to the second floor, a phenomenon that prompted a journalist years ago to observe that piano playing in Lock Haven had become a lost art.

Bald Eagle Mountain is the first of the massive ridges the West Branch will encounter on its trip downstream.[5] It is said that the Indians called the

4. By comparison, some of the tributaries of the West Branch drop at a rate of 1,000 feet per mile.
5. Although it is a dominant feature along the river today, 900 feet high in some places, the mountain is a tiny vestige of a once-soaring anticline known as the Nittany Arch, which

thirty-seven-mile stretch of river along Bald Eagle the Long Reach, for its quiet, level descent. The region attracted a few settlers before the Revolution, but the lack of easy transportation seriously slowed development. Travel up the West Branch was grueling and, once there, life was difficult. Early inhabitants complained of the "prodigious swamps" that dotted the landscape amid the many streams that cascade from the Allegheny Front.

One stream that helped with transportation instead of hindering it was Bald Eagle Creek, which enters the West Branch just below Lock Haven and provided access to the south. Today, the creek still benefits the river. Because it and its tributaries flow through beds of limestone, Bald Eagle brings a cargo of much-needed alkalis into the Susquehanna—neutralizing large quantities of the acid flowing down from the mines.

Bald Eagle Mountain is capped by Tuscarora quartzite, sandstone metamorphosed into a rock that is extremely resistant to erosion. Ben Marsh calls Tuscarora quartzite "the ridge-former," and at this moment the Bucknell bus is groaning away in first gear as it struggles to reach the crest of another quartz-capped ridge, North White Deer Mountain, south of and parallel to Bald Eagle. In between sits the Nippenose Valley.

On an aerial map, the Nippenose (named for an Indian chief who once lived there) resembles the shallow crater of some extinct volcano. The valley's limestone floor has given it certain unusual characteristics, and Marsh ushers his students through a wildflower-filled woods to see one of them.

"What's wrong with this picture?" he asks the group. A pretty little creek flows a short distance and suddenly disappears in the ground. That sort of thing is common in the limestone valleys along the Susquehanna, including those farther south. Here, water rarely flows on the surface, but instead goes underground through cracks and channels worn into the soft limestone. Hiking a short distance through the woods, Marsh scrambles down a trail. There stands what was once a large cavern, its roof long since collapsed, revealing just where the tiny stream had traveled and what it accomplished en route. Water cascades down the limestone wall and flows a short way before descending underground again.

"Can you drink this water?" a student asks. "You won't die, but you might wish you had," Marsh replies. "You'll see what I mean in a minute."

---

towered over a large portion of north-central Pennsylvania. Bald Eagle is the stump of the northern leg of that arch, long since eradicated by the persistent force of erosion.

As the bus crosses the valley, Marsh points out the sinkholes that dot the landscape and inquires, "What do you think those might be used for?" No one had an answer.

The bus pulls into the entrance of a quarry and Marsh promises the students "one of your peak lifetime experiences." They file off the bus and instantly recoil from a pervasive stench of decay. Marsh is delighted. "So why did God give us these sinkholes?" he asks again, crossing the road, his students tentatively following. "Landfills!" he exclaims, gesturing with his shovel. There, filling a deep limestone sinkhole, are old tires, a baby crib, a refrigerator, bags of garbage, a television set, car parts, and at least one deer carcass. "You put it into a sinkhole and it's gone. It's slowly making a giant garbage teabag, which just leaches out into the ground." Nobody asked again about drinking the water.

As on the previous week's excursion to the anthracite field, Marsh has a grand finale planned for the Nippenose. Walking across a field, he leads his students to a stand of tall trees. Here, amid ferns and mayapples, Solomon's seal and columbine, are several spectacular moss-lined sinkholes, thirty or forty feet deep. The students are startled. "You mean, just a little bit of water could do all this—make these giant holes?" a young woman asks.

From one of the sinkholes springs the bubbling water of Antes Creek, a lovely stream that flows three miles out of the valley through Bald Eagle Mountain and into the West Branch near Jersey Shore.

The geology lesson completed, Marsh cannot resist showing his class a manmade curiosity along the stream. There, standing incongruously amid the trees, is a tall granite column that once had been part of the state capitol building that burned in 1897. The inscription on the column, added after it was transported here from Harrisburg by the property's eccentric owner, reads: "Wi-Daagh, King of the Susquehanna Indians whose wigwam was here. Executed treaty with William Penn, Sept. 13, 1700 conveying Susquehanna River and lands adjoining in consideration of a parcel of English Goods."

"This was the center of Indian life once," says Marsh. "We look at it and say, 'It's nowhere.' But our definition of what is *somewhere* is how we define resources—a coastline, cities, roads. Yet this was the center of what the Indians wanted. It provided them everything they needed."

After leaving Lock Haven and Jersey Shore, the West Branch flows past Williamsport before making a sharp curve around the foot of Bald Eagle

Mountain.[6] The river weaves its way between two ridges and passes the towns of Muncy, Montgomery, Milton, and Lewisburg. Finally, with little fanfare, it slides beneath the great rocky promontory opposite Northumberland and mingles with the North Branch.

The Susquehanna River, wide and commanding, is at last whole. It swings resolutely to the south, headed for the Chesapeake Bay and, ultimately, the sea. For the next 123 miles, the river will grow steadily in volume, thanks to numerous tributaries, including its largest, the Juniata. With branches extending into southwestern Pennsylvania, the Juniata drains 3,404 square miles before joining the Susquehanna at Duncannon. Even with the addition of such an important tributary, this final stretch earned the Susquehanna its nickname of the "mile-wide, foot-deep river." But those who dismiss the Susquehanna as uninteresting because of its phlegmatic appearance would be making a serious mistake.

While geologists find much to investigate in the Susquehanna's upstream reaches, the main stem of the river is a siren, repeatedly drawing them to its banks. The geology here is intense; it can be dramatic and, of course, perplexing.

That's especially true when you're trying to advance a new theory to a skeptical audience of your peers. Frank Pazzaglia, the geologist from Penn State, was doing just that. He was attempting to prove that tectonic activity—earthquakes and tremors—had played a much greater role in the modern geologic history of the Susquehanna than anyone recognized. In furtherance of his hypothesis, he had been up and down the river collecting rocks from its terraces since 1989, when he began his doctoral research.

"The terraces," explains Pazzaglia, an outgoing young man with short dark hair, "are just the river's old floodplain," made up of glacial rubble that got washed far downstream. The stony terraces line much of the river, in places appearing as stairsteps, signaling a series of glacier-induced floods. It is Pazzaglia's theory that in certain places the terraces were warped upward in ways that only earth tremors could have caused. (Earthquakes in the region aren't entirely theoretical. In 1984, an earthquake in Lancaster measured 4.1 on the Richter scale. "That wasn't as big as they get elsewhere," he notes, "but the epicenter was quite close to the Peach Bottom nuclear plant.")

Whatever the fate of Pazzaglia's theory, his research on the age and

6. Geologists theorize that the Susquehanna once flowed over the top of Bald Eagle Mountain. A small water gap at its peak indicates that. But as the mountain emerged from the soft sediments covering it, the river slid down and around its base.

history of the terraces will enhance the scientific understanding of the Susquehanna watershed and all East Coast geology. But many of those who have wandered along the river with rock hammers and notepads have been driven by something more tangible: money. Even today, most of the research of the Pennsylvania, Maryland, and New York geological surveys is used by those who wish to develop the land in some way and want to know what lies beneath its surface.

It was this same desire for wealth that sent the first adventurers into the wilderness long before America gained its independence. For them, the Susquehanna proved to be a logical starting point, for reasons practical as well as scientific. The river offered the only access to the interior.[7] Captain John Smith might be labeled the earliest prospector on the Susquehanna. Untrained in science but a keen observer of everything around him, Smith set out in the summer of 1608 dreaming of finding a passage from the Chesapeake Bay to the South Seas. Choosing the most promising of the four rivers flowing into the head of the bay, he and his crew soon encountered what they described as large boulders strung across the wide stream. There was no way past them. "Though canoes may go a day's journey or two up it, we could not get two miles up it with our boat for rocks," the captain wrote of the river. Designating the obstacle as "Smyth's Fales," the Virginian and his men turned back in defeat. It might have consoled them to know that countless others would also see their grand schemes for the Susquehanna foiled by this vein of rocks.

Two hundred years later, at the beginning of the nineteenth century, geology remained a science known only to a few. But that was about to change, for America's rapid growth made a better understanding of its natural history essential to anyone hoping to capitalize on its resources—and there were plenty of people eager to do that along the Susquehanna. Road construction required a knowledge of rock formations; so, too, did the digging of canals and the erection of bridges. The discovery of coal on

7. In notes accompanying a map he prepared in 1755 after extensive travels along the Susquehanna, Welsh cartographer Lewis Evans wrote, "The Mountains are almost All so many Ridges with even Tops and nearly of a Height. To look from these Hills into Lower Lands, is but, as it were, into an Ocean of Woods, swelled and depressed here and there, by little Inequalities, not to be distinguished one Part from another, any more than the Waves of the Real Ocean." Although the two maps Evans produced were of extraordinary quality given the limited knowledge of his day, many others printed in the eighteenth and early nineteenth centuries were as much advertising tools as informational guides, intended to attract investors in land or resource development. An 1833 map of New York State, for example, showed the coal fields of Pennsylvania extending as far north as Cayuga Lake, economically enticing if not geologically accurate.

the riverbanks gave rise to questions about where else this new fuel might be found. As more and more farmers recognized the value of limestone as a soil supplement, deposits were located and quarries opened. Valuable minerals lay hidden among the rocks. For these reasons, interest in geology among men of science and commerce soared along the Susquehanna and across America.

Between 1820 and 1845, geological surveys of most of what was then the United States were completed. The quality of the work varied widely, as did its motivation. Maryland's first geological survey, authorized in 1834, was directed by the state agency in charge of transportation development, with most of the later work done by faculty members and students of the Johns Hopkins University. New York's Geological Survey, authorized in 1836, occasionally operated without funds, sustained only by the hard work and devotion of its long-time director, James Hall. (Hall's primary interest was in paleontology, and the New York survey amassed a huge collection of fossils. When funds ran low, Hall would sell some of the collection to continue his activities.)

The desire to know more about the potential riches of the Susquehanna and lands to the west prompted formation of the Geological Society of Pennsylvania in 1832.[8] While the society's founders were men "of science," as an early history notes, they were by no means political babes in the woods. In hopes of winning state funding, they prepared their list of areas ripe for geologic survey—and subsequent economic development— making certain to include the hometowns of influential legislators. Even so, it would be four years before the lawmakers decided to allot $6,400 annually for a five-year survey. The post of state geologist went to Henry Darwin Rogers, a 26-year-old professor at the University of Pennsylvania.[9]

At the start, the task facing Rogers and his contemporaries was daunting. No one had catalogued the various rock formations in the state.

8. By 1840, the much-expanded organization changed its name to the Association of American Geologists and eight years later it became the American Association for the Advancement of Science. The Pennsylvania Geological Survey dates its founding to 1836.

9. Two years earlier, Rogers had been appointed professor of natural sciences at Dickinson College in Carlisle, Pennsylvania, the youngest member of the faculty. He apparently made such a favorable impression that the trustees agreed to buy him new laboratory equipment. Relations cooled rapidly, however, when college officials discovered Rogers's liberal views toward education. He was dismissed in 1831 at the conclusion of the spring semester, and at least one historian reports it was the result of Rogers dancing with a student. Minutes of the trustees' meeting at which he was fired noted only that he was not acting "in perfect accordance in relation to all matters of discipline and internal regulation." He was then hired to teach at the University of Pennsylvania.

Information they gathered often seemed to be in conflict with what they were seeing. A sequence of rock layers recorded in one spot would show up again elsewhere—but with certain layers inexplicably missing. Rogers and his staff grew discouraged. And then, in a stunning revelation, they realized what was wrong: in places, erosion had obliterated eons of geologic history. The missing rock strata didn't represent an error; the rocks had simply worn away. Rogers's work in stratigraphy—the order of rock strata—served as the framework for all subsequent mapping of the Appalachian Mountains up and down the East Coast.[10] It remains unaltered today.

Modern-day geologist Bill Sevon, a pleasantly woolly-looking man with thick silver hair and a penchant for plaid flannel shirts, still gets excited when describing Rogers's moment of discovery. He even wrote a play about the incident to mark the 150th anniversary of Pennsylvania's first geological survey. One of Sevon's favorite rock specimens, resting atop a bookcase in his cluttered office overlooking the Susquehanna, is his own reminder of the geologic complexities produced by erosion. The lower half of the rock is limestone, dating back 500 million years or more; the upper portion is conglomerate, about 400 million years old. Completely erased from this chunk of rock are 100 million years or so of geologic time.

Geologists in the mid-1800s found themselves under increasing pressure for more information. Despite the great progress in the science, its practitioners remained unable to explain much of what they saw on the river.[11] Especially tantalized was Harvard geologist William Morris Davis, who

10. Rogers's older brother, William Barton Rogers, had been appointed state geologist of Virginia (which then also included West Virginia). The two men, who closely collaborated, are generally credited as being the first to understand the complex geology of the Appalachian Mountains.

11. It was 1858 before Henry Darwin Rogers completed his two-volume *Geology of Pennsylvania,* accompanied by the first Geological State Map, both of which he published at his own expense. By then, he had become a professor at the University of Glasgow in Scotland, regarded as the international center for geologic study. This was a considerable achievement for a young American.

Although it appeared belatedly, Rogers's work was exceedingly valuable. In all likelihood, his map of rock formations—the best available at the time—was used in planning the battle at Gettysburg. Certainly Union officers would have had access to the map, and it is likely William Rogers would have had a copy of his brother's map in his files at the University of Virginia, rendering it available to Confederate leaders as well.

The early geological reports prepared by Rogers and others were printed in English with separate editions published in German, regarded then as the true language of science. The quality of the German editions of Pennsylvania's reports was somewhat erratic, however. In a pinch, the authors apparently dreamed up some of their own Teutonic-sounding words, confusing every reader, German *and* American.

found in the Susquehanna clues to the history of the entire Atlantic coast. His research on the river later in the century also enabled him to piece together most of the geologic history of the Appalachian Mountains, expanding greatly on the work of the Rogers brothers.[12]

The mystery of the five sandstone ridges north of Harrisburg and why the Susquehanna cuts through them especially intrigued Davis, just as it does geologists today. Although there have been several theories proposed, the currently accepted explanation is this: the ridges were buried beneath sediments 2½ miles thick that washed from the massive offshore mountain range, eventually creating an expansive plain. At the time, the north-flowing Susquehanna was lazily nibbling its way south and happened to flow across the top of the ridges. When uplift occurred, the Susquehanna simply reversed its flow across the ridges, cutting deeper as its velocity increased. After that happened, no force of nature could change the river's mind.

The Susquehanna hasn't quite completed its meal of the five ridges. As the river flows through the mile-wide gaps it has carved, the remnants of the rocky barriers can still be seen in the form of rapids that traverse the channel. Early entrepreneurs put to good use the water that backed up behind these rapids, or "riffles" as they're called on the river. They became favorite spots for ferry crossings. The riffles are especially visible at what's known as Dauphin Narrows, where the Susquehanna comes out of a series of curves and heads through Blue Mountain. Canoeists know they can squeeze a good ride out of the river there.

Having cut through Blue Mountain, the last ridge, the Susquehanna begins its travels through country whose valleys lured early settlers and served as hospitable avenues to the interior of the country in the seventeenth and early eighteenth centuries. It was possible to leave Philadelphia and follow the Great Valley to the Lebanon Valley, the Cumberland Valley, and on to the Shenandoah or the wild Ohio country.

From the river it is difficult to sense the transformation of the terrain, for now the Susquehanna is densely populated, its banks crowded by modern civilization—trainyards, shopping strips, industries, homes and

---

12. Davis's scholarly treatise, "Rivers and Valleys of Pennsylvania Then and Now," was published in the first volume of the *National Geographic* in 1889 and today remains a respected and oft-cited work. In fact, Bill Sevon suspects it may be the most frequently cited work in geology. Sevon marvels at the accuracy of Davis's theories in light of how little was known at the time about the forces that formed the earth. Noah and the Great Flood had not been discarded as an explanation all that long before Davis tackled the subject.

highrises, interstate highways and bridges, the buildings that house the government of Pennsylvania and all those who do business there. This intrusion is short-lived, though, for below Harrisburg and its clutter of satellite communities, the riverbanks turn green again, hillsides descend to the water, islands dot the surface, and the Susquehanna again dominates the landscape. Only the white, hourglass-shaped cooling towers of the Three Mile Island nuclear power plant interrupt the picturesque river scene.

There, at Middletown, the river crosses a band of shale and red sandstone marking the end of the Valley and Ridge Province. To the south is the broad expanse of Great Valley limestone that has produced some of the best farmland in the world. The Great Valley joins the Piedmont, with its poorer soils of mica, schist, and quartzite and large rock outcroppings that complicate the Susquehanna's journey to the Chesapeake.[13]

The distinctive bands of rocks along this section of the river manifest themselves in a variety of ways. In Lancaster County, for example, it is possible to see where the sandstone-shale belt gives way to limestone, because there the umber soil turns dark and loamy. Across the river in York County, a tributary of the Susquehanna marks the same geologic boundary: Conodoguinet Creek runs along the divide between the sandstone-shale belt and the limestone. To the south, Yellow Breeches Creek in turn separates the limestone from the sandy, poorer soils that stretch into Maryland. As a result of their geology, the two streams are quite different. Although the Conodoguinet is fed by cold-water springs at its origin, it is a warm-water stream, drawing much of its flow from surface sources. The Yellow Breeches, however, is a cold-water stream, fed primarily by deep underground springs that well up from the limestone strata. Trout fishermen love the Yellow Breeches; the Conodoguinet is a bass angler's haven.

After passing Three Mile Island on his way south for some field work, Frank Pazzaglia pulls his truck into a boat-ramp parking lot and points out the first examples of igneous rock on the Susquehanna: the famed Con-

13. Early in the nation's history, this part of the Susquehanna also provided an assortment of commercially valuable rocks and minerals. Peach Bottom slate from York County was regarded as the best roofing material available; by the 1850s, there were eighteen slate quarries on the west side of the Susquehanna. Two mines in Lancaster County provided the world's major source of chrome; all the nickel mined in North America came from a Lancaster County mine, which also produced small quantities of copper. Iron ore was extracted in both Lancaster and York counties, with York County alone having 126 mines. Deposits of fire clay sustained a thriving brick-making industry in York County. The early industrial sites that grew up around these resources still fascinate scholars.

ewago potholes, one of two sets on the river near here. These are composed of diabase. The other potholes, located about thirty miles south at Holtwood, are bored into schist.[14]

"One of the strongest influences on what a river does is the rock bed it's flowing over," says Pazzaglia. "Wherever you see a waterfall or a rapids in the river, you can almost always see some change in the rocks. The river tends to be extremely sensitive to these things."

Although the Susquehanna here was far removed from the glaciers, it still has terraces formed of glacial litter: rocks known as clasts that were carried downstream by meltwater. As Pazzaglia stands on the well-trodden bank frequented year-round by thousands of anglers seeking the fish that love the shelter of the rocks, his eyes automatically scan the stones at his feet. "Even though this has been pretty much reworked by man, you can pick up rocks of all different types," he says, leaning over and fingering a small pebble. "Oh, that is beautiful! This is not an Appalachian rock. That single clast alone tells you that you're looking at an igneous rock. This could be from the Canadian Shield. Who knows where it came from? It had to be brought down by the glaciers."

The small towns of Marietta and Columbia, once thriving commercial hubs that drew their prosperity from the Susquehanna and its resources, are the last communities of any size along the river until Havre de Grace, Maryland. About five miles below Columbia, near the summit called Turkey Hill, is the dividing line between the Great Valley and the Piedmont. As a testament to the complexity of the rocks here, the site spawned one of the most famous and long-lived geological debates in North America, which continues today. The subject is the Martic Line, where two quite different rock types abut. Some geologists believe it to be a major thrust fault, in which billion-year-old rocks were lifted atop much younger rocks. Others, however, argue that it is simply that—two metamorphic rock types of differing ages in unusual sequence.[15] Although Pazzaglia sides with the

14. These veins of hard rock are common across southern Pennsylvania. In several places they create odd knolls, including Little Round Top and the Devil's Den at Gettysburg National Military Park. The rock formations also provide ideal sites for power plants because of their geologic stability. Three Mile Island is composed of diabase, which is also the bedrock beneath the York Haven power plant, just downstream at Conewago. Holtwood is built on a metamorphic base of schist.

15. One of the more colorful adversaries in the Martic Line fight was Florence Bascom, the first woman geologist in the United States. Bascom, born in 1862, received her Ph.D. from the Johns Hopkins University in 1893—the first woman to receive a doctorate from the all-male university—and went on to a distinguished teaching career at Bryn Mawr College. There, she

thrust fault school, he adds with a grin, "The river doesn't seem to care one way or the other. It flows right across."

At Turkey Hill, the Susquehanna enters a narrow gorge, and its transformation couldn't be more extreme. "From its first entrance into the Turkey Hill, to the tide, there is no part that deserves the name of a sheet of smooth water," wrote Benjamin Latrobe, the brilliant engineer who in 1801 was assigned the task of recommending ways to render the Susquehanna navigable. Here, the river once again becomes wild and remote. Even today, crossing the Susquehanna at its southern end is difficult; in the thirty-mile stretch between Columbia and the Conowingo Dam in Maryland, there is only one bridge, and that wasn't completed until 1968.

Indeed, as with one of Ben Marsh's field trips, the river is saving its best for last. More than a mile and a half wide as it approaches Turkey Hill, the Susquehanna is compressed to less than a quarter of a mile across as it races through the gorge to Perryville, Maryland. Descending at a rate of 7.3 feet per mile, the river gains speed as it passes beneath walls that stand 200 to 500 feet above. And then there are the rocks. Observed a visitor in 1894:

> The whole lower region of the Susquehanna . . . makes one think that nature must have been either angry or else in a playful mood the day in which it was created. See these bold, jagged precipices, jutting clear out into the waters, those ponderous bowlders [sic] in the very bed of the channels weighing thousands of tons. What are they doing here? How did they get here? Was it by some mighty convulsion of nature, such as is unknown at the present day? Why these unique, unnatural, and grotesque shapes? It is as if Jove had been hurling his thunderbolts at his enemies and to their absolute discomfiture.

---

trained a whole generation of female geologists while also mapping the Piedmont region of southeastern Pennsylvania for the U.S. Geological Survey. Bascom corresponded with William Morris Davis and others, and her work was regarded as extremely thorough and accurate.

Bascom encouraged two of her brightest graduate students, Anna I. Jonas and Eleanora Bliss, to study an area east of the Martic Line known as Doe Run for their doctoral dissertations. Their research generally endorsed Bascom's interpretation of the region's geology, including her rejection of the thrust-fault theory. Later, the two women repudiated their views, and then did all they could to discredit Bascom. Jonas's husband, George Stose, who at the time was chief editor of geologic maps for the U.S. Geological Survey, withheld publication of Bascom's work for years. When the work eventually was printed, it had been revised to reflect the Stose-Jonas interpretation of the rocks Bascom had mapped.

Eleanora Bliss renounced her former teacher as well. She married Adolph Knopf, an editor of the *American Journal of Science*, which refused to publish Bascom's works. Up until her death in 1945, Bascom vigorously rejected the thrust-fault interpretation.

The complexity of the rock structures intimidates geologists today. "People are afraid to work here," says Sam I. Root, a former colleague of Bill Sevon's at the Pennsylvania Geological Survey who now teaches at the College of Wooster in Ohio. Root and his students occasionally make the ten-hour trip to the lower Susquehanna to examine its peculiar features.[16]

On one such trip on an April weekend, Root's entourage scrambles atop an outcropping of schist that towered above the riverbank, the rock face so gnarled as to resemble the roots of an ancient tree. Alongside it, a waterfall cascades over a flat slab of schist. Somehow it had escaped the forces that twisted the adjacent rocks into tight knots. "To me, the Susquehanna's a wonderful place," says Root. "Forget its intrinsic beauty. It has created a tremendous amount of rock exposures, so you can see much of what happened geologically on the East Coast right here."

It is in the potholes at Conewago and Holtwood that the Susquehanna really shows off, however. Nowhere else in the United States is there such an extensive display of similarly sculptured river rocks, or a better place to study river hydraulics.[17]

This is Bill Sevon's domain. The potholes were formed when the river, engorged with glacial melt and carrying huge quantities of abrasive sediments, attacked these hard rock sills like thousands of mighty drills. What amounted to a series of underwater tornadoes bored cylindrical holes vertically into the diabase and schist. Rocks from the entire Susquehanna watershed and beyond can be found in and around these potholes, and some of the holes are large enough to hold an adult.

Although the existence of the potholes at Holtwood was well known to geologists by the early 1900s, the ones upstream at Conewago Falls were not discovered until October 1947, when they emerged from beneath the river's surface during a severe drought. After a newspaper reported their existence, 10,000 people flocked to the Susquehanna to see the rocks.

Of equal fascination to geologists is the odd configuration of the river bottom in the Susquehanna Gorge along the Pennsylvania-Maryland border. There, the river has carved a series of spoon-shaped depressions known as "deeps" on the eastern side of the channel, but not on the west. They are so deep that early settlers believed anything dropped into the river

---

16. It is a natural linkage because some of the geology that dominates their area of Ohio is a direct result of events along the Susquehanna. The tremendous weight of the sediments eroding from the offshore mountain range onto the Valley and Ridge Province initially caused the land to sink. That, in turn, created a bulge in the rock strata in central Ohio. The students are merely seeing the cause of the effect in their backyard.

17. Another set of potholes exists along the Lackawanna River near Archbald.

there would not surface until it reached the mouth of the Chesapeake Bay. When the Holtwood power plant was built in 1910, the river was diverted by a cofferdam to the west bank and six of the deeps were exposed. Some are carved more than 100 feet into the rock bottom, which means they are below sea level. These are not remnants of an old river bed, for they are unconnected.

"We still don't know how they were formed," says Bill Sevon. He and fellow geologist Glenn H. Thompson, Jr., who teaches at nearby Elizabethtown College, have devised a theory, however. The two men believe that during the Ice Age a "micro-climate" developed on the river, with the sun melting ice and opening a channel to the east. That allowed large volumes of sediment to surge through the gorge there, scouring out the deeps.[18]

The Holtwood potholes are breathtaking, filling the river channel as it winds through a wooded gorge. With the rush of the current the only sound, the river here is a natural wonder. "Nature's handiwork on display," says Pazzaglia, gazing out at the rocks. "This could be a national park." Seconds later, he adds glumly, "But if people knew this was here, it would be ruined."

People already have treated this scenic corridor of the Susquehanna with a heavy hand. Although geology thwarted many schemes to transform the Susquehanna into a riverine highway, it conspired to satisfy another of civilization's needs—electrical power. Situated in the Susquehanna Gorge are the dams of four hydroelectric plants. These have tamed the wildly flowing river into a series of slackwater lakes, now popular with fishermen, houseboaters, and waterskiers. Not so popular is the stretch below the southernmost dam at Conowingo, Maryland, where engineers have occasionally used their ability to stop the river's flow altogether.

But as soon as it can, the Susquehanna runs free again, racing over rocks in its final sprint to the Chesapeake, ten miles away. Not far downstream from the Conowingo Dam, at a site near Port Deposit, where the water cascades over its last hurdle of rocks, stands a small historical marker. "In 1608," the marker reads, "Capt. John Smith ascended the Sus-

18. A similar "deep" was discovered upstream during construction of a railroad bridge across the river. The gully in the river bottom cuts diagonally through a bed of limestone. Modern-day engineers may have been surprised, but the deep was well known to early residents along the river, including the operator of one of the first ferries on the Susquehanna. The deep provided the route followed by ferryman John Harris, who ultimately would sell some of his riverfront land to the state of Pennsylvania for its new capitol.

quehanna River until stopped by the rocks. On his map he calls this point Smyths Fales."

The marker might also have borrowed a line Ben Marsh often uses to conclude a field trip with his Bucknell students: "Thus do rocks determine the future of man." And, in this instance, a river.

Chapter Two

Economic Development

"A race for the river!"

The odd-looking train, with its muscular black locomotive, 1940s-era coaches, and glass-walled touring car, attracts stares as it rumbles north through the town of Columbia, Pennsylvania. This eclectic string of rail cars bears no resemblance to the long freight trains that normally frequent these tracks. The 130 or so passengers gaze back with equal curiosity, taking in the empty brick factories, the vacant lots, and the down-at-the-heels business district that spreads away from the Susquehanna.

If anyone onboard knew that because of the river Columbia had almost become the capital of the United States, or that it once was possible to depart for Europe from its wharves, or that the town built fortunes for many, including an ex-slave who became the richest black man in America, there was no mention of it. Viewed from the windows of this train, Columbia seems like dozens of other small river towns whose spark has been extinguished.

Filling the seven cars are invited guests—business people, officers of economic development groups, utility managers, real estate brokers, and a handful of state and local public officials. The excursion along the Susquehanna has one purpose: to lure business and industry back to the river, and to the rail lines that hug nearly every mile of its banks.

The host of the trip is Conrail, the amalgam of several railroads that once plied the Susquehanna. Today Conrail carries almost all the freight that moves by rail anywhere in the Susquehanna Valley. Railroad tracks march through the hearts of many river towns, and hundreds of buildings along the river still have rail sidings at their loading docks, a reminder of the once-dominant role trains played.

For decades, railroads carried away the resources of the Susquehanna to a world eager to consume them. The rail lines ultimately gave way to highways, just as a half century before canals had succumbed to the railroads. Before all that, the Susquehanna itself had been the prime source of transportation. It was not a burden the river bore gracefully.

In the last car of the Conrail train sits Frances Cunningham, an economic development official who works in Harrisburg. An effervescent woman, Cunningham is paid to lure new businesses to Dauphin County, and she has used just about every tool she can think of to sweeten her pitch. Quite often, she says, the Susquehanna helps do the selling. When a prospective client arrives at her eighth-floor office, "I stand by my big picture window with the river behind me. I pull back the curtains and say, 'The best thing about this area is the quality of life!' It makes a big impression. People just don't know about the river."

That can also be a severe handicap for Cunningham. As the train leaves Columbia behind, her attention is fixed on the rapids in the Susquehanna as the tracks passed below the promontory known as Chickies Rock. "I get one or two calls a year from industries, generally in the South or Southwest, that are interested in locating here," she says. "They've heard about the river and figure they can move some of their goods by water, which is a big selling point. We then have to explain why they can't, about how shallow the river is. And about the rocks."

Too many rocks. Not enough water. In a resigned voice, Cunningham echoed the theme that dominates the economic history of the Susquehanna. Here was a river that seemed destined to take people from the sea into the heartland. That offered access to rich resources—furs, and then lumber, and coal, and produce, and more—and the power to process them, and the markets to sell them. Dreams of taming the Susquehanna into a great trading river have persisted since European explorers first laid eyes on it. To be sure, millions of dollars worth of goods did move on the river, but always at great risk, and only a small fraction of what might have come. Despite exhaustive efforts and extraordinary expenditures, the Susquehanna would not be tamed.

For those who first called the Susquehanna home, its peculiar features posed no problem. The Indians, with canoes and light loads, utilized the river as a highway that allowed them to move between the fecund Chesapeake and the northern and western fur country. Trade and travel along the river was brisk, as evidenced by artifacts still being unearthed. Spear points made of rhyolite, a hard rock found near Gettysburg, have been found in the Wyoming Valley, and at an archaeological dig on Canfield Island, near Montoursville on the West Branch, which contains artifacts dating to 5000 B.C.

In 1608, when John Smith's expedition stalled amid the boulders on the Susquehanna near where Port Deposit is today, a welcoming party of about sixty Indians came downstream to greet him. They were part of a riverside village of about 1,600 or more at the present-day town of Washington Borough, just south of Columbia. This was the Indian capital of the entire Susquehanna Valley at the time, its inhabitants having been lured there perhaps by the prospect of trade with the handful of Europeans arriving on the Delaware River and, later, in Virginia. By mid-century, the Indians' numbers may have reached 3,000 or 4,000—far larger than the area's current population.

While no one knows for certain what the Indians called themselves, they eventually were designated Susquehannocks.[1] Agrarian people closely related to the Iroquois who lived to the north, the Susquehannocks were prospering in the lower river valley. Crops were plentiful; the Susquehanna was full of fish, and the adjacent forests teemed with wildlife, berries, and nuts.

For the Indians, the rocks at the lower end of the river were a source of inspiration, not frustration. Aboriginal tribes predating the Susquehannocks had decorated the massive boulders with intricate carvings of fish and mythological characters. These petroglyphs—still mysterious to archaeologists—were gouged deeply into the hard mica schist, indicating that those who labored to carve the inscriptions wanted them to endure.[2]

1. The map Smith drew of the upper bay and rivers draining into it identified the tribe as "Sasquesahanougs." The name may have been a Nanticoke word, and it was only the English who identified the tribe that way. The French called the tribe Andastes, and the Dutch and Swedes Minquas.

John Smith, who may have been engaging in some self-aggrandizing hyperbole, described the Indians who met him as "a Gyant like people and thus atyred." Their voices, he wrote, "may well beseem their proportions, sounding from them as a voice in a vault." It may have been the "atyre" of the Indians—including a full bearskin worn as a cloak, or the wolf-head pendant—that put Smith in such awe, for the Susquehannocks averaged only about five feet four inches in height, according to Barry C. Kent, who has written extensively about them for the Pennsylvania Historical and Museum Commission. According to Kent, little else is known about their physical appearance. The chances of learning more has been greatly reduced in recent years. Changes in the types and quantity of fertilizers used by farmers have hastened the decomposition of the remains. Graves excavated in recent years have contained only teeth, whereas a generation or two previously whole skeletons could be found.

2. Little did the tribes know, however, that the people who would eventually occupy the valley would choose to dam the Susquehanna to produce electrical power and flood the rocks on which they had labored so painstakingly. In 1930, as work began on the Safe Harbor hydroelectric dam, the Pennsylvania Historical Commission undertook a project to rescue some of the rocks and the drawings they contained. Humans had already extracted a toll on the artifacts. Sightseers had carved doodles and initials alongside or atop the Indian engravings.

Simply locating the petroglyphs was a problem, for in some places they were buried under coal sediments four or five feet thick that had washed downstream. Nevertheless, a team working under the direction of archaeologist Donald A. Cadzow copied the petroglyphs

Archaeologists and historians speculate that the first inhabitants of the Susquehanna arrived about 10,000 to 12,000 years ago, when glaciers still were sculpting the upper watershed. These Indians established flourishing communities on the river's banks and islands, migrating upstream and down—at first to suit their own needs, and later to escape the growing numbers of white settlements.[3]

John Smith's account of his expedition to the Susquehanna, published in London in 1624 with what would serve for years as the most accurate map of the region, captivated fortune-seekers. In 1631, William Claiborne established two trading posts—one on Palmer's Island at the mouth of the river and another on Kent Island in the Chesapeake—and bought furs from the Susquehannocks. In 1634, Cyprian Thorowgood retraced Smith's steps, seeking trade with the Indians, but he too was thwarted by the rocky river bed.

By the time William Penn arrived in 1682 to inspect the colony deeded him by Charles II, he had heard glowing accounts of its natural bounty. Even so, Penn was impressed with the diversity and abundance of this new land. Others had their eyes on the territory, too, and Penn immediately found himself embroiled with his neighbors to the north and south over the boundaries of his possession. They also claimed the Susquehanna lands. He would die never knowing the extent of the colony that bore his name.

Penn's was one of the last colonies to be chartered by the Crown, and was, in effect, squeezed in among existing ones, which were loathe to relinquish territory to the newcomer. In addition, the deeds granted to Penn and the Duke of York were vague, leaving in doubt ownership of the sixty-mile zone between the forty-second and forty-third parallels. With ownership went control over the enormously valuable fur trade with the Iroquois.

located on several islands destined to be underwater. Then, the rocks were cut into pieces and with great difficulty, due to the strong currents in the area, were ferried in a small motorboat to shore. They remain today in the collection of the State Museum.

3. The Susquehannocks abandoned their village near Columbia about 1675, perhaps looking for better hunting, or perhaps fleeing another tribe. Some moved south to the Patuxent River in Maryland, but tensions and suspicions between the Susquehannocks and white settlers there led to several bloody outbreaks of violence. After enduring a long siege, a starving band of Susquehannocks, remnants of a once-thriving tribe, slipped past a group of militia in the dark of night and fled farther south to the Potomac. They eventually would return to the Susquehanna, locating along Conestoga Creek.

Another part of the tribe relocated at the junction of the North and West branches in a settlement they called Shamokin—"the place of eels," according to one translation. Today it is known as Sunbury. The Susquehannocks also inhabited the Wyoming Valley and the fertile delta at Tioga Point, where evidence of their presence occasionally still turns up after a flood.

The northern boundary eventually was peaceably drawn at the forty-second, and New York got the furs. Penn was not, however, about to cede his claim to the southern portion of his colony, despite the vehement—and sometimes violent—efforts of the Calvert family of Maryland, who asserted ownership of land to the fortieth degree of latitude (which passes through Philadelphia and just south of present-day Lancaster). Penn planned to establish a city equal to Philadelphia on the Susquehanna near the current site of Columbia. He was drawn there, he wrote, by "the known goodness of the soyll and scituation of the Land, which is high and not mountainous; also the Pleasantness, and Largeness of the River being clear and not rapid." The Susquehanna, he continued, would serve as a highway for his own colony. It would also provide the settlers in interior New York with an outlet to the sea, and a chance to trade along the way. To unify his farflung holdings, Penn proposed building a canal that would connect the Schuylkill and Susquehanna rivers.[4]

Penn's dreams for his city on the Susquehanna never materialized, for the bitter boundary dispute with the Calverts strained his family's resources and complicated settlement efforts west of the river. After years of legal wrangling, the King's Council in 1767 ordered the boundary fixed at 39 degrees, 44 minutes, its present location. That line had been laid out earlier by two astronomer-surveyors from England.

Because there were no scientists in the colonies considered skilled enough to perform the measurements, the Penns and Calverts had summoned Charles Mason and Jeremiah Dixon to undertake the task. The two men arrived in Philadelphia late in 1763 and immediately began to construct a small observatory to fix their precise position and launch their survey. It would require nearly four years of often grueling and dangerous travel through the wilderness for Mason and Dixon to survey the 332-mile border, which they identified with limestone markers shipped from England.[5]

4. Nearly 100 years would pass before the project, known as the Union Canal, carried its first traffic from Philadelphia to Middletown in five days. Built at an enormous cost of $6 million, the canal included a 729-foot-long tunnel west of Lebanon, the second tunnel built in the United States. Although a remarkable engineering feat, the canal was plagued by many problems. Not only was it too small to carry heavy freight boats, but water continued to seep out of the canal bed because it passed through porous and fractured beds of limestone. Despite an additional $6-million-dollars' worth of improvements, the canal never fulfilled its owners' hopes for success. It was abandoned in 1885.

5. These markers didn't always remain where Mason and Dixon so painstakingly installed them. It was not uncommon for them to be appropriated for fence posts, and one was even found serving as the fireplace lintel in a settler's cabin.

To Marylanders, however, a line on a map was a meaningless formality. Control of the region was dictated by geography. And in their hearts, the citizens of Baltimore believed the Susquehanna rightfully belonged to them.

The struggle to rule the river valley, begun by the Calverts before Penn's arrival, would be waged for another century. The cost would be high. Bloody skirmishes would be fought, and Pennsylvania would be driven to the brink of bankruptcy to solidify its hold. But nothing seemed too great a price, for the Susquehanna was a coveted prize.

Wilderness greeted Susanna Wright and her family when they moved to the Susquehanna in 1726. The transition could not have been more extreme for this extraordinary woman, whose intellect and independence had already earned her a valued place as counsel and confidante to Benjamin Franklin, James Logan, and other visitors to her father's house in Upland, south of Philadelphia. Capable of speaking several languages, educated in science and medicine in her native England, Wright, then 29 years of age, must have shared her father John's sense of discovery about the move.

Joining the Wrights were Robert Barber and Samuel Blunston, fellow Quakers who also had resided comfortably outside Philadelphia and consorted with the leaders of the colony. The site chosen for their settlement was 1,000 acres of heavily timbered land on the east bank of the Susquehanna, which Barber had purchased with an inheritance.

The location seemed ideal, just as it had to William Penn. Here the river was wide and shallow. To the east, the fertile limestone valley had filled with German and Swiss farmers, and already settlers were spilling across the Susquehanna to carve homesteads for themselves to the west, despite the ongoing dispute over whose land it was. A handful of ferries offered passage, including one that began carrying passengers in 1695 at the mouth of the river in Havre de Grace, and another, to the north, started by John Harris about 1712.

Wright, Blunston, and Barber put their political connections in Philadelphia to work immediately. The Pennsylvania Provincial Assembly obligingly created a new county, which John Wright named Lancaster, after his birthplace in England. And when it came to making key appointments, there were only three candidates: Blunston became county clerk; Barber, sheriff; and John Wright, justice of the peace. Soon after, John Wright was granted a charter to operate a ferry across the Susquehanna, and the settlement became known as Wright's Ferry.

Colonial officials in Philadelphia had a strong motive to encourage the Quaker foothold on the Susquehanna. They regarded it as the first line of defense against Maryland. John Wright soon discovered he would be called on frequently to enforce Pennsylvania's claim to the west side of the river as well.

His archrival was a Marylander named Thomas Cresap, who arrived from Baltimore in 1730 and settled on the west bank, four miles south of Wright's Ferry, opposite what is now Washington Borough. He, too, began transporting passengers across the river. Cresap was more than a business competitor, however; he was generally regarded as an agent of Maryland, assigned to cement the Calvert claim by encouraging settlers to pledge their allegiance to Baltimore, not Philadelphia. Cresap, whom Wright and Blunston described as having "loose morals and turbulent spirits," also created trouble with the Indians, who had had good rapport with the settlers at Wright's Ferry.

Over the next eight years, the friction between Cresap and the Quakers grew increasingly violent. When a Lancaster County posse attempted to arrest Cresap for attacking John Wright, gunfire was exchanged and Cresap fatally wounded a member of the posse. In retaliation, the settlers of Wright's Ferry set fire to Cresap's home, seizing him as he fled from the blazing building. Cresap was jailed in Philadelphia, freed by a raiding party from Maryland, and recaptured. Finally, the king ordered a halt to the fighting and Cresap was released. The land dispute simmered on.

Despite the hostilities, the little settlement at Wright's Ferry grew. Wright and Blunston petitioned the county to lay out a road west from Lancaster to the Susquehanna, to be known as the King's Highway. Barber was chosen to select its route, and he placed its terminus between the properties of his two friends. The future of the enclave was guaranteed. The Susquehanna would prove to be a generous benefactor.

Susanna Wright lived near the ferry landing that bore her family's name until she died in 1785 at age 88. With remarkable energy, she raised crops, tended an orchard, and experimented in her garden with various native and European plants. The queen of England wore a dress of silk produced by silkworms Susanna Wright raised.

From London, Wright received shipments of china, books, and prints. Furniture built by Lancaster County craftsmen mingled with fine period pieces from Philadelphia and England. Her library contained hundreds of volumes in several languages, as well as her own poetry and essays.

Wright frequently was called upon to adjudicate legal disputes and to dispense home remedies to ailing neighbors. An astute businesswoman, she presided over the growing domain of her family, which ultimately spread across the Susquehanna to a landing on the west bank that became Wrightsville.

Over the years, Benjamin Franklin sent her books, candles, and items from his store in Philadelphia, concluding his letters with "regards to all my Friends at the River." In return, Susanna shipped the Franklin family baskets of her favorite apples—Spitzenburgs and Pippins. On one occasion, she sent them pickled pike, known as "Susquehanna salmon," packed in a borrowed barrel that was accompanied by an apology to Franklin's wife, Deborah: "When you have taken it out, you will please to let a serv[ant] return the Kegg to the waggoner, as it is a borrowed one and the people insist on having it again. This is ill manners, but with you our good friend, we can be quite free. We rejoiced to see Mr. Franklin here for a quarter of an hour, and to hear of you and Sally [the Franklins' daughter]."

The correspondence between Susanna Wright and the Franklins was lively, reflecting the breadth of their mutual interests, but it also conveys the depth of their friendship. When Benjamin Franklin traveled to England in early 1765, Susanna eagerly awaited news of his safe arrival. "We were under no great degree of anxiety at being so long without any account of him," she wrote to Deborah Franklin after receiving word of his journey, "not as politicians but as Friends, old fashioned friends and in that character we pay our ardent wishes for healthy felicity and a safe and happy Return in due course to his affectionate family and native Soil."

Although Susanna Wright and others in the community lived peaceably with the few Indians remaining in this region of the Susquehanna, there was trouble elsewhere along the river. The French and Indian Wars had left much of the frontier in turmoil, and a number of settlements to the north of Wright's Ferry suffered from marauding bands of Indians.

It was left to small local militias to defend these communities. The most infamous group was comprised of Scotch-Irish Presbyterians who lived north of Harris's Ferry and called themselves the Paxton Boys. Operating without sanction from provincial leaders in Philadelphia, but with the blessings of people who feared for their lives, the Paxton Boys conducted a series of attacks against Indians along the Susquehanna, including a raid in the summer of 1763 into the Wyoming Valley to avenge the deaths of newly arrived Connecticut settlers.[6] In their view, any Indian was a ready target.

6. Like New York and Maryland, Connecticut also became embroiled in a boundary dispute with Pennsylvania. According to its 1662 charter, Connecticut's western boundary was the Pacific Ocean, excepting land possessed by any other "Christian prince or state."

The Boys were especially infuriated by the presence of a small band of Indians along the Conestoga Creek—the pitiful remnants of the "gyant" people "of an honest and simple disposition" who had welcomed John Smith with venison, tobacco, and other gifts, and who had lived peaceably along the Conestoga Creek for generations. These Conestogas, as they now were known, had become little more than charity cases, dependent upon the generosity of the Penn heirs to support them, and reduced to selling handcrafts they made. On December 14, 1763, about fifty Paxton Boys descended on their tiny village and murdered three men, two women, and a boy.

Fearful for the safety of the remaining fourteen Conestogas, Lancaster County officials offered to shelter them in the county workhouse, the most secure building in the area. But on the evening of December 27, the Paxton Boys rode into Lancaster, broke down the door of the workhouse, and slaughtered the last of the Susquehannock tribe.

A short time later, Benjamin Franklin published a heart-wrenching description of the slaughter, purporting to be an eyewitness account of the Indians' final moments. "They fell on their Knees, protested their Innocence, declared their Love to the English, and that, in their whole Lives, they had never done them Injury; and in this Posture they all received the hatchet! Men, women and little Children—were every one inhumanly murdered!—in cold Blood!" It was widely believed that Susanna Wright's horror and outrage over the massacre had influenced Franklin's report.

Even in Wright's later years, her legendary intellect drew visitors to her home on the Susquehanna. Dr. Benjamin Rush wrote of finally meeting "the famous Suzey Wright, a lady who has been celebrated above half a century for her wit, good sense and valuable improvement of mind." She

---

Skipping over New York, Connecticut asserted its claim to northern Pennsylvania and beyond. In 1750, a few settlers from Connecticut moved into the Wyoming Valley and sent word home about the region's fertility.

Encouraged by the Susquehanna Company, a private land developer, 1,000 people moved to the valley from Connecticut during the 1760s. It was an Indian attack on the first of those settlers—known as the Wyoming Massacre—that prompted the Paxton Boys' revenge.

The land dispute between Connecticut and Pennsylvania intensified as additional Yankee settlers flocked to the valley. Troops from Pennsylvania were dispatched to the Susquehanna to roust the Yankees, but by 1771 more Connecticut emigrants had arrived. The outbreak of the Revolutionary War halted the disputes, but with independence they resumed anew. A special commission created by the new Congress awarded the land to Pennsylvania in 1782, but was silent on how to compensate the Connecticut settlers. When Pennsylvania attempted to seize the land, brutal fighting erupted. Finally, in 1787, Pennsylvania agreed to honor the Connecticut land titles, ending what had become known as the Yankee-Pennamite Wars.

told Rush that "the pleasure of reading was to her a most tremendous blessing."

In her lifetime, Wright witnessed countless changes in the fortunes of her river and the community grown up along its banks. From the windows of her neat house on a small rise above the Susquehanna, she could glimpse the wagons waiting to be ferried across the river, and on occasion spy a crudely made raft bobbing downstream from the north, bearing goods to trade. Even so, she could not have foreseen what the Susquehanna had in store for the former wilderness outpost after her death in 1785.

It was her nephew, Samuel Wright, who dreamed the grandest dream for the little community, which in 1788, in a moment of patriotic zeal, he renamed Columbia. The ferry across the Susquehanna had provided a critical link between the colonies during the Revolutionary War, carrying troops, weapons, and supplies along an inland route relatively safe from British interference. Peace had hastened the movement west to the expanding frontier. The volume of goods coming downriver was growing steadily, putting Columbia at the hub of north-south and east-west travel in Pennsylvania. Wright divided 100 acres he owned into building lots and sold them in a lottery. He reserved the banks of the river for cargo, and soon the owners of the large new homes along the Susquehanna found themselves looking out at towering piles of lumber and coal unloaded from the rafts and arks that appeared each spring.

With buoyant optimism, Wright also reserved land east of his home on Second Street for the permanent capitol of the United States. At the time, Congress was debating where to put a new seat of government, and the east bank of the Susquehanna was a favorite site. A measure to that effect passed the House, perhaps aided by an impassioned speech from Congressman Thomas Hartley of York, who "assured the honorable gentlemen who were disposed to pay attention to a dish of fish, that their tables might be furnished by prime good ones from the waters of the Susquehanna." A commission was named to study sites on the river for the capitol, and Congress authorized $100,000 to acquire land.[7]

But members of Congress had another matter to resolve at the same

---

7. Hartley's hometown had already had its moment of glory as the nation's capital. In the fall of 1777, with British troops occupying Philadelphia, members of the Continental Congress fled west, convening for a day in Lancaster and then putting the Susquehanna between them and the enemy. Crossing the river at Wright's Ferry, they conducted the affairs of state in the courthouse at York, where they remained until June of the following year. It was in York, on November 15, 1777, that the Articles of Confederation were enacted, using for the first time the term *United States of America.*

time—the question of whether the new federal government would assume the debts of the individual states. The Southern states opposed the idea; the remainder supported it. To lessen Southern opposition, the Susquehanna was passed over in 1789 in favor of land along the Potomac River.

While Wright's grand plan for Columbia came to naught, the little town was destined to prosper on its own. With more than 26,000 square miles of the Susquehanna watershed spread out above it, Columbia was situated at "the bottom of a great bag or sack, into the upper part of which natural and agricultural produce is poured from the north-east, from the north, and from the west," wrote one of the essayists who promoted development of the region. Coal was being mined in Wilkes-Barre; a few sawmills were operating in the wilderness of the West Branch of the Susquehanna; rafts carrying lumber, grain, and whiskey had floated downstream from both the North and West branches; and thousands of acres were being cultivated throughout the watershed. With America now independent of Britain, its citizens looked to themselves for financial security. For some, the Susquehanna seemed ripe for transformation into an avenue of commerce.

Although Maryland's legal claim to the vast Susquehanna region had been rejected decades before, the economic ties between Baltimoreans and Pennsylvanians along the river continued to strengthen. Not only did geography encourage the flow of goods to the south, but Philadelphia seemed uninterested in the prospects of the river communities. The prevailing attitude was expressed by a Philadelphia newspaper editor who wrote that "the back countries are a dead weight upon us; they pay very little towards the support of the government." Pamphleteer Tom Paine added his disparagement, complaining of the Susquehanna citizenry, "They come here to legislate and go there [Baltimore] to trade."

Emboldened by such attitudes, Maryland quietly began to lay plans to tap the bountiful watershed that washed up on its doorstep. In 1783, a group of Baltimore investors announced plans to build a canal—the first in the nation—from tidewater to the Pennsylvania boundary.[8] Overnight, all indifference evaporated. Philadelphians became obsessed with fears that Baltimore would steal the bounty of the Susquehanna. Suddenly, the future of Pennsylvania seemed to turn on control of a river few had ever even seen.

Pennsylvania countered with a proposal of its own. But what began as an ambitious plan to render the river more useful ballooned overnight into

8. Tidewater, or the fall line, on the Susquehanna is located just above Port Deposit. Geographic references to tidewater on the river generally include the area from Havre de Grace to Port Deposit.

a public works project that has few rivals in American history. Driven by greed and jealousy, it flaunted geology, economics, and common sense.

Since 1771, the Susquehanna had been designated a "public highway"—accessible to all, according to an act of the Pennsylvania Assembly. Even if nature had not given the lie to the lawmakers' actions, Pennsylvanians were not about to include Marylanders in their definition of "public." The rocks in the lower Susquehanna forced most downstream cargo out of the river at Middletown, Marietta, or Columbia, well above the state border. Thus it became obvious even as work on Maryland's nine-mile Susquehanna Canal got underway that unless Pennsylvania helped by removing the rocks, the project would be of little value. (In fact, the Susquehanna Canal never was a success. Its round-sided design and swift-running current made passage difficult. Eventually the canal was sold at a sheriff's sale.)

Several wealthy Philadelphians did take an interest in commerce a short distance upstream, investing $100,000 to construct a canal around Conewago Falls, the only obstacle impeding downstream traffic bound for Marietta or Columbia. Completed in 1797, it was the first canal to be built in Pennsylvania. (Today the York Haven hydroelectric station makes use of the falls, where the river drops nineteen feet in a quarter-mile.)[9]

Construction of the Conewago Canal certainly didn't hurt Columbia, which by now was on its way to becoming a major port. Here goods were unloaded from rafts and arks and transferred to stout wagons, which departed for Lancaster and Philadelphia on the road laid out years earlier by Robert Barber.[10] The fortunes of Columbia improved even more when in 1801 Pennsylvania—finally acceding to its citizens' pleas to improve the river—retained the services of engineer Benjamin Latrobe to carve out a channel in the Susquehanna from Columbia to tidewater, and to complete a survey south to Havre de Grace. The British-born, German-educated Latrobe was between professional triumphs when he headed for the Sus-

9. Although the Philadelphia investors who underwrote construction of the canal believed it would become a major navigational improvement and provide a handsome return, the project never lived up to their expectations. Even as laborers were digging, a German-born miller by the name of Kryder who had traveled down the Juniata and Susquehanna bound for Baltimore navigated an odd-looking craft laden with barrels of flour over the falls and through the rocks without incident. He arrived in Havre de Grace in time to unload his cargo to a bay shallop that docked in Baltimore the following day. Soon, arks like the German's became commonplace on the river, bypassing the canal.

10. The rise of Columbia came at the expense of Middletown, which until the canal was completed had been the southernmost destination for most river traffic and had developed into a major milling center because flour was cheaper to haul to market than wheat.

quehanna. He had already designed and built the first major steam-powered waterworks, which gave Philadelphians safe drinking water, and he had exhibited his talents as an amateur zoologist, geologist, botanist, and artist in what would become many sketchbooks, diaries, and journals.[11]

The modest improvements notwithstanding, the Susquehanna remained what it always would be: a one-way river, and not an especially hospitable one at that. What evolved was a peculiar triangular trade. Goods would come downstream to the river towns or even to Baltimore and be sold, but the proceeds derived from those sales would be spent in Philadelphia on merchandise that could be hauled overland to the Susquehanna's upper reaches. As the volume increased, downstream merchants grew increasingly frustrated and demanded some action to even out this trade imbalance.

While a few venturesome souls did try to ascend the Susquehanna, it was a daunting task. Surveyors hired to lay out what would become the Susquehanna and Tidewater Canal from Baltimore to the Conewago Falls summed up the challenges vividly:

> The roused up, mighty river, as it pours along, charged with the drainage of its millions of acres, resistless, roaring, dreadful, tumbling down through rocks abrupt, seems to hold in scorn all human efforts and contrivances to ride on its bosom, and run counter to its thundering course.

According to another account, the effort to move goods up through the Conewago Falls

> required 30 or 40 men a greater part of the day . . . for the men are obliged to perch and scatter themselves (as it has been humorously expressed) like *black-birds* on the rocks, and to drag their burden shifting from rock to rock through the whole length of the falls.

The growing number of farmers, coal miners, and lumbermen upstream observed with great interest the efforts to improve the Susquehanna.

---

11. Latrobe's arrival on the river was a homecoming of sorts. His late mother, Anna Margaretta Antes Latrobe, had been born and raised in a frontier outpost built by her father on the West Branch of the Susquehanna along a creek that bore her family's name. Upon her death in England, she deeded her son land in Pennsylvania. The young Latrobe, grief-stricken over the death of his wife during childbirth, fled to America, hoping to find solace and a receptive audience for his professional skills. He would go on to earn renown as the architect of the U.S. Capitol and other federal buildings, including the President's Home (as the White House then was known), specifying as an integral part of their construction the white pine that grew in abundance on the Susquehanna's banks.

"Clear your river, and you will command the whole of our trade," wrote a wealthy New Yorker along the Genessee River, who personally pledged to construct a canal or turnpike link with the Susquehanna if it was rendered passable downstream. But New York State had plans of its own, and suddenly Pennsylvania saw a second threat to its attempts to control Susquehanna Valley commerce, this time from the north.

The Erie Canal, traversing the state from Buffalo to Albany and providing a cheap and fast means of moving bulky goods to market, was completed in 1825, eight years after it was begun. If Maryland's plans for a canal to tidewater had sparked fears in Pennsylvanians, the opening of the Erie Canal ignited a bonfire. The Pennsylvania legislature, which until then had only paid lip-service to publicly funded internal improvements, was seized by the canal fever that had infected the nation, fueled in large part by newspaper editors, pamphleteers, and speculators whose rhetoric about economic windfalls became more inflated with each turn of the press.[12] Although slow to start, Pennsylvania overnight made up for its tardiness, driven by Philadelphians whose financial fortunes already were slumping badly.[13]

Maryland's activities also were exerting pressure on Pennsylvania. The first federally sponsored construction project, the so-called National Road linking Baltimore with the untapped resources of the Ohio Valley, opened in 1820, and Pennsylvanians—particularly Philadelphians—feared the highway would siphon off western trade that otherwise might have flowed to Philadelphia.

Following close on the heels of that development came the announcement that a group of Baltimoreans planned to launch steamboat service on the Susquehanna. The steamboats promised something no one had ever enjoyed from the river: two-way trade. And the vessels held out for Pennsylvanians and Marylanders the prospect of transportation far superior to the dangerous, seasonal descent by rafts or arks, or the long, jolting ride over

12. There was enormous reluctance in Washington to involve the federal government in improvement projects. Many people believed that the Constitution prohibited it. Congress authorized the first river improvement project in 1819, appropriating $6,500 for surveying rivers to the west of the Mississippi and the Ohio. As public sentiment for such projects mounted, legislative and constitutional limitations disappeared. Support for public works projects became a major plank of the newly created Republican Party.

13. By 1800, Philadelphia had been surpassed by New York as the nation's largest port, abandoned as capital of both the nation and the state. Politically, it no longer held exclusive control, for citizens in outlying counties possessed no fondness for the Quaker elite that had ruled the colony and state for so long. Many of the newcomers to the western counties were of Scotch-Irish descent, and, as such, found greater ethnic allegiance with Baltimore.

rugged roads. But the investors' grand dreams soon fell victim to the stubborn Susquehanna all in one brief season, the spring of 1826.

The three boats were the *Codorus* (the first sheet-iron boat built in the United States), the *Susquehanna,* and the *Pioneer.* The *Susquehanna*'s maiden voyage ran from York Haven to Northumberland and back. The *Pioneer* made it as far as Williamsport, then headed downriver past Harrisburg and never sailed again. The *Codorus,* which weighed 6,000 pounds, was rolled through York on wheels. It arrived in Binghamton on May 20 amid much celebration and thence returned to York Haven. That was the *Codorus*'s lone trip.

The *Susquehanna* was the only one of the trio to return on the river. The second voyage, six weeks after its first trip, came at the behest of the Susquehanna River Commissioners of Maryland, who hoped to determine how far up each branch a steamboat could travel. Their decision was keenly awaited by Baltimore merchants and citizens. Having successfully reached Sunbury on May 1, towing a loaded keelboat behind it, the *Susquehanna* set out for the Wyoming Valley. Impeding the way, however, were the Nescopeck Falls near Berwick. As the big sternwheeler labored through the rapids, one of the boilers exploded, fatally injuring several onboard, among them a state legislator. That loss didn't faze the newspaper editors in Baltimore, however. They proclaimed steamboat travel on the Susquehanna a success and declared that soon the wealth of the great river would fall squarely into their laps.

Philadelphians were driven to a state of near panic, rendering them susceptible to the increasingly fantastic claims of the swelling number of promoters of a canal system in Pennsylvania.[14] The barrage of canal hyperbole continued. Not only would canals restore Philadelphia to its place as the preeminent city in the nation, but every other community along the canal route would reap incalculable benefits, backers promised. To some extent this latter claim was accurate; many towns grew because of their proximity to the canals.

Facts rarely got in the way during a canal discussion, however. A Philadelphia senator with unusual map-reading skills proclaimed that a mere seventy-five miles separated "the Schuylkill at the Market Street Permanent Bridge [in downtown Philadelphia], and the mouth of the River Columbia on the Pacific Ocean . . . !!!" It was only a matter of time, he

14. An early backer was Robert Fulton, who had been born not far from the Susquehanna in Lancaster County in 1765. Although best remembered for his work on steamboat design, Fulton was intensely interested in canals and advocated their use in his native state before his death in 1815.

predicted, before Chinese silks and teas were floated down the Schuylkill to Philadelphia households.

Revenue derived from canal tolls, declared another influential writer of the day, "would support the government and educate every child in the Commonwealth." If that weren't enticing enough, he added that the revenues would "soon pay off the state debts and provide a surplus of funds so great as to free the inhabitants forever from the burdens of taxation."

Pennsylvania's growing canal fervor alarmed Maryland's citizenry. They were receiving goods via the Susquehanna, and feared the loss of that cargo upon completion of the Commonwealth's canal system—precisely what Pennsylvania had in mind. The Baltimore editorialists and pamphleteers manned the printing presses, hoping to drive their own state into the canal frenzy. "A race for the river!" trumpeted one headline. "The desert daily advances upon the city, and in such cases the very spirit of pestilence seems to have driven from its streets *the busy hum of industry,*" warned a Baltimore scribe. The merchants of Baltimore pleaded for a well-designed canal linking their city directly to the Conewago Falls.

Lost amid all the rhetoric was the fact that despite the hazards involved, the amount of goods descending the Susquehanna itself was increasing each year, attesting to the growth of the upstream settlements. Hezekiah Niles of Baltimore, whose *Weekly Register* dutifully recorded traffic on the river, estimated the value of goods arriving at tidewater in 1826 at more than $1.5 million. Pennsylvania officials valued the goods descending the river at $5 million. To a large degree, the difference in the two figures represents cargo that left the river at Columbia.

"A vast and unprecedented amount of property has passed down the Susquehanna the present season," noted the *Harrisburg Chronicle* on April 6, 1826. "For three weeks past, the river has been literally covered with boats, arks and rafts laden with coal—bituminous from Clearfield county, and anthracite from Susquehanna county—lumber of every description, plaster, whiskey, potatoes, cheese, wheat, flour, pig metal &c. &c." The *Lycoming Gazette* reported that as of April 19, 785 arks and rafts passed Columbia, the most ever to descend the river. Eight million feet or more of lumber from the Susquehanna were arriving each spring in Washington, D.C.

That same year, a century after John and Susanna Wright had arrived on the banks of the Susquehanna, their little settlement boasted nearly 2,000 citizens and a robust economy, thanks to its location. Columbia "was the place where expeditions West made their first rally and base of supplies for all projects into the new and undiscovered sunset land," wrote one traveler. Added another:

> Columbia too is one of those places where we always liked to tarry longer than for a change of horses. It contains an intelligent and enterprising population, several of whom we have found very agreeable companions. As to the story that the merchants of this place lay in annually a stock of blind horses, and of watches without works, to trade away to up country people, whose rafts or arks chance to be wrecked on the rocks near the town, and who must, therefore, sell for any price or lose all. We hold it to be a sheer fabrication, got up in malice, or in envy . . . Still, it must be admitted, they are a shrewd and long-headed people—tight hands at a bargain—who do all they can to make hay while the sun shines, or rather to make money while the river is high.

By the early 1800s, it was common for up to 150 wagon teams to congregate on the east bank, waiting two or three days for their turn to be ferried across the Susquehanna. (The ferry operator happened to own the nearby tavern.)

To alleviate the congestion at the ferry crossing, the world's longest covered bridge opened in 1812, underwritten by the newly formed Columbia Bank and Bridge Company.[15] But the east-west traffic was almost incidental to the town. The Susquehanna was the engine that drove its economy. During the spring, each freshet—a surge of water from rains or melting snow that briefly elevated water levels—would bring with it 1,500 to 2,000 rafts, arks, and keelboats from the farthest reaches of the Susquehanna. Anthracite from the Wyoming Valley fueled iron furnaces in the vicinity of Columbia, and by 1820 more than 6,000 tons a year were being sent downriver.

The arrival of the lumber rafts alone created such a traffic jam on the

15. The bridge, which cost $233,000 to construct, was destroyed by ice in 1832 and rebuilt two years later. It was this second bridge that played an integral part in the Union's defense against Confederate invaders bound for Philadelphia in 1863. With rebel troops advancing toward Columbia from York, a contingent of Pennsylvania militia took up a position at the western end of the mile-long bridge, prepared to do battle. Outnumbered and without artillery in the face of the larger, better-equipped Confederate brigade, the Pennsylvanians retreated under fire across the bridge, but not before a charge of dynamite was detonated under the westernmost span. The mighty bridge quivered but didn't collapse. The militia commander ordered the bridge set ablaze as the Confederate troops raced onto it. The timbers sent up flames that could be seen for miles. Sparks ignited fires in Wrightsville, and to the surprise of terrified residents, the Confederate troops manned buckets and helped quench the blaze. The advance of the rebel troops was halted, and they returned to York before setting out once again to join troops massing at Gettysburg.

Susquehanna that the citizens of Columbia sought help from the state legislature in 1817. "The owners of rafts who bring lumber down the river, occupy so much space along shore, as to render it either impracticable or dangerous for boats loaded with grain to approach the warehouses for the purpose of unloading, which, in unseasonable weather renders the produce liable to loss, or damage," noted a Senate committee report. The Columbia residents requested permission to regulate access to the wharves and landings, and to impose fines for violations; the legislature complied.

While some vessels would continue on to Port Deposit or Havre de Grace, Columbia was the destination of choice. The decision to leave the river there was a financial one. In the 1820s, the cost of navigating a forty-ton ark 250 miles from Oswego, New York, on the shores of Lake Ontario, to the canal at Conewago was about $50. The remainder of the trip downriver, some 50 miles, cost an additional $50 to $70. Special pilots had to be hired to navigate the unwieldy boats through the lower end of the river. Insurance also rose sharply if the boat continued past Columbia. As a result, the little town's shores filled with warehouses, wharves, and freight yards, and Columbia and its sister community on the west bank, Wrightsville, swelled with people who worked in and profited from them.

For those with goods to sell, the Susquehanna was an endless source of frustration. The shipping season lasted only a few weeks each year, almost all of it in the early spring. As a result, "the whole trade of the Susquehanna descends at nearly the same time; the markets, which are at all times, uncertain, in the towns and villages along the river, are overstocked; the owners have incurred expenses which they cannot meet without sales, and they are frequently obliged to sell at a ruinous sacrifice," wrote one of the newly appointed Pennsylvania canal commissioners in 1827.

That Pennsylvania was about to embark on a canal-building program was no longer in question. Its planners, following New York's example, opted to traverse the state from east to west. The needs of those in the rich heartland with goods to move north and south were largely ignored. The system was intended to direct trade toward Philadelphia, and away from Baltimore. Indeed, the canal system was planned to make the lower Susquehanna even less hospitable to downstream traffic than it had been.

The second bit of news for Pennsylvanians along the Susquehanna was that they would be taxed to pay for this project that offered them no benefits. Almost without exception, transportation improvements in the past had been financed by private investors, who then charged the users tolls. The idea of *public* works projects was only beginning to be considered.[16] In the case of the proposed canal system, however, the state seized the project—and the promised gigantic profits—for itself.

On July 4, 1826—the fiftieth anniversary of the nation's independence as well as Columbia's centennial—ground was broken in Harrisburg for the Pennsylvania Canal, which was also known as the Main Line Canal, and later, when the project grew to include other canals and improvements, as the State Works. Governor John Andrew Shulze declared, "There can be no doubt of the superiority of transportation by water. It brings the articles and produce so much nearer to market, that it gives a value to what would otherwise have rotted on the surface, or lain neglected in the bowels of the earth."

Despite the years of lobbying by the state's newspapers for the canal system, the groundbreaking received only passing mention in the press. The editor of the *Pennsylvania Intelligencer* used the occasion to respond to criticism that the state had waited too long to follow New York's lead. What has Pennsylvania gained by waiting? the editor asked. "*Experience*—and *demonstration*," he wrote.

> If she had not the example of New York before her now, the calculating policy of her industrious citizens, would revolt at the prospect, as a project that was idle and impracticable—as calculated to involve the state, in unextinguishable debt without a hope of ever accomplishing her object, or ever deriving the least benefit from her expenditures.

New York *had* set a good example; Pennsylvania chose to ignore almost every aspect of it. As a result, the *Intelligencer* editor unwittingly described an uncannily accurate scenario.

Just what was Pennsylvania committing itself to? For starters, a public works program without the slightest idea of how to finance it. The state began borrowing money for the project even before it was fully authorized. A commission to study how to pay for the canals was appointed some time later. Construction began before the route was agreed upon, and before anybody had figured out how to cross the mountains in the middle of the state. A key component of the system was to be a rail line linking Philadelphia and the Susquehanna at Columbia. No reliable steam engine had yet been invented.

---

16. Over the years, Pennsylvania had invested in a number of private construction projects, buying stock in companies that were building turnpikes and bridges and making similar improvements. Maryland engaged in the same activity, notably helping to underwrite several turnpike roads into the Pennsylvania countryside west of the Susquehanna.

To finance *its* canal, New York had imposed a tax on land along the right of way, correctly assuming that the real estate would increase in value once the waterway was built. Revenue from other special taxes was set aside to retire the construction debt. As a result, the Erie Canal paid for itself nine years after it opened for business. That was the same year— 1834—that Pennsylvania's canal system began operation, already deeply mired in debt.[17] Pennsylvania chose to rely strictly on tolls to pay for the Main Line Canal—which might have worked if the lawmakers hadn't gotten greedy.

Work on the original plans had barely been completed in 1826 before major alterations were made. Those first plans had authorized a twenty-four-mile-long canal along the Susquehanna from Swatara Creek at Middletown to the mouth of the Juniata, and a thirty-mile canal along the Allegheny River between Pittsburgh and the mouth of the Kiskiminetas River. Within a year, the scheme had mushroomed into an unconnected series of canals up the Juniata to Lewistown, up the Susquehanna to Northumberland, and an additional forty-four miles along the Kiskiminetas, plus studies for canals along the North Branch to the New York state line, along the West Branch, and in western and eastern Pennsylvania. Also included was the link to Philadelphia: the eighty-two-mile Columbia-Philadelphia Railroad, the first railroad in America built with public money.

The reason for the construction explosion was simple. No legislator worth his salt would vote for a canal in someone else's district without ensuring that his own would be provided for. "It was impossible to get an appropriation through the Legislature for any one piece of work, without including others of doubtful utility," wrote an engineer involved in the Columbia-Philadelphia Railroad project.

And cost was no object in this logrolling contest. As 1829 came to a close, $8.3 million had been spent on canal construction, an additional $1.4 million in debts had been incurred, and $2.1 million in contracts had been awarded. That represented a sizable increase over the original $300,000 the legislature had appropriated for the canal project three years

17. Despite claims that Pennsylvania's east-west Main Line Canal would steal the business of the Erie Canal, that never happened. Although it was longer by nearly 100 miles, the Erie Canal's rates were half those on the Main Line. The Erie had half as many locks and no rail divisions that required cargo transfers. And if that weren't enough, operators of the Erie Canal continued to make improvements while Pennsylvania never even resolved initial design problems.

earlier. And not a penny in revenue had been generated. Banks grew so worried about the state's solvency that they became reluctant to loan money to Pennsylvania. Lawmakers solved that problem; they amended the banks' charters to require them to make the loans.

It quickly became apparent that the canal designers—to say nothing of the politicians—had been overly optimistic. The thirty-nine-mile Susquehanna Division Canal, from the mouth of the Juniata to Northumberland, was estimated to cost less than $600,000; it totaled about $1 million. As for the Columbia-Philadelphia Railroad, engineers had promised it could be built for $1.4 million, but the actual figure was $5.3 million, a cost overrun of 279 percent. (When equipment and track improvements were factored in, the final cost was $11.1 million.)

Revenue projections weren't any more accurate. The Susquehanna Division generated less than $142,000 during its first nine years of operation. That did not cover the $314,000 spent for maintenance, let alone the $1-million construction cost. The North Branch Division Canal, which ran seventy-three miles from Northumberland to the mouth of the Lackawanna River, fared even worse. It cost nearly $1.5 million to build, produced $63,000 in revenue during its first six years of operation, and required nearly $400,000 in repairs.

Earlier claims by promoters that the canals would pay for the education of every Pennsylvania child rang a little hollow now; it seemed unlikely the state could even afford pencils. "The great mistake on our part has been in undertaking too much at once," lamented Gov. George Wolf. In 1831, he proposed a personal property tax to help defray the drain on the treasury. It was repealed by the legislature five years later, after generating $1 million.

The massive cost overruns were not solely the fault of the engineers. With millions of dollars flowing from the state treasury, everybody and his uncle got into the canal contracting business. Rarely were jobs doled out on the basis of competence. The construction superintendent was ordered by the canal commissioners to ascertain a bidder's "moral character or religious principles"—in other words, his politics—before awarding a contract. On election day, it was not uncommon to see work crews traveling up and down the canal route, stopping at every polling place to vote for their party's slate. In the 1838 gubernatorial election, Morris Township along the Juniata delivered 1,060 votes; the township had 200 residents. A conscientious canal repair crew was working in the vicinity.

Contractors frequently abandoned their work, forcing the state's canal commissioners to rebid the job. When a new, more expensive contract was awarded, the winner often was the man who had just defaulted on the work.

Undaunted by this theft of public funds and the state's worsening financial condition, the canal commissioners decided to press on with the most complex portion of the State Works project—the route over the Allegheny Mountains, linking the canals along the Susquehanna with those to the west. The thirty-eight-mile railroad passage included a series of ten inclined planes, five on each side of the summit. Canal cargo arriving on boats at Hollidaysburg on the Juniata River was loaded on rail cars and lifted 1,400 feet to the top of the mountain, then lowered 1,150 feet to a station on the Conemaugh River, not far from Johnstown. Drawn along by stationary steam engines, horses, and gravity, the cars were attached to a continuous loop of hemp rope.[18]

The Allegheny Portage Railroad made its first trip on November 21, 1833, carrying members of the Philadelphia Board of Trade and ten tons of bacon. It officially opened for business the following spring. Considered an engineering marvel, it drew worldwide praise and was a freight-hauler's nightmare. The Allegheny Portage Railroad sealed the fate of the troubled State Works.

Despite failing to deliver most of what its promoters glibly promised, the canal system did cause a sharp drop in freight costs, and it opened unlimited new markets for the resources of the Susquehanna. The per-ton rate for hauling goods from Philadelphia to Pittsburgh decreased from $120 to $30 once the through route was completed in 1834.

Locally, the impact of canals was also significant. In the Wyoming Valley, 7,000 tons of coal were shipped to market in 1829; the following year, 43,000 tons left the valley via the Delaware and Hudson Canal to the east and the North Branch Canal along the Susquehanna. Although the trip from the Wyoming Valley to New York City via the State Works, the Chesapeake and Delaware Canal, and other waterways constituted a

18. The hemp rope was replaced with a cable of twisted wire, the invention of John August Roebling, the German-born engineer who began his American career on the State Works in 1837. A story is told that Roebling was motivated to devise a safer cable for the Allegheny Portage after seeing two men crushed by rail cars released when the rope snapped. No record of such an accident is contained in the official reports of the Allegheny Portage. This may mean that the story is apocryphal or, as some speculate, it may simply reflect selective recordkeeping by officials worried about public acceptance of the project. In either event, Roebling's wire cable was installed. He went on to earn world renown for his engineering successes, including the Brooklyn Bridge.

700-mile journey, a good deal of coal was shipped that way. Much also went to markets in Baltimore, and the first outsider to acquire an anthracite mine in the valley lived in that city.

Canals along the West Branch also meant that timber cut from the steep hills and valleys could be processed before it was shipped to market, instead of floated or rafted as rough-hewn timber to mills in places such as Columbia or Havre de Grace. Soon, sawmills and finishing plants were erected in Williamsport, Lock Haven, and other West Branch communities, radically changing the lumber industry and triggering its exponential growth.

The canal barges carried a variety of cargo, including the U.S. mail and even the pieces of the transportation system that ultimately would replace the State Works: railroad ties, engines, and rails. Freight soon was joined on the canals by floating saloons, missionary craft, and boats fitted out as general stores. P. T. Barnum's Grand Colossal Museum and Menagerie, featuring Tom Thumb, played the West Branch valley via canal, and a trio of showboats plied the Main Line Canal offering "Minstrels, Ledgerdemaine and Acts of Trained Dogs, Monkies and White Mice." One hundred delegates from Williamsport, accompanied by the town's famed Repasz Band, traveled by canal to the Baltimore political convention that nominated Henry Clay for president.

The canals also carried passengers eager to sample the adventure of this new means of travel on what was regarded as one of the most scenic routes in the country. In 1835, the Pioneer Fast Line offered a trip from Philadelphia to Pittsburgh in 3½ days, via the Columbia-Philadelphia Railroad (a trip of seven to eight hours' duration, not including a night spent in Lancaster), and then packet boat up the Susquehanna, over the Allegheny Portage, and on to Pittsburgh. There, it was possible to board steamboats bound for Cincinnati, Louisville, St. Louis, and New Orleans.

A first-class ticket on the packet boats cost $12 for the 395-mile trip across Pennsylvania, and for the money, the traveler got more than just pretty views. "A canal packet boat is a microcosm that contains almost as many specimens of natural history as the Ark of Noah," observed Philip Houlbrouke Nicklin, a Philadelphian who in 1835 wrote *A Pleasant Peregrination through the Prettiest Parts of Pennsylvania, Performed by Peregrine Prolix.*

Nicklin boarded an eighty-foot boat in the canal basin at Columbia, "a thriving and pretty town" of 2,500 citizens, he noted. Atop the barge sat a cabin that was converted into sleeping quarters in the evening. Passengers squeezed themselves into narrow bunks hung by ropes from the ceiling.

"The number of berths, however, does not limit the number of passengers; for a packet is like Milton's Pandemonium, and when it is brim full of imps, the inhabitants seem to grow smaller so as to afford room for more poor devils to come in and be stewed," Nicklin wrote. To while away the time, passengers were free to walk on the roof of the cabin, although constant vigilance was required to avoid the bridges. Or they could stretch their legs on the towpath, for the barges moved at a rate of three and a half miles per hour, pulled by teams of horses.

Charles Dickens also traveled by canal during an American trip in 1842, departing from Harrisburg and heading up the Susquehanna and Juniata, bound for Pittsburgh. He, too, commented on the sleeping accommodations, which to him resembled "three long tiers of hanging bookshelves." "I began dimly to comprehend that the passengers were the library, and that they were to be arranged edgewise on these shelves till morning." Despite a less than restful night (the constant spitting of his cabinmates disturbed him),

> there was much in this mode of travelling which I heartily enjoyed at this time, and look back upon with great pleasure. Even the running up, barenecked, at five o'clock in the morning, from the tainted cabin to the dirty deck; scooping up the icy [canal] water, plunging one's head into it, and drawing it out all fresh and glowing with the cold, was a good thing. The fast, brisk walk upon the towing-path between that time and breakfast, when every vein and artery seemed to tingle with health; the exquisite beauty of the opening day, when light came gleaming off from everything; the lazy motion of the boat, when one lay idly on the deck, looking through rather than at, the deep blue sky; the gliding on at night, so noiselessly, the shining out of the bright stars, undisturbed by noise of wheels or steam, or any other sound than the liquid rippling of the water as the boat went on; all these were pure delights.

While Charles Dickens and Peregrine Prolix waxed eloquent about the wonders of canal travel, Harriet Beecher Stowe was not as charmed.

> There is something picturesque, nay, almost sublime, in the lordly march of your well-built, high-bred steamboat . . . But in a canal boat there is no power, no mystery, no danger; one can't blow up, one can't be drowned unless by some special effort; one sees clearly all there is to the case—a horse, a rope, and a muddy strip of water, and that is all.

Writing in *Godey's Lady's Book,* Stowe advised anyone making a trip on the Pennsylvania canals to take "a good stock both of patience and clean towels with them, for we think that they will find abundant need for both."

One of the more unusual boats to appear on the canals was that of Jesse Christman, who sold his farm on the Lackawanna River, intending to move to Illinois. Opting to travel by water versus land, Christman loaded his family, poultry, pigeons, and household belongings on a boat he built and named the *Hit or Miss*. He headed down the North Branch and Susquehanna canals and then up the Juniata Canal. Although Christman's original plans were to sell the *Hit or Miss* at Hollidaysburg and build another boat on the west side of the Allegheny Portage, he was talked into loading the vessel on a rail car and hauling it over the mountains, where it resumed its trip west. The idea worked so well that portable boats became popular. The boats were built in sections separated by bulkheads, and simply taken apart to be transported by rail. By the 1840s, there were packet boats whose passengers could remain in their sections while crossing the mountains, something akin to today's containerized cargo ships.

Despite the huge investment in the canal network, these manmade waterways suffered the same problem as the Susquehanna: there was either too much water or not enough. The canals were drained from November until early spring to protect them from ice. In other seasons, flooding caused severe damage to the locks and aqueducts that were an integral part of the system. More often, however, it was low water that brought traffic to a halt.

Rejecting New York's example, Pennsylvania had failed to invest in the necessary reservoirs, relying instead on the unreliable Susquehanna to provide water. Dams were built along it to supply feedwater to the canal system, and these obstructions proved a constant source of irritation to those who still wanted to use the river. Both Maryland and New York strongly protested the construction of the dams, which, they argued, denied them their rights to free access to the Susquehanna guaranteed by Pennsylvania years before. When dams washed away during a flood in 1830, Maryland petitioned Pennsylvania not to replace them. The request fell on deaf ears.

Raftmen along the West Branch of the Susquehanna still relied on the spring freshets to move their white pine and hemlock downstream, and they also were bitterly opposed to the dams. While the structures were supposed to have openings for such cargo, these were not always adequate, and the raftmen often were forced to navigate their bulky craft over the top at great risk to themselves and their lumber. Drownings and serious injuries were common. The dams also seriously reduced shad populations along much of the Susquehanna; the migrating fish could no longer swim upstream.

Frustrated in their efforts to preserve free navigation on the Susquehanna, and suffering from the competition offered by Pennsylvania's canal system, Baltimore businessmen renewed their efforts to build a canal that would tap the Susquehanna, tying into the State Works opposite Columbia. The long-discussed Susquehanna and Tidewater Canal would include a twenty-six-mile segment within Pennsylvania and therefore would require the Commonwealth's approval. The project was bitterly opposed by Philadelphians, who argued that it was "completely subversive to the principles" of the State Works, and would render the $25 million already spent on the canals "tributary to a rival state."

The Marylanders' plan had the support of Pennsylvanians west of the Susquehanna who had not realized much benefit from the State Works. Joining them were lumbermen and coal operators upstream, who saw Baltimore as a market for goods too bulky to be shipped via the Columbia-Philadelphia Railroad. In April 1835, the Pennsylvania legislature granted a charter to the Susquehanna and Tidewater Canal Company. After fifty years, Maryland finally was to have its canal to the Susquehanna country.

Construction of the forty-five-mile canal began immediately, and immediately the project encountered problems. A shortage of available laborers (most were engaged on the State Works) and the unexpected ruggedness of the countryside drove up the cost to $80,000 per mile, or a total of $3.6 million, earning the Susquehanna and Tidewater Canal the honor of being one of the most expensive built in the United States before the Civil War. Nevertheless, with great celebration, on May 28, 1840, guests from Baltimore and Philadelphia arrived in Havre de Grace to mark its completion.[19]

Just how important this costly, long-delayed link to the Susquehanna would be to Baltimore's economic future had already been foretold. The out-of-town guests traveled to the dedication ceremony by train. And, just thirteen days before the Susquehanna and Tidewater Canal opened for business, the Baltimore and Susquehanna Railroad completed an extension from York to Wrightsville, an event that also merited a large celebration. Guests from Baltimore made the seventy-mile trip to Wrightsville in just over four hours, leaving them plenty of time to walk across the river for

19. To facilitate travel back and forth across the Susquehanna, a low dam was built just south of Columbia, which created a slackwater pool. Canal boats were towed to the opposite shore by teams of horses that used a special walkway on the bridge.

a banquet in Columbia, which they honored with a toast: "May her prosperity be as unceasing as the flow of her river."[20]

Indeed, that is what the future seemed to hold for the town at the axis of this new transportation network. Train travel to and from Philadelphia had commenced in the fall of 1834.[21] With the completion of the Susquehanna and Tidewater Canal, it was a simple matter in Columbia to board a barge destined for Baltimore, whose famed clipper ships could carry passengers anywhere in the world. To the north fanned the maze of Pennsylvania canals. Even the reliable old Lancaster Turnpike remained in use, although by now it was driven primarily by farmers too poor to transport their goods by other means.

Still, it was the cargo descending the Susquehanna that sustained Columbia. And among those who reaped the enormous bounty of the river was merchant Stephen Smith, who was born a slave in 1796 and died seventy-seven years later as the richest black man in America.

At age six, Smith was indentured to a Revolutionary War hero, Gen. Thomas Boude, who lived in Columbia and was married to John Wright's granddaughter. Boude was one of the first citizens of the Susquehanna to buy vast tracts of timberland upstream and float logs down the river for sale.

Lancaster County historian Samuel Evans later wrote of Boude's introduction to Smith, using an anecdote to illustrate Smith's early head for business. It took place as the boy was traveling to his new home, accompanying Boude and Boude's daughter. Young Smith had his dog with him,

20. Officials in Philadelphia and its newspaper editors once again were full of dire predictions. Referring to his hometown, a legislator from the city worried that the rail link would "drain the very life blood from her veins." If the rail connection with Baltimore was approved, warned one of his colleagues, "the state will soon be like the old Commodore who died in the West Indies and who was sent home in old Jamaica rum; the sailors tapped him (as Maryland wishes to tap this state), and on his arrival he was found lying on his beam ends, as dry as this tapping would leave us, if we do not put a stop to it."

21. At first, horses were used to move the cars along the rails, and anyone who wanted to pay a fee could simply lift a cart onto the tracks and proceed in either direction. This created enormous confusion and, frequently, fistfights, as faster-moving traffic would get stuck behind a plodding freight wagon. Three steam engines soon were added to the rail line, but horses were not banned for a decade.

Such modern advances didn't always ensure a smooth and uneventful trip, however. One summer, a plague of grasshoppers made the rails so slick that the iron wheels of a train simply spun. Someone proposed sanding the tracks, and the train eventually proceeded on its way. The trains initially burned wood, and farmers along the route often discovered missing fence sections. Later, the trains burned anthracite and then bituminous coal.

but when the three stopped briefly in Harrisburg, he sold the pet to another boy for fifty cents. Evans wrote:

When the General started for Columbia with his purchase [Smith], this dog followed his old master, and the boy who lately purchased him followed the dog but was not able to coax him away from Steve who took it upon his lap and would not give it up, nor would he fork over the fifty cents, the purchase money. Of course the Harrisburg boy set up a howling, and he was not appeased until the General gave him a half dollar and told Steve to keep the dog which he brought with him to Columbia.

Smith worked in Boude's lumberyard. Before he reached 20 he was managing the general's extensive business. Upon turning 21, Smith asked to be released from servitude, paying Boude $50 for his freedom. His fortune rapidly grew as a result of wise investments in real estate and timber, and soon Smith owned one of the biggest lumberyards along the Susquehanna. He was the largest stockholder of the Columbia Bank, and had he been white would have served as its president. As it was, he chose the man to fill the job.

Blacks were not uncommon in Columbia; 400 lived there in 1832, nearly 20 percent of the town's population. For years Columbia had been a well-known stop on the Underground Railroad. The river in effect served as a safety zone, with the counties on the west side regarded as unsafe for runaway slaves. But once across the Susquehanna, amid the strong Quaker community that had existed in Columbia since the days of Wright, Barber, and Blunston, slaves finally felt secure. A large number of ex-slaves chose to remain in Columbia, and many were employed in the coal and lumber yards.

The peacefulness of the community was shattered in 1834, at a time when racial unrest stirred a number of northern cities. A mob of about fifty whites marched to the black section of Columbia, shooting out windows and hurling stones at some homes. Stephen Smith, whose success particularly rankled many in the town, was the mob's next target; his office was ransacked. Shortly thereafter, Smith announced his intention to sell his business and leave town. He apparently was persuaded to remain by members of the Wright family and others in Columbia who denounced the assaults. Despite continued racial troubles, most blacks followed Smith's example and stayed. Real estate records show that they continued to purchase land in Columbia during the period and took an active role in the community.[22] Although Smith eventually did move to Philadelphia, his

---

22. Among those in the front lines defending the Columbia-Wrightsville Bridge against the oncoming Confederate troops in 1863 were black residents of Columbia.

business in Columbia thrived, as evidenced by an inventory of its holdings in 1849: several thousand bushels of coal, 2.25 million feet of lumber, and twenty-two of the best freight cars running to Philadelphia and Baltimore. Smith's company owned $9,000 worth of stock in the Columbia Bridge Company and $18,000 worth in Columbia Bank. He died in Philadelphia in 1873, leaving no children.

With its direct links to major cities, Columbia became a surprisingly sophisticated community. Readers of the *Columbia Spy,* the local newspaper, were briefly treated to the work of a special correspondent, hired about 1845 to write of events in Philadelphia and New York—and presumably to boost readership. The correspondent, Edgar Allen Poe, had recently published *The Raven,* and *Spy* owner Jacob L. Gossler offered Poe $5 per weekly column. "We thought this a moderate compensation, but it was really extravagant in comparison with, as we afterwards learned, the salary of ten dollars per week that he received for editing the *Magazine* [probably *Putnam's Monthly Magazine*], which at the time, after the *North American Review,* was the most popular and considered the highest literary authority, in this country," Gossler recounted later. Although the five columns Poe authored for the *Spy* were not remarkable, according to Gossler, the editor took pains to note that Poe's handwriting and spelling were good. "The *i*'s were all dotted, every *t* crossed, and there were no blots or erasures. They were a delight to the compositor."

Pennsylvania's love affair with canals ended as quickly as it had begun. There were plenty of reasons. The manmade waterways were often impassable—damaged by floods, clogged by silt, or closed by weather. The Allegheny Portage was an impossible bottleneck, requiring thirty-three changes in equipment and a crew of fifty-four men to move goods across the mountains. Shippers on the Erie Canal showed no intention of switching to Pennsylvania and replenishing its coffers. What caused the real change in public opinion, however, was the discovery in 1842 that Pennsylvania was on the verge of bankruptcy, incapable of paying the soaring debt it had incurred with its State Works program. Activity on a number of canal projects, including the North Branch Extension from Pittston to the New York line, was abruptly suspended.[23]

23. The principal engineer of the North Branch Extension was William B. Foster, Jr., who was joined at his temporary base of operations in Towanda by his 14-year-old brother, Stephen. As a student in nearby Athens, young Foster composed his first song, "Tioga Waltz." William Foster went on to gain celebrity in his own right, serving as one of the first

How could things have soured so quickly? As newly elected governor David Rittenhouse Porter noted upon taking office in 1840, the answer was obvious: everybody talked about canal revenues, but nobody ever mentioned costs—and the costs of repair were monumental. From the very beginning, Pennsylvania had borrowed to pay the interest on its construction loans. Tolls generated by the State Works between 1835 and 1839 amounted to $4.4 million. Operating and maintaining the canals (poorly at that) soaked up almost $3.9 million of that amount, leaving about $500,000 a year toward $1.8 million in interest on the $34-million debt. "The people have been told again and again that our fiscal condition was flourishing and prosperous, while in fact, our prosperity was all based on paper calculations and loans," said Porter. And those loans, he added, "are some day to be paid." But apparently tomorrow was soon enough; to finish the system, Porter urged the expenditure of another $4.5 million that the state did not have.

That is nòt to say that Governor Porter and the legislature completely ignored the looming fiscal emergency. A new tax was enacted, intended to retire Pennsylvania's debt. The levy was imposed on household furniture, carriages, watches, and the salaries of state employees. Even if it had been collected aggressively, which it wasn't, the new tax would have generated just $600,000 annually. In fact, only $33,000 was collected the first year, less than 1 percent of the state's debt.

By 1842, it was impossible to deny the inevitable, and Porter announced it was time to sell off at least portions of the State Works. Topping the list was the Columbia-Philadelphia Railroad, together with a segment of canal along the Delaware River. The decision was widely supported by Pennsylvanians. When the bids were opened, however, a group of investors offered just $3 million for the eighty-two-mile railroad, on which the state had spent more than $11 million. The offer was brusquely rejected.

But when the fiscal year closed that November, the ledgers looked grim. To date, Pennsylvania had spent $53.3 million building and running the State Works. The canals had yielded $9.3 million in revenues. Interest payments amounted to $16.2 million, and the state still owed $39 million

---

engineers of the Pennsylvania Railroad. His canal project didn't fare as well, however. Ninety-four miles long, through extremely rugged terrain, the canal eventually was completed in 1856, sold two years later to the Sunbury and Erie Railroad, resold for $1.5 million, and destroyed by floods in 1865. During its brief existence, the canal, which cost taxpayers $4.6 million to build, produced no revenue.

for construction loans. Pennsylvania had exactly $115,466.91 in its treasury.[24]

That same year, the legislature approved the sale to private investors of the railroad between Philadelphia and Columbia as well as the Allegheny Portage and the east-west network of canals that terminated at Pittsburgh. The price was set at $20 million, about two-thirds of its cost to the state. Even then, there were no takers. Part of the problem may have been a requirement that the buyers maintain the system in good working order "forever"—something the state hadn't been able to do even for a decade.

A project that turned out to be a financial disaster for Pennsylvania taxpayers would prove to be a financial windfall for a fledgling business on its way to becoming one of the country's most powerful corporations—the Pennsylvania Railroad. All traces of the canal fever of two decades before had vanished. It was time for railroad fever. A host of railroad companies were incorporating, and investors flocked to back them. Included was the Pennsylvania Railroad, chartered in 1846.

The lure of railroads was not grounded in speed or cost; trains simply were more dependable than any previous method of transportation. Coal companies along the Susquehanna's North Branch now had customers up and down the East Coast who demanded reliable deliveries; lumber firms on the West Branch knew they could supply the world with pine and hemlock if they could get it to buyers without risking devastating losses to floods or accidents; farmers in the rolling valleys along the river had grain, livestock, and produce that could command top dollar in urban markets, but they needed guaranteed shipment schedules.

The railroads were the logical buyers for the failed canal system. The network of canals that crisscrossed the state offered them several options. Those sections of the canals which operated reliably and at a profit—and a number did, especially those that hauled anthracite—could remain in use under new ownership. Those that were unprofitable could be filled in and the graded canal beds converted inexpensively to carry tracks. (The frequency with which that occurred is evidenced by the miles of rail lines along the Susquehanna, many of which were built atop the old canal network.)

Even so, a number of people in Pennsylvania—especially along the Susquehanna—protested vigorously that the canal system should be pre-

---

24. Among the most outspoken critics of the state's freefall into insolvency were the British, who had heavily invested in the State Works. The periodical *Punch* noted in 1844 that Pennsylvania was celebrating the bicentennial of William Penn's birth with "appropriate exercises," including "the exciting and national sport of 'Beggar my Neighbour.'"

served, arguing that the canals would serve as competition and hold down rail rates, particularly for the bulky cargo—coal, lumber, and grain—that still dominated the river trade.

Knowing that time was on its side as far as Pennsylvania's asking price for the State Works was concerned, the Pennsylvania Railroad began construction of a rail line from Harrisburg to Pittsburgh. It was completed by 1852. Passengers from Philadelphia could ride to Lancaster on the Columbia-Philadelphia Railroad, change trains for Harrisburg, and board a Pennsylvania Railroad car there for the westward journey.[25] Traffic on the canals dwindled markedly, for trains cut travel time by 80 percent.

In 1855, when Pennsylvania once again put its State Works up for sale, J. Edgar Thomson, the Pennsylvania Railroad president who had helped design the Columbia-Philadelphia Railroad a quarter-century before, offered $7.5 million. He also attached one condition: that the state repeal a rail tonnage tax, which at the time was generating $200,000 a year. Pennsylvania asked for another $1 million from the rail company in exchange for dropping the tax, and title was transferred on August 1, 1857. Railroad officials had gotten a real bargain.

Nine months later, the state sold the canals along the North and West branches of the Susquehanna to the Sunbury and Erie Railroad Company for $3.5 million. The railroad in turn sold them to raise revenues to complete a line across the northern part of the state, giving rail access to the lumber industry, which was about to experience enormous growth.

In the end, the State Works generated $43.8 million in revenue for Pennsylvania, a figure that includes both tolls and the income from its sale. Losses, however, amounted to $57.8 million—and Pennsylvania was saddled with an additional $40 million in debt.

It was a high price to protect the Susquehanna from economic incursions by its neighbors. And a needless defensive tactic, for the Susquehanna possessed more than enough resources to go around. As transportation and access improved along the river, the race to develop those resources began in earnest. Coal production soared, and in the 1860s Pennsylvania became the world's leading lumber-producing state. Manufactured goods, iron, and other raw materials were also hauled out of the river basin to Philadelphia, Baltimore, and the world.

The rivalry to control the Susquehanna trade, which had dominated the economies—and politics—of Pennsylvania and Maryland since colonial days, faded away quietly in the years before the Civil War.

25. The Allegheny Portage was eventually replaced by the famed Horseshoe Curve.

Long after people stopped trying with steamboats, dams, and canals to make the Susquehanna a navigable river, it became one—on no less authority than the U.S. Congress. With the passage of the 1890 Rivers and Harbors Act and subsequent amendments, Congress elevated the Susquehanna to a status shared with the Mississippi, Hudson, Columbia, and other busy rivers of commerce.

Today, the Susquehanna is deemed officially navigable from its mouth as far north as Athens and up the West Branch to Lock Haven. "Oh, yes," says Tom Filip, who has been enlisted to confirm this designation, "it's true." Filip, a former schoolteacher and part-time Chesapeake Bay waterman, now is assistant chief in the regulatory branch of the U.S. Army Corps of Engineers' Baltimore district, and, as such, is responsible for protecting the navigability of the Susquehanna River—and explaining why his job exists in the first place.

His initial piece of advice is to forget the dictionary. Congress invented its own definition, "which is part of the problem," according to Filip. "Once the term got into the law, it began to lose the practical meaning of what we all consider navigable, which means you can get a boat up and down."

But there is a reason for Congress's interpretive approach. Being designated *navigable* makes a river eligible for certain federal programs, meaning U.S. taxpayers foot the bill for such operations as channel dredging and flood-control.

Just as navigability can be bestowed by Washington, it can be removed as economic and political needs dictate. In 1904, fourteen years after being declared navigable, the Susquehanna above the Maryland border was designated as nonnavigable by Secretary of War William Howard Taft. That cleared the way for large obstructions to be built on the river. It just so happened that at the time the Pennsylvania Railroad wanted to build a bridge at Havre de Grace. (Secretary Taft was kind enough to personally wire the railroad president, A. J. Cassatt, notifying him of the decision.) Taft's action also cleared the way for construction in Pennsylvania of two hydroelectric dams, the first of which—York Haven—was completed the same year. A dam at Holtwood followed soon after. Maryland also approved a proposal to build a hydroelectric dam near Conowingo.

A decade passed before the navigability issue surfaced once more. In an impassioned speech on the floor of Congress, Rep. J. Hampton Moore of Philadelphia sought votes to overturn Taft's decision. "I do not know of any other river in the country so capable of public service that has been so signally overlooked," he declared. As a result of dams built along the river, "the people of Pennsylvania and New York have quietly been deprived of their right of an outlet to the sea."

Referring to the newly completed dam at Holtwood, Moore observed,

It was a great piece of engineering, but it escaped the scrutiny of the Federal Government, which it could not have done had the Government exercised its ordinary jurisdiction. No lock or passageway for vessels seeking an outlet to the Chesapeake Bay or to the sea was provided. Even the shad fishermen above the dam were shut out of their usual occupation, and although a fishway has since been set up, there is no method for fishing vessels to pass the dam. The structure is a barrier to commerce above and to commerce below; it is as much a barrier to the potatoes and tobacco of York and Lancaster Counties as it is to the coal from Wyoming or Luzerne.

Moore proposed a series of federally constructed dams and locks to render the river navigable "all the way up to Harrisburg." Although Congress supported him in designating the Susquehanna navigable once again, Moore's grand plan for transforming the river into a thoroughfare went the way of other such schemes.

It would be nearly seven decades before the question of free access on the Susquehanna heated up again, and this time the beneficiary was a shiny visitor who traveled hundreds of miles to reach the Susquehanna, only to be turned back by manmade obstructions.

Columbia sits at the northern end of a slackwater lake created by the dam at Safe Harbor, the fourth to be built on the lower river. Today, says Philip Glatfelter, retired banker and lifelong Columbia resident, the Susquehanna provides the town "with drinking water and recreation. That's about all." (It's also good for some occasional excitement in the form of high water and massive ice jams, adds his wife, Bernadette.)

The old industries that once filled the town—sawmills, coal yards, shad fisheries—are long gone. So, too, is the big roundhouse operated by the Pennsylvania Railroad. "We used to boast that more rolling stock passed over the tracks at Front and Walnut streets than anywhere else in the United States," says Glatfelter. Now a passenger train draws second glances, and the large brick factories and warehouses that relied on rail links are in disrepair. "No new industries came to replace the old," Glatfelter continues. Nearby York and Lancaster, and their suburban malls, have hurt Columbia's downtown, and residents commute elsewhere to work.

"A number of years ago, the town decided its future lay in its history," says Glatfelter. Columbia, Wrightsville, and Marietta have banded together to promote their historical heritage, hoping to lure tourist dollars to this stretch of the Susquehanna. Among the attractions is the small stone house once inhabited by Susanna Wright, furnished exactly as if she still resided there. Adds Glatfelter, "If you were ever going to build a transportation museum, this would be the place."

The intensive competition between Pennsylvania and Maryland to win the loyalties of those living along the river hasn't disappeared completely. "On this side of the Susquehanna, we watch the Philadelphia Phillies," says Glatfelter. "Over there, they follow the Orioles."

The schemes to convert the Susquehanna into a grand waterway failed, but its banks still serve as a vital transportation network. The river is lined by nearly 500 miles of railroad track, on which move more than 160 million tons of freight each year. Although Conrail's east-west line across Pennsylvania is regarded as one of the railroad's "primary" lines, the Susquehanna Valley route is "in the upper ranks of our secondary lines," says Larry A. DeYoung, regional market manager for Conrail.

Every day, scores of Conrail trains snake along the river, carrying cargoes as diverse as those that once came careening downstream on the high waters of spring: coal hauled from the Clearfield area, bound for power plants on the North Branch and main stem; logs from the West Branch, bound for Baltimore and the export market; cocoa beans, sugar, corn syrup, and milk, headed for the Hershey Foods Corporation; tank cars of chemicals for industrial facilities up and down the river, grain, automobiles, steel, iron ore, and machinery. Often the only signs of civilization on the West Branch are the long, rumbling freight trains pulled by blue Conrail locomotives.

As Conrail officials circulated among their invited guests on the special Susquehanna tour train, they stressed repeatedly that they were looking to add more to their manifest lists. When the train passed Lancaster County's new multimillion-dollar incinerator, talk turned to hauling trash to the site by rail. A short time later, as the cars traversed autumn-brown corn fields, Jim Fallon, who manages Conrail's Harrisburg division, mentioned that soon he hoped to whisk just-picked crops from the rich farmland of the lower Susquehanna overnight to markets in New York City.

As a newcomer to the Susquehanna, Fallon is still discovering the volume of resources of his home base. "There's no shortage of things from this region that we could ship out," says Fallon. "It sometimes amazes me just how much there is."

Chapter Three

Logging

"The trees came down like tall grass"

The old scars of the Susquehanna's forests are plainly visible to a knowing eye. The narrow, leaf-littered hiking trail ascending a steep hillside was once the grade for a logging railroad. Flowering apple trees occupy the site of a bustling lumber camp, once home to a hundred men or more. The deep pools that shelter brown trout are the byproduct of old timber dams. Ralph Harrison sees them all as he travels through this country. As a district ranger in the 198,000-acre Elk State Forest in north-central Pennsylvania, Harrison is reminded every day of the amazing history of the West Branch of the Susquehanna River.

One of the largest sawmills in Pennsylvania sat where Harrison's office is today along Hicks Run, the eleven-mile stream that flows into the Bennett Branch of Sinnemahoning Creek, which in turn joins the Susquehanna at Keating. The mill operated around the clock, processing the million or more logs cut from this small, unremarkable valley, one of scores in the mighty West Branch watershed. Now, all that remains in Hicks Run in addition to the ranger station are a few rag-tag hunting cabins and an overgrown cemetery. In some seasons, there are more elk than humans in these hills, a fact Ralph Harrison and his two colleagues in this part of the forest, Marsha Jeffrey and John Sidlinger, regard as one of the major benefits of their jobs.

They are an unlikely trio, these guardians of the forest, yet their common love of this particular piece of the Susquehanna country has forged a strong friendship. The West Branch and its tributaries here flow through some of the remotest parts of the state, now wild and empty, dotted by tiny communities whose size and dreams have shriveled as their valuable resources—timber and coal—were extracted and the profits spent elsewhere.

Ralph Harrison is a Lincolnesque, silver-haired man of few words who has lived all his life in these woods, joining the Bureau of Forestry in 1953, he says, because it offered an opportunity to work outdoors. This bit of personal history prompts a quick retort from his partner, grinning at him across a battered desk in the corner of the garage-workshop that also serves as their office. "Admit it," teases Marsha Jeffrey, "you took it because nobody else wanted the job."

Jeffrey, a lanky ash blonde, is as outgoing as Harrison is taciturn. Raised in the gritty, industrialized corridor south of Philadelphia, she played as a child in a polluted creek. "I never knew you could drink from the ground," she says. The only deer she had ever seen were in a petting zoo. Determined to leave the city, Jeffrey enrolled in Penn State's wildlife technology program, and after graduating worked as a seasonal employee for the Bureau of Forestry and at other odd jobs while doggedly outwaiting the state's ponderous civil service process. Her goal: to land the first full-time position that became available in the Elk State Forest. The fact that the job was heavy-equipment operator deterred her not at all. She had to lift weights to pass the training course and still keeps a set of barbells in the living room of her tiny creekside house. "I'm a heavy-equipment operator so I can be here. I'm not here because I'm a heavy-equipment operator," she explains with a smile. Sitting behind the green ranger station is her massive yellow road grader, whose tires tower above her. Her bulldozer is parked alongside.

The third member of the crew is forester John Sidlinger, who can recall the exact date he arrived at Elk State Forest: June 8, 1978. "My wife wasn't real happy about coming here," he says. "On the drive from State College where we had been living, she started crying at about Emporium because she hadn't seen a shoe store in an hour. But she loves it now," he adds quickly. "Space is what I like about this place. You know you're pretty much your own person here."

Sidlinger, a handsome dark-haired man in a traditional red-and-black plaid wool jacket, is responsible for managing the timber production from this sprawling forest. It is he who decides which stands of mature trees are ready for harvest and who authorizes the removal of certain smaller trees, those that interfere with the growth of valuable commercial species, such as red oak and black cherry, which thrive in this climate. "We are growing a garden here and we have to wait 100 years for our tomatoes to get ripe," he explains. "All we're doing in the meantime is weeding. But we can sell the weeds."

Trees rank as Pennsylvania's most valuable natural resource, ahead of coal. Some of the finest hardwoods in the world grow in the state, and lumber valued at $4 billion is delivered to domestic and international markets each year. That amounts to about 1 billion feet of lumber. Much of it comes from the rugged hills and valleys drained by the West Branch of the Susquehanna.

Sidlinger designates a total of about 2,500 acres per year to be selectively logged. From each acre, six or seven century-old trees may be cut. The "weeds" are lesser-quality young trees, which are converted to paper or pulp. Logging is possible in only about half of Elk State Forest; elsewhere, the terrain is too rugged, or the area is regarded as so scenic that lumbering is prohibited. There are pressures from both sides to open more forest for timber-cutting or close more to commercial uses. There also is intense lobbying to cultivate commercially valuable trees, such as oak, at the expense of natural forest diversity. "It's a real juggling act to keep everybody happy," Sidlinger says.

He acknowledges a deep appreciation for the old trees that remain in this forest. "Sometimes I think those old guys should stay around," he says. "The loggers don't have enough respect for them when they're on the ground." Sentiment aside, the state forests of Pennsylvania currently are being managed to generate about $8 million in revenue annually. That figure may rise in the near future as a new generation of trees reaches maturity. Nearly 12 billion feet of valuable hardwood timber currently is maturing in Pennsylvania's forests.

The last time the lumbermen swept through these valleys and mountain ridges, they literally left nothing behind. Pennsylvania's hills were so devoid of vegetation that even deer couldn't survive. It has taken nearly a century for the forest to recover.[1]

On an October day, the woodlands of the West Branch burn with the vivid colors of sugar maples, cherry, beech, oak, and ash, interrupted occasionally by cool green clumps of hemlock or the unmistakable starburst silhouettes of white pine, the two species that once reigned unchallenged in these forests. It is a glorious spectacle. It is also a testament to nature's ability to erase man's most egregious insults.

Once, 99.8 percent of Pennsylvania's 28,692,480 acres was covered with trees.[2] Small wonder, then, that Pennsylvania is the only state named for its forests. The property deeded to William Penn by Charles II is conservatively estimated to have contained 700 billion feet of lumber. That would build 63 million of today's single-family homes, or about two-thirds

1. The deer rebounded in less than three decades. By the late 1930s, deer overpopulation was a problem in many areas of the state. It has worsened since then.

2. Today, the state has 16.5 million acres of forest, about 57 percent of its total area.

of all the housing units currently in the United States. And there may have been twice that much.

The settlers who first arrived regarded the uninterrupted expanse of trees as a burden, not a blessing, and they set about civilizing this endless wilderness by eradicating it. Wrote a British visitor:

> They have an unconquerable aversion to trees, and whenever a settlement is made they cut away all before them without mercy. The man that can cut down the largest number, and have fields about his house most clear of them, is looked upon as the most industrious citizen, and the one that is making the greatest improvements in the country.

In the New World, the first lumberman was, in fact, the first settler.

Penn only reluctantly agreed to the name Pennsylvania (meaning "Penn's Woods") to please the king.[3] Before he set foot in his province he drafted stringent conservation rules for the "adventurers and purchasers" about to settle there. One acre of trees was to be retained for every five acres cleared, with special care taken to preserve oak for shipbuilding and mulberries for silk production. While silk played a minor role in the colony's early economy, shipbuilding provided a critical means of facilitating trade with England.

Penn knew full well the value of timber. England had eradicated its dense forests by the thirteenth century and even the royal timber preserves had been depleted by Charles II's day. As a result, the crown depended on foreign sources to meet its ever-growing defense and domestic needs and was desperately seeking a new, dependable supply of raw materials. The forests of the New World seemed a godsend, and the settlers there were all too happy to oblige, for timber proved to be an easy commodity to trade for badly needed hard currency and manufactured goods.[4]

Because of a harmonious blend of cool climate, constant moisture, and

---

3. Penn favored the name "New Wales" because of the colony's hills.

4. The settlers of Jamestown shipped a load of mast timber to England in 1609, one year after Capt. John Smith ventured up the Susquehanna. By 1652 an active trade with England had been established from several colonial ports. Yet there were early indications that Penn's concerns about depleting this resource were warranted. By 1670 some Massachusetts towns were experiencing timber shortages, and in 1685 the British admiralty, fearing that the booming colonial lumber trade might deprive it of ship-building materials, reserved for its own use the best timber in America, to be identified by a blaze shaped like a broad arrow. Surveyors fanned out across the forests of New England and New York, reaching as far as the headwaters of the North Branch of the Susquehanna, to mark trees reserved for the Royal Navy. The so-called Broad Arrow policy was roundly despised—and ignored—by settlers, who regarded the woods as their own to use as they wanted. Penn's plea for conservation also went unheeded.

deep, though rocky, soils, the mountain valleys of northern Pennsylvania possessed timber the likes of which no modern-day visitor can comprehend. So dense were these forests, wrote naturalist John Bartram, who traveled up the Susquehanna in 1743, that "it seems almost as if the sun had never shone on the ground since the creation. We observed the tops of the trees to be so close to one another for many miles together, that there is no seeing which way the clouds drive, nor which way the wind sets." Others found the dark forests foreboding. "Shades of death," lamented one early traveler. Two- and three-hundred-year-old white pines, more than ten stories tall and in excess of forty inches at their base, were everywhere.

There may be no more versatile or valuable building material than white pine *(pinus strobus)*. More than any other single species, it contributed to the internal commerce and development of the young United States. The first house in America was built of white pine; by 1805 half a million homes had been constructed of the wood. So integral to daily life in America was white pine that it was chosen to adorn the first flag of those seeking freedom from British rule.

The grain of white pine is straight and true; it does not warp or rot. It is light and easy to work, yet remarkably strong. Its durability is obvious even today: white pine stumps still dot the steep hillsides of the West Branch a century or more after the trees were felled. Such trees could be cut in arrow-straight lengths of 90 or 100 feet that carried neither a blemish nor a knot. Often there were no limbs for 100 feet or more on the trunk; the overstory was so dense that no light penetrated below that level. A legendary white pine cut in Clearfield County, near the headwaters of the Susquehanna, measured 168 feet and produced a 150-foot-long plank.

The value of white pine was further enhanced by its location—dense stands crowded creek- and riverbanks and the steep hillsides along them. The deep snowfalls of the West Branch region made moving logs through the woods to frozen streams a simple task in winter—which was when white pine was cut, for in warm weather the sap would stain the wood and slash its value. Thus, farmers, idle during cold weather, could supplement their incomes by cutting trees and preparing them for market in the early spring, when even tiny creeks along the Susquehanna swell with melting snow. With the streambeds full, it was possible to move the massive pine logs hundreds of miles downstream to market.

Early settlers along the Susquehanna soon discovered that white pine floated easily even while carrying heavy loads, and it was a simple matter to fashion the logs into rafts. Logs destined to become masts or spars were carefully bound together with pliant hickory sticks, which left no marks on the valuable wood; other timber, headed for sawmills, was squared by axes and fastened with oak or hickory pins into floating platforms ranging in length from thirty to eighty feet. A farmer and his sons, hired hands, or neighbors clambered aboard, and wielded long oars fore and aft to negotiate the twisting curves and shoals of creeks that eventually joined the Susquehanna. It was not uncommon for these rafts and their crews to float 300 or more miles to Marietta, Columbia, and even Havre de Grace. There the pine raft was disassembled and sold to eager buyers from Baltimore and Philadelphia. By 1796, rafts from both the North and West branches of the Susquehanna were making the trip downstream, some traveling as far as Norfolk.

Of the two branches, the West Branch was *the* rafting river, often jammed with thousands of floating platforms in the spring. Far more common on the North Branch were crudely constructed arks, shallow flat-bottomed boats designed to survive a one-time trip downstream bearing cargo from the fertile farmland of New York State. Whether by raft or ark, for the men who journeyed downriver the freshets of spring heralded the beginning of an adventure; for those who watched the vessels pass, they signaled the end of winter.

Wrote poet Nathaniel Parker Willis, who lived along the Susquehanna in Owego, New York:

> As it swells in March, the noise of voices and hammering come out from the woods above, warn us of the approach of an ark, and at the rate of eight or ten miles an hour the rude structure shoots by, floating high on the water without its lading (which it takes in at the village below), and manned with a singing and saucy crew, who dodge the branches of trees, and work their steering paddles with an adroitness and nonchalance which sufficiently shows the character of the class . . . It is a curious sight to see the bulky monsters, shining with new boards, whirling around in the swift eddies, and when caught by the current again, gliding off among the trees, like a singing and swearing phantom of an unfinished barn.

Glamorous, perhaps, but also dangerous and grueling. "A voyage across the Atlantic does not involve so much danger to life and property, as the navigation of the river," wrote one observer. Added another:

> Now a Susquehanna waterman . . . will go on board an ark or a raft somewhere about the New York line, in March, April and May, descend to the tide water of the Chesapeake, and then return home on foot, through mire, rain, and all sorts of weather, at the rate of 50 or 60 miles a day. When

he gets home he jumps upon another ark or raft, and enacts the same feat over again—making five or six trips during the season of high water.

Between 1840 and 1860, the heyday of rafting on the West Branch, as many as 50,000 men traveled downstream on these crude log platforms. The uppermost put-in point was three miles above the community called Cherry Tree, which sits at the intersection of Clearfield, Cambria, and Indiana counties.[5] From these shallow waters each March and April were launched some of the river's tallest and finest timber. The men who guided the unwieldy rafts developed a culture all their own, and the tall tales that rafting inspired would live on long after the last white pine had been sent downstream.

So efficient was the Susquehanna as a one-way river road that the growth of population and trade actually slowed. As long as demand for timber was high, the ease of getting the logs downriver lessened the need to bring the markets closer to the trees. The rugged terrain and frequent conflicts with the Indians who lived in this wilderness also discouraged the spread of population up the West Branch. On occasion, the settlers were forced to flee their homes and seek shelter in frontier forts and larger settlements to escape Indian attacks.[6] That prompted the Pennsylvania legislature in 1795 to create Lycoming County, a move intended to boost population and improve local defense. With a total of 12,000 square miles—about twice the size of Connecticut—the county was named for a stream that flowed south into the West Branch.[7]

5. A wild cherry tree growing there marked the southwestern boundary of lands acquired in the 1768 treaty signed at Fort Stanwix, New York, by the heirs of William Penn and the Six Nations, who agreed to relinquish lands as far as a man could push a canoe up the West Branch. The site originally was known as Canoe Place.

6. The largest evacuation of the West Branch, known as the Big Runaway, occurred in 1778 in the midst of America's war for independence. It was an outgrowth of two simultaneous battles being waged along the Susquehanna—one against the British and their Indian allies and the other against Connecticut settlers claiming ownership of the Wyoming Valley. The handful of Pennsylvania residents along the river were forced to flee for their lives, taking refuge at Fort Augusta at the junction of the North and West branches, or in towns further downriver.

7. The choice of the county seat was fraught with controversy. Williamsport, which at the time consisted of just one building—an inn—finally was chosen despite strenuous objections from residents of other communities who argued that the site was nothing but a swamp, prone to regular flooding. (The fact that William Hepburn, a former state senator and newly appointed judge, owned property along the Lycoming may have influenced the selection.)

Williamsport's new status failed to boost its fortunes measurably, however. In 1800 the village had just 131 citizens. The county itself had slightly more than one adult male for each ten square miles. This was enormously valuable, but unforgiving, country, linked to the outside world only by the Susquehanna.

In November 1817, Chauncey Brockway, his wife, Rhoda, and their infant daughter, Louisa, left their home in New York State, bound for land they had purchased in what is now Elk County at the western edge of the Susquehanna's drainage area. The road along the West Branch, barely more than a wide trail, ended at Lock Haven, and the young couple, accompanied by two hired men, transferred their belongings to a canoe and poled upriver. They were forced to abandon the canoe on the Sinnemahoning Creek when the rocky stream froze solid. Setting out on foot in a heavy snowfall, they continued on, fording the creek and scrambling over fallen trees. Brockway carried the baby, and his wife a satchel of clothing. Brockway, 24 years old, wrote in his journal,

> Sometime between three and four o'clock in the afternoon, Mrs. Brockway asked me if we were almost through. I told her that I did not know but thought it was a good way off yet. At this saying she stopped and said that she could not go another step, as she was completely exhausted, had eaten nothing since daylight, her clothes were wet and heavy and frozen on her and her stockings were frozen fast to her shoes. We were in the wild woods alone and I did not know what to do, as there were no prospects of any help from any source but in ourselves. I told her for us to stop there would be certain death for her and her baby, and perhaps for myself also, for we had no way to make a fire and she was then almost frozen.

They made it to a cabin as night fell. After resting there, they pressed on until they reached their property.

> Here we were, just ready to begin life for ourselves, and this was our situation, our family and our prospects. We had our log cabin to make out of timber then standing, and provisions enough for eight or ten days and some 20 or 25 dollars in cash, and about 100 miles from our base of supplies, or where any provisions could be bought, except some 16 bushels of corn I bought on my way coming up the river, and it was 30 miles down the stream. This looked a good time, or a fair chance, at least, to starve.

The Brockways and their hired workers erected a small cabin and spent Christmas Day filling in the cracks between the logs. Their sole source of food for a month and a half was unground corn.

> For breakfast we had hulled corn and water porridge, for dinner we had water porridge and hulled corn, and for supper we had a change, water broth and hulled corn. We all stood it very well and worked hard.

About the first of March, the ice broke up and "let us out into the world again." Brockway headed to Jersey Shore, the nearest river settlement, and bought supplies, including two milk cows.

Sharing this country with the Brockways were a few settlers along the creeks of the region, including Hicks Run. Canoes, not wagons, provided transportation, and food came from the forests and streams. Brockway wrote,

> As you go up the river bank, instead of cows and oxen, you will meet from 4 to 6 big, fierce bear hunting dogs, and sometimes more, and no plows or harrows, but a log cabin, with stone chimney on the outside and a number of fish spears, a torch light stand made of wire or small iron, for night fishing or hunting. You take a look around you, and see a bushy-haired bluff-looking frontiersman, and his wife is a full match for him in looks, and a whole lot of tough looking children and perhaps two or three great strapping, strag[g]ling hunters.

Brockway, who had planned to farm his seventy-two acres, wrote despairingly of the land: "Nothing but bleak, rocky, barren sides of the mountains in view, and a high, rough, broken mountain in the rear." It was, he noted in dismay, covered with dense stands of white pine, hemlock, and oak. No crops would grow. After three years of struggle, he and his family moved on.

Tales of the Susquehanna and its forests were told wherever lumbermen gathered. A seventy-five-mile-wide swath of pine, plus huge stands of hemlock that formed a buffer zone around the pine, ran northeast to southwest along the Appalachian Plateau. The best logs had been cut from the forests in New England and New York by the 1830s and 1840s, and the Susquehanna was virgin country that beckoned like a beacon. The forests that had intimidated the first settlers enticed the next wave of arrivals. Even so, the Susquehanna was not about to give up its treasure easily.

The opening of the West Branch Canal in 1834 finally linked the Lycoming County seat, Williamsport, with the rest of Pennsylvania. While the Susquehanna would remain the principal route for moving timber for many decades, access to canal transportation meant that finished lumber could be manufactured in Williamsport mills and delivered to buyers practically anywhere. It also meant that profits derived from processing the lumber could remain in the bustling town of 1,200 people rather than traveling downriver with the logs. In 1838 a Philadelphia firm erected

Williamsport's first sawmill. Nicknamed the "Big Water Mill," it contained four up-and-down, water-powered saws. The enterprise was not a financial success and was sold at a sheriff's sale a short time later.

But logging on the Susquehanna was nonetheless about to be transformed from a sideline of idle farmers to an *industry* that created millionaires. In 1835, a Maine logging firm dispatched one of its agents, John Patchin, to assess the timber resources of the West Branch. He apparently never reported back, and instead settled near the tiny upriver community of Curwensville in Clearfield County, forty miles from the river's source. Patchin promptly began buying white-pine land for himself for about five dollars an acre. He established his base of operations in what is still known as Patchinville, a handful of weathered houses in the southwest corner of Clearfield County. Ultimately, John Patchin would own or control 40,000 acres of the best timberland on the West Branch. Those who knew him claimed he had the ability to smell good pine. Some even called him "the Spar King," a tribute to the number of masts and spars he sent downriver for America's sailing ships. Patchin was not above digging new channels for the Susquehanna to follow to get his spars safely to market.

Unlike most lumbermen of the day, John Patchin rarely cut from his own land. Instead, he bought stands of timber from others, many of whom were all too eager to have their land cleared. When Patchin's son Aaron died in 1897, the family still owned 2,600 acres of virgin white pine, including some that John Patchin had purchased more than half a century earlier.

Today, Roger Rorabaugh logs the land John Patchin once controlled, cutting primarily red oak as well as some cherry and maple from the valleys and mountains around Burnside, just a few miles downstream from Patchinville. The annual production of the family-owned Rorabaugh Lumber Company is 3 million feet, making it slightly larger than most sawmills along this stretch of the West Branch. Roger Rorabaugh and his brothers, Bob and Dan, are the first generation of the family to have made lumbering a full-time occupation. Their great-grandfather, born in 1843 in a log cabin on the ridge behind the mill, was a farmer, as were his son and grandson. They augmented their incomes by lumbering when the demands of planting and harvesting allowed.

"They used to raise livestock for the lumber camps and grain to feed the horses and mules," says Rorabaugh, a friendly young man who has left the enclosed cab of the giant saw he was operating to show a visitor around the mill.

"Technology's made this a full-time business," he explains. The

Rorabaughs no longer just cut trees into logs and logs into lumber for someone else to process. They produce "everything from ax handles on up," including high-quality, furniture-grade oak, which they dry in a kiln at the mill. Nearly 80 percent of the best hardwood logs cut in Pennsylvania today are exported to foreign manufacturers for furniture production; the Germans are especially fond of red oak, the Japanese of cherry.

Even so, observes Rorabaugh, who reads everything he can find on local history, "we're not that far removed from the days of John Patchin." At the rear of the millyard, the remnants of a dam built by Patchin still can be seen in the swift-flowing West Branch. Just how high the Susquehanna can rise is apparent by the mud line near the top of the banks. "I've seen it increase three feet in no time," says Rorabaugh.

Perhaps heeding the example set by the Patchins, Rorabaugh's great-grandfather refused to allow the best timber on his land to be cut, and a few years ago Roger and his brothers came across an eleven-acre tract of family property that contained a stand of massive hemlocks, some more than fifty inches in diameter at the base. "Just a hundred years ago, they wouldn't have been anything unusual. But we'd never seen anything like them," he says. After much family debate, and in concern that the aged hemlocks might blow down in a storm, a decision was made to cut the trees. "One tree produced 3,000 feet of lumber." The wood was used to build a home for his brother. "That made cutting those trees a little easier."

John Patchin wasn't the only outsider drawn to the stands of prime timber along the West Branch. One by one, they arrived along the river and made their mark.

John DuBois had learned the lumber business at his father's sawmill on the North Branch in Owego, New York. At age 17, he made his first trip downstream on a log raft; soon he was routinely descending to Columbia and even to the Chesapeake Bay to sell the lumber cut in his father's mill. Striking out on his own in 1838, DuBois moved to Lycoming County, erected a sawmill, and began buying large tracts of land, including several sizable parcels in Williamsport. On 500 acres on the south side of the river, he built another mill, and the community that grew up alongside it became known as Duboistown. He logged many of the valleys along the river and its network of creeks, including Hicks Run, which he bought, sold, and repurchased. DuBois and his brother Matthias also acquired more than 32,000 acres of choice white-pine land in Clearfield County, much of which proved to be underlain with coal. There a second, larger community named for John DuBois sprang up. Several years before his death in 1886,

DuBois was estimated to be worth between $12 million and $20 million; his mills employed 600 men and were capable of producing 200,000 feet of lumber a day. A thousand men worked in the woods cutting his timber, and another 600 mined his coal.

James Perkins arrived in Williamsport in 1845. A native of New Hampshire, Perkins came via Philadelphia, where he had sold his interest in a calico manufacturing plant. He was looking for another lucrative business venture and found it in a plan promoted by John Leighton, a Maine woodsman who had walked most of the West Branch in the 1830s. Leighton had an idea that would transform logging on the river, but his efforts to find backers had been fruitless until he met Perkins.

Large sawmills had yet to be built on the West Branch, in part because investors were leery of a business that operated only a few months a year—when the Susquehanna and its tributaries were high enough to float the logs to the saws. Leighton and Perkins reasoned that if they could create a means of storing logs, then the mills could run much longer, justifying major capital investments, ensuring greater production—and reaping greater profits. It was Leighton who looked at the West Branch at Williamsport and knew he had found the perfect location—the Long Reach, where the river levels out and the current swings gently toward the south against the steep flank of Bald Eagle Mountain, creating a secure holding basin.

Leighton's plan was simple: build a floating barrier, or boom, across the Susquehanna to catch logs as they came downstream. No longer would it be necessary to assemble rafts and shepherd them hundreds of miles to market. Nor would lumber owners be forced to station men in the middle of the river round-the-clock to catch logs as they came racing along in the current and then wrestle them to shore to be cut into lumber. Trees felled in winter could be hauled or skidded to the closest stream and simply released en masse on the current in early spring. Once in the log boom, they would remain impounded until sawmill operators were ready to retrieve them.

This was not a new idea; a log boom had been built on the Androscoggin River in Maine in 1789. But it was new to the Susquehanna, and meant change more far-reaching than the lumber economy of Williamsport. Free use of the river was about to end. The boom would become, in effect, a toll gate, with the fees collected from those using the Susquehanna reserved for Perkins and a few others.

Perkins's and Leighton's idea for the boom was greeted with skepticism from the lumbermen themselves, including John and Matthias Du-Bois, who nevertheless invested in the project. Although the Susquehanna

Boom Company was incorporated in 1846 and 100 shares of stock were issued, each valued at $100, it fell to Perkins to finance the project himself. But when the river flooded in 1849 and two temporary booms withstood the high water, even the DuBois brothers, who owned twenty-five shares apiece (Perkins owned twenty-four), were convinced. It may have been one of the most profitable investments of the era. For fifty-eight years, every log that descended the West Branch represented money in the pockets of the boom-company stockholders. Rates for storing logs in the boom ranged from 75 cents per thousand feet in the early years to $1.25, and during its lifetime the boom held more than 7 billion board feet of logs. That translated to about $7 million simply for letting the logs sit in the Susquehanna. The boom company also charged fees to haul them out of the river.

When the boom was full, it held enough lumber to build the equivalent of 534,000 modern-day houses. A person could walk for miles upriver on a solid bed of tightly packed logs. The boom itself consisted of 252 timber cribs twenty-two feet high, which were built into the river bottom at fifty-foot intervals and filled with rocks.[8] The cribs, linked by iron chains and floating logs at the water's surface, formed a diagonal line upstream for a distance of seven miles. At the upstream end along the north shore, an angular arm known as the sheer boom channeled the logs into the main holding pond. From the sheer boom extended a 250-foot-long fly boom that served as a gate to allow river traffic—primarily the thousands of timber rafts plying the West Branch each spring—to pass downstream. Although free access to the river for these rafts was a requirement of the boom company's state charter, the boom operators flouted that provision—much to the consternation of the raftmen, who had to pay for passage through the barrier. For nearly two decades, an uneasy rivalry— marred on occasion by bloodshed—existed between the lumber companies and the raftmen, who simply wanted to get to market to sell their winter harvest of timber.

As soon as the Susquehanna freed itself of its mantle of ice, the chains with their log floats were strung across the river at Williamsport, and a rider headed up the West Branch announcing, "Boom's hung, let the logs come." (Later, a phone line was dedicated specifically to relay the announcement.) A season's worth of pine and, in later years, hemlock was

8. John DuBois later sued the Philadelphia, Wilmington and Baltimore Railroad Company, claiming the firm stole his idea for constructing underwater piers to build a bridge across the Susquehanna at Havre de Grace. In 1871, the U.S. Supreme Court ruled against DuBois, noting that he had publicly described the construction process before he obtained a patent on it.

released into the water to hurtle downstream in the swollen current. The loggers had to act swiftly for, as Roger Rorabaugh knows, water levels on the West Branch fluctuate dramatically with rainfall, and even an hour or two can affect stream flows.

The changeable spring weather posed a problem for the many Scotch-Presbyterians in the region. They believed Sunday was the Lord's Day, but also were loathe to waste a precious moment getting their logs to market, where the earliest timber commanded the highest prices. The conflict finally was presented to the governing body of the Presbyterian Church, and according to one widely repeated story, the elders finessed the issue by noting that God wouldn't send high water on a Sunday if He didn't intend for the Presbyterians to put it to good use.

The woodsmen also aided their cause by erecting dams on the hundreds of creeks draining the watershed. These dams could be closed and opened at will to augment stream flow. By carefully synchronizing releases from these "splash dams," a lumberman could move his logs downstream on a manmade wave of water.

A few splash dams still remain in the remote reaches of the West Branch. One is just a short distance upstream from the Hicks Run Ranger Station. From the road, it is not obvious, but Ralph Harrison knows precisely where to stop the dusty green Jeep with "Bureau of Forestry" emblazoned on the side. One of four such dams that once spanned Hicks Run, this one has withstood nearly a century of springtime floods. Yellow birches now grow in the sediment that has built up behind it, but the clear water reveals the submerged remnants of a breastwork that once stood twelve to fifteen feet tall. Nearby, an apple tree in bloom stands as mute evidence that this site also served as a logging camp, one of several that advanced up the valley felling timber on its way. "You can always tell where the camps were because of the apple trees," says Harrison. "The loggers would throw out the cores or bury them, and the trees just took root."

Canal boats at Beach Haven, east of Berwick, ca. 1900 *(opposite, top)*. Although the network of canals built along the Susquehanna greatly improved transportation, the canals suffered from the same problems as the river—there often was either too much water or not enough. (James V. Brown Library, with permission)

Canal Basin at Columbia, Pa., ca. 1895 *(opposite, bottom)*. Even after railroads were built along the Susquehanna, bulk cargo, especially coal, was transported by water. (Pennsylvania Canal Society Collection, Hugh Moore Historical Park and Museums, Inc.; Easton, Pennsylvania)

Virgin forest, Sullivan County, Pa. *(above)*. This photograph was taken by Dr.
Joseph T. Rothrock, who launched Pennsylvania's forest conservation move-
ment in the 1880s. Alarmed at the destruction of the state's primeval forests,
Rothrock traveled around the state with a collection of photographic slides
depicting the beauty of the remaining woodlands as well as the extent of logging.
(Philadelphia Museum Commission, Division of Archives and Manuscripts,
Pennsylvania Historical and Museum Commission, with permission)

This was a far more common view in Pennsylvania between 1880 and 1910
(opposite, top). The scrap wood left behind was hauled away to make cellulose.
In less than a century, loggers had all but eradicated the virgin forests that once
covered 99.8 percent of the state. (Philadelphia Museum Commission, Division
of Archives and Manuscripts, Pennsylvania Historical and Museum
Commission, with permission)

Pine logs were fashioned into rafts and navigated hundreds of miles downstream
to markets on the lower Susquehanna *(opposite, bottom)*. Here a log raft is
negotiating the chute, or opening, in the Susquehanna Boom. The long oar, or
"sweep," was used to steer the unwieldy raft. (James V. Brown Library, with
permission)

In 1938, to commemorate a century of logging on the West Branch, the "Last Raft" began a descent of the river, drawing huge crowds along its route. As the raft approached the railroad bridge at Muncy, it struck a pier, careening out of control. The stern then struck another piling, and the raft tilted, dumping all but one passenger into the icy water. Seven people drowned. (Courtesy of Florence Leiby Smith)

Not far from the ranger station, Harrison stops the Jeep again on the rutted dirt road, grabs an axe, and heads toward the creek, which today is a favorite of trout fishermen. As he walks, he gestures toward the steep hillside behind him. The loggers working there would make a tree fall so its top was pointed downhill, he says. They would trim off the branches and leave it there until the hillside was covered with snow. Then they would give it a push. "Running, it was called," says Harrison. Some mighty pines would hit the valley floor with such force that the tops would pierce the ground like arrows. "So they'd just cut off the tree at ground level, leaving the rest in the dirt." As he speaks, Harrison raises his axe and strikes a weathered gray limb sticking up from the soil. The steel blade cuts into the pale yellow wood, which smells strongly of fresh pine—as it must have when it hit the forest floor, a century before.

Harrison once found a pine log that had been in the creek for a hundred years or so, and made a bookcase from the wood. "It was a good piece of lumber."

Just as the newly arrived lumbermen were about to change the face of the Susquehanna, so too would they transform Williamsport. At one point in its history, Williamsport had more millionaires per capita than any other city in the United States—18 among its 19,000 citizens—all of them drawn there by the forests of the Susquehanna River.[9]

It was James Perkins and his boom that ignited the city's growth. But another outsider would dominate nearly every aspect of community life for a quarter-century. Peter Herdic arrived on the West Branch in 1853 at age 29, a New York native whose formal education consisted of learning to write his name. He appears to have been a man of sharp contrasts: charitable, perhaps visionary, yet driven and not above exerting his enormous political power to get what he wanted. At his peak, he controlled an empire of 54,000 acres of timberland as well as almost every major enterprise in Williamsport: several sawmills, a newspaper, large amounts of residential and commercial real estate, the city's most luxurious hotel, its trolley company, a gas and water works, and a bank. He donated land and money

9. There is very little record of the interaction among these successful entrepreneurs, either professionally or socially. The lack of documentation of this fascinating part of Williamsport's history is attributable to several severe floods over the years and a fire at the county historical society. But it also undoubtedly is a result of the transitory nature of the business that created this concentration of wealth. The lumbermen made their fortunes and either lost them as the forests were depleted, or moved on to other logging towns.

for churches and underwrote construction of low-cost housing, employing out-of-work loggers.

The stories of Herdic are legion.[10] When his plans to convert land along West Fourth Street into a millionaires' enclave were threatened by rival real estate developers, Herdic secretly bought some of his rivals' land, erected tenements and a boarding house on it, and then filled them with undesirable tenants. When his candidate for county judge was narrowly defeated, Herdic persuaded the state legislature to abolish the judicial district and eliminate the judgeship.

In 1857, Herdic and two other newcomers to Williamsport, Mahlon Fisher and John G. Reading, bought the Susquehanna Boom Company from Perkins, DuBois, and the other investors—at a time when the timber industry on the West Branch was about to experience exponential growth. Then, exerting his influence in Harrisburg, Herdic won approval from the legislature to raise the fees, ostensibly to underwrite construction of a new dam below the boom. Over the next eight years, the income of the boom company totaled more than $2.25 million. Much to the consternation of loggers all along the West Branch, the fee increase remained in effect long after the dam was paid for, contrary to terms set by the lawmakers. (The legislation itself was said to have mysteriously disappeared from the state vault.)

While lumbering occupied some of his time, and provided working capital, Peter Herdic also speculated heavily in Williamsport real estate. In 1856 he erected an ornate Italian villa-style home at one end of West Fourth Street. Soon, land along the street, which he owned, became *the* fashionable address. There was no shortage of would-be neighbors, for the Susquehanna and its forests had provided many Williamsporters with undreamed-of wealth. They hired Herdic's favorite architect and built ostentatious mansions. One contained a stained-glass window featuring Mozart and John Milton; its fireplace was adorned with tiles depicting the tales of King Arthur. Mahlon Fisher's Greek Revival home was so pretentious in its day that it became known as the "million-dollar mansion." Touring theater companies, musicians, and renowned lecturers, including Mark Twain, made regular stops in Williamsport.

The glory days of the West Branch were just dawning, however, for America was about to begin consuming lumber voraciously. In 1850, the

10. There remain almost no personal records of his life, however, except a handful of court documents.

United States produced 5 billion board feet of lumber.[11] Within a single decade production increased 60 percent, and Pennsylvania surpassed New York to became the nation's leading lumber producer. The towering white pines that lined the Susquehanna and its tributaries were responsible for boosting the state into first place. In 1860, Williamsport proudly proclaimed itself Lumber Capital of the World.

The exploitation of Pennsylvania's forests was driven primarily by economics, of course. But overriding the pure commercialism of lumbering were two popular beliefs that gave it a certain moral mandate.

Since the first pioneers headed into the American wilderness, a belief persisted that the plow would follow the ax. Thus, clearing the land was a means of putting it to a "higher" purpose—the production of food. In reality, however, very little of the nation's forest land is suitable for farming; forest cover *is* its highest purpose. In Pennsylvania, only about 15 percent of the land is arable; the remainder is capable of sustaining just one thing— trees. As Chauncey Brockway and countless others discovered, the soil beneath the trees was too poor, too rocky, or simply too steep to farm.

Another popular belief of the era held that cut-over forest land would follow a natural progression: hardwoods would replace the pines and hemlocks, and after the hardwoods were cut down, pines and hemlocks would grow again. Thus, the theory went, timber resources could never be depleted and were a gift that Providence plainly meant people to use. As it happens, that progression of species is exactly what has occurred in Pennsylvania's forests. But in the nineteenth century, human greed came perilously close to outstripping nature's regenerative powers. The natural-progression theory also ignored one destructive force active in the forests: fire. And it failed to take into account what would happen to those living downstream when the hills to the north and west were rapidly denuded of their protective cover.

The outbreak of the Civil War unleashed an unprecedented demand for lumber—to build ships and fortifications, rail cars and supply depots— and Pennsylvania did its part for the Union cause. As the postwar recovery began, demand only increased, and the forests of the Susquehanna quenched much of the nation's appetite. By the end of the 1860s, more than a million logs were reported in the Susquehanna boom, and the race to harvest the centuries-old virgin forests of the West Branch was on. "Into the

---

11. A board foot is a unit of measure twelve inches long by twelve inches wide by one inch thick. The terms "foot" and "board foot" are used interchangeably.

West Branch forests marched an army of loggers, and the trees came down like tall grass before a giant scythe," wrote Pennsylvania historian Paul A. W. Wallace.

First, Lycoming Creek rang with the sound of axes and saws; then the phenomenally productive Pine Creek; Kettle Creek; the Sinnemahoning, and on up the Susquehanna. The rapaciousness of the lumbering is illustrated by a log drive in 1868 that began on the Bennett Branch of the Sinnemahoning and consisted almost entirely of white pine. Making the trip were John DuBois, who owned much of the timber, and Hiram Woodward, an employee of timber magnates John G. Reading and Mahlon Fisher. Journals maintained by DuBois preserve details of the trip.

Record snowfalls during the winter of 1867–68 had facilitated the movement of large numbers of logs from the steep hillsides to the stream banks. On March 19 word reached the loggers along Bennett Branch that the boom at Williamsport, 100 miles away, had been hung. The drive could begin.

Thirteen thousand logs, measuring over 4 million board feet, were pushed into the boiling current that day. At various landings along the river, more logs were added: 550,000 feet of pine from Mountain Run; more than 40,000 logs from a camp two days downstream; 348,000 feet from another. More than 2 million feet were added at Tyler's Flats; 3 million from another landing, and 3.6 million at yet another. In all, 100 men and eight teams of horses were kept busy hauling stranded logs from shoals, repeatedly entering the frigid water to keep the logs moving. The river by now was a solid mass of bobbing timber. Behind it floated a specially constructed ark that contained bunks, a galley with a new $51 cookstove, and a company store from which the men could purchase tobacco, rubber boots, gloves, and other supplies. Along the way, additional food was purchased from local residents—150 cabbages at eight cents a head, a barrel of sauerkraut, a barrel of flour—all of which DuBois noted in his account book.

Sixty-four men were dispatched up Kersey Run to help bring down 3 million more feet of pine. The water levels dropped, slowing the downstream movement and enabling DuBois, then 59, to make a hurried trip to St. Marys to obtain more cash to pay his crew and purchase supplies. He withdrew $400 from the bank. On April 4 and again three days later snow fell and quickly melted, raising the water level. By April 9, Bennett Branch was running "bank full," according to a journal entry. At Benezette, a blacksmith reshod the horses and repaired the hand pikes used by the drivers to free stranded logs. More than 4.3 million feet of timber was added at Trout Run; from Mix Run came 300,000 feet.[12]

The drive reached the confluence with the Sinnemahoning at Keating on April 19, and sixteen men were discharged, their services no longer needed because the deeper water simplified moving the logs. The last group of logs—810,000 feet cut from the First Fork of the Sinnemahoning—was added to the drive just before it came upon another flotilla of timber bound for Williamsport. The logs were allowed to commingle; the brands stamped into the butt ends of each one, similar to those used on cattle, would establish undisputed ownership upon arrival. Through this teeming mass of loose pine logs passed 400 to 500 timber rafts bound for the lower Susquehanna.

As the drive neared Lock Haven, itself a thriving logging community with sawmills—and saloons—lining the riverbank, twenty-six of the crew requested a night off and advances on their wages of between $5 and $20, according to the journal entries. Strung across the river at Lock Haven was a log boom capable of holding 100 million feet of timber. All hands were required to carefully shuttle the logs bound for Williamsport past those floating in the Lock Haven boom.[13] As the drive grew closer to Williamsport, more crew members were discharged, collecting pay that averaged about $4 per day and included a $2.80 train ticket for the return trip home. Those remaining were assigned the task of bringing up the rear to ensure that all logs were accounted for.

By mid-May, nearly two months after it had begun, the DuBois-Woodward log drive arrived at Williamsport. In the Susquehanna boom it deposited logs estimated to contain 44,430,000 feet of timber cut from 2,221 acres of land. This represented more than one-fourth of the amount received by the boom in 1868.

The *Lycoming Daily Gazette* took brief note of the loggers' arrival. "It is, after all, the laboring man, whose daily efforts return him daily wages, which gives life and permanent prosperity to any community. They are the real strength, the real wealth and the real power. Their money keeps mov-

12. Mix Run would produce something other than fine timber. It was the home of one of America's best-known silent-movie cowboys, Tom Mix. Mix was born in 1880 along the small creek that bears his name. His father worked as a horse handler for John DuBois's lumber drives. Tom Mix was hired for his first movie role by Thomas Edison, who was filming in Oklahoma. In all, Mix made 370 movies.

13. It is still possible to see the remnants of the old boom cribs in the water just upstream of Lock Haven, thanks in part to the clarity of the water—perhaps the only benefit to be derived from its acidity. The size of the logs, impressive even underwater, gives a modern-day observer a hint of the magnitude of the trees that once flourished along the West Branch and came careening downstream.

ing. Seldom, indeed, do they allow it to rust under lock and key." The paper also duly reported that several drunken brawls had broken out in town.

Within days, heavy rains flooded the West Branch and threatened the logs in the boom, estimated to be worth $2 million. At particular risk was the sheer boom, which was designed for only ten feet of water, whereas the remainder of the boom could hold back logs at water depths of up to fifteen or sixteen feet. On May 18, a portion of the sheer boom burst and between 12 and 15 million feet of logs went hurtling downriver. Thousands eventually reached Havre de Grace and the Chesapeake.

This was not the first time a portion of the boom had broken, nor would it be the last. In 1860, John DuBois alone lost 4.5 million feet of timber when the barrier gave way. It broke again in 1861 and 1865. Recognizing a way to turn misfortune into profit, the savvy DuBois built a sawmill in Havre de Grace and bought up the salvaged logs at cents on the dollar.

Williamsport was a gilded city with a seemingly unlimited future—as long as the river delivered trees and the mills kept humming. In the summer of 1872 the mills fell silent.

Unusually heavy spring rains that year had filled the Susquehanna boom to near capacity, and more logs waited upstream to be processed at the three dozen or so sawmills along the river. About 3,000 men and boys were employed in those mills, earning between 80 cents and $2 for a workday that began at 6 A.M. and ended at 6:30 P.M., Saturdays included. The stirrings of the labor movement had begun in Pennsylvania nearly a half-century earlier, when the Journeymen House Carpenters of Philadelphia had called for a ten-hour workday.

On May 7, 1872, the national Labor Reform Union, then a year old, held its state convention in the Lycoming County Courthouse in Williamsport. Chief to the union's platform was a shorter workday. It should have come as no surprise to the mill operators that their workers might be receptive to joining such an organization.

On June 27, the *Daily Lycoming Gazette and West Branch Bulletin* reported that workers had assembled "to take action in relation to demanding the ten hour system in the various mills of the city." Noting that laborers elsewhere were demanding a reduction in their workdays from ten hours to eight, the group declared, "we believe that if ten hours is too long a day's work for them, 12 and 13 are certainly too much for us." The members voted to stop work until their demands were met. "The working man must have time to read and inform himself of what is transpiring in the nation," a worker told his colleagues at the rally. Leading the unionists were Thomas H. Greevy, who at age 22 lived with his innkeeper mother and who later would become a prominent lawyer; A. J. Whitten and Thomas H. Blake, who worked in the sawmills; and James C. Bermingham, a Williamsport policeman who was fired the day after the initial meeting by the mayor, S. W. Starkweather, who owned a sawmill. They and other Williamsport workers formed Local 10 of the Labor Reform Union.

Commenting on the union's creation, the *Gazette*'s city editor, John Meginness, urged "prudent counsel" on both sides. "Both parties have legal and equitable rights which should be carefully considered," he wrote. Throughout the summer, the newspaper would reflect a sympathetic view toward the workers' actions. Peter Herdic, whose holdings included several sawmills, also owned a controlling interest in the *Gazette*.

Herdic's role in the strike was a curious one. While his counterparts rejected the call for a shorter day, he pledged a ten-hour workday with an hour at midday for "rest and refreshment." In addition, Herdic promised to pay each worker extra "for all the hours and parts of hours that he works over the ten." It was an unprecedented offer. Buoyed by Herdic's promise, the workers—led by a small contingent of black mill hands, chosen to symbolize the strikers' desire to be freed from "slave labor conditions"— visited the thirty or more sawmills in and around Williamsport and urged nonstriking workers to walk off the job. Many did, and the saws were shut down. With a few exceptions, the mills would remain closed for three weeks. The Sawdust War, as it became known, had begun.

By nightfall, rumors were flying. A trainload of 500 union sympathizers reportedly was headed to Williamsport from Baltimore. Mayor Starkweather petitioned the governor to send in troops to quell the strike— then not yet twelve hours old. The sympathizers never materialized, and it would be nearly three weeks before Gov. John W. Geary finally dispatched any troops. In the meantime, the strike was so peaceful and uneventful that at one point the newspaper reported: "There is nothing to-day that requires special mention." When an offer of an 11½-hour day and a 25-cent wage increase was rejected, the mill owners voted to close down not only all the mills, but also the boom. That produced an outcry from lumbermen above Williamsport and sawmill operators below the boom, who were also forced to curtail operations.

The mill owners, however, were not as unified as their workers. On July 15, the *Gazette* reported that a large crowd had gathered outside P. Herdic and Company upon learning that it was about to become the fourth mill to resume operations with a ten-hour work day. Herdic sweetened the deal at his mill by also offering a 25-cent-per-day pay increase. It was at this meeting that strike leader A. J. Whitten was reported to have said to the crowd, "It is twelve hours and no sawdust, or ten hours and plenty of sawdust," giving the strike its rallying cry.

Tensions mounted, stirred by the fact that some mills had reopened with nonstrikers. On the morning of July 22, a group of about 300 strikers approached the Filbert and Otto mill, one of those defying the union's demands. The marchers were greeted by special policemen and warned to stay off the property. According to a reporter on the scene, "After considerable conversation of an exciting nature, a yell was given and the strikers moved toward the mill." The police drew their revolvers, and were met with "a shower of brickbats." Sheriff Samuel Van Buskirk would later testify that he saw a crowd of fifty women nearby cheering on the strikers with cries of "Clean them out!"

In a telegram to Governor Geary later that morning, the sheriff pleaded for help. Williamsport's two national guard companies—including the Taylor Guards, which consisted of forty-six black men—were mobilized. "Law and order must be sustained," Geary cautioned. A short time later, Van Buskirk and Mayor Starkweather wired the governor again: "The mob is becoming more infuriated. Send not less than 500 troops with sufficient ammunition. Send them tonight on special train." Overnight, five train cars of soldiers arrived and the following day the *Gazette* reported that a total of 303 soldiers were bivouacked at the Court House. Soon, arrest warrants were issued for the strike leaders, charging them with assault and battery and "riotously and tumultuously" entering several mills.

The strikers' anger apparently dissipated with the surrender of their leaders, and the militia spent most of its time parading through town. By August 1, the troops had begun to depart, which prompted the *Gazette* to wryly note,

> The West Branch army, with its sweeping lines of glittering steel, has retired from the carnage fields of the Susquehanna, and by a wave of the military baton ceases to exist . . . They return home with ammunition well preserved, having fought a bloodless battle, leaving behind memories of oblique movements, division fronts and ranks of four through the streets of this American Paris, besides desparate [*sic*] charges for ten hour men through gardens, where plump and healthy cabbages, stout and lofty tomato vines, have went down before the tread of conquering men.

On September 3, the case of *Commonwealth vs. James S. Bermingham et al.* began in the Lycoming County Court of Common Pleas; presiding was Judge James Gamble—the jurist whose job had been legislated out of existence at the request of Peter Herdic. Restored to the bench by the State Supreme Court, Gamble waded into the dispute that had torn apart the community.

After four days of testimony, the judge cautioned the jury against regarding the matter before them as a struggle between the wealthy and the working man. He told the jurors:

> We are emphatically a nation of laborers. The capitalists of this decade are largely made up of the laborers of the last, and those of the next decade will be as largely composed of the laborers of this. In this country labor is as honorable as capital, and the man who entertains any other sentiment only subjects himself to universal ridicule.

In less than an hour, the jury returned with a verdict. Twenty-one of the strikers were found guilty. Most received light sentences (some had been in jail since their arrest two months earlier), but Judge Gamble ordered the four leaders to serve a year of labor at the Eastern Penitentiary in Philadelphia. "It is marvelous that human life was not sacrificed," he told them. Two days later, Governor Geary stunned the mill owners by issuing pardons for all those convicted. *Gazette* editor John Meginness later wrote that Peter Herdic persuaded Geary to grant the pardons.

Demands for the ten-hour day were largely forgotten as the mills resumed operations. Even with a twenty-one-day work stoppage, the Susquehanna boom experienced a record year. Nearly 300 million feet of lumber was processed in Williamsport mills in 1872. (Thirty years later, workers in many mills along the West Branch were still earning between $1.25 and $1.50 for an eleven-hour day.)

Williamsport's prosperity mirrored that of the nation. America was in the midst of an economic surge, fueled by postwar growth which, in turn, set off a wave of speculation the likes of which this nation had never seen. Government was corrupt, fraudulent business dealings were commonplace, and many of the nation's leading entrepreneurs had built their empires on worthless paper. Americans fell deeper in debt, as more and more capital was transferred from production to speculation. At the forefront was Jay Cooke, who had been made a junior partner in a leading Philadelphia banking house by age 21 and went on to help finance the Civil War. On September 17, 1873, Cooke's banking house collapsed, the New York Stock Exchange closed its doors for ten days, and the United States slid into a depression. The number of bankruptcies soared, factories closed, and thousands lost their jobs.

The Panic of 1873 did not wreak all its damage overnight, and for Williamsport the year was a prosperous one. Nearly 1.6 million logs floated into the boom, setting an all-time record for lumber produced. Samuel Filbert, owner of the mill where the Sawdust War had erupted the previous summer, purchased a second West Fourth Street property from Peter Herdic and commissioned an elaborate Italian villa as a wedding present for his daughter Lucy. That fall, Herdic purchased 200 acres on the east bank of Lycoming Creek, consolidating his holdings on the fashionable west side of town. As with most of his business ventures, Herdic borrowed heavily to finance the land, apparently undaunted by his own spiraling debts.

All around, the economic signs grew more ominous. Even the nation's appetite for timber was slowing and in Williamsport much of the 221 million feet of white pine and 20 million feet of hemlock lumber that had been cut in 1873 remained unsold by the following spring. Some mill owners questioned the wisdom of sending crews into the forests over the winter of 1874–75 to cut new timber, and many men found themselves without jobs or means to feed their families. In response, Peter Herdic underwrote construction of more than sixty new buildings, ranging from low-cost multifamily dwellings to two large brick residences. It may have been this project that was his financial undoing, although as late as 1877 he was still hosting legendary July Fourth festivities at the elegant resort and health spa he owned in Minnequa, forty miles from Williamsport. That year, 7,000 people attended.[14]

But time finally ran out. On August 30, 1878, Peter Herdic—once said to be worth $10 million—filed for bankruptcy, with debts of more than $1.8 million. The news stunned Williamsport and was reported around the United States. Almost immediately, rumors spread that Herdic had looted his own accounts and businesses, secreting his vast funds to avoid paying his debts. Others speculated that he was the victim of powerful and ruthless men who had manipulated his downfall to acquire property worth a half-million dollars for a few thousand. The *New York Times* published an article to that effect on its front page. Records preserved as a result of years of lawsuits provide no conclusive answer.[15]

14. The year before, guests had included the governor, the president of the Pennsylvania Railroad, and other prominent men, all of whom arrived on a plush-covered seat mounted on the front of a steam engine.

15. Herdic's largest creditor was his former business partner in the Susquehanna boom,

Herdic's financial dealings also attracted the attention of the Commonwealth of Pennsylvania, which charged him with conspiracy to defraud investors in his brother-in-law's bank, and in a separate prosecution, with obtaining money under false pretenses. Although he was convicted in the first matter, he was granted a new trial; the charge subsequently was dropped. In the second case, he was found not guilty.

Peter Herdic fled the Susquehanna and started over. He moved to Philadelphia and, after briefly managing a hotel frequented by the state's lumbermen, formed in 1880 the Herdic Personal Transportation Company, which built passenger coaches. (The source of his capital remains a mystery.) The vehicles, which had been in service in Williamsport for several years before that, were painted bright yellow and known there as "canaries," but elsewhere were called simply "herdics." They were popular in several cities, including Washington, D.C., where they remained on the streets until about 1918.

In another business venture, begun in 1886, Herdic built water-treatment plants. It was on an inspection tour of his waterworks in Huntingdon, Pennsylvania, in February 1888 that he slipped on some ice and severely injured his head. He died a month later of a massive blood clot on the brain. Herdic left no will.

A few years after Herdic's death, a local historian proposed erecting a monument with the following inscription: "To the memory of one who found Williamsport a village, and made it a beautiful city—Peter Herdic." The saga of Peter Herdic ends in 1900. In a handwritten letter, the two men who had served as trustees in the long-running Herdic bankruptcy asked a federal judge for permission to distribute the last $147.55 in the estate for "the relief of a daughter of Peter Herdic by his first wife who although married, unfortunately was led astray and is now in actual want."[16] On

---

John G. Reading, who claimed to be owed more than $175,000. Another creditor, owed almost $63,000, was William Weightman, a chemist who owned the monopoly on quinine and was the richest man in Philadelphia. Many of Herdic's friends believed it was Weightman who had masterminded Herdic's financial collapse. In the frenzy of selling that took place after the bankruptcy, Weightman acquired many of the 630 parcels of real estate Herdic owned throughout the Susquehanna region. Sixteen thousand acres containing coal deposits and 14,000 acres of timber were sold to Weightman for $4,000. The luxurious Herdic House hotel he built on West Fourth Street in 1864 at a cost of $225,000 went to Weightman for $1,200; the uncompleted Herdic Block—a sprawling brick office-apartment-theater complex overlooking the hotel and its adjacent park—was purchased for $50 by Weightman, who renamed the block for himself.

16. This apparently is the same daughter who was married in the $80,000 Episcopal church on West Fourth Street that Herdic paid to have built. The ceremony was attended by

May 5, the request was granted. Today Peter Herdic's restored pink mansion, with its ornate columns and elegant interior, is a restaurant. Nearby, a small street bears his name. No monument was ever built.

The Susquehanna still possessed vast stands of prime timber awaiting harvest. The economic slump that undid men like Peter Herdic passed, and demand for lumber, still an important measure of the national prosperity, again began to climb. In 1883, the Susquehanna boom held 1,874,655 logs—the most it would ever contain.

With each passing year, the river bore an increasing number of hemlock logs mixed amid the white pines, for the mighty pine along the West Branch was rapidly being depleted. By 1880, hemlock comprised one-quarter of the logs sawn on the West Branch; just a few years before, it had amounted to one-tenth. "Merchantable pine has now almost disappeared from the state," wrote noted arborist Charles S. Sargent in his *Report on the Forests of North America,* commissioned as part of the 1880 census. Sargent's report estimated that 1.8 billion feet of white pine remained in Pennsylvania, with 1.3 billion still standing along the West Branch and being cut at a rate of 380 million feet per year. (The remainder was located at the headwaters of the Allegheny River.) In contrast, 4.5 billion feet of hemlock stood across the northern tier of the state.

Before logging began, twice as much hemlock as white pine grew in Pennsylvania, but the hemlocks were not highly valued as lumber. For generations, the stately trees were cut down solely for their bark, which contained an acid used in tanning. Fifteen hundred feet of hemlock were needed to produce one cord of bark, and the nation's tanneries were consuming 1.5 million cords of bark annually. Often the trees were felled, stripped, and then left behind, a practice that fueled an increasing number of major forest fires.

The hemlock era of Pennsylvania lumbering began in the early 1870s, driven in part by the rising prices and scarcity of white pine.[17] But a modest new invention just coming into common usage also enhanced its appeal: the wire nail. Carpenters discovered that, unlike the hand-wrought and

---

the state's political elite, and a listing of the gifts received by the bride filled a half-column of Mr. Herdic's newspaper.

17. Upon removing all the white pine from a tract that also contained hemlock, many early lumbermen sold the land for two or three dollars an acre and moved on. By 1890, however, hemlock stands were selling for as much as $80 per acre, and the average acre would produce between 15,000 and 20,000 feet of lumber.

machine-cut nails available until that time, wire nails held solidly in hemlock wood.

With hemlock suddenly obtaining commercial value, a new surge of logging swept the West Branch, and the Susquehanna's hemlock forests fell in its wake. "To consume the forests as speedily as possible, satisfied with what can be realized from them in the operation, appears to be the spirit which rules this region," reported an aide to Charles Sargent. He noted that lumbermen spoke of the stands of hemlock as "'inexhaustible,' which is not strictly true, for it is doubtful if it holds out to supply the increasing drain made upon it by tanneries and saw-mills for more than twenty-five years to come." His predictions were not far off the mark.

Even though the Susquehanna boom broke records with the number of logs it captured in 1883, that in no way approached the total amount of timber cut from the West Branch, for the river no longer offered the only means of getting the logs to market. To be sure, the West Branch still was full of logs each spring. But the logging industry had undergone another fundamental change, one that would ignite its final spurt of growth in Pennsylvania.

The average life of a sawmill is about twenty years; then the adjacent timber is exhausted and the mill is forced to relocate or close its doors. The presence of the Susquehanna, and the low-cost transport it provided, had extended the lives of some Williamsport mills, but now their time was running out. Increasingly, lumber companies were dispersing throughout the West Branch region, erecting their giant saws closer to the remaining stands of timber and converting to a more reliable, if costlier, means of getting the lumber to market: the railroad.

It was during the 1860s that logging railroads first arrived in the West Branch region to transport timber growing far from streams. These tramroads, as they were known, consisted of wood rails over which traveled horsedrawn cars carrying logs. Horses were eventually replaced by a tenton locomotive built by the Climax Manufacturing Company of Corry, Pennsylvania. The appeal of the Climax engine was its simplicity, light weight, and ability to operate on extreme grades and sharp curves—of vital importance in the rugged mountains. More powerful engines later replaced the Climax.

By the 1880s the valleys of the West Branch and its many tributaries were laced with small lumber railroads, linking the mills and the logging camps that grew up alongside them. No other state possessed as diverse an assortment of types and sizes of railroads; few rail lines covered more than fifteen miles.

But the cost of building a railroad into a rugged valley or over a mountain made it even more essential to squeeze every penny from the timber as quickly as possible. It was unusual for a railroad to remain in one place for more than a decade because even small logging companies consumed timber voraciously. The railroads themselves became huge buyers of lumber. By the turn of the century, the nation's 190,000 miles of railroad rested on 700 million untreated wooden ties, which were replaced at a rate of 140 million per year.

At the same time, a large new market for scrub timber, heretofore of no commercial value, developed as the coal industry experienced its own period of rapid expansion. For every hundred tons of coal mined, two tons of timber were needed for props and planks. Loggers found that even immature and low-grade wood had buyers in the mines or railroads, or in the growing market for paper products and "chemical wood," used in the manufacture of cellulose. Thus, nothing was left behind.

A latecomer to lumbering on the West Branch was Frank Henry Goodyear, son of a New York country doctor, who from the 1880s until 1910 was the leading producer of hemlock in Pennsylvania. Goodyear owned 200 square miles of prime timber land around the headwaters of the West Branch of the Susquehanna and the Allegheny River. He and his brother Charles instituted round-the-clock, year-round operations. An ingenious man, Frank Goodyear even found a way to market the useless slab wood created when the trees were squared into lumber; it was split and tied into bundles and sold to New York City tenement dwellers for starting stove fires. With two mills at Austin on Freeman Run and another at Galeton on Pine Creek, the Goodyear firm could produce nearly 1 million feet of lumber per day. Only one other company, the Central Pennsylvania Lumber Company, may have cut more timber from the state's forests. (Today, Pennsylvania's largest lumber firms average about 20 million feet per year.)

Logging was wastefully indiscriminate. For each tree cut, as many as fifty young saplings—the forest's next generation—were destroyed by carelessness. White pine and fine hardwoods were being used when lower-quality wood would have sufficed. "Most of our lumber is furnished at present by trees over 200 years old," lamented the chief of U.S. forestry. The mills were then only utilizing between 20 and 30 percent of the tree; the remainder was discarded as waste.

The specter of a timber famine, first raised after the Civil War, grew gradually from an abstract idea espoused by a few to a matter of concern

even for some Susquehanna lumbermen—but not all. One direct consequence of the timber plunder was hard to ignore, however: worsening
floods in watersheds that had been stripped of trees. To be sure, flooding
was historically common on the West Branch, but in the years since the
boom had been strung at Williamsport, it seemed as if the flows grew in
intensity. None, however, rivaled the disaster that began on May 30, 1889,
when a storm system swept in from the Midwest and stalled above the
Susquehanna. Williamsport, lying downstream from one-quarter of the
Susquehanna's entire watershed, took the brunt of the storm.

There, floodwaters rose to thirty-three feet, six feet higher than the
previous record flood in 1865. The river current exceeded ten miles an
hour, carrying with it "houses, furniture, stables, out-buildings, trees, logs,
great piles of sawed lumber, bridges, fences and farming implements,"
according to one news account. "The deep, hollow, rumbling sound caused
by the shifting stones, and the plunging, thumping and dragging of logs
and trees, could at night be heard miles away from the river." Fifty people
were killed along the West Branch.

As destructive as the flood was, there were some who saw it as a
vindication. Until that time, their warnings about the consequences of
deforestation had largely been ignored. Now there could be no dispute.
The despoliation of the West Branch became a symbol for a new movement
in the United States: forest conservation.

"There are few places in the east where the natural beauties of mountain scenery and the natural resources of timber lands have been destroyed
to the extent that has taken place in northern Pennsylvania," concluded a
turn-of-the-century report by the U.S. Geological Survey. "One may journey for miles without encountering a mature tree. The situation is an
excellent one in which to consider the value and possibilities of intelligent
forestation."

Long before the flood, Pennsylvania had taken a few steps toward
protecting its dwindling forest resources (following the lead of New York,
which also had seen its reserves decimated). In 1870 Pennsylvania enacted
the first law in the nation that made it a crime to set a forest fire. Despite the
law, losses from fires—those naturally occurring as well as those inten-
tionally set—remained high, frustrating what few reforestation efforts
were underway. "There is very little of this land that can be farmed, but the
young timber grows very fast," wrote an Elk County lumberman to the
state Division of Forestry in 1897. "If fire could be kept out there would be
a good growth of timber in twenty-five years."

Congress, warned by experts that the timber shortage was "so near as to be practically tomorrow" and so severe that "our existence as a nation will end," responded by creating the Division of Forestry within the U.S. Department of Agriculture. What was lacking, however, was significant public support for conservation. Americans still believed the forests inexhaustible, their value solely as lumber—a view encouraged by the federal government, which was selling some of its finest western forests for $2.50 per acre.

Pennsylvanian Gifford Pinchot, who returned from studying forestry in Europe in 1890, later recalled the prevailing mood: "The nation was obsessed, when I got home, by a fury of development . . . The man who could get his hands on the biggest slice of natural resources was the best citizen. While forest devastation was going like a runaway locomotive, forest protection was pursuing it like a manpower handcar, and falling farther behind with every mile."[18]

Pennsylvania's nascent conservation movement attracted some unusual advocates, among them an adventuresome medical doctor and a small group of socially prominent Philadelphia women. Dr. Joseph Trimble Rothrock, who taught botany at the University of Pennsylvania and had accompanied several western expeditions as staff surgeon, launched a public campaign to save the state's forests. His efforts attracted the attention of the Philadelphia women, and in the spring of 1886 they invited him to address what would be the first of many meetings. Rothrock was a stirring speaker, an engaging writer, and an astute politician. (He was also determined; his first speech on the subject attracted just three people—the lecture's sponsor, a janitor, and a man who wandered in off the street.) And he prevailed. Although Gifford Pinchot is often credited with inspiring Pennsylvania's forest conservation movement, in fact the effort was well underway by the time Pinchot returned from Europe, thanks to the dedication and charisma of Joseph Rothrock. Tirelessly, he traversed the state with his limelight lantern and box of photographic slides to show Pennsylvanians just how bleak the situation had become.

In 1893, Pennsylvania belatedly recognized that "forests were of enough importance to the state to be looked after, even if the oversight must be paid for," as Dr. Rothrock later wrote. The state created a forestry commission. Soon afterward, it began a large-scale land acquisition program, predominately along the Susquehanna. (Only one other state, New York, embarked on a similar effort.) In 1899, Pennsylvania owned just

18. Pinchot would become chief of the division of forestry in the U.S. Department of Agriculture in 1898. Seven years later, when the U.S. Forest Service was created, he headed that agency. He later would serve two terms as Pennsylvania's governor.

20,000 acres. By June 1907, the state holdings had spread to twenty-four counties and totaled 735,000 acres, most of which had once been covered with prime white pine and hemlock, but now stood naked and useless. By the end of 1913, the state owned almost 1 million acres. Today, Pennsylvania owns 2 million acres of state forest.

Many logging companies were only too happy to part with their cut-over land. Huge tracts were simply abandoned and allowed to revert to the state for unpaid taxes; others were sold for a few dollars per acre. In some instances, however, property owners discovered coal beneath the rugged hillsides, and the extraction of that resource by strip mining took its own heavy toll on the river—one that continues a century later.

By now the lumber industry was well into its long decline, but in pockets along the Susquehanna logging continued at a frenzied pace. At Hicks Run, more than 500 men, some with their families, lived in a community that flourished between 1904 and 1912. The little town even boasted a street dubiously known as "Red-Headed Women's Row." News of the outside world was provided by the weekly newspaper *Grit* published in Williamsport. A twenty-one-mile-long railroad with five locomotives ferried the giant logs up and down the valley, a double-band sawmill could cut 200,000 feet of lumber a day, and stacks of finished lumber stretched for a quarter-mile. John DuBois had logged this same creek decades earlier, leaving behind enough timber, primarily hemlocks, to invite a second invasion.

Life in the logging camps varied widely. It was often said that loggers would endure dirty living conditions as long as the food was good. Board was part of a worker's wages, and the operator who provided the best meals could attract the best men. A visitor to the DuBois camp at Hicks Run once commented on the quality and quantity of food provided and asked DuBois how he could afford such a luxury. "I can't afford not to do it," DuBois is said to have replied. In a ten-month period, the cook in one Hicks Run camp baked 12,000 pies for the logging crew, who dined beneath a sign that advised: "Better To Eat Than To Talk." Native brook trout abounded in Hicks Run, as did eels, which migrated hundreds of miles from the Atlantic Ocean; both were popular meals. Bear and venison also were served.

Like the hemlock and pine, hardwoods—primarily oak and chestnut—growing along these creeks were of enormous size. When the builders of the Panama Canal sought the largest timbers they could find, the mill at Hicks Run sent white oak thirty-six inches square and thirty feet long. During its seven years of existence, the Hicks Run mill produced 280 million feet of lumber, plus 153,000 cords of bark.

In July 1912, when the trees were gone from Hicks Run, the camp was abandoned. The loggers and their families packed their belongings and departed by train, many for points farther west, searching out new forests. Slowly the little valley began to heal its scars.

For Williamsport, where lumber had been the lifeblood for six decades, the collapse of the industry brought severe economic repercussions. City services, once the envy of the rest of Pennsylvania, deteriorated. By the turn of the century, the town was so poor that its police officers transported prisoners in a wheelbarrow; there was no money for a paddy wagon. The Susquehanna boom was rarely crowded; most logs went elsewhere via rail. In May 1908, the officers of the Susquehanna Boom Company voted to disband, noting that "the business of the company seems to be over." The following year, the boom was dismantled—an event that didn't even warrant a newspaper story.

Even the mighty Central Pennsylvania Lumber Company determined that the timber was now too distant for its Williamsport mill to operate profitably. Shortly before 1 P.M. on December 17, 1919, a lowly maple log, twelve feet long and twenty-four inches in diameter, encrusted with ice and snow, was guided against a whirring band saw and converted into two-inch planks. A few commemorative photographs were taken, and with that, the last sawmill operating in Williamsport—a city that a few decades before had been the lumber capital of the world—closed its doors. The Williamsport mill, which once employed more than 200 men, was torn down to make room for a new high school, whose athletic teams were known as the Millionaires. The heritage of lumbering on the West Branch faded into family stories and memorabilia.

On a small patch of grass far upriver in Cherry Tree, where the Cush Cushion Creek flows into the West Branch, there stands a rectangular granite marker, erected in 1955. "All people that on earth do dwell, Speak softly—tread lightly, To honor the raftmen—the loggers, Their mothers and wives, Of Penns Woods, carry on," proclaims the simple slab. It is there to memorialize an ill-fated attempt to relive the glory days of logging on the Susquehanna.

In 1938, R. Dudley Tonkin, a third-generation West Branch lumberman, commissioned what he called the "Last Raft" to commemorate his grandfather's arrival to the river a century before and his own half-century in the business. Not only would the raft be almost an exact replica of the

112-foot-long "pup," or half, rafts that once plied the West Branch, but its crew was to consist of former raftmen, many of whom were by then in their seventies. (As a concession to modernity, an outhouse was installed on the raft's stern.)

The voyage of the Last Raft was an idea that seized the entire region. The day before it was launched, 10,000 people poured into the tiny village of Burnside—barely a wide spot in the road—to view the white pine platform. More than a quarter century had elapsed since a raft had headed down the West Branch, and many had only heard stories of the adventures of rafting. Tonkin's Last Raft had as its destination Harrisburg, where the governor was scheduled to receive a ceremonial auger and the raftmen were to be feted.

As with all things, the passage of time had significantly altered the Susquehanna, and some observers expressed doubts about the wisdom of the trip. Lock Haven had erected a dam that had no chute to accommodate rafts; a flood in 1936 had damaged the chute in the Williamsport dam; and at Muncy, the Reading Railroad had doubled the number of piers on its bridge. Yet Tonkin and the aging raftmen were not deterred. They could master the Susquehanna.

On the morning of March 14, 1938, amid the mist that frequently fills the West Branch valleys, the Last Raft was "tied loose" at McGee's Landing, not far from Burnside. Harrisburg lay 200 miles downstream. A crowd of over 5,000 filled the riverbanks to witness the departure. Grandfathers carried grandchildren; fathers and sons, mothers and daughters stood shoulder to shoulder. Few along the muddy banks did not have some familial tie to the once-dominant logging industry. The crew of ten men, with veteran pilot Harry Connor, 75, at the forward steering oar, swung the raft into the current. The Susquehanna obliged the old men; the descent began.

Roads along the river were jammed with the cars of spectators, and several enthusiastic onlookers leapt onto the raft from bridges as it passed beneath. Souvenir-hunters in Clearfield stole most of the kitchen utensils. At one place on the riverbank, an elderly woman waved a large American flag while her husband played "The Star Spangled Banner" on a glistening cornet.

Newspapers around the country reported the progress of the Last Raft, and letters addressed to "The Last Raft, somewhere on the Susquehanna" were delivered at each stop. Among those onboard was newsreel cameraman Thomas Proffitt, filming the historic trip for the nation's movie theaters.

The raft reached Williamsport on March 19 and the next morning set off again with forty-eight people onboard—a number that taxed the buoyancy of the unwieldy craft. Its surface was at times below the water. While some believed the most dangerous part of the trip was now over, ahead lay two bridges spanning the Susquehanna. One carried the highway between Muncy and Montgomery, and the other, just downstream, the Reading rail line.

High spirits notwithstanding, the Susquehanna was never to be taken for granted. At the first bridge, the raft struck a piling and the crew grappled desperately to straighten it out. The sightseers on the bridges and riverbanks had a clear view of what happened next.

The current beneath the rail bridge flowed at an angle, requiring the pilot to aim directly for a stone pier and then let the raft drift diagonally through the narrow opening. The rear of the raft could not be allowed to swing. At the last minute, in a frantic moment of confusion, someone ordered a change of course and the raft struck the fifth pier head-on, shattering the wooden shanty atop the platform and killing Proffitt, who was swept overboard, his camera still rolling. (The film was later retrieved intact and shown in movie houses around the United States.) The stern swung into another pier and the raft tilted, dumping all but one passenger, a woman, into the icy river. Despite valiant rescue efforts, seven people drowned, including Harry Connor.

Among the hundreds of people on the bridge was Florence Leiby, a 23-year-old nurse who brought her box camera and boyfriend to see the raft. "Everyone was lined up, waiting," Leiby—now Florence Smith, wife of the mayor of Montgomery—recalled fifty-four years later. When the raft crashed, she began snapping pictures. "All we could do was yell, 'Get out there with the boats!' I could see people falling from the raft. We didn't know what had happened underneath the bridge."

As volunteers dragged the river for bodies, a coroner's inquest was convened. Seventy-nine-year-old Ed Sunderlin, who was manning the rear sweep at the time of the crash, blamed it on having "too many pilots on board." In the end, the deaths were ruled accidental and the raft, little damaged, was allowed to complete its journey.

Low water plagued the remainder of the trip. The raft was grounded twice and ultimately tied up at Fishing Creek, eight miles above Harrisburg, with just three of its original crew onboard. There, the raft was disassembled and its timber sold to a lumber dealer.

Today, the West Branch of the Susquehanna once again flows through dense woods. The flat-topped hills drop to the water's edge like green shoulders, rank after rank of them, endless and beautiful. Nearly 75 percent of the 7,000-square-mile drainage basin is forested, but the trees of this generation are predominately hardwoods. The devastating fires that swept the barren hillsides after the loggers departed are responsible for that change. The heat destroyed conifer seedlings, but those of the oak, cherry, and other species survived and, without competition for sunlight, took root and thrived. But that, too, will change.

In the not-so-distant future, perhaps half a century from now, the mountains and valleys of the West Branch will again revert to white pine and hemlock, according to James C. Nelson, who has worked for the state's Bureau of Forestry for thirty-seven years and now serves as its chief. "It is really a cyclical process," he says.

Two forces will combine to end the reign of the hardwoods. Repeated assaults on the many stands of oak by gypsy moths and other pests have already destroyed many of these grand trees across the Susquehanna watershed. But humans and insects no longer are the prime players in forest composition these days; that honor goes to the state's million-plus population of white-tailed deer.[19]

While they would far rather spend their days with the 200 elk that range through their territory, Ralph Harrison and Marsha Jeffrey devote an increasing portion of their time to trying to outsmart the deer, which eat almost any growing thing but are especially fond of young hardwoods. In areas that have been logged, seedlings stand no chance against the voracious deer and natural reforestation has failed. Electric fencing has proven successful in giving the young trees a head start against the deer, but it is costly and difficult to install in remote areas.

Yet the natural value of a thriving forest—whatever its composition—is undisputed. If all the Susquehanna watershed resembled the woodlands of the West Branch, the sediment and agricultural runoff that jeopardizes the Chesapeake Bay today would be greatly diminished. To date, however, little attention has been paid to reforestation among the many programs and millions of dollars devoted to the bay cleanup. Some fear that as the stands of hardwoods along the West Branch reach maturity another logging boom will be triggered, wreaking havoc on water quality throughout the drainage basin.

19. These are the offspring of the thousand or so imported into Pennsylvania at the turn of the century after logging and overhunting eradicated the native herd.

On a corner of the metal desk she shares with Ralph Harrison at the Hicks Run station sits Marsha Jeffrey's collection of animal skulls, picked up in the course of her work in the forest—black bear, beaver, red fox, gray fox, coyote, field mouse, bobcat, opossum. A rattlesnake skin dangles from one wall and wild turkey feathers adorn another. Beneath these displays is an assortment of books on the North American elk. Once common here, the elk were eradicated by hunters and then reintroduced to these mountains about the same time the deer were restored. Unlike the deer, however, they have been very slow to reestablish themselves.

On a bitterly cold February day, shortly after dawn, Ralph Harrison and Marsha Jeffrey come across a herd of twenty-one elk grazing far up a forest road. No matter how many times they see these animals, they pause in awe. This is an unusually large group. Frost covers the elks' heads and antlers like a silver veil, and they stand quietly, alert but not frightened by the human visitors.

"There are three generations in that herd," whispers Marsha, her words creating clouds as silver as the frost on the elk. Moments later, the animals majestically move on, disappearing into a dense grove of beeches, maples, and oaks. As they depart this small glade, they thread their way past a few white pine seedlings that are poking up from aged stumps of their ancestors.

The Susquehanna is nurturing another generation of trees.

Chapter Four

Floods

"We are going to try to beat the river"

Ten thousand people could not hold back the flood-swollen Susquehanna. At 10:30 on the morning of June 23, 1972, the raging river topped a thirty-seven-foot dike and the nation's most destructive natural disaster at that time struck the Wyoming Valley. Exhausted volunteers, who had been battling the rising water since dawn, raced from the mountains of sandbags they had stacked along the levees. Within hours, the Susquehanna had inundated much of the valley in fast-moving, murky water twelve feet deep.

As the river began spilling over the dikes, Jim Jiunta abandoned his home movie–making and returned to his house in South Wilkes-Barre, a block from the Susquehanna, to remove fuses from the circuit box and collect a few prized items from the basement—two bottles of liquor, a new coat of his wife's, his hunting rifles, and a favorite power saw. He carried the belongings to a bed on the first floor of his ranch house and went back downstairs, planning to bring up one more armload of possessions and then depart. He was taking no chances; he had even left his hard-to-start Volkswagen running outside. But Jiunta miscalculated how much time he had. Suddenly he could see mustard-colored water filling the window wells of his basement. The details of the next few moments are etched in his memory.

"All of a sudden, there was an explosion and the air roared toward me. It sounded like Niagara Falls. The hair on my head and on my arms was standing straight up." As he watched in horror, the water blew out the windows and surged into his basement, carrying before it a refrigerator, a freezer, and heavy tables. He raced up the stairs, the water rising at his feet. Air forced up from the basement by the torrent made the living-room carpet billow beneath his feet. "It was like walking on a cloud," he says. Dust poured "like steam" from the electrical receptacles around the house. In one of those curious acts that make no sense in retrospect, Jiunta carefully changed into old clothing before abandoning his home and all his belongings, neatly folding his good pants and leaving them on the bed.

It would be four days before he returned. The coat, liquor, rifles, power saw, and pants were ruined, caked with mud. The mattress they had rested upon was wedged against the bedroom door. Like everything else in the house—and a large portion of the entire valley, home to 225,000 people—it was fouled with the stinking slime of the Susquehanna.

Not even Jim Jiunta's rooftop television antenna was spared. A Coast Guard rescue boat that had passed over his house looking for flood victims became entangled in the wires, pulling them loose. The government paid him $69 to replace the antenna; he never was compensated for the propeller marks on his roof.

When the Susquehanna River finally crested in Wilkes-Barre at 7 P.M. on Saturday, June 24, it was eighteen feet above flood stage, and flowing at more than twenty-six times its usual rate. The amount of water racing past the measuring gauge *each second* could have satisfied the daily water needs of 43,000 people. The force of the water swept stately brick homes from their foundations and tore caskets and bodies from a cemetery. By nightfall, the Wyoming Valley had become a nineteen-square-mile lake, dotted with a few manmade structures standing like tiny islands. When finally tallied, the damages in the valley exceeded $2 billion, making the 1972 flood the most costly disaster in terms of property losses in the nation's history at the time.

Once again, the Susquehanna had demonstrated who was and will forever remain the undisputed sovereign of this valley.

Rivers have always served as magnets to development, for along their banks the land is fertile and flat. The settlements in colonial America spread outward beside rivers, which offered cheap and easy transportation. The occasional flood was welcomed by farmers, for it brought rich sediments that replenished tired soils, and the losses incurred in the regular spring freshets were offset by the benefits derived from them. But people soon came to regard the riverbanks as their own, their tenancy on them as permanent, and the *river* as the intruder. Dirt trails carved by Indians along the floodplains became roads and, later, rail lines and superhighways. Small settlements became large communities, with river frontage a coveted possession. Industries sought the river for power to run their machinery and to carry away their waste.

Growth along the Susquehanna was no different, despite the probability of flooding. The Wyoming Valley is especially susceptible to high water, for here the river slows as it zigzags five times across the valley before exiting through the narrow gorge at Nanticoke. Early settlers learned to expect floods each spring, when the thick ice on the river clogged the gorge.

They soon came to respect the old Indian adage that serious floods occur about every fourteen years on the Susquehanna. They also discovered that the Susquehanna abides by no rules.

On the West Branch, floods were recorded in 1744, 1758, and 1772, precisely in accordance with the Indian maxim. An ice flood on March 15, 1784, swept away houses and all the cattle in Northumberland. The same day on the North Branch, floodwaters crested at thirty feet and swept away 150 homes in the Wyoming Valley, killing a resident of Forty Fort and a horse in Wilkes-Barre. An unusual autumn flood that occurred on October 5, 1786, became known as the Pumpkin Flood because rising waters in the Wyoming Valley lifted the ripe fruit from their vines. "Heavy pumpkins came tumbling downstream like great orange cannonballs and had much the same effect when houses or men stood in their way," wrote one observer.

The foolhardiness of building along a river was recognized early on. Nathaniel Parker Willis, the poet who lived on the North Branch of the Susquehanna, wrote in his 1840 book *Letters from Under a Bridge:* "I intend to get up a memorial to Congress, praying that the banks of rivers in all towns settled henceforth, shall be government property, to be reserved and planted for public grounds." Poets may have seen the wisdom of such a policy; politicians never have. As a result, flood damages have steadily mounted. Yet this loss of life and property has never deterred people from settling—and resettling—along the river. That, in turn, has guaranteed that the damages always are greater when the next flood comes, as it assuredly will.

The first flood for which there remains more than anecdotal data struck the Susquehanna Basin on St. Patrick's Day, 1865, with waters cresting at 33.1 feet in Wilkes-Barre and 27.5 feet at Williamsport. A warm southwest wind and early spring rainfall had hastened the melting of ice and snow from an unusually severe winter. On the West Branch, all bridges between Farrandsville, upstream from Lock Haven, and Northumberland were heavily damaged or destroyed, and homes along the river were flooded. Details of damages along the North Branch are sketchy, in part because they were lost in subsequent floods. Even so, 1865 became the flood of record on the North Branch until it was surpassed by that of 1936, which in turn was exceeded by the disaster of 1972. Hardest hit in the 1865 flood were the remnants of the canal system that followed the Susquehanna. The Pennsylvania Railroad reported millions of dollars in damages.

Nearly a quarter-century would elapse before the next major flood struck, this time on the West Branch. In the interim, small communities along the river had become large ones; Williamsport, for example, had tripled in size, thanks to its thriving timber industry. Spawned by a freak storm, the rains began on May 30, 1889, and continued in places for thirty-six hours. "It seemed that the windows of heaven had been opened and the water descended in a solid sheet," wrote West Branch journalist and historian John Meginness.

Eight inches of rain, an estimated 6.7 billion tons of water, fell on a 12,000-square-mile area of central Pennsylvania, from Johnstown to Harrisburg and into the northern counties of Pennsylvania. By noon on May 31, the magnitude of the storm was becoming frighteningly apparent. Along the West Branch, humans were about to witness the deadly force of the river.[1]

News of a major flood in Clearfield reached Williamsport by telegraph early on the morning of Friday, May 31, but not until about 2 A.M. Saturday did the log-filled river begin to rise. All the while, the rain continued. At 9 A.M. Saturday, the floodwaters had equaled the record set in 1865; twelve hours later, much of Williamsport was under seven feet of water. As it rose, the Susquehanna toyed briefly with the incursions on its banks, bursting through the crowded log boom, hurtling logs and even an entire sawmill ahead of it. Engineers later would estimate that the river was flowing at 120 times its normal rate. Flood damages were reported as far south as Harrisburg. Fifty people were killed along the West Branch. No official estimate was made of damages to property, but John Meginness calculated losses at between $25 and $30 million.

Among those killed were nine members of the Youngman family and three others who lived on Antes Creek, which flows into the river near Jersey Shore. George and William Youngman operated a woolen mill along the creek that produced blankets for the lumber camps; their homes were located a short distance downstream. In the early hours of June 1, the two brothers watched in horror as the water burst through a dirt embankment at the mill. George Youngman raced back to his house, roused his family, guests, and servants from their beds, and gathered them where he believed they would be out of danger. Giant timbers borne on Antes Creek slammed into the frame house, tearing it apart, piece by piece. Soon, just one room remained.

---

1. The same storm swept away the poorly maintained South Fork Dam above Johnstown, on the other side of the Alleghenies. In what became known as the Great Johnstown Flood, a twenty-foot wall of water, moving at speeds of up to sixty miles an hour, bore down on the city and its 28,000 inhabitants. In ten minutes it was over; 2,200 people would die as a result and 967 more were missing.

George Youngman later described the final moments:

Miss Phelps, the governess, heroically endeavored to calm their fears by declaring that this house and family should not be destroyed. They had carried with them into the room a large family Bible from the flooded room below. She turned to the second verse of the 43rd chapter of Isaiah and read it aloud. ["When you pass through the waters I will be with you; and through the rivers, they shall not overwhelm you . . . "].

Two minutes [later], the east side of the room fell into the fierce torrent with a crash, and the twelve inmates were engulfed!

Youngman was swept a half-mile down the creek, but managed to rescue a niece. His wife, Tillie, and five children drowned, as did Eliza Phelps, the governess; two sons survived. William Youngman's wife and two children drowned, as did two members of a neighboring family.

In Williamsport, bridges were gone and large sections of the town were underwater. The situation of its people became desperate. Hungry residents looted grocery stores seeking food, but little had escaped the ravages of the Susquehanna. A correspondent for the *Philadelphia Times* relayed an urgent plea from the city's mayor to the outside world: "Send us help at once, in the name of God, at once . . . Such a thing as a chicken is unknown here; they were all carried off."

Help, when it did come, was provided by private citizens and relief committees established in cities around the United States and the world. Philadelphians dispatched clothing and disinfectant; the Pittsburgh Relief Committee raised and sent $560,000. Subscribers to New York City newspapers contributed funds, and people in Wales sent $1,300. Even the Sultan of Turkey contributed toward the $3 million raised to assist Pennsylvania flood victims. (Most of that money was sent to aid Johnstown and its residents.)

As for the state, it played a minor role in the recovery, and only after grappling with the legality of providing such assistance. "It was found that the only constitutional method by which the assistance of the State, as such, could be given was through and under the direction of the State Board of Health," wrote the secretary of the Flood Relief Commission, appointed by the governor. Public moneys were expended only to remove debris from streets and to clear clogged streams. The workers themselves, and the supplies they used, were paid for from private contributions.

Assistance to victims was disbursed by a committee of prominent citizens. The response from the recipients ranged from humble gratitude to greed. The commission's secretary wrote,

As a rule, no payment was made to persons having a remaining property, real or personal, of the value of $2,000, though circumstances sometimes required that exceptions be made. Some of the claims were remarkable as coming from a presumably self-respecting people, who would only accept help when in great necessity. Claims for damage to "vegetables in the cellar," or "damage to garden," or "wetting of carpets," were common, which, in view of the fact that many thousands of families in the State had their homes submerged almost or quite to the second floor and who have not asked for assistance, emphasises [sic] the fact that many looked for money only because their neighbors had received help.

All told, the Williamsport relief committee, which dealt with claims from almost all of Lycoming County, examined 2,838 petitions, and authorized payments in amounts ranging from $5 to $592, for a total in flood relief of $155,911.82. This was more than half of the dollar amount of all the relief grants awarded to West Branch residents.

The magnitude of the 1889 flood convinced its victims that they dared not allow the river to remain untamed any longer. For help, they looked to an unlikely source—the federal government. Washington had assumed a limited responsibility for the nation's major rivers following an 1824 decision by the Supreme Court which said that authority to regulate commerce extended to interstate navigation.[2] The ruling coincided with the soaring interest in internal improvements around the United States, and Congress took the opportunity to slowly but surely expand the federal government's involvement in such projects. The first services it could offer were river surveys. The Army at the time contained the largest corps of trained civil engineers in the nation. They had built forts on the frontier and operated the U.S. Military Academy at West Point. Although some lawmakers voiced doubts about the Corps of Engineers doing survey work to benefit private development, their concerns succeeded only in holding down early appropriations.

It was not until after the Civil War, when Republicans in Washington

2. The landmark decision, written by Chief Justice John Marshall, grew out of a dispute over the rights to operate a steamboat in New York waters, initially awarded to Lancaster County native Robert Fulton. The New York legislature had granted exclusive rights to Fulton and Robert Livingston, who in turn had transferred it to a third party, Aaron Ogden. Another steamboat operator, a man named Gibbons, claimed he was licensed under federal law to operate in the same waters and that New York had no authority to exclude him. Recognizing the rapid development of transportation over the previous decade and the harmful effect of state-issued monopolies on interstate commerce, Marshall found for Gibbons, declaring that regulating such commerce was a proper federal responsibility.

launched a national rebuilding program, that federally funded public works projects—and the politics attendant upon them—came into their own. As recently as 1917, the prevailing view in Washington—and locally—was that those who benefited from flood control should pay for it. That view softened after a series of floods hit the lower Mississippi River Valley. When the residents petitioned for help in preventing future disasters, Congress obliged, offering to underwrite a share.

The nagging question of the legal authority to get into the flood-control business was sidestepped. Those in Congress who urged federal involvement—perhaps foreseeing the political benefits to be derived—successfully argued that a levee system would not only enhance navigation on the Mississippi, but also open more land along the river to development. Both were deemed to be in the national interest.

Those with a vested interest in building these manmade flood-control projects, notably the Army engineers and their friends in Congress, fostered a cruel, and costly, hoax on the American public. Such structures, they led people to believe, could *control* flooding. In fact, they could only mitigate flood losses. But it proved to be an ingenious strategy, for nature conspires to keep the builders perpetually employed.

When another disastrous flood struck the Mississippi Valley in 1927, killing 200 people and destroying $236 million worth of property, Congress magnanimously swept aside the local cost-sharing requirement. That produced the threat of a veto by Pres. Calvin Coolidge, so a compromise was worked out, which remained in effect for more than half a century: the federal government would build the project, and local governments would maintain it.

Another fiscal conservative in the White House, Ronald Reagan, would in 1982 return some of the burden to those deriving direct benefits. The federal government, said Reagan, should not be in the business of financing, and thus encouraging, people to live in flood-prone areas. But that was not before Congress had expended tens of billions of dollars to subsidize development on land that—levees, dams, and reservoirs notwithstanding—would be recurrently damaged by floods.

This federal role in local land-use planning, especially along the nation's waterways, always has been fraught with conflict, as political agendas frequently overwhelm sound judgments. That's as true today as it was in the decades following the Civil War when Corps of Engineers surveyors fanned out over the nation's river systems. They compiled data and studied the basins with an eye toward a host of manmade improvements. The Susquehanna was no exception.

The first survey of the West Branch was conducted the year after the deadly 1889 flood. The Corps reported back to Congress that not only could the West Branch never be made navigable, as some had hoped, but "there is no practicable method of confining its water, in times of great flood to the general course of the channel which can now be undertaken . . . the river is not worthy of improvement." If modern politics is any indicator, those words were not what the local congressional delegation had hoped to hear, and the Corps would return to the West Branch on a number of occasions. Eventually it recommended the construction of four reservoirs in the upstream reaches of the river, plus levees in several communities along its banks.

Then, as now, some requests from Congress must have strained the credulity of the Army engineers. In 1902, after his election rival promised to make the Susquehanna navigable to oceangoing vessels as far upstream as Northumberland, U.S. Rep. M. E. Olmsted used his legislative prerogative and directed the Corps to conduct a study. With thinly concealed sarcasm, the Corps reported back: "The problem presented for consideration is that of improving for purposes of navigation a nontidal river which drains an area of nearly 30,000 square miles, has worn a channel through hard primitive rocks, is generally shallow, has a steep gradient, and much of the way abrupt rocky banks, and is subject to destructive floods." While it would be possible to provide for large-sized ocean vessels, according to the Corps, the construction of such a waterway would compare "in magnitude with the Nicaragua Canal." Estimated cost: nearly $1 million per mile. Olmsted was reelected.

At some point, the Corps learned that candor did not always win allies on Capitol Hill at budget time. Quite often, popular projects received the engineers' go-ahead despite clear evidence that the costs were understated and the benefits inflated. It has been the meaty Rivers and Harbors bills, funding highways, bridges, dams, channel clearance, and a host of other public works projects over the years, that have earned a permanent place in the American political lexicon for the term "pork barrel."[3]

After floods in December 1901 and March 1902 swept through Wilkes-Barre, the Army Engineers surveyed the North Branch of the Susquehanna.

---

3. William Safire in his *Political Dictionary* notes that the phrase dates to a pre–Civil War practice of occasionally distributing salt pork to slaves from huge barrels. In their eagerness, the slaves would attempt to grab as much as they could for themselves. Members of Congress are said to engage in the same conduct to win federal projects for their home districts.

They blamed several dikes, built to improve coal-barge navigation on the river, for worsening flooding downstream. But as for ordering their removal, the engineers said diplomatically, "There may be room for a difference of opinion." The survey also took note of the huge amount of coal-mine waste dumped in the river at Wilkes-Barre, extending like a hill fifty feet or more into the river channel.

The debris remained until the river flooded in 1904, at which time it was washed away. A January thaw had caused thick ice to break up, and a February cold snap froze it again in jumbled piles like towering icebergs. Spared for the moment, the people of the Wyoming Valley flocked onto the Susquehanna to see the strange spectacle. Hundreds viewed one massive tower of ice, rising thirty-six feet above the river, which some said bore a striking resemblance to George Washington. When heavy rains fell throughout the Susquehanna basin on March 6 and 7, the ice again broke apart and the river rose, cresting at 30.6 feet in Wilkes-Barre before the force of water eventually flushed the ice chunks, ten feet thick in places, out the Nanticoke Gorge and on downstream. Islands below Harrisburg were obliterated by the grinding action of ice and debris. As the ice jam entered the narrow stretch of the river in southern Lancaster County, it stalled for a few hours, then burst loose, only to jam again before escaping to the Chesapeake. Damages along the Susquehanna amounted to $7.7 million, with nearly $2 million of that occurring in the Wyoming Valley. The state reported $800,000 in damage to bridges alone.

A book commemorating the 1904 flood took note of the damage to the Wyoming Valley, observing that until a few years before the low-lying land on the outskirts of the city had been vacant and the valley had not been plagued by floods. The authors noted:

> It was during this lull that the people who were ambitious to have homes of their own looked away from the congested portions of the city to these wide acres, where land was cheap and where they might establish their domestic circles at comparatively small cost. In the course of a few years populous communities arose upon these lowlands and beautiful homes transformed the waste regions into residence auxiliaries to the main city.

Soon, however, the new homeowners "were brought face to face with the mighty power of the Susquehanna."

The Corps came back to the Wyoming Valley to consider flood-control measures, concluding in 1917 that "the only practicable way to protect the communities . . . is by means of such levees or embankments." The project would cost about $900,000 but the Corps determined that, because no national interest would be served, the expense should be borne locally. Local officials did nothing.

A decade later the Army engineers visited again. By then the price tag for the recommended levees had jumped tenfold, to $9.4 million. Again, the Corps saw no national interest to be served in the improvement. The engineers also offered some blunt words. "Flood heights have been increased and the damages aggravated" by development in the floodplain. "There is much evidence along the river of a great indifference on the part of the individual and the public to the necessity of a waterway sufficient to care for floods. For either profit or convenience, there have been established residential subdivisions on areas subject to overflow."

The Wyoming Valley has always suffered from a shortage of space in which to grow because it is hemmed in by mountains on both sides and traversed by the meandering river. Thus, land is at a premium. The scarcity was compounded by the voracious appetite of its premier industry: coal mining.

Initially small in scale and locally owned, the mining operations were transformed in 1831, when a group of Baltimore investors purchased a 410-acre tract at Wilkes-Barre and began mining there. Anthracite was hauled to the Susquehanna, loaded onto arks or canal boats, and shipped downstream. Soon other large mining concerns followed. The expanded industry consumed scarce property and honeycombed the ground beneath it with tunnels and chambers. At the same time, the population of the valley was growing. Wilkes-Barre leaped from 23,339 inhabitants in 1880 to 37,651 within a decade. Similar increases were reported elsewhere in the valley. Most of those new arrivals were immigrant laborers lured to the mines by the availability of jobs. Tenements crowded onto tiny lots were commonplace, and long after the collapse of the anthracite industry Wilkes-Barre remained one of the state's most densely populated communities. As the Corps of Engineers predicted in 1927, the concentration of population along the river ensured that flood losses would be substantial.

It was March 1936 when the Susquehanna rose up again, this time wreaking $67 million in damages throughout its length. Wilkes-Barre and its neighbor across the river, Kingston, reported losses of $7 million; 15,000 residents were evacuated, and floodwaters crested at 33.07 feet—a new record. South Wilkes-Barre was especially hard-hit. In Williamsport, damages exceeded $5.6 million. Two-thirds of Sunbury was underwater and 6,000 residents were evacuated. "The sight, as the hundreds boarded the trains, looked like an exodus of exiles, from a town of revolution. They bore boxes, paper bags, dogs, canaries and parrots—anything they had time to clutch when the rescue boats came up to their windows," recounted one journalist in Sunbury. Rescues were complicated by ten-mile-per-hour currents. In Harrisburg, cavalry horses were employed to evacuate residents and to tow rescue craft through currents so strong that men could not row against them. With the water-treatment system destroyed, it temporarily became a crime to take a bath in the state capital.

Members of Congress whose districts had felt the wrath of the Susquehanna lobbied their colleagues to enact a comprehensive federal flood-control program.[4] Two months after the flood, Congress enacted the National Flood Control Act; $27 million was appropriated for projects that the Corps of Engineers promised would control the Susquehanna in Pennsylvania and New York.

The new law declared that flood-control projects were justified when the benefits outweighed the costs. "The great flood of March 1936 has demonstrated that the flood problem on the Susquehanna River is much more serious than was previously realized," wrote the Army's Chief of Engineers in a report outlining major improvements within the basin, including dams and flood walls.

Recognition of the problem was one thing; protection was another. In 1940, the Susquehanna flooded again, killing 14 people and forcing 30,000 Wyoming Valley residents to flee. That spurred completion of levees and other improvements in sixteen communities up and down the river. Despite people's vivid memories of the flooding, a number of those projects encountered stiff opposition, including some from Harrisburg residents. "Property owners have expressed a preference to risk occasional flooding rather than to have their view obstructed by levees or walls," noted an Army engineer. The price of preserving this riverine view would eventually become apparent.

The largest flood-control project in the basin was constructed on the Wilkes-Barre and Kingston stretch of the Susquehanna—a $9.1-million levee system designed to contain thirty-seven feet of water, four feet higher than the 1936 crest. If anyone in those parts had any doubts about the wisdom of returning to the riverbank to live, the reassurances uttered by

4. The year before, a measure calling for construction of dams, levees, and floodwalls along the Susquehanna had passed the House, but died in a Senate filibuster by Sen. Millard E. Tydings of Maryland. The federal government didn't have the money for such things, Tydings said. "This is not a bill to make employment for people. This is a bill to make a deficit in the Treasury, to make a debt for future generations to pay, an unnecessary debt in most cases, although some of the projects may have individual merit."

federal and local officials should have assuaged them: the dikes were designed to keep out the worst flood in the history of the valley. A book of
photographs commemorating the 1936 disaster reiterated the prevailing
view: "Perhaps never again will [the] Wyoming Valley witness such a fear-
some spectacle of a river gone wild. To its taming by protective dikes, a
need we have too long ignored, this volume is dedicated."

Along the Susquehanna, areas that had felt the fury of the river were
turned into housing developments, industrial parks, shopping centers, interstate highways, and revitalized business districts. Wilkes-Barre was no
different. In 1936, 5,000 buildings occupied the 800-acre portion of the
city that was evacuated during the flood. By 1972, 25,000 structures occupied the same tract. One of them was Jim Jiunta's white frame ranch house.

Jiunta and his wife, Columbia, paid $48,000 for the three-year-old house
on Haldeman Street in South Wilkes-Barre in 1958. Located in a quiet
neighborhood of well-maintained homes, the house suited the Jiunta family's needs perfectly. His pharmacy was a short distance away and his three
children could walk to school, the playground, and the homes of friends.
The proximity of the river meant nothing to Jiunta or his neighbors, for in
those years it still was heavily polluted with acid mine waste and sewage,
and was rendered inaccessible by the levees even if anyone had wanted to
reach it. The days when Wilkes-Barre children proved their bravado by
swimming out to Richards Island were just a memory.

Jim Jiunta, who had grown up in Wilkes-Barre and whose parents still
lived nearby, clearly recalled the 1936 and 1940 floods, when water was a
foot deep on Main Street and sewage backed up into homes. Like everyone
else, he believed that the dikes ensured such a disaster would never be
repeated. As he jumped into his Volkswagen on the morning of June 23,
1972, and left his rapidly flooding home behind, Jiunta realized the false-
ness of such security. The Susquehanna, gorged by rainfall from a freak
tropical storm, would drown his house to within two inches of the top of
the chimney. The dikes, and those who labored to reinforce them, had been
defeated by the river.

Tropical Storm Agnes was born in the waters off Mexico's Yucatan Peninsula, growing to become the first hurricane of the season by June 18, 1972.
After striking land in Florida, the storm system weakened and headed up
the Atlantic coast in predictable fashion. After strengthening again, it was
designated a tropical storm on June 21. On the afternoon of June 22, Agnes
veered inland near New York City to merge with a broad low-pressure

system stalled over central Pennsylvania. Agnes thereupon dumped about 28.1 trillion gallons of water—1½ times the capacity of the Chesapeake Bay. Nearly half of the total fell on the Susquehanna basin. Already that June, fifteen inches of rain had drenched the upper reaches of the river. Every place that water could go—even the 300-foot-deep buried valley beneath the Susquehanna in the Wyoming Valley, even the miles of abandoned coal shafts—was already full.

On June 19, when Agnes was still over Florida, the Luzerne County Civil Defense office began to monitor the storm's path, relying on data from the National Weather Service and Pennsylvania's Flood Forecasting Service in Harrisburg. A holdover from the days when every community had air-raid shelters and stockpiles of food and water, the agency and its six full-time employees were housed in the subbasement of Wilkes-Barre's riverfront courthouse—not a bad place to be in the event of nuclear attack. But this time the enemy was the Susquehanna. One of the first evacuations was the Civil Defense office itself.

Heading the agency was its volunteer director, a retired brigadier general and Ivy-League educated lawyer by the name of Frank Townend. Before long, his voice would become well known to Wyoming Valley residents glued to their radios, for it was he who made the decisions affecting their lives.

Outside the valley, others were bracing for what already had been declared a devastating storm. At mid-afternoon on June 21, the President's Office of Emergency Preparedness in Washington had warned its regional offices along the Atlantic coast to expect a "major disaster." The National Weather Service predicted record flooding. Evacuations in Elmira, New York, were begun, and more than a foot of rain was predicted for the entire east side of the Alleghenies.

Townend's chief aide was Nicholas Souchik, a retired lieutenant colonel who had served under Townend in the Pennsylvania National Guard. Years of experience with the Susquehanna initially convinced the two men that the experts elsewhere were overreacting. They were sure that the river would not breach the dikes. The levees were designed to withstand a crest of thirty-seven feet, although in some places they had subsided—the result of mining beneath them—and probably could contain only about thirty-four feet of water.

Relying on early estimates, the local newspaper being printed for delivery to doorsteps the following morning proclaimed: "34 Foot River Crest Predicted." It wasn't the only newspaper to misjudge the storm. The *Harrisburg Patriot-News* reported, "There appears to be no immediate threat that the main channels of the Susquehanna, the Juniata and West Branch will reach flood levels along the river basin." By nightfall, the paper's presses were flooded.

With rain still pelting the 250 miles of river above the Wyoming Valley, its residents uneasily waited out the night of June 22. For some it would be the last time they slept in their homes for a year or more.

As additional data poured in, the pace and mood intensified at the Civil Defense headquarters. Shortly before 11 P.M., Townend ordered residents of low-lying areas of Plymouth Borough, on the west side of the river, to evacuate. A large cut in the dike had been made that spring for sewer construction and the hole had yet to be closed. Many packed their belongings and went to stay with friends or family in Wilkes-Barre or Kingston, believing they would be safe from the rising water. They would soon be forced to flee again.

Townend returned repeatedly to the airwaves, his emergency broadcasts relaying the growing threat of flood.[5] Using revised data from the state Flood Forecasting Service, he announced at 2:10 A.M. on June 23:

> The flood situation on the Susquehanna River for Wilkes-Barre and Kingston is much more serious than we had figured . . . It's more serious than the 1936 or 1940 floods. Now to put it as succinctly as possible, we believe on the basis of the advice from the state, from our own figures, and from other information, that the river Friday afternoon about 3 o'clock will be at least 38 feet and maybe at a 40-foot level.

The Civil Defense team was grappling with a big question: Could the river be contained? If the answer was yes, it would require an enormous commitment of manpower, with no guarantee of success. The choice was made. A short time later Townend delivered the following announcement:

> Now this is addressed to everybody in the Wyoming Valley area and to a certain extent the people outside of [the] Wyoming Valley. What we want is everybody who thinks it's worthwhile not having the river come over the dikes to come out and do his share in preventing it. It is not a job for 400 men or 600 men or a thousand men. If we do it, if we succeed, it's probably going to take at least 10,000 people . . . It takes a lot of sandbags, a lot of material to raise the level of the dike by one foot or two feet or three feet

5. Official tapes or transcripts of the broadcasts have not been retained, according to county officials. Tapes made of emergency messages, apparently by a radio reporter, were later compiled by local historian and journalist Anthony J. Mussari, author of a book on the Agnes disaster. It is from his transcript that Townend's announcements are derived.

which will be our eventual objective. It has to be a lot wider than it is high. We are going to do this with sandbags, if we get the sandbags . . . What we need is people who can use a shovel and that's all you need to know. If you have your own garden shovel we want you to bring that . . . let me say again we're not thinking about 500 men, we're thinking about 10,000 persons working on this. If we do this, there's a possibility of keeping the river inside the dikes. If we don't do this, we would only be sitting back and watching the river come in. Now that's our appeal for volunteers for the work on the dike . . . Stay on your own side of the river, bring a shovel if you can. Please eat your breakfast before you get there, please come in work clothes and not until 6 o'clock in the morning . . . We hope it works. This is the only plan that any of us know that possibly can work. Thank you.

Two hours later, Townend's news was grim:

This is General Townend at Luzerne County Civil Defense headquarters. It's now 4:20 A.M. on Friday morning. The information we have now still indicates that the river will go over the dikes. What is getting worse is that it may be sooner than we expected. The river at 4 A.M. is at 32.3 feet . . . It's a rise of 3.4 feet in the past three hours; it's been rising at the rate of about one foot per hour. Now at this time we have to ask the people in Wilkes-Barre and Kingston in the level areas to get out of those areas to high ground . . . We expect a crest between 38 and 40 feet . . . We've made arrangements with the city that we will use the Civil Defense sirens that usually only sound on noon on Saturday to signify the point at which the river starts coming over the dike. If you hear those sirens, it will mean that the river on one side or the other or possibly on both is then coming over the dike and although the water may rise slowly, it is time to get to high ground.

Now we're going to have people start working on the dike at 6:00 A.M. and what we hope [is], we are going to try to beat the river.

As dawn broke, Townend's call for volunteers produced a flood of its own: a wave of men, women, and children—an estimated 10,000 strong— streaming to the levees. Trucks belonging to local contractors, summoned by Civil Defense authorities, rumbled through town full of dirt and sand, headed for the dikes. As the available supply of sandbags was quickly depleted, a call went out for more. Volunteers combed the community for anything that could be filled. Homeowners deposited plastic trash bags on their doorsteps for pickup; the U.S. Postal Service donated mail sacks; local merchants contributed Christmas shopping bags; a downtown hotel supplied pillowcases.

Those laboring at the dikes probably didn't hear Townend's radio message at 6 A.M. It was brief: the river had broken all records, surpassing the 1936 crest of thirty-three feet, and was still rising. The task ahead was herculean—a term Townend himself used. It would require 130,000 sandbags to raise the fifteen miles of dikes just one foot. From there, the numbers grew geometrically: 330,000 bags for a second foot; 530,000 for the third foot. As they toiled, the grimy, rain-soaked volunteers heard water splashing at the top of the levees, and saw it seeping through the earthen dikes. Still the effort continued.

> This is General Townend at ten minutes of eight from Civil Defense headquarters in the Courthouse. We've just moved up from the [sub]basement . . . the water is getting a little too deep . . . The river at 7 o'clock was at 35.38 feet. This, most of you know, is 2.37 feet higher than it was in '36 which was the previous record . . . We are quite sure that this will be relatively short duration. It may be only two or three days, maybe less, but at this point the chances are less than 25 percent that we'll be able to contain the river. If we do, that's great. But the chances are not good and people should be evacuating, and as of now I would only say you only have a short time to get out. No panic because . . . there may be some boats around later, but it's much better to get in your car than it is later on in a boat. So I hope you make it.

About 10:30 A.M., the Susquehanna topped the dike at Ross Street and Riverside Drive and the exhausted volunteers fled. Within a matter of minutes, their massive labors were swept away by the raging waters. The elegant brick and stone homes on well-to-do Riverside Drive bore the brunt of the river's fury. At 11:10, the sirens sounded, and those who had not already headed for higher ground departed. Soon, much of the valley was under eight to ten feet of water, and it was still rising.

Townend's decision to delay evacuation until virtually the last minute—and to instead encourage a sandbagging effort that some believed was doomed from the start—remains a subject of great local debate to this day. Many residents say that with adequate notice they could have moved their belongings to safety, rescued precious heirlooms now gone forever. "If only . . . " is a phrase that recurs in discussions of the Agnes disaster. Yet there is no arguing with the fact that 72,000 people were safely evacuated from their homes in the valley and no one was killed by the floodwaters.

Shortly after 1 P.M., the dike at Forty Fort on the west side of the river broke, and floodwaters surged into the historic riverside cemetery. Caskets and the bodies they contained were ripped from the earth, some carried for several miles downriver. With no hope of identifying the remains, most were reburied in a mass grave.

By 5:00 that afternoon, the Wyoming Valley was on its way to becoming a large, dirty lake. The refugees had crowded into makeshift shelters or bunked with friends, struggling to comprehend their fate. When the Susquehanna finally crested the following day, at 7 P.M., it had risen to 40.91 feet, nearly four feet above the official height of the levees. At its peak, the river was flowing at a rate of 345,000 cubic feet per second, or almost 2.6 million gallons per second. Three days before, its flow had been 13,100 cubic feet per second. At Marietta, downstream from nearly 26,000 square miles of Susquehanna watershed, the river was flowing at a rate of more than 1 million cubic feet per second on the evening of June 23, or more than 650 billion gallons in a twenty-four-hour period. At the ninety-five-foot-tall Conowingo Dam, the water rose to just seven feet from the top, despite engineers' frantic efforts to release as much water as the floodgates could handle.

Along the river, whole communities were inundated. At Harrisburg, the Susquehanna crested four feet above the 1936 record, flooding the downtown and many riverfront homes, those whose views had been so carefully preserved. Among them was the Governor's Mansion.[6]

The Chemung River between Corning and Elmira had swollen to a four-mile-wide lake. Two hundred bridges were destroyed in New York and Pennsylvania, isolating large segments of the population and complicating rescue efforts. In all, 5,000 square miles were flooded; 118 deaths were attributed to the storm. The youngest victim was 10-month-old Benjamin Kauffman, son of Samuel E. and Sarah Kauffman, a young Amish couple from Ronks, Lancaster County. The buggy in which they were riding was swept into the Pequea Creek. As recounted by Amish historian Gideon Fisher, Sarah grabbed and clung to a tree branch, but her husband and son were carried away by the current.

One area spared from the ravages of the Susquehanna was Sunbury. There, a concrete flood wall, completed by the Army Corps of Engineers in 1948 over the protests of some residents concerned about losing their views, held out the worst of the waters, which crested at 35.8 feet, one foot

---

6. Water was five feet deep in the mansion in 1972 and destroyed a baby grand piano and some draperies. Everything else had been moved to the second floor. Although a widely distributed news photograph showed Pennsylvania governor Milton Shapp and his wife Muriel in a motorboat at the front door of the mansion, they were not living there at the time of the flood. Instead, they occupied a smaller house across the river and were just inspecting damage at the official residence when the photo was taken.

higher than the 1936 record. Any residual doubts about the value of the wall—which a critic once said gave Sunbury "the feel of an empty swimming pool"—were swept away with the receding waters. A joyous bit of graffiti, proclaiming "We Love You Wall!", appeared soon after.[7]

Property losses attributed to the Agnes storm in seven states exceeded $4 billion. In terms of property damage, no area in Agnes's path was harder hit than the Wyoming Valley, where losses topped $2 billion. Twenty-five thousand homes and apartments were destroyed or damaged; in Kingston alone, only 20 of the town's 6,600 homes were spared. Wilkes-Barre's entire business district was underwater, and in the valley more than 2,700 commercial establishments sustained damages; utilities suffered heavy losses, and large segments of the valley were without electrical service for weeks. Motorists were forced to drive as far as sixty miles to find a bridge still capable of carrying them across the river.

The valley resembled a battle zone, with as many as 9,000 military personnel dispatched to aid in rescues, provide security, and assist in the initial cleanup. Stunned residents were prevented from returning to their stricken neighborhoods by National Guardsmen and police, who manned barricades. Their orders were to turn away all who sought entry, not just to keep out looters but because of fears that buildings, as well as the ground itself, might collapse. The deserted, flooded streets were patrolled by boats.

Not everyone had heeded General Townend's advice to evacuate, however. A few refused to go, including Elwood Disque, who lived a block from the river in South Wilkes-Barre. He watched the wall of water racing into his neighborhood on June 23. Rather than join his fleeing neighbors, Disque, a teacher at nearby Wilkes College, took a loaf of bread, peanut butter, a knife, a can opener, and a package of meatloaf, plus a mattress, bedding, and blankets, to the attic of his home on Birch Street. He filled the bathtub with water, and prepared to wait out the flood, maintaining a diary of his experiences.

7. Damages were reduced along the West Branch by four flood-control reservoirs, at Curwensville, Blanchard, Kettle Creek, and the First Fork of the Sinnemahoning Creek (the last of which was completed in 1969, thirty-three years after first being proposed). Williamsport's levees also held back the Susquehanna. Elsewhere on the river, at Muncy, Milton, and Lewisburg, which have no levees, flood crests in 1972 all exceeded the 1936 records. Since 1972, the citizens of Lock Haven, where flooding has always been a serious problem, have been split over the proposal to build a fifteen-foot-high levee to run six miles along the West Branch. Critics claim it will destroy the river vistas—and character—of the historic town. Construction began on the Lock Haven levee in 1992. Because of changes in federal law, a part of the cost of the $86-million project is being borne by the community, whose share is $4.4 million; the state is paying $11 million, and the federal government the remainder.

I woke up about 8:00 A.M. [June 24] hearing the furniture banging against the ceiling of the first floor. I did feel rested. Then I looked out the window. The ranch style homes were well covered by the water. I turned on the [portable] radio. The Susquehanna River now extended five miles on both sides of its bank—a large lake of mud filled with acid and oil and a roof top jutting out here and there. I suddenly realized I would be living in the attic longer than one day. I rationed myself to three slices of bread a day plus snacks.

I could see several cats and small wild animals sailing by on bits of lumber. A flood certainly cleans out a lot of cellars and backyards.

[June 25:] I attempted to flag down a helicopter from the attic window. There had been friendly waves before as they flew by. I knew they were on more important missions than picking up one person. They were just trying to keep me cheerful. Finally one arrived. But the trees around the house and the high voltage wires prevented them from coming close enough to pick me up. The huge waves created by the propeller just washed over the two-story houses across the street.

[June 26:] No boats—no one has passed today. The water has receded considerably and one can now begin to see the ground once more. I am amazed at how much animals that are stranded on roofs can endure. One particular dog gives off mournful wails, walks back and forth on the roof but is much weaker. His wailing cries carry so far over the water at night. It gives one a haunting feeling.

[June 27: By now, much of the water had subsided, but Disque discovered that all the doors and windows in his house had swollen shut and he needed help to get out.] Woke up rather early this morning after a good night's sleep. Had V-8 [vegetable juice], peanut butter sandwich and pineapple for breakfast . . . Two young men were checking a neighbor's house. I ask them to lean the ladder against the hall window so that I could get out— then to bring me bread, cold cuts and to mail the letters I had written . . . Will read old *Life* magazines until dark and then go to bed. The young men rescued the dog from the neighbor's roof and reported it to the Humane Society. There are so many stray, hungry animals.

The morning of June 27 dawned unseasonably hot and humid, and thousands of distraught Wyoming Valley residents crowded behind National Guard barriers awaiting the go-ahead to return home. When it came, many found that their familiar neighborhoods were now unrecognizable. Houses, torn apart, spilled out the contents of a lifetime. Trees, cars, riverborne debris and personal possessions lay where the receding water had dropped them. Everything was covered with a lung-clogging coating of dust or mud. The stench of rotting fish and food, the residue from the millions of gallons of untreated sewage and industrial wastes discharged into the river during the flood, and the powdery mud itself filled the air. The pervasive stink remains one of the most vivid memories of the disaster.

If the refugees from Agnes thought their nightmare was over, they were mistaken. Many would later say they were victims of not one but two disasters. The second came at the hands of their own government. Even before the Susquehanna's floodwaters had crested, advance teams had begun arriving to assess damages. Soon, the full force of the federal bureaucracy would descend on the Wyoming Valley. Before its last representative departed—several years later—U.S. taxpayers would have spent more than $2 billion there, or nearly $28,000 for every man, woman, and child who had suffered some loss. Never before has a single disaster-stricken community received such an outpouring of federal largess. It was as if every taxpayer in America had a vested interest in seeing the valley rebuilt. That nobody stepped forward to seriously challenge such a financial commitment was due in large part to a former Shakespearian actor who sported a Salvador Dali–style waxed mustache, wore red, white, and blue sneakers and ruffled shirts, and happened to be one of the most powerful men in Congress: Rep. Daniel J. Flood. This role was to be the finest of his career.

Hearing of the impending disaster in his district, Flood, a Democrat, telephoned Secretary of Defense Melvin Laird, a Republican, and announced that he was commandeering Laird's helicopter to head home. As the craft landed, the 67-year-old congressman turned to an aide and declared, "This is going to be one Flood against another!" Flood traded his purple suit for a set of khaki fatigues and set up a command post at a nearby naval reserve base. A few hours later he appeared on local television to announce, "Today I have ordered the Army Corps of Engineers not to permit the Susquehanna to rise one more inch." That may have been the only order issued by the congressman that went unheeded by federal bureaucrats. Even so, the Susquehanna halted its rise within a half-block of his Wilkes-Barre home.

A consummate politician who wielded his position as chairman of a House Appropriations subcommittee masterfully, Dan Flood was revered in the Wyoming Valley due to his ability to deliver federal programs and services to his constituents. Although Congress had the ghettos of New York and Chicago in mind when it enacted the 1960s Model Cities legislation, the first community to obtain funding was Wilkes-Barre. So extensive was his list of IOUs, accumulated since he entered Congress in 1944, that there was little Dan Flood couldn't achieve. And he was about to prove it. Flood returned to Washington and pushed a $1.6-billion Agnes relief bill through a receptive Congress with almost no debate.[8] It was, Pres. Richard Nixon would proudly proclaim, "the single largest amount ever allocated to a recovery effort in this country." The fact that 1972 was a presidential election year, and Pennsylvania was important to Nixon's reelection, didn't hurt its chances, either.

Among the bill's provisions were $1.3 billion for the Small Business Administration to provide loans for home owners and business people at 1 percent interest, with the first $5,000 of the loan forgiven. (The state did its part too: the Pennsylvania General Assembly authorized outright grants of $3,000 to the head of each household with Agnes losses.) At the time, the average annual family income in Wilkes-Barre was a mere $8,100. Thus, a number of residents received the equivalent of a full year's wages from taxpayers.

Another $200 million was earmarked by Congress for temporary housing, and millions more were appropriated for repairs to roads, bridges, and other infrastructure. In its haste to get the Wyoming Valley back on its feet, the federal government opened the treasury doors.[9] The total payout in the valley for Agnes—$2.2 billion—was nearly double the combined federal expenditures for the five previous natural disasters around the nation.

Two years after Agnes, the *Philadelphia Inquirer* published a series of articles examining the outlay of federal funds and what taxpayers—and flood victims themselves—received for the money. Based on its review of the government's own records, and on conversations with officials and Wyoming Valley residents, the newspaper concluded that the absence of planning and oversight had resulted in tens of millions of dollars being wasted. In the Wyoming Valley alone, the Small Business Administration

8. The only apparent nay-sayers were two California congressmen who called the measure an "invitation to fraud" and cited instances following the 1971 earthquake in their state in which "whole neighborhoods" with minor damage obtained federal loans, the first $2,500 of which was forgiven. "The little old lady whose house was washed down the river will not get help because she can't repay the loan. But somebody with a stain on his rug will get a loan he does not have to repay," predicted Democratic Rep. James C. Corman.

9. Victims of the flooding that struck Rapid City, South Dakota, two weeks before Agnes also were included in the bill's benefits. There, 238 people died and property damages exceeded $200 million. Senator George McGovern of South Dakota, who was challenging Nixon for the White House, was an active supporter of the massive federal relief bill. Like a host of other politicians—including Richard Nixon—he toured the Wyoming Valley to console residents, assess damages, and greet voters.

would write off $40 million in loans never repaid. What the relief effort produced was a community driven deeply into long-term debt for property on the banks of a river that will once again deliver a devastating flood.

Major changes eventually were made in federal-disaster assistance programs. Included among them was elimination of low-interest Small Business Administration loans. In 1982, when the Maumee River flooded Fort Wayne, Indiana, disaster recovery loans were available, but at rates nearly equal to prime, and local governments were required to pay 25 percent of the cost of repairs to roads, bridges, and other public structures. The Wyoming Valley and the Susquehanna had emptied the public purse.

When Jim and Columbia Jiunta returned to their house on Haldeman Street on the steamy morning of June 27, a 1948 Chrysler was propped up against a nearby tree. The doors and most of the windows of their house had swollen shut, so they climbed in through a bathroom window. Blissfully swimming in water trapped between the thermal panes of the sliding glass doors to their patio, they found what Jiunta describes as "pollywogs," denizens of the river water that had submerged the ranch house. Like thousands of other residents of the Wyoming Valley, the Jiuntas began the wrenching labor of discarding most of their fouled possessions. Jiunta borrowed a gas mask from his Army Reserve unit so he could work without gagging from the stench.

For weeks, curbsides throughout the valley were piled high with belongings. More than 8 million cubic yards of debris were removed from Wilkes-Barre alone; abandoned strip mines were converted into landfills to handle the discards.

But sorting through personal belongings was just one emotionally draining task ahead of the flood victims. Their benefactor—the federal government—also expected them to make decisions whose consequences would remain with them all their lives.

"You just didn't know what to do," recalls Jim Jiunta of those first weeks and months. "That was your greatest fear—of making the wrong choice." So confusing and complicated were the assistance programs that some flood victims walked away financially better off than before, while others were plunged into debt. Jiunta still seethes over a former neighbor who received $51,000 for his flood-damaged home, which had cost $22,000 to build. The same neighbor also was paid $15,000 in relocation expenses—money he used to "relocate" exactly where he had lived before, building a new house where his old one stood, positioned neatly alongside an undamaged swimming pool and shrubbery.

As for Jiunta, after inexplicable delays, program officials deemed that his home had not been damaged enough to qualify for a similar buyout. He was forced to borrow $50,000 for repairs. The same happened with his ravaged pharmacy; it was judged salvageable, so he took out another $80,000 loan to make those repairs. "March 5, 2003," says the retired druggist; that's when he will have repaid his loans from the federal government. By then, he will be almost 80. "And remember, before Agnes, everything I owned was debt-free."

Despite the agonizing uncertainties, there were moments of humor in the chaos. When Jiunta first arrived at his pharmacy, "there were bedpans and pills everywhere. I had a display case with $300 worth of Timex watches. I picked one up, hosed it off and it ran. I still have that watch. We thought it would have made a great commercial."

As promised assistance failed to materialize, tensions mounted in the Wyoming Valley. Delays in providing temporary housing kept thousands of victims confined to crowded shelters. Then, hordes of contractors—lured to the valley by stories of fortunes to be made—swarmed in and soon the going rate to replace a pane of glass had risen to $300. Confusion reigned among the dozen or more federal agencies overseeing repair programs. Victims watched first in amazement, and then in disgust, as one federally funded crew would arrive to tear out the repairs just completed by another federal crew working under a different program.

In a community that had always regarded welfare assistance as a handout for the lazy, the waste and greed embittered many. One flood victim, who received a furnace he didn't need and plumbing for a bathroom he didn't have, kept everything. "If the fruit is fallin' off the tree, you'd be a damn fool not to pick it up," he explained.

While the federal government was willing to commit billions to the recovery along the Susquehanna, it used no sticks with its carrots. Never once did it question the determination of local and state officials to rebuild on the floodplain. In fact, that was a criterion to qualify for some federal money. Even many of the flood victims were appalled by the fact that they had no option but to return. Min Matheson, a retired organizer with the International Ladies Garment Workers Union who became an admired and effective advocate for the flood victims, repeatedly labeled the plans "lunacy."

"The city is shaped like a saucer," Matheson said, referring to the densely populated valley. "But instead of moving the city up to the edges of the saucer, they are encouraging development in the lowest point of it."

This seemingly mindless course had a concrete motive: tax revenue.[10] Officials of the two dozen or so communities that had suffered the worst flooding faced a loss of their tax bases if riverfront properties were declared unsuitable for habitation. For many of the small towns, whose industry was gone and whose mines had closed, residential real estate provided the bulk of operating revenues. Personal factors also played a role. Families had lived in the little towns for generations and were loathe to pack up and leave. After all, they said, their parents and grandparents had survived past floods, and now they would, too.

So Wilkes-Barre and the other communities sidled right back up to the Susquehanna. Lots cleared of their water-damaged buildings were sold cheaply. That is what lured Robert W. Smallcomb to acquire three city-owned lots on Riverside Drive for $4,000 and build a split-level home in 1980. "Whenever the Susquehanna gets high, I get worried," he concedes. "But I guess if the city isn't worried about it, I shouldn't be."

Two years after Agnes, Wilkes-Barre authorized residential development on the last remaining large tract of undeveloped land within its borders, a property known as the Barney Farm—despite the fact that in 1972 the farm had been under ten feet of water. City officials hoped the expensive homes planned for the development would attract upscale buyers who otherwise might locate—and pay taxes—elsewhere. Their dream materialized. Today, curving streets with names like Mercedes Drive are lined with some of the highest-priced homes in the city.

The pretty gray-and-white Victorian on Mercedes Drive is owned by Tom and Maria Mattern. At the rear of their property sits the levee that is meant to protect them from the Susquehanna. "It's a long way down to the river," observes Tom Mattern, who was a teenager during the Agnes disaster. On a summer evening, with baskets of red geraniums swinging gently in the breeze on the front porch, the young couple talked about their decision to move to the river's edge. "We looked elsewhere," explained Tom, "but all the surrounding areas have hazards, too. In the winter, the roads get icy up in some of the other developments."

"We're a lot safer than our neighbors," adds Maria, gazing down the gentle hill toward the neighborhood where Smallcomb and the Jiuntas live. Mattern, who operates his family's flower shop in Wilkes-Barre, is unlike many residents of the Wyoming Valley. He has flood insurance.

---

10. In Rapid City, a different choice was made. Local officials there cleared out a five-mile strip through the heart of the city along Rapid Creek and converted the area into a park, with former residents relocated to higher ground.

While Congress has a consistent record of funding projects that encourage development in flood-prone areas, its view of who should pay for flood damages has changed several times over the decades.

In the 1950s, Congress backed away from a plan to offer subsidized flood insurance, and instead elected to continue providing outright assistance in the event of natural disasters, including floods. But by 1966, federal disaster relief topped $1 billion, and flood insurance once again was discussed. Two years later, the National Flood Insurance Act was passed, creating the Federal Insurance Administration. The law made available low-cost insurance to residents of communities with federally designated flood-prone areas. In return, local officials were expected to adopt and enforce land-use measures to limit development and thereby reduce future flood damage.

Criticized by some as federal intrusion into local land-use decisions, the act might have had the desired effect if Congress had adequately funded it. In its first year of existence, only 4 out of an eligible 20,000 communities with flood hazards were enrolled in the program because the necessary paperwork had not been completed. Even more disabling was the manner in which the law was interpreted. The definition of what comprised a flood-prone area initially was construed so loosely that in Wilkes-Barre, for example, the "flood plain" was the river. Everything else, including flood-prone South Wilkes-Barre, was regarded as safe for unlimited development.

Sales of flood insurance were extremely low, despite federal subsidies that made the policies extremely inexpensive—forty cents per hundred dollars' worth of coverage. In 1972, when Agnes tore through the valley, only two homeowners in Wilkes-Barre had purchased the insurance. (After Agnes, the rates were reduced to twenty-five cents per hundred in an effort to attract more buyers.)

With the staggering price tag of the Agnes disaster fresh in their minds, members of Congress tightened controls on flood insurance in 1973. Henceforth, they declared, it would be impossible to obtain a loan from a federally insured lending institution to buy or build in a flood-prone area without flood insurance. Also, no such community would be eligible to receive disaster assistance (even for nonflood disasters) if it did not participate in the insurance program. That created a furor in many towns. It wasn't long, however, before Congress again began weakening the act to appease unhappy constituents. Lending institutions also discovered that they need not fear federal sanctions if the insurance requirement was ignored.

Then, in 1982, the Reagan administration overhauled federal water policy as part of its budget review. The time-honored tradition of full federal funding for flood-control projects was scrapped; local and state governments together would now be required to pay a quarter of the costs. And, the Reagan budgeteers decided, the American taxpayer should no longer be subsidizing development along the floodplain. Full rates would be charged for coverage on new structures built in flood-hazard areas, and private insurers would sell the policies and administer the program. As a result, rates began to climb; sales of policies stalled, but began to rise again several years later.

Today, nationwide, only about 20 percent of those living in flood-prone areas have flood insurance.[11] That ratio applies to the Wyoming Valley as well and includes many families who lost everything in 1972 and still reside within several hundred yards of the Susquehanna. What is their reasoning? Psychologists call it "cognitive dissonance"—the ability to believe, despite the evidence, that disaster will strike somewhere—and someone—else.[12]

Ask a Wyoming Valley resident why he or she still lives along the river, and you are likely to get an answer not easily understandable to an outsider. "Family ties," says Jim Jiunta, whose two sons and a daughter live nearby. "And, I don't like it anyplace else." He tried living on higher ground, but soon returned to his old neighborhood. What of the risks of another flood? "I'll take my chances," he replies.

If the flood did anything for its victims, it left them with a keen sense of what's important in their lives and what isn't. "The furniture, the television set, the clothes you can replace. It's the pictures, the family things that are gone forever," says Jiunta, fingering one item he managed to salvage—a mildewed, barely legible high school diploma awarded to one of his children. In 1975, when the rain-swollen Susquehanna threatened to again inundate South Wilkes-Barre, Columbia Jiunta took no chances. She and a son stuffed everything in the house into one of the last remaining rental vans to be had in northeastern Pennsylvania. "Even our toothbrushes were on that truck." The neighborhood was spared, but "it was close," she says.

The residents of the valley believe their security rests in a long-awaited, much discussed, $200-million federal levee-improvement project, first pro-

11. Of an estimated 11 to 13 million households in such areas, only about 2.3 million are insured.
12. Many Californians living in earthquake-prone areas do not have insurance either.

posed shortly after Agnes. It was among several ideas considered to reduce the risks of flooding. One that was popular with residents, but ultimately rejected by the Corps of Engineers, involved dredging twenty-five miles of the Susquehanna to deepen the river by twelve feet. This would have produced 62 million cubic yards of dredge spoil, enough to create a 2.5-mile-high mountain covering an acre of ground. Another proposal entailed clearing the floodplain by removing the 20,000 residences and 3,000 businesses located there. The Corps nixed that one, too, and instead recommended raising the floodwalls by an average of three to five feet. That would still leave them lower in places than the 1972 crest, but Corps experts say that the risk of another cataclysmic flood like Agnes has been practically eliminated with the construction of the Tioga-Hammond and Cowanesque reservoirs on tributaries of the Susquehanna.

Not everyone is enthusiastic about the levee-raising idea. For one thing, it would increase the severity of flooding in downstream communities that have no levees. Residents there have demanded that they, too, receive some protection. The project also has come under scrutiny in Washington. Federal auditors in 1989 determined that the benefits to be derived did not offset the cost—technically a death knell for the project under new federal austerity guidelines. Even if the funds eventually are authorized, it would take years to complete construction. "Which just puts us that much closer to the next big flood," said Anthony J. Mussari, a historian and professor at King's College in Wilkes-Barre. "The question is, Have the people of the Wyoming Valley become disaster-conscious? The answer is No. People just wanted to return to a semblance of order and then, once that was achieved, to pretend that it won't happen again."

Some changes have been made in the aftermath of the Susquehanna's rampage. Luzerne County Civil Defense is now Luzerne County Emergency Management. And Kevin O'Brien, the personable operations officer, proudly shows a visitor the sophisticated computer equipment and automated rain gauges that enable its five-person staff to track weather and river levels. "Oh, we're much better prepared for a flood than we were in 1972," says O'Brien, who was a high school sophomore then. That's probably a good thing. The office is still located in the subbasement of the courthouse.

Pollution

"A trifling inconvenience"

Every morning, rain or shine, cold or hot, they are drawn to this piece of the Susquehanna. Charlie Rittner is usually the first to arrive, about 5. He starts the coffee and then heads out onto the river to fish, no matter what's biting. Over the next few hours, the others drift in. By 8:30 or so, the regulars are all here, a half-dozen men, most in their 50s, 60s, and 70s, who grew up within sight of the Susquehanna and have never left for long. Joe Millward. Rusty Beckey. Harry Myers. Joe Mesaric. Bud Wilbern comes in from his island. It is Bud who explains this daily assembly: "We are river rats."

Their rendezvous is an incongruous place. The concrete-and-steel span of the Pennsylvania Turnpike's bridge across the Susquehanna looms overhead, carrying a never-ending stream of trucks and cars. The drone of traffic would be constant if it weren't frequently eradicated—along with all conversation—by a plane landing or taking off at nearby Harrisburg International Airport. On the southern horizon stand the four cooling towers of the Three Mile Island nuclear plant, steam belching from two, the other pair lifeless. To the north sprawls the monstrous, rusty hulk of the Bethlehem Steel Corporation's four-mile-long Steelton plant. And Conrail freight trains rumble over tracks that mark the eastern perimeter of Bud's property.

To find the "river rats," it's necessary to bounce over abandoned railroad tracks and a cratered roadway, pass by heaps of broken concrete and littered loading yards, and squeeze through a narrow opening in an aged, soot-stained railroad overpass. Once beyond Bud's ominous "No Trespassing, Members Only" sign, you've entered an unexpectedly serene world. Here, the Susquehanna flows a mile wide and as far as the eye can see in either direction. Islands break the smooth surface of the water—some merely tufts of emerald-green marshgrass, home to thriving colonies of migratory waterfowl; others large enough to bear thriving colonies of summer residents. The sounds of all the cars and trucks and planes heading somewhere else are quickly forgotten, for when you've arrived at Bud

Wilbern's boat landing it seems there could be no other destination.

The Susquehanna has been part of daily life for Bud Wilbern and Joe Millward since they were youngsters growing up a few blocks away in the small mill town of Highspire. They trapped muskrats together among these islands, occasionally getting lost in the fog on their way home. They've fished more days than they care to count. When World War II broke out, these boys from central Pennsylvania joined the Navy. They have been through two major floods, '36 and '72, and plenty of less memorable bouts of high water. They have watched massive ice jams grind landmarks away, reshaping the face of the river they know so well.

While others measure the health of the Susquehanna in laboratories, Bud and Joe simply walk down to its edge and look. During their six-plus decades of careful observation, they have witnessed the gradual regeneration of a river ravaged by humans.

Not all that long ago, there were no fish in this part of the Susquehanna—nor in plenty of other places, for that matter. The currents carried the filth and waste of 24,100 square miles of upstream watershed past this landing. "You couldn't put your feet in for the oil. You would get a ring around your ankle," says Bud. Many days, the water stank from millions of gallons of untreated sewage and industrial waste poured into it; the surface glistened with a rainbow sheen of chemicals. The bottom was black with thick silt from the upstream coal mines. Waves of dead fish, suffocated by the lack of oxygen or poisoned by acids, floated by.

Today, Charlie Rittner and others often can be found fishing near the outfall of the Bethlehem Steel plant. Local anglers boast that the bass fishing here can't be topped anywhere, and Bud's thinking of expanding the small parking lot at his boat landing to accommodate the weekend crowds. When shad fishing resumes, he says with mixed emotions, "this place will boom." The swimming's fine off the landing, and even better from the island where Bud lives most of the year.

There is a downside to all this, of course, and it worries Bud. Once in a while someone who has seen the landing from the turnpike bridge will arrive to ask about keeping a boat there. "I always say to them, 'Leave your name, and if there's an opening, I'll let you know.'" When they're gone, Bud discards the information. "I don't need the money. I need the privacy, and I want to keep this place nice."

Like the Susquehanna's long, slow slide into squalor, its rejuvenation has been years in the making, and it is far from completed. Despite the river's awesome capacity to survive even the most egregious insults, the weapons wielded by humans and the forces of nature are so powerful that

Bud and Joe one morning may walk to the river's edge and see that the progress of recent years has been swept away overnight. Nature did that in 1972. Human beings came close in 1979.

The river rats have been accused by the uninitiated (a group that includes most of the wives) of doing more gossiping and lounging than anything else, but this morning the prevailing mood is one of industry. The rats are building new quarters, and the impending arrival of fall has hastened preparations—to some extent at least.

Until recently, the landing's only amenity was a fifty-five-gallon drum filled with scrap wood, around which the river rats would gather to warm themselves when the weather turned nasty. That didn't satisfy Joe Millward, a regular since retiring in 1980. "We decided we wanted something over our heads to keep the rain off, and some sides to keep out the wind," he explains. So he and Bud scrounged around the neighborhood, locating discarded shipping crates, old highway signs, and scrap lumber, and erected a clubhouse, one wall of which, according to the address stenciled on its side, started life in Nuremburg, Germany. Soon, a coffeepot appeared, then two television sets (three, if you count the one that's never worked), a rug, some old chairs, and even pictures for the walls. Although the metal drum remained outside—a kind of shrine to the bygone era—an old iron stove fashioned from pipe forged in the Bethlehem Steel plant provided heat indoors.

Nice as it was, the place did have one flaw. "The river'd get a little high and our feet would get wet," says Joe. That set in motion the current construction project, also a decidedly low-budget effort. A wonder of engineering, a monument to recycling, the new clubhouse rises from the hull of an old pontoon boat, which has been hoisted high onto cement blocks and anchored down with stout cables so it won't wash away in the flood everyone knows will come. Someone offered a Franklin stove that had survived the 1972 flood. Somebody else donated a large bay window, so the rats cut a hole in the boat's rear wall to accommodate it. A set of tires appeared one day, but Bud plans to use them on his truck.

For a while, the grand plans for the new place seemed a bit too optimistic, and even Bud had occasional doubts. (He fidgeted one morning as some of the regulars milled around waiting for instructions from Rusty Beckey, who was savoring the last of Charlie Rittner's coffee. "You don't get Rusty started too early in the morning," Bud observed. "He's a private contractor.") But Rusty, who used to be a long-haul truckdriver before he became a roofer, and the other rats shared Bud's vision. Now the Franklin stove sits beneath a wooden mantel adorned with two black porch lights, which, as

Bud demonstrated, give off a pleasant glow from their blue lightbulbs. Rusty proved the value of a back door to nowhere by opening it and catching thirty catfish when the river rose after a heavy rain. "I kept the fire going and just sat here fishing," he said. All that remains to do now, according to Rusty, is to lay the carpet and get some curtains for the windows.

When Bud retired from his job at a local road construction firm in 1988, he took over management of the landing from his brother, Stu, who was in poor health. Stu had acquired the place years before from Henny Etnoyer. Henny used to mine the river for coal and lived in a shack he built atop a coal barge beached at the landing. Henny raised a young girl in the shack and two hogs out back. Although nobody can remember the name of the girl, including Joe, who went to school with her, they remember the pigs. "It was the cleanest hog pen I ever saw," says Bud, a handsome, silver-haired man whose real name is David.

As kids, Bud and Joe used to come to this spot, lured out of bed by the curious sights and sounds of the Susquehanna's Hard-Coal Navy, a fleet of battered steamboats and barges that plied the river as far north as Sunbury. For nearly a century, the fleet vacuumed up hundreds of thousands of tons of coal particles and silt each year from the riverbottom, waste that had washed down from the anthracite fields of the Wyoming Valley. The fine riverbed anthracite was prized by power plants, Bethlehem Steel, and other industries. To get it, the steamboats slowly winched their way against the current on steel cables attached to anchors far upstream, their huge T-shaped hose nozzles sucking up the river bottom. Some of the barges would unload at the landing Bud now owns. Obliging steamboat captains would allow Joe and his friends to tie their little boats to the trailing barge and hitch a slow ride up to Harrisburg.

The last vessels of the Susquehanna's Hard-Coal Navy left the river in the mid-1950s. The fleet had once numbered 200 or more, and in some years extracted as much as 300,000 tons of anthracite in this process of submarine mining.[1] Not only did the fleet owners turn a handy profit (their only major expense was the purchase of coal; the boilers on their boats couldn't use the fine river anthracite) but they performed a public service. Without the dredging, bathers headed to Harrisburg's City Island bathhouse could have walked over from the shore. Joe Millward remembers

1. Dredging continued on Lake Clarke, the expanse of Susquehanna behind the Safe Harbor Dam, until 1973. The coal extracted from the river bottom was used to power the steam generator at Holtwood, owned by Pennsylvania Power and Light Company. During the twenty-two years that the dredge operated, nearly 10 million tons of coal were recovered.

when his brother waded out to an island to spend the day but was forced to swim back after a barge passed by.

Submarine coal-mining was one of the first, and more unusual, casualties of the long effort to clean up the Susquehanna basin. Other radical changes were in store for the river and those who lived along its banks. At long last, society began to accord the Susquehanna a value other than that of a limitless waste receptacle.

Throughout history, people have used rivers for transportation and power, for drinking water and waste removal, for recreation and aesthetic pleasure. The conflicts built into these multiple demands on a single resource long have been recognized, but it has only been in recent years that each function has been given equal stature in public policy.

The Susquehanna was far from unique in its descent to a foul and tainted watercourse. As recently as 1972, the United States had tens of thousands of miles of polluted rivers and streams. Today, the nation's waterways largely have been transformed. The once improbable goal of rendering them "fishable, swimmable"—the target set by the 1972 federal Clean Water Act—has nearly been attained, thanks to the passage of federal laws, the infusion of hundreds of billions of dollars for waste treatment, and the embrace of the principle that *no* American has the right to deprive another of a clean stream.

But long before Washington paid attention to water pollution, long before it became a subject of public discussion and concern, a small group of Pennsylvanians who believed good fishing was one step short of Paradise decided that the desecration of the state's rivers must end. Many would not live to see the fulfillment of their dream, and those who remain know the victories are not secure. "People still have no conscience about what they do to the river downstream," says John C. Youngman, born along the Susquehanna in 1903, and one of its most zealous guardians ever since.

The Susquehanna was never harnessed as a workhorse river like the Delaware, the Hudson, or the Mississippi, but that did not rule out polluting development along its banks. Canals, followed by rail connections, lured entrepreneurs, who found that the Susquehanna could provide two important services: it could run machinery and it could remove waste.

The river served America's first steel mill, which occupied the site of the Bethlehem Steel complex in Steelton today. Tanneries, attracted by the abundance of hemlock bark, sprang up along the West Branch and the Juniata, disgorging lime, animal flesh, and bleaches. Slaughterhouses were built near farms along the North Branch, their effluent laden with blood and offal. Dairies and food-processing firms along the fertile southern end of the river spewed out wastes that coated the water with foul-smelling foam. Elsewhere on the river, factories discharged pickling liquors, dyes, oils, cyanide, phenols, and acids. Towns along the Susquehanna grew, doubling and tripling in population, and sending their sewage into the river. All this development had one thing in common: waste disposal consisted of laying a discharge pipe to the closest waterway; sometimes the industries didn't even bother to lay the pipe.

Concern about the contamination of the Susquehanna was muted by the fact that it was never an important source of drinking water, and by a prevailing belief that rivers generally could assimilate whatever poisons humans deposited.[2] And had the Susquehanna been asked merely to endure the burdens of industrial and domestic pollution, perhaps the harm would have been minimal. But people demanded more of the river in their drive to exploit its rich resources.

The problem was not lumbering. While this wreaked havoc along the Susquehanna by increasing its natural propensity to flood, the loggers did little to upset the basic chemistry of the river itself. It was the exploitation of the river's other phenomenal resource—coal—that nearly killed this mighty waterway.

More than 100 billion tons of coal were once buried beneath Pennsylvania, and historically the state has produced far more coal than any other—nearly one-fourth of that mined in the entire United States. Almost 80 billion tons still remain in the ground, three-fourths of which is soft, or bituminous coal. That is located almost exclusively in the western half of the state, with much of it concentrated in the drainage basin of the West Branch of the Susquehanna. The world's largest known deposits of anthracite, or hard, coal are found in a 500-square-mile area of northeastern Pennsylvania.

The coal is the end product of the extraordinary pressure applied by the earth's changing crust to the swamps that existed over 300 million years ago. As the land folded into the ridges that stretch from northeast to southwest, beds of coal were formed—some hard, some soft, depending on

2. Only a few communities—among them Binghamton, Lancaster, Danville, and Havre de Grace—depend even today on the Susquehanna for municipal water. Although Baltimore has the capability to draw water from the river at the Conowingo Dam and transport it via pipeline to the city, it does not do so.

Nearly all river towns have always drawn their water from tributaries, wells, or reservoirs that remained largely free of pollutants even when the Susquehanna itself was seriously degraded.

the pressures exerted. The anthracite lies in separate fields—the Northern Field which underlies the Wyoming Valley; the Western and Eastern Middle fields, drained by the North Branch before it reaches Northumberland; and the Southern Field, drained in part by Swatara Creek, which empties into the Susquehanna at Middletown, south of Harrisburg.

The Northern Field is a canoe-shaped trough of coal that begins in Forest City in Susquehanna County and extends fifty-five miles southwest to Shickshinny in Luzerne County, following the Wyoming Valley most of the way. Consisting of eighteen workable seams that reach down 2,100 feet or more, the Northern Field, like the others in Pennsylvania, still contains huge quantities of recoverable coal—as much as 7.3 billion tons.

In 1917, the peak year of anthracite production in Pennsylvania, 156,148 men descended into the bowels of the earth to blast and chisel away vast caverns in the glistening anthracite, bringing to the surface more than 100 million tons of coal. So exhaustively did the miners work beneath the Wyoming Valley that by the turn of the century it was possible to walk the twelve miles from Pittston to Nanticoke and never leave the underground maze of tunnels and shafts.

While Indians presumably experimented to find a use for the black rocks jutting from the steep hills or lying in the streambeds of the Susquehanna, the U.S. Geological Survey attributes the discovery of coal to some Yankees from Connecticut who in 1762 had settled in the Wyoming Valley. Wilkes-Barre blacksmith Obadiah Gore was using it by 1769, and during the Revolution, coal was shipped down the Susquehanna in arks, transferred to wagons, and hauled to the armory at Carlisle to fuel the forges there.

The hard coal produced tremendous heat and little ash, but it had a major disadvantage: it would not burn without a constant flow of oxygen. That rendered it of little value to the average user, as one businessman discovered in 1807. Abijah Smith's grand scheme to mine coal from the seventy-five acres he owned in Plymouth and ship it downriver to Columbia collapsed when he could attract no customers. For the first time, but definitely not the last, coal was dumped along the banks of the Susquehanna.

The following year, Wilkes-Barre tavernkeeper Jesse Fell stacked some of the coal in an iron grate. It burned briskly, his inn became a landmark, and the coal industry of the Wyoming Valley was born.

Getting coal to market proved difficult and costly at first. Coal imported from Wales cost less in New York and Philadelphia than anthracite from the Susquehanna. That equation changed with completion of the first canals, and ready markets were assured. A Baltimore newspaper in 1840 carried an announcement of the imminent arrival of bituminous coal from the north via the Tidewater Canal, noting, "This is a new item of trade here, and will, we have no doubt, become a very important one."

Once entrepreneurs saw the potential for delivering this valuable resource to the rest of the East Coast, pressure mounted to extend the canals—and eventually rail lines—directly to coal country. The railroads themselves became the biggest consumers of coal, and after the Civil War most of the mines were controlled, if not owned outright, by rail companies. (Although such monopolies were illegal in Pennsylvania, no one, least of all the complaisant state legislature, paid any attention to that. The law eventually was repealed.) Coal and the railroads became a politically invincible combination that lasted more than a century, winning enormous concessions from the state government. These included, for the coal industry, exemptions from Pennsylvania's clean-streams laws. The exemptions were repealed in the mid-1960s, but long before then much of the Susquehanna and its tributaries had been seriously contaminated.[3]

Perhaps nowhere was the desecration of a landscape as complete as in the Wyoming Valley, where the river was lined with hundreds of collieries. In 1870, more than 7.8 million tons of coal were mined from the anthracite field there. Describing this once green and peaceful vale, Peter Roberts, a sociologist and clergyman, wrote in 1904:

> The fish are exterminated, and the forests where solemn grandeur and majesty impressed the souls of men are no more. The children of mine employees are to-day raised among surroundings that are dismal and dreary. The huge culm and rock heaps, polluted streams, bare and barren hills, cave-ins and strippings, make up the landscape which greets the eyes of these thousands, and if they are polluted in mind and body we need not be surprised. Man can turn a wilderness into a garden, but it needs intelligence and forethought. In these regions hardly a spot can be found in the villages and towns that is not cursed.

Although miners once broke up the large chunks of coal underground, the introduction of the coal breaker in the 1840s brought that process to the surface. The amount of coal waste increased one and a half times. Coal operators also dumped low-grade coal, slate, and other mine debris into piles on the ground. These culm banks literally became combustible mountains, towering over many mining communities. Small coal pieces and the

---

3. The Pennsylvania Railroad so tightly controlled politics in Harrisburg for years that its lobbyist was widely known as the state's fifty-first senator. Anyone needing to speak with him knew exactly where to look—in the office of the Senate president.

fine sediments created as the chunks were sorted were dumped into or alongside the closest stream. The freshets of springtime could be counted on to sweep these waste piles away. Coal destined for market was washed, and the water, now an inky soup, was poured back into the river.

In its 1917 survey of the North Branch, the Army Corps of Engineers noted that coal silt was fifteen to twenty-five feet deep in the river channels. This was carried by the currents 100 miles and more downstream to sustain the Hard-Coal Navy.

For the operators of coal mines, both bituminous and anthracite, water has always proved as much a curse as a blessing. When coal is removed from the underground seams, water seeps—or sometimes flows—into the openings. As early as the 1860s, mine engineers in the Wyoming Valley were working on ways to get rid of this water. Even so, anthracite production from the valley steadily increased, growing from 4 million tons in 1860 to 9 million tons in just a decade.[4]

In most cases, the only way to get water out of a mine is to pump it away. The problem is that once the water and air come into contact with the coal-bearing strata, a chemical reaction takes place—a process that in nature would be nothing more consequential than weathering. But mining hastens the course of nature, particularly in Pennsylvania, whose geology features a wealth of the chemical ingredients that combine to produce acids. In coal seams pyrite, a mineral compound of iron and sulfur, combines with air and water and oxidizes to produce ferrous sulfate and sulfuric acid. As these new substances move through the mine, additional oxidizing takes place, creating ferrous iron and other acid compounds.

By the time the water leaves the mine it can be a potent mix of sulfates, acid, and iron hydroxides, plus aluminum, calcium, manganese, and ferrous iron. It is the presence of iron hydroxides in the discharge that give the receiving streams a bright orange color, and as the pace of mining along the Susquehanna increased, more and more streams took on this telltale hue. The streams themselves became sterile, for no living thing could survive the levels of acid.

Acid is formed in bituminous coal, too. Fields of this coal, softer than anthracite and far more accessible, underlie more than half of the

4. The Wyoming Valley accounted for about half the anthracite mined in Pennsylvania, with the remainder produced in the so-called Western Middle and Southern fields. These are drained not only by the Susquehanna but also by the Schuylkill and Lehigh rivers. They, too, suffered severe pollution and siltation. About 800,000 tons of coal silt were dredged from the Schuylkill annually in the 1940s, much of it winding up as fill at the Philadelphia International Airport.

6,900-square-mile West Branch drainage area, as well as portions of the Juniata and Tioga rivers. Unlike the moribund anthracite industry to the east, bituminous mining continues today, in the boom-bust cycles common to many extractive industries. Much of the same land first stripped of its virgin forests was destined to be stripped next of its coal, and before the scars from one had healed, the rust-colored wounds of another began to appear.

Clearfield, Chest, Bennett Branch, Moshannon, Sinnemahoning— stream after stream fell prey to the acidic waters from the mines, and all emptied their pollution into the West Branch of the Susquehanna. In some portions of the river, geology lessened the impact. For example, Bald Eagle Creek and its tributaries flow over large beds of limestone and add about 130,000 pounds of alkalinity each day to the river, nearly neutralizing the heavy loads of acid flowing in from above. Fish are abundant as far north as Bald Eagle Creek, which joins the river just below Lock Haven. For much of the remaining 100 miles to the headwaters, the West Branch is still virtually an aquatic dead zone. The transformation of the river at Bald Eagle Creek is impossible to miss. Upstream of Lock Haven the West Branch is startlingly clear, with every rock on the bottom plainly visible. At the mouth of Bald Eagle, however, the river turns a more normal green, and almost immediately bass and other species can be seen in the shallows.

John Youngman recalls that it was 1907 or 1908 when the first wave of acid water swept down the Susquehanna and reached Williamsport. Over time, these slugs of acid, as they are called, would arrive with increasing frequency. They usually came in late summer when the river was low, its life-sustaining oxygen nearly depleted. A heavy rainstorm in the headwaters would flush out the mines and, like clockwork, the massive infusions of acid would come rolling downstream twenty-four hours later. Youngman remembers the riverbanks strewn with dead fish, the ones that inhabited the Susquehanna of his childhood: trout, bass, and pike—the same fish that Susanna Wright sent to Benjamin Franklin. "We didn't know what was causing it at first, but we knew it meant the end of good fishing," he says.

While acid produced the most dramatic effects on the Susquehanna, the river's service as a sewer also was grossly apparent. If the tenants of the state Capitol building, which sits a mere two blocks from the river, didn't know this, their olfactory senses were severely impaired. "The liquid between the river banks in most of our industrialized sections is no longer water in its strict sense, but a conglomeration of human excretia and industrial wastes," lamented a Pennsylvania health official in 1937. Outbreaks of disease were common. The Commonwealth wasn't unique in this regard.[5]

Like a number of other states, Pennsylvania had made some feeble attempts to control sewage discharges. In 1905 it passed the Purity of Waters Act; compliance was voluntary, and pollution continued unabated. In 1923 the Pennsylvania General Assembly created a Sanitary Water Board, comprised of three members of the governor's cabinet and three citizens, whose job was to issue sewage discharge permits. Guiding the board's activities, however, was this basic assumption: the public welfare depended upon industrial prosperity and, given a choice between pure water and economic vitality, clean streams ranked a distant second.

To facilitate its efforts, the board created a caste system for Pennsylvania streams—those still pure and deserving of protection; those polluted but still capable of supporting some aquatic life; and those so foul they could serve just one purpose—as sewers. For reasons unclear today, the board calculated that Pennsylvania had 100,000 miles of streams (the actual number is about 45,000 miles). The members decided that of this total, more than one-third was so polluted that it was "not economically practical" to attempt any cleanup. One-fourth were still "virtually in their natural state." The remainder, the board found, endured varying degrees of pollution. The fate of those streams was to be determined by how much it would cost to reduce the wastes flowing into them. While the actual number of stream miles was erroneous, the percentage for each classification *was* accurate.

The fact that Pennsylvania officials had declared one-third of the state's waterways not worth saving—and weren't going to be aggressive in protecting the rest—did not sit well with John Youngman, who returned to Williamsport in 1927 with a law degree from Harvard, a feisty sense of right and wrong, and deep, deep roots on the West Branch of the Susquehanna River.

His family history, including his own, is the history of the river itself. It is a tale he never tires of telling. At the conclusion of a day-long tour of his beloved West Branch country, John Youngman stops in a sun-dappled cemetery guarded by a mighty black cherry tree. Here rest the remains of some of his ancestors, including his great-great-great-grandfather, John

5. United States Surgeon General Thomas Parran, in testimony before Congress a decade later, painted a graphic picture of just how much untreated sewage polluted the nation's streams. If the solids from these wastes were dead and disintegrating mules, weighing 1,100 pounds each, Dr. Parran calculated, it would be as if 8 million were being dumped into America's waterways each year.

The staff of the *Williamsport Sun and Banner* outside the newspaper office after the devastating 1889 flood *(above)*. The billboard reads: "Extra! Friday. Is It An 1865 Flood? The biggest river for years on the West Branch." In fact, water rose to 33 feet in Williamsport, six feet higher than the 1865 flood. Fifty people were killed along the West Branch. (James V. Brown Library, with permission)

Tropical Storm Agnes in 1972 broke all records on the flood-prone Susquehanna *(opposite, top)*. After toiling for hours in a futile attempt to raise the levees in Wilkes-Barre, volunteers fled for safety as the raging Susquehanna topped the dikes. Within minutes, their work was washed away, and much of the Wyoming Valley was under water. (Photograph by John Walton)

In the Wyoming Valley alone, damages from Tropical Storm Agnes exceeded $1 billion *(opposite, bottom)*. More than 2,700 businesses sustained losses, including these in Kingston, across the river from Wilkes-Barre. Despite the damage, federal recovery programs encouraged rebuilding on the flood-plain. (*Philadelphia Inquirer*/Michael Viola, with permission)

157

The Susquehanna and its tributaries offered a convenient means of disposing of coal waste *(above)*. In places along the North Branch, coal silt was 15 to 25 feet deep. The Bradley Washery #1 on the Lackawanna River was typical of many in the anthracite region. (Department of Forests and Waters, Sanitary Water Board, Division of Archives and Manuscripts, Pennsylvania Historical and Museum Commission, with permission)

The coal silt washed down the Susquehanna, sustaining what became known as Hard-Coal Navy, a fleet of battered steamboats and barges that plied the river as far north as Sunbury until the 1950s *(opposite, top)*. The fleet vacuumed up hundreds of thousands of tons of coal particles and silt each year from the riverbottom and sold them to utilities and industries. Here, some of that coal is unloaded. (Department of Commerce, Division of Archives and Manuscripts, Pennsylvania Historical and Museum Commission, with permission)

Until 1970, coal mine operators in Pennsylvania could simply walk away from a mine with no liability for the pollution it caused *(opposite, bottom)*. As a result, thousands of miles of streams were rendered lifeless. (Department of Health, Division of Archives and Manuscripts, Pennsylvania Historical and Museum Commission, with permission)

Henry Antes. While the names of other relatives have eroded from the small headstones, they have not faded from John Youngman's keen memory.

In 1773, Lt. Col. John Henry Antes settled on the West Branch at the mouth of the limestone creek that has since borne his name, just upstream from Jersey Shore. There he built a log stockade and a grist mill, raised a family that included the mother of renowned engineer Benjamin Latrobe, and defended this wilderness outpost from Indian attack. "It's all because of a calico dress that the Youngmans acquired this land from John Henry Antes"—thus John Youngman begins the tale. Amelia Antes, granddaughter of John Henry, was apprenticed at age 16 to a seamstress and sent downriver via raft accompanied by her tuition, a heifer. When she came home six months later, Amelia donned a stylish dress she had made, provoking a jealous outburst from a foster daughter being raised by the Antes family. Amelia was ordered by her father to change out of the calico dress and into homespun, but instead she took a horse and rode off to visit an aunt who lived in Youngman's Town, now Mifflinburg. There she met and fell in love with Elias P. Youngman. The couple returned to Antes Creek, were married, and eventually set up housekeeping on her father's homestead, raising thirteen children. There have been Youngmans watching over the valley ever since, their great-grandson is now saying, and always will be, for two of the lushly forested hills that soar above Antes Creek are Mount Elias and Mount Amelia.

Over the years John Youngman has purchased property traversed by the creek, and today he owns two miles of the stream, an insurance policy of sorts for Antes Creek. About midway along its glistening tumble over

The price of lax regulation of coal mining in Pennsylvania was more than just environmental damage. The owners of the Knox Coal Co. ignored warnings about digging too close to the river bottom, and on January 22, 1959, the Susquehanna broke through the ceiling of the mine *(opposite, top)*. The bodies of 12 miners were never recovered. (Department of Mines and Mineral Industries, Knox Mine Disaster, Division of Archives and Manuscripts, Pennsylvania Historical and Museum Commission, with permission)

In an effort to plug the giant cataract created by the Susquehanna at the Knox Mine, a rail line was diverted, and more than 200 rail cars were dumped into the hole *(opposite, bottom)*. Truckloads of rocks, railroad ties, utility poles, and hay were thrown in as well, disappearing without a trace. By then, however, the Susquehanna had flooded almost all mines in the Wyoming Valley, and the anthracite era came to a virtual halt. (David L. Lawrence Papers, Division of Archives and Manuscripts, Pennsylvania Historical and Museum Commission, with permission) limestone ledges is the two-story frame "cottage" built by his father, a Williamsport doctor, in late 1888. The homes of John Youngman's uncles, George and William Youngman, and their families formerly sat upstream. Nine of John Youngman's relatives died when the Antes became a torrent during the legendary flood of 1889. Because of its location on a small rise, the cottage built by his father escaped the avalanche of water. Youngman recently located the family Bible that was read by the children's governess as the terrible flood bore down on them.

Nearly every weekend, John Youngman and his aged dog Lassie make the trip out from Williamsport, piling their belongings into a taxi, for he no longer sees well enough to drive. To reach the cottage, it is necessary to cross a swinging bridge over the sparkling creek, where brook and brown trout now thrive and stocked rainbows dart among the ripples. Youngman, a slight man with thinning white hair, leans on the smooth walking stick he cut from a sugar-maple sapling just behind the cottage. He stops at midspan to point out what he calls the Courthouse Steps Dam, built of large granite slabs that once adorned the front of the Lycoming County Courthouse and cost him $60 to acquire ("They had me bidding against myself," he grumbles) but $750 to haul away. "Seven people walked across those steps to their hangings," says Youngman. "My father, who was 15 at the time, shinnied up a telegraph pole to watch one of them."

The musty cottage is crammed with the memorabilia of generations of Youngmans: a photograph of his Uncle William, who at age nine hopped on a troop train bound for the Battle of Gettysburg and wasn't heard from until after the war ended; a small pile of fossil-bearing rocks that John Youngman collected as a boy, including his favorite, which bears a large paw print ("Noah's dog, I always thought"); skins of rattlesnakes from the mountain behind the house; and dozens of photographs of fishing expeditions over the years. Inspired, he takes a rod and reel and heads slowly up Antes Creek, only to find that the trout lurk teasingly in the shadows, but aren't biting this morning.

Trout have always thrived in the pure waters of Antes Creek, but it was the exception among Susquehanna tributaries when John Youngman returned to the West Branch in the 1920s. Like a small group of others around Pennsylvania at the time, Youngman—who has as much vinegar as blood coursing through his veins—grew increasingly troubled by the decline in the state's water quality and the unresponsiveness of those in Harrisburg. If the Susquehanna was cleaned up, he reasoned, then fish would return. He knew one other thing: "No trout making its way up the Susquehanna could bypass the sweet, cold water of Antes Creek." When that day came, he planned to be there to greet the fish, rod in hand.

Youngman soon found that he wasn't alone in his frustrations. A Philadelphia lawyer by the name of Grover Cleveland Ladner had championed clean water for years, in part because of the terrible condition of the Schuylkill River in his hometown. Ladner was an outspoken critic of the Sanitary Water Board, accusing it of placating polluters. It was he who recognized the potency of Pennsylvania's thousands of sportsmen and the impact of elevating clean streams to a political issue. "But he said if we were just going to talk fish, we'd never get anywhere," Youngman recalls. "Talk about public health, he said, and don't worry about the fish. He was right."

Thus it was that the Pennsylvania Federation of Sportsmen's Clubs was born on February 11, 1932.[6] Time and time again, the federation would rally its membership (today numbering 65,000) on a host of conservation and environmental issues. Ladner, the organization's first president, also helped write the landmark 1937 Clean Streams Act and then campaigned hard for its passage. The law set what were then stiff penalties for water pollution ($25 to $100 per day) and empowered the Sanitary Water Board to inquire just what was contained in the discharges being dumped into state waterways—a novel concept at the time. Significantly, however, the coal industry was exempted from compliance until a means of treating its acid discharges could be discovered.

In 1939, Youngman replaced Ladner as president of the federation; he is its last surviving founder. Ladner continued his strong advocacy for clean water and years later, after being appointed to the Pennsylvania Supreme Court, wrote the decision upholding an important provision of the Clean Streams Act—the very law he had helped to write. "I don't suppose they would let him do something like that today," chuckles Youngman.

The clean-streams campaigners discovered allies in some unexpected quarters. When the federation sought contributions to seal abandoned coal mines and reduce the flow of acid water, female textile workers in Williamsport each gave fifty cents. "They just wanted to be able to swim in the river again," Youngman recalls. "You can believe we spread word of that around."

---

6. One of the first questions to provoke heated debate within the federation was whether to lift the 143-year-old ban on Sunday fishing in Pennsylvania. Many, Youngman included, wanted to continue the prohibition for reasons having nothing to do with the Sabbath. "I feared the counter-jumpers [city dwellers] would come up here and clean out our streams." Ladner, however, favored Sunday fishing. "He said, 'If they come all the way up here and can't catch any fish because the water's polluted, it will make them mad and they'll be on our side forever.'" The ban was abolished and Ladner's predictions proved correct.

Despite good intentions and small campaigns, the Susquehanna and its tributaries were doomed to remain polluted until the wastes went elsewhere. The problem, according to Youngman, was "how to make people understand they now had to pay for something they had free for years." It was a tough sell.

In 1936, Maurice K. Goddard, a young teacher at Mont Alto, the state forestry school, collected two water samples from a small creek that flowed through Chambersburg, in south-central Pennsylvania. One was taken above a tomato-processing plant operated by the H. J. Heinz Company and the other just below the firm's discharge pipe. The upstream sample was pure; the downstream water dark and murky. Goddard persuaded the owner of a local sporting goods store to display the two jars of water in his shop window. "Do you know how long that lasted?" Goddard asked. " 'Til that evening. The local chamber of commerce and officials from Heinz forced him to remove the jars or they threatened to boycott his store. That's how powerful polluters could be." Goddard went on to become one of Pennsylvania's legendary environmental watchdogs, who for more than half a century has devoted his life to protecting and conserving the state's resources.

In many respects, Doc Goddard, as he is widely known (the result of honorary doctorates awarded him), filled the shoes of conservation giants Dr. Joseph Rothrock, father of forest conservation in Pennsylvania, and Grover Ladner. Like Rothrock and Ladner, Goddard believes that no single interest has the right to deprive Pennsylvanians of the natural resources intended for all. Goddard served twenty-three years as the state's conservation chief before retiring in 1979, and has remained an outspoken and vigorous campaigner ever since.

Slowly, public resentment of polluted streams began to build. Sensing the anger, the Pennsylvania General Assembly passed amendments in 1945 intended to halt the discharge of untreated sewage. This led to no end of novel excuses from communities expected to comply with the new law. Wilkes-Barre city engineer Guy B. Walker stoutly proclaimed that the sewage from his town in fact served a beneficial purpose—it counteracted the acid in the river. (Actually, the raw sewage and coal sediments coagulated into gooey clots and dropped to the bottom of the Susquehanna.) Harrisburg officials argued that they shouldn't be required to process the capital's sewage until upstream communities treated their wastes. The discharges continued.

Still no one was regulating coal wastes, despite the rapid deterioration of streams throughout mining country. Between 1945 and 1951, the Sanitary Water Board turned down just 175 of the 2,500 applications for mine drainage permits it received. State officials maintained that there were no known means of controlling acid discharges. (More accurately, there were no *inexpensive* means.) The coal industry offered Pennsylvanians an either/or alternative. "You can't have both fish in inland streams in coal mining districts *and* coal. One must give way to the other," a Pennsylvania coal executive told a congressional committee in 1947. "And certainly, coal, being one of our basic industries, must be protected." In Pennsylvania, it certainly was.

As public concern grew, the courts were called upon with increasing frequency to resolve disputes pitting the rights of coal operators to pollute against the rights of citizens to have clean water. It is in these opinions that the gradual shift in attitudes toward pollution can be detected.

For eighty-eight years, until the mid-1960s, the prevailing law in Pennsylvania was spelled out in a state Supreme Court case called *The Pennsylvania Coal Company vs. Sanderson and Wife*. Eliza McBriar Sanderson sued the coal company for severely polluting a brook that flowed through her property. The high court ruled against her. Noting that coal-mine owners would not be able to do business if they were held liable for damage caused in the course of normal operations, the judges wrote, "The trifling inconvenience of particular persons must sometimes give way to the necessities of a great community." That sentence would be repeated again and again—long after other states had rejected such views.

Just how entrenched this attitude became in Pennsylvania law and public policy is evident in a 1935 opinion, written by a judge with a penchant for florid writing. "We cannot give Mediterranean skies to the plaintiffs, when by doing so, we may send the workers and bread-winners of the community involved to the Black Sea of destitution," wrote trial judge Michael A. Musmanno in a lawsuit involving smoldering coal wastes.

Nineteen years later, when the Pennsylvania Supreme Court took up a similar case, the court majority relied in part on Musmanno's 1935 opinion. The judges cited it in finding that pollution must be weighed against "the utility of the [coal-mining] operation," and that in this case the fumes did not constitute a public nuisance.[7] Dissenting was none other than Michael A. Musmanno, by then a justice on the high court, having defeated Grover Ladner for the seat. Justice Musmanno explained his change of heart on the pollution question by noting, "In the preservation of human

---

7. In this instance, the fumes were literally destroying the paint of a nearby house.

life, even bread is preceded by water, and even water must give way to breathable air."

But it was newly elected governor James A. Duff who declared enough was enough. In 1947—in a bare-knuckles display of political will rare in Pennsylvania—he announced, "No business is either big enough or important enough" to impede the cleaning up of the state's streams. Duff, a fiercely independent Republican and an avid outdoorsman, launched a dizzying program to improve water quality, committing $35 million to the effort.[8] In February 1950, Duff ordered communities along the Susquehanna to build sewage-treatment plants—and have them operating by June 1, 1952.[9] Construction soon began on thirty new treatment plants on the river. Two continuing holdouts were Harrisburg, which didn't stop dumping untreated sewage into the Susquehanna until 1962, and Wilkes-Barre, which found another creative reason for not complying. Officials there claimed to be unable to install sewer lines because of the threat of mine subsidence. In 1962 a judge noted that even in earthquake-prone California engineers had figured out how to lay sewer lines, and ordered the city to proceed. The Wyoming Valley sewage-treatment works finally began operating in November 1969.

Although the subsidence problem offered a convenient excuse for Wilkes-Barre, the consequences of nearly two centuries of deep mining beneath the Wyoming Valley were very real—as became terrifyingly apparent on January 22, 1959. That morning, eighty-four men were working the Pittston vein, a thick seam of high-quality anthracite that ran beneath the Susquehanna. The vein belonged to the Pennsylvania Coal Company— the same firm that had destroyed Mrs. Sanderson's brook ninety-one years before. Pennsylvania Coal had leased the workings to the Knox Coal Company, which had been mining the seam for years. Extracting coal beneath the Susquehanna was an extremely complex proposition because of the buried valley beneath the river, which made it difficult to gauge with confidence the thickness of the rock strata above the seam itself. To be safe, most companies left between thirty and eighty feet of rock to support the tremendous weight of the river passing overhead. Pennsylvania Coal printed

8. The Susquehanna wasn't Pennsylvania's only befouled river. The Delaware, which received 350 million gallons of untreated sewage daily from the city of Philadelphia alone, plus a witches' brew of chemicals from industries along its banks, had become so polluted that the commandant of the Philadelphia Navy Yard complained that river water was eating the paint off his ships.

9. Duff's aggressive policies on pollution cleanup did not hurt him politically. In 1950, he was elected by a wide margin to the U.S. Senate, where he served one term.

warnings on its maps, barring mining where the strata were less than fifty feet thick as determined by bore holes drilled from the surface.[10]

But Knox officials, apparently tempted by the value of the coal their men were digging in the River Slope Mine, ignored the warnings. By the autumn of 1958, the mine tunnels were actually ascending toward the river. Even though ordered by a state mining inspector on January 12 to halt work in that area, Knox continued, removing twenty-six cars of coal from the top of the seam the following day.

The Susquehanna also was at work. A midwinter thaw had caused the river to rise thirteen feet by the morning of the twenty-second, and the water was filled with large chunks of ice. At about 11:45 A.M., two miners heard a wooden beam break in the chamber that had been carved from the top coal seam and went to investigate. With an earth-shuddering roar, the Susquehanna crashed through the ceiling in a deadly torrent. Above, a giant whirlpool was formed in the river, with 100,000 gallons swirling down into the hole each minute as if into a huge sink drain. Only sixteen feet separated the mine chamber from the bed of the river. Almost immediately, thirty-nine miners were lifted out of the rapidly flooding chamber, joined by an additional seven several hours later. Another twenty-six miners walked for seven hours in icy water up to their armpits before reaching safety. The bodies of the twelve others were never found.

By 7 A.M. on January 24, the Susquehanna had completely filled the mine. Now it threatened to flood other mines in the valley, flowing through the miles of tunnels that linked them. In a desperate attempt to stem the flow of water into the chasm, state and federal officials rerouted a rail line to the river's edge. Forty gondola cars and 560 mine cars were dumped into the hole. Truckloads of rocks, railroad ties, utility poles, hay—anything officials could get their hands on—were thrown in as well, disappearing without a trace.

A few weeks later, Maurice K. Goddard—now the secretary of forests and waters—authorized the first of several projects to divert the river, fill the hole with concrete, and seal it. All told, Pennsylvania would spend $5.75 million on the recovery and repairs. By then, however, many other mines were flooded. Criminal charges, including involuntary manslaugh-

10. There was also ample historical evidence about the dangers posed by the hidden valley. In December 1885, at the Susquehanna Coal Company's mine in Nanticoke, a torrent of water and rounded stones broke through the mine shaft, killing twenty-six miners whose bodies were never recovered. Twelve years later, at the nearby town of Wyoming, the post office was swallowed in a hole 300 feet in diameter and 25 feet deep, created when mining activities ruptured the protective rock layer and allowed water to pour in.

ter, were filed against the foreman and superintendent of the mine, three officers of Knox Coal Company, and two officials of Pennsylvania Coal Company. But no one went to jail for the mine collapse.

Almost overnight, the Susquehanna brought a virtual end to the anthracite industry in the Wyoming Valley, which had seen a steady decline of markets since the conclusion of World War II. River water filled the vast underground caverns; pumping it out was deemed too costly by the owners. One mine after another closed its doors, never to reopen. The Northern Anthracite Field, which the year before had produced 7.7 million tons of coal and employed 11,636 people, was all but silent. Today, just a few hundred people earn their living from anthracite in the valley, stripping rather than deep-mining, and pulling less than 1 million tons annually from the black veins.[11]

Mining may have ceased on the North Branch, but acid from the coal-bearing rock strata kept flowing into the Susquehanna. Conditions continued to deteriorate on the West Branch as well. Asked to describe the river at its worst, John Youngman recalls times in the late 1950s and early 1960s when "the water would be clear. It didn't look horrible at all. But it was like a bottle of dilute sulfuric acid." In places, that's still true today.

Throughout this period, the Sanitary Water Board issued encouraging progress reports about river cleanup. Its newsletter, "Clean Streams," was filled with articles and photographs of treatment plants under construction and new industrial-waste processes, as well as reports of coal operators being warned about pollution. Coal silt on the North Branch had been reduced by 6 million tons annually, one survey declared proudly—although this had more to do with the collapse of the anthracite industry than with the effectiveness of enforcement. Even Maurice Goddard, who was on the board by virtue of being secretary of forests and waters, was

11. Until the late 1980s, there remained one last, assured market for anthracite coal, thanks to the Wyoming Valley's powerful godfather in Congress, Rep. Daniel Flood. After discovering in 1960 that the 8,000 furnaces at Army bases in West Germany were burning German coke, but could be converted to use anthracite, Flood made sure they were. No matter that it cost taxpayers a small fortune to buy the anthracite and ship it overseas; no matter that the Army had to hire an additional 1,000 employees to stoke the fires. Pennsylvania anthracite companies could not find enough miners to fill the contracts with the government (they considered importing foreign miners to do the job), and the shipments routinely were late.

The small favor to an influential member of the Appropriations Committee mushroomed into a $20-million annual expense to the Army by 1970, and even the Pentagon began complaining. Flood responded by sponsoring legislation making it a crime to burn anything but anthracite in the furnaces. Flood left Congress in 1980, but the anthracite shipments continued for nearly another decade until the last contract expired.

talking boldly of major recreational development along the Susquehanna. But there was a growing sense among some Pennsylvanians that things weren't quite as rosy as the announcements proclaimed. Boaters on the Susquehanna frequently found their mooring lines coated with human feces. A 1962 editorial published in the *Philadelphia Evening Bulletin,* entitled "When a River Is Ruined," noted that the Susquehanna was "the color of a rotten orange" between Wilkes-Barre and Sunbury. Acid levels there were so high that bridge work had to be halted because the concrete would not cure, the newspaper said. The Catawissa Boatmen's Club erected a billboard at a bridge near Bloomsburg that announced: "You are now about to cross the filthy Susquehanna River. It wasn't always this way, but the political bosses haven't the guts to stop pollution."

The Sanitary Water Board was not ignoring all polluters, however. In late 1962 it came down hard on the North Branch community of Nescopeck, population 2,000, ordering it to build a $350,000 sewage-treatment plant. Yet Wilkes-Barre and Harrisburg—with combined populations of 144,000, and presumably a bit more political clout—continued to discharge raw sewage into the river unimpeded. Wilkes-Barre alone contributed 15 million gallons a day.

It was the fish kills that stood as undeniable proof that the Susquehanna was still a very sick river. Scientists had begun to recognize that they could look to fish as indicators of the health of an entire ecosystem. If polluted water killed those living in it, the experts correctly assumed, then the water could not be very good for humans, either. The worst fish kill in Pennsylvania's history occurred in October 1961. It involved three large pumps installed as part of a federal-state program to control flooding in the Wyoming Valley's deep mines—a legacy of the Knox disaster. Early that month, the pumps began disgorging about 25 million gallons of extremely acidic water to the Susquehanna each day, enough to raise the river level three feet. The pumps were located at the Glen Alden Coal Company's mine just south of Wilkes-Barre. Soon, fifty-five miles of the Susquehanna were littered with dead and dying fish.

Describing it as "the most serious pollution situation ever," the executive director of the Pennsylvania Fish Commission, Albert M. Day, predicted that three years would pass before the river could again sustain any form of aquatic life. The discharge prompted a public squabble between two branches of state government—the Sanitary Water Board, which had ordered the coal company to shut down its pumps, and the Department of Mines and Mineral Industries, whose secretary argued that the order might leave 1,080 miners without work. The old debate—clean water or jobs—echoed once again. Congressman Daniel Flood interceded, obtaining permission for Glen Alden to pump the water to an impounding basin owned by the Army Corps of Engineers, and that allowed the few remaining mines to stay open.

The legal reverberations of the Glen Alden spill continued for several years, however. The Sanitary Water Board ordered the mining company to design and build a treatment plant for its acid discharges. The company challenged the order, and in late 1964 an appeals court ruled that the board lacked authority "to require treatment of acid mine drainage to unclean streams." No one would have characterized the Susquehanna otherwise.

It was becoming increasingly clear that the Susquehanna was doomed if the state only tackled mine drainage problems *after* the acid was in the water. In 1960, nearly 3,000 miles of Pennsylvania's waterways had high levels of mine acids, and more were falling victim each year. Thus, attention shifted to requiring more responsible mining practices. Because most of the coal then being extracted came from surface mines, regulations were drawn up for those operations. Chief among the proposals were stricter rules governing land reclamation in an effort to reduce the formation of acid. That effort died in a Senate committee chaired by John Haluska, a Democrat from coal-rich Cambria County, where the West Branch begins. Haluska's allegiances were clear. He commuted to his job in Harrisburg in a Chrysler Imperial owned by one of the state's largest strip-mine operators. Asked about the chances that the mining bill would leave his committee, Haluska quipped to a newspaper reporter, "Many are called and some are frozen." He then made good on his word.

But times had changed and the brazen assault on the legislation prompted a full-scale counterattack from the Pennsylvania Federation of Sportsmen's Clubs and the man who would become its president, John Laudadio of Westmoreland County. Laudadio was joined in the battle by William E. Guckert, a professional taxidermist and outdoorsman who would later become the irascible head of Pennsylvania's Bureau of Surface Mine Reclamation. The pair awakened many Pennsylvanians to the severity of mining degradation in their state. At election time, the sportsmen's federation also targeted those in the General Assembly who had opposed strong mining regulation. Among the lawmakers turned out of office was John Haluska.

Laudadio was elected to a state House seat in the 1962 election. There he led the fight for a strip-mining bill said to be the strictest in the nation. It required restoration of the land to its original contour, control of acid discharges, and higher bonds for coal operators to ensure compliance with the rules. The measure won approval in 1963, despite the emotional pleas of 970 women and children from Clearfield County who told lawmakers that the bill would eliminate the jobs of their miner husbands and fathers.

It was not until 1965, however, that the General Assembly took its most aggressive step to clean up the state's streams. Coal and steel officials protested that the proposed legislation would force both industries to leave the state, but Laudadio and a handful of others in the Assembly pressed for enactment.[12] With the backing of citizens as diverse as mineworkers, garden club members, and sportsmen, they succeeded.

Declaring that the special privileges granted to the coal industry "discriminate against the public interest," the lawmakers took note of the price of decades of inaction: Pennsylvania had more miles of water polluted by mine drainage than any other state in the nation. The lawmakers then ended a century of pollution exemptions for the coal industry; henceforth, coal wastes were to be treated like any other harmful waste in Pennsylvania.

The coal industry's grip had been severely weakened—but by no means broken. A law was only as good as its enforcement and that was an entirely different matter. Coal-mining enforcement in Pennsylvania has always been erratic and subject to political pressures.

The 1965 legislation set a lofty goal for Pennsylvania—to prevent any further degradation of its waterways and to restore every polluted stream to cleanliness. To achieve that, more muscle was needed. Coal companies had to be made liable for acid discharges even after they halted active mining. As things stood, the companies could simply walk away from the mines—and from any responsibility for what they did to Pennsylvania's streams.

The ink from Gov. Raymond P. Shafer's pen had barely dried on amendments to the Clean Streams law in late July 1970 when the law was put to the test. Shafer had armed himself well for what would be a long and critical fight. Heeding the advice of Attorney General Fred Speaker, the governor gathered a team of talented young lawyers and gave them the heady title of Environmental Strike Force. Their mandate: "To go out and

12. In one dramatic moment at a crowded legislative hearing, lawmakers listened as a coal-industry witness testified that acid mine discharges posed no health hazard. That was the moment Laudadio had been waiting for. Reaching beneath the desk, he pulled out a bottle of bright-orange, foul-looking water taken from a nearby mine and asked the witness to stand by his assertion. The witness put a glass of the water to his lips, but did not swallow. Afterward, the witness was heard to say, "Boy they got me that time!"

enforce the laws of Pennsylvania," recalled the young lawyer chosen to head the strike force, William Eichbaum, then all of 29 years old and the veteran of one environmental lawsuit. "We had to be legally aggressive, creative, and scientifically solid." Shafer promised them free rein and the backing of his administration. Their first target: the Barnes and Tucker Coal Company.

Located not far from where the West Branch begins, in a rugged basin that once was covered by white pine and hemlock, the Barnes and Tucker mine had produced more than 29 million tons of coal during its fifty-four-year working lifetime. Operations were halted in May 1969 and the mine opening sealed because the company said it could no longer afford to pump out and treat the water that was flowing in. The mine quickly filled and in June 1970 a million gallons a day of highly acidic water began to spew out. The pollution swept 200 miles down the Susquehanna, causing a major fish kill. In an effort to minimize the impact on the West Branch, the state spent $1.5 million adding lime and other neutralizing chemicals to the water.

Barnes and Tucker officials argued that the company was not liable for treating the discharges flowing from its abandoned mine, or for the expenses incurred by the state, because it was operating under a permit issued before the new regulations went into effect. With the likes of John Laudadio in the legislature and Bill Guckert, the state's surface-mining chief, demanding that Barnes and Tucker be prosecuted to the fullest extent, Bill Eichbaum and the Strike Force carefully built their case.

Times indeed had begun to change. K. W. James Rochow, who would argue the Barnes and Tucker case before the Pennsylvania Supreme Court on two occasions, and litigate many subsequent pollution cases for the state, recalls that no one—legislator, lobbyist, newspaper, or citizen—pressured the Commonwealth to soften its enforcement stance against Barnes and Tucker.

In a legal rollercoaster ride, the Barnes and Tucker case produced a series of victories and defeats. On its first trip to the state Supreme Court, the justices took the occasion to finally reject the 1886 Sanderson "trifling inconvenience" doctrine, declaring that the pollution caused by the Barnes and Tucker discharges was, indeed, "against public policy" and "a public nuisance." When the case again came before the justices in 1977, they upheld the state's authority to make the company treat the discharge.

The decision represented a turning point in environmental oversight of the coal industry and a tremendous morale boost for those doing battle to clean up the Susquehanna and other waterways. It also sent a clear signal to other polluters around the state. "It legitimized the laws," said Eichbaum, who went on to oversee federal surface-mining laws and later to develop regulations in Maryland protecting the Chesapeake Bay. But it did not relieve the state of the staggering burdens left by an industry that had operated carte blanche for generations. (Nor did it guarantee by any means that the coal industry would henceforth operate responsibly.)

The coal companies were not the only polluters along the Susquehanna to come under pressure in the spring and summer of 1970. Another long-time sacred cow felt the heat: the Pennsylvania Railroad, by now Penn Central. When Governor Shafer asked the state health department for a list of the state's worst air and water polluters, the railroad ranked number one for water pollution—because of its sprawling Enola Yard and Shop, located directly across the river from Harrisburg. For years, large quantities of oil, cleaning solutions, fuel, and other chemicals used in servicing the rail system's fleet were routinely dumped on the ground or allowed to run directly into the river. Despite the fact that everyone on the river knew exactly where the pollution was coming from, the Sanitary Water Board over the years had done nothing to halt it. For Governor Shafer, that was the last straw. The governor summoned members of the board to his office and declared himself "completely dissatisfied" with their performance. By the end of 1970, the Sanitary Water Board had been disbanded and re-placed by a new agency, the Department of Environmental Resources (DER).

The department had a strong public mandate. In 1971, the voters of Pennsylvania overwhelmingly endorsed a constitutional amendment intended to protect the state's resources. In language eloquent and simple, the amendment declared,

The people have a right to clean air, pure water, and to the preservation of the natural scenic, historic and esthetic values of the environment. Pennsylvania's public natural resources are the common property of all the people, including generations yet to come. As trustees of these resources, the Commonwealth shall conserve and maintain them for the benefit of all the people.[13]

The Susquehanna no longer was at the disposal of a few.

13. Among the authors of the amendment was Ralph W. Abele, who had gone to Harrisburg in 1969 to help shape the state's environmental programs as executive secretary of a newly formed legislative committee on air and water pollution. Abele would go on to head the Pennsylvania Fish Commission, and for nineteen years, until his death in 1990, work tirelessly to fulfill the pledge contained in the amendment.

Now the building and improving of sewage-treatment plants along the Susquehanna, underwritten with generous grants from Harrisburg and Washington, began in earnest, and by the 1980s water quality had improved markedly. Not only were dozens of new waste-water treatment plants in operation, but untreated industrial discharges to the river had been reduced. Under terms of the 1972 federal Water Pollution Control Act, sewage effluent had to meet certain criteria and, in theory at least, penalties could be imposed when it did not. In practice, many plants were allowed to keep operating even though they provided only minimal treatment of human and industrial wastes. The most notorious plant on the watershed was that of the Wyoming Valley Sanitary Authority in Wilkes-Barre, which until the late 1980s provided only primary treatment—meaning that it screened out solids and little else from the wastes pouring from its outfall pipe.

Every day along the Susquehanna, hundreds of samples of water are taken to measure the health of the river and its tributaries. The water is tested for fecal coliform bacteria, which connote the presence of human and animal waste, and for heavy metals and suspended particulates that can foul expensive machinery. It is checked to determine the levels of dissolved oxygen, critical to sustaining life in the water, and for excessive nutrients that spur unwanted growth. On occasion—usually only in emergencies—the water is analyzed for the presence of toxic chemicals and radiation, indicators of potentially serious public health risks.

The testing equipment may fill a sophisticated laboratory, or it may be packed in a cardboard box stowed in the trunk of Bob Alexander's Honda. Alexander is one of a new breed of water-quality chemists on the Susquehanna River, drawn to his task by a deep concern for the environment. Once a week, he drives to the bridge on Fiddler's Elbow Road near his home outside Hershey and drops a plastic milk jug attached to a rope into the Swatara Creek below. For the next hour and three-quarters, he carefully measures and records the health of this piece of the Susquehanna watershed.

Alexander is part of a volunteer network established by the Chesapeake Bay Foundation to monitor water quality around the Susquehanna drainage basin. He takes his samples downstream from a sewage-treatment plant that receives wastes not only from a fast-growing area of suburban Dauphin County but also from the huge Hershey Foods Corporation plant. He, and his partner at this site, Roger Giberson, belong to

Telephone Pioneers of America, a service organization of Bell of Pennsylvania employees, which enthusiastically responded in 1990 when asked to undertake the project by the foundation. In fact, there were more volunteers than could be used to staff the four sampling stations on the Swatara and four others along the Yellow Breeches Creek on the west side of the Susquehanna. Those participating in the program receive training in the chemical analyses and recordkeeping they are expected to perform, and Alexander meticulously follows a detailed instruction form to ensure he doesn't leave out any step.

"This was all new to me," he explains while carefully recording that the nitrate level in the water is 24.2 milligrams per liter this morning, that dissolved oxygen averages 8.5 milligrams per liter, and that pH levels are 6.75. The information will be forwarded to the foundation, to the state Department of Environmental Resources, and, if deemed appropriate, to the U.S. Environmental Protection Agency. "We've never seen anything bad in the water here," says Alexander. "Since we've been doing this, there haven't been any notable changes in the water quality." That is just the kind of report that makes Diane Alwine happy. As a senior environmental specialist with Hershey Foods, she works to make sure that Bob Alexander's data *doesn't* fluctuate.

It was the abundance and purity of water (as well as the availability of fresh milk from nearby farms) that lured Milton Hershey to this part of the Lebanon Valley in 1905 to open a chocolate-making plant. Today, the wastes discharged from the Hershey plant are of particular concern because of their exceedingly high organic content, the result of the large amounts of milk and sugar used. At first, they were sent directly into Spring Creek, which flows into Swatara Creek. Then, the waste was sent to the local sewage plant. Long-time residents recall that foul odors often enveloped the town when the stuff of candy bars and cocoa decomposed. Hershey now pretreats its wastewater, using bacteria to digest the organic contents. Then the effluent is sent to Derry Township's sewage-treatment facility for final processing before being discharged into the Swatara not far from Fiddler's Elbow Bridge.

Pretreatment of industrial wastes is the exception rather than the rule along the Susquehanna, however. Its value is not disputed; the procedure can be customized to extract specific chemicals that might damage municipal waste-water treatment equipment, or cause harm to the environment. The problem is its cost. Although existing federal law requires pretreatment, regulators have been slow to force industries to spend the money to install the necessary equipment. That hesitancy may evaporate as the danger of toxic chemicals in the nation's water supply becomes more clearly understood.

Although Bob Alexander's samples show consistently good water quality, others involved in various grassroots water-quality monitoring efforts throughout the Susquehanna basin see far different results. The pH levels on a number of streams, such as Pine Creek and its tributaries in Potter, Tioga, Clinton, and Lycoming counties, are poor. The obstacle to the river's recovery is its old nemesis: acid mine drainage.

Abandoned-mine drainage is the major source of water pollution in Pennsylvania, accounting for about half the total miles of degraded streams. Agriculture is a distant second statewide, although along the lower Susquehanna, for example, it is the leading polluter. Other, lesser sources of pollution affecting the Susquehanna are inadequately treated municipal sewage-treatment discharges; so-called nonpoint sources, such as runoff from paved surfaces; "natural conditions," which include acid rainfall; and "inadequate on-site treatment systems," namely septic tanks.

In the state's most recent survey of water quality along the Susquehanna, "resource extraction" repeatedly was cited as the source of problems. Nowhere is this more evident than on the portion of the West Branch patrolled by Nancy Rieg, where more than 97 percent of the contamination comes from mine drainage.

Rieg's first job in the coal fields was as a youngster, when on weekends she would descend into the mines owned by her grandfather to water the ponies that lived and worked in the shafts far below ground. The daughter of a miner who spent forty-two years underground, Rieg these days devotes her time to the coal fields between Curwensville and Clearfield, a portion of the Susquehanna so polluted that until recently it was almost devoid of fish and even aquatic plants.

Rieg is a mining inspector with the Pennsylvania Department of Environmental Resources. She began working with DER in 1972 as a certified clinical chemist, analyzing about 10,000 water samples a year. One day, she says, "I discovered that some of the samples came from areas where my family had mined coal." She abandoned her lab coat for a hardhat and a pair of steel-toed workboots and became an inspector. "I thought, maybe I owe the environment this much." She's the only woman among the fifteen inspectors assigned to DER's busy Hawk Run district, which oversees mining in five coal-rich counties around Clearfield and State College.

The scars of mining—past and present—along the Susquehanna and its tributaries are pervasive here. Many stream bottoms and banks are flame-colored. Steep hillsides that once harbored coal have been recontoured and planted with trefoil or corn or hay; others stand naked to the elements, awaiting reclamation that may never come. Mighty earth-moving equipment is silhouetted against the ridges as it claws out the bituminous coal that eventually will be shipped to power plants and industries.

Clearfield County, near the headwaters of the West Branch, has more active coal mines than any other county in Pennsylvania—200. Many are located in areas that can never be mined without some form of environmental damage. Critics often cite Clearfield County as the most flagrant example of DER's continuing willingness to issue mining permits without requiring the operator to first prove that he or she can work in compliance with the rules.

Most of the 6 million tons of coal mined in the county annually lie in the so-called Lower Kittanning seam, which because of its geologic composition has always generated lots of acid water. "So the odds are, we'll have lots more discharges," explains Rieg, whose job begins only after the permits are issued in Harrisburg.

Much of her work involves figuring out how to keep water from reaching the coal, an almost impossible task in many mines. "You don't have to be a chemist," she says with a grim smile. "You have to be a plumber. I've learned one thing after eighteen years: You cannot turn the water off after it starts flowing."

Nancy Rieg is responsible for inspecting between thirty and thirty-five active mines once a month. She visits a dozen or so inactive mining sites four times a year. This afternoon, she's headed out to visit a small surface mine owned by the Penn-Grampion Coal Company of Curwensville. As she navigates the beige DER Jeep Cherokee along a rutted dirt road, a construction crew laying water pipe appears over the crest of a hill. The sight causes Rieg to give a little cry of joy. "Look!" she exclaims. "Finally, they're going to have water!"

More than a decade ago, mining destroyed the water supply of twenty families in this portion of rural Pike Township, Clearfield County. Blasting to extract the coal fractured the rock strata and allowed contaminants to seep into the homeowners' wells. The mine's owner provided bottled water, and ultimately—after a lengthy battle with DER—was ordered to connect the homes to a public water supply. The sight of the new pipeline snaking miles across rural countryside is something Nancy Rieg has waited to see for a long time. "The greatest environmental impact of mining now is on drinking-water supplies," she explains.

The Penn-Grampion mining site is a few hundred yards from the banks of the Susquehanna. The company has posted a bond of $3,000 per acre for the thirty-five-acre site, and Rieg knows that this particular location is extremely difficult to mine without causing problems for the river. The loss of forest cover as a result of heavy logging on land above the mine already has lowered the pH levels of a small, nameless creek flowing nearby, leaving little capacity for any additional acid. The sandy composition of the soil also complicates matters; erosion could occur easily. Even the local rocks aren't very hard; they crumble under the slightest pressure. Rieg theorizes that this site was once part of the riverbed itself. The coal seam, which runs from twelve to forty-five feet below the surface, is U-shaped, as if it had been worn down by water. Rieg has spent much time learning the geology of the region—partly through reading, but mostly by looking and listening to those who work the river valley. "After all these years," she says, "I'd better know a lot!"

Bob Newpher and Cloyd "Pappy" Miles, who mine this site, wave to Rieg as she parks the Jeep. A large earthmover with a hook-like coal "ripper" extending from the rear, a coal truck, a shovel, and two men are all that are needed to remove the coal here. Tiny operations such as this are common on the West Branch. Newpher and Miles uncover only a small area of the coal seam at a time, extract it with the ripper, and replace the overburden as quickly as possible. The goal: to minimize the buried coal's exposure to air and water. Although Rieg has criticized some aspects of the operation, she generally gives the two men good marks for their sensitivity to a difficult mining situation.

Situated at the lowest point of the mine site, near the river, is a siltation pond positioned to collect any runoff before it reaches the Susquehanna or the small tributary that flows along the edge of the property. Newpher, an avid fisherman, stocked the pond with a few bass as an experiment. They're thriving. "The only time we have any problems in the pond is after a heavy rain," he explained. "The rainfall is so acidic that it screws up the pH of the pond."[14]

14. Pennsylvania receives the most acidic rainfall in the United States, with the pH averaging 4.1. Lemon juice has a pH of 2.2 and normal rainwater a pH of 5.6. Many of Pennsylvania's trout streams already have suffered as a result of the acidity. Increasingly, biologists and water-quality experts on the river and the Chesapeake Bay are factoring acidic precipitation into their pollution equations. Its long-term effects on aquatic life and cleanup efforts are unclear.

Rieg heads to a spot near where the little tributary enters the Susquehanna, parking the Jeep on a path leading to the river. An orange ribbon attached to a shrub shows where a water sample is to be drawn. "We mark it like that so we can always be sure we take it from the same place," Rieg explains. On the short walk to the riverbank, Rieg assumes an odd goosestep stride as she moves through the tall grass. "You have to be careful," she volunteers. "Snakes. This time of year they'll strike at anything."

Soon she is gazing out at the deep green Susquehanna as it glides swiftly past in the late afternoon sun. A steep and heavily forested hillside dips down to the water on the opposite shore. "I've seen herons along this stretch of the river," Rieg remarks. When she returns to the Jeep she discovers Bob Newpher waiting in his pickup, the engine idling. As she backs the Jeep out of his way, Newpher waves and drives on down to the river. It's quitting time, and he's come to fish for the pike, bass, and muskie that have begun once again to inhabit the upper reaches of the West Branch.

While there are success stories along this part of the West Branch, there also are flagrant violations of the law. The power and influence of the coal industry remains very strong in Pennsylvania, and the environment has often taken a back seat to other political agendas. Even if every regulation were enforced to its maximum extent, however, the devastation caused by generations of rapacious mining would forever haunt the river. The price tag for cleaning up acid mine discharges in the Susquehanna ranges between $1.5 and $2.5 billion. Across the state, the cost of reclaiming abandoned mine land—much of which lies in the Susquehanna watershed—will be a whopping $13 to $15 billion. Pennsylvania's annual budget is slightly over $12 billion.

Nancy Rieg heads up one of her favorite creeks, intent on making a point. Almost every acre of Hogback Run's 3.25-square-mile drainage area has been mined, yet there are long stretches of the little creek that are more reminiscent of the heart of Vermont than the heart of coal country, filled with native rhododendrons, ferns, and velvety moss-covered ledges. As the Jeep hits a hole in the road, sending a spray of muddy water down the steep banks, Rieg winces, then observes wryly, "If a mining company did that, it would cost them $10,000. Siltation violation."

Near the top of Hogback, a steep hill, planted in trefoil, rises on the right. Less than two years before, it had been a large surface mine. Rieg follows a rushing rivulet as it carves a gully along the edge of the reclaimed mining site. The water is flowing from an abandoned deep mine on an adjacent property. The mouth of the mine is barely visible through dense underbrush. "Bears love these old mine openings," she says, as she twists through the trees and vines, heading toward it. "The water from this one stays about 50 degrees year-round and is of good quality." If there were any bears, they wanted no part of a brown-haired mine inspector, the mother of three children.

"I want to show you something that infuriates me," says Rieg, climbing back into the Jeep, her inspection of this site completed. As she reaches the valley head, where Hogback originates in a spring, she points to a dump filled with old tires, refrigerators, and assorted household debris. "There must be forty feet of garbage in there!" she fumes. "We make the coal operators put everything back and then people come up here and just dump!"

A month after Nancy Rieg guided a visitor around the coal fields of Clearfield County, she forwarded the water-quality analysis of the sedimentation pond just below the Penn-Grampion mining site. The pH level was 6.7, heavy metals were all below one milligram per liter, and sediment loads were well under allowable limits. A good report. The bass in the pond were thriving, Rieg noted, and in an addendum to the technical information, she wrote that brook trout had been seen in the lower portion of Hogback Run.

It takes about a day for the water leaving the Penn-Grampion mine and Hogback Run to make its way down the Susquehanna to Williamsport. John Youngman, who can see the river from his law office atop a downtown bank building, remembers when everyone knew such things, because the arrival of mine water could mean trouble for the city.

In another thirty-six hours or so, the water will have made the trip from Williamsport to Bud Wilbern's landing south of Harrisburg. Bud is standing on the bank this morning, taking a break from the construction and absorbing the scene around him. The water is cocoa-colored. "Rained upstream yesterday," he observes to no one in particular.

A few minutes later, Joe Millward makes a similar trek to the riverbank to stare out at the three or four boats in the rising mist and sunshine. "Too muddy to catch anything today," he observes. "Tomorrow will be a lot better."

Chapter Six

Nuclear Development

"There is absolutely no danger"

Of all the disasters to befall the Susquehanna, the most frightening was the one no one could see. That was what scared Bud Wilbern and the rest of the river rats. That and the fact that nobody seemed to know what to do. Floods were one thing; you waited for the water to recede and went in to clean up. But the events that began in the early hours of March 28, 1979, were entirely different. "You couldn't detect anything," says Bud, standing in the doorway of the nearly completed clubhouse, less than four miles from Three Mile Island—home of America's most famous nuclear reactor.

"They'd be up there saying that everything was just fine," he says, "and the next thing you know, somebody else'd be up there telling you it wasn't." Suddenly, all the reassurances of safety, the boasts about modern technology, the pledge of zealous government oversight were revealed for what they were: hollow promises. It became evident to everyone, the river rats included, that nobody really knew what was going on. "Pretty soon you figured everybody was lying," adds Bud.

On this morning, eleven and a half years later, the subject of TMI is fresh on everybody's minds. The day before, 98,000 homes and businesses had received in their mailboxes a twenty-five-page booklet listing evacuation centers, emergency telephone numbers, and instructions on how to minimize radiation exposure in the event of an accident at TMI. Rusty Beckey thumbed through the copy lying around the clubhouse, stopping at a map. "This tells us what we're supposed to do," he says, a note of cynicism in his voice. The map shows little blue arrows along the area's complex network of highways and back roads, arrows that are meant to direct 160,000 fleeing citizens out of harm's way beyond the official ten-mile danger zone.

As a former long-distance truckdriver, Beckey sees a certain irony in a safety plan that relies on swiftly moving whole communities of frightened people over the region's narrow, winding roads. "How the hell do they think that would work?" he asks Bud and Harry Myers, who has just arrived after finishing his shift as a fireman at Harrisburg International Airport. This is not a new topic of conversation.

Tens of thousands of residents in the five Pennsylvania counties on the lower Susquehanna annually receive this reminder of the price of having nuclear neighbors. Some get two mailings a year, for they live or work not only near Three Mile Island, but also within ten miles of another nuclear plant, Peach Bottom to the south. A similar booklet is provided to those living near the twin reactors upstream, at Berwick.

Only the Mississippi River has more nuclear power plants along its banks than the Susquehanna, and it is five times longer. There are the two reactors at Three Mile Island, one of which is still operating. The Peach Bottom Atomic Power Station has two working reactors plus a small one that has been shut down since 1974. The Susquehanna Steam Electric Station on the North Branch also has two reactors. Total: seven. And if the utilities had had their way, the Susquehanna would have five more.

Once, that seemed a perfect use for the river. Indeed, in their view of the Susquehanna, the utility executives were no different from the lumbermen and coal barons before them. It was a resource to be exploited, in this case for its ample supply of necessary cooling water and its proximity to expanding markets for electric power. Those were the days when America was in love with the atom and no application for this amazing energy source seemed inappropriate, from lighthouses to car parts to jet engines. The Susquehanna was integral to many people's plans for cashing in on nuclear technology. Yet, as with other human activities on the river, they paid no heed to the consequences. While sewage and industrial wastes, the effluent from coal mining, and the loss of its forests degraded the Susquehanna and made life along the river unpleasant, this lackadaisical alliance with the atom has posed—and continues to pose—the greatest threat to its very existence.

The fishing's good near Three Mile Island, and the river rats occasionally head down that way when they leave Bud's landing. The island itself is home to lots of wildlife, and tour groups not only get to drive by the infamous reactor and cooling towers but also get to visit the scenic tree trail and the waterfowl refuge.

All along the Susquehanna, wildlife populations are thriving, and nowhere is this more apparent than on the islands that dot the river from Sunbury to the Chesapeake. Eagles, osprey, herons, canvasbacks, bitterns, tundra swans, buffleheads, and river otters—all have been sighted. Less exotic species have taken up residence as well, in part because development along the banks has encroached on their mainland habitats.

The Pennsylvania Game Commission owns several large Susquehanna islands and maintains refuges on them. In late 1990, the state officially recognized the value of river islands and launched a campaign to acquire those that are in private hands. Odd as it may seem, Pennsylvania has no idea how many islands exist in the Susquehanna, let alone who owns them. The project is a favorite of Jacob Sitlinger of the Game Commission staff, who says the islands are more than just choice wildlife refuges. They also minimize the impact of upstream development by catching the tons of sediment that wash downriver each year, sediment that otherwise would wind up in the Chesapeake Bay.

"I have seen these islands grow," Sitlinger says, and describes one north of Harrisburg that expanded from one acre to twenty in less than a century. It takes very little to form an island in the sediment-laden Susquehanna. Some have even grown up around the old pilings that held the log boom at Williamsport in place. But just as these bits of land can grow, they also can be erased. The 1972 Agnes flood altered the size and shape of many islands, sweeping some away entirely.

Bud Wilbern bought Green's Island in 1976, after Agnes destroyed the cabin he owned on another island. Now he lives there much of the year in a neat red frame cottage that sits amid a grove of chestnut trees, a small orchard, and several tall pines. Not far away is an oddly shaped barn housing a 1929 Model A Ford that came over by boat. Bud occasionally takes a spin around the island. "It's complete solitude here," he says. "You're away from it all."

A concrete pier for the turnpike bridge across the Susquehanna serves as a kind of dividing line on the thirty-three-acre island. Bud allows one or two friends to set up camps on the three acres south of the pier, with the clear understanding that they are not to bother him on the north end. Joe Millward, of course, is one of the friends, and the mere mention of Bud's island prompts Joe to begin a story. One summer, Joe and his thirteen-year-old grandson from Texas were out on the river fishing, while Joe's wife and his niece waited behind at the island campsite. "We heard them screaming and figured they were in trouble," says Joe. "We hurried back and there were the women standing on top of the picnic table and two raccoons were on the ground." He pauses, a smile spreading across his face, his eyes twinkling. "I've heard of people treeing a coon, but never a coon tabling two women." No matter that the rats have heard the story a dozen times, it still gets a laugh.

Three Mile Island is the largest and indisputably the best known of the Susquehanna islands. Despite its name, it is two and a half miles long and situated ten miles south of Harrisburg. Part of a 4,000-acre estate inherited by Hannah Cookson of Lancaster from her late father in 1760, the island was farmed and supported a profitable shad fishery for many years. As far back as 2,500 years ago, it served as a way station for Indian tribes traveling the Susquehanna. They left behind a treasure trove of artifacts—pottery shards, arrowheads, and tools—which were unearthed by archaeologists before construction of the reactors began in the late 1960s.

When the Metropolitan Edison Company joined scores of other American utility companies, large and small, aboard the great nuclear bandwagon and announced plans to erect its first and only nuclear plant, the island seemed an ideal site to company leaders. Others weren't quite as enthusiastic. Some feared that hot-water discharges from the plant would harm fishing, which had finally begun to improve as the river was cleaned up. Others worried about the reactors' proximity to Harrisburg International Airport. But cooling towers minimized the hot-water problem, and federal authorities ordered that the two reactor containment buildings, which encase the deadly nuclear core, be strengthened to withstand the impact of a Boeing 707 jet. With that, the plant won the go-ahead from the Atomic Energy Commission in 1968, the same year the AEC granted construction permits for two more reactors on the Susquehanna, at Peach Bottom, forty miles to the south.

There were proposals for nuclear development all along the river in the late 1960s. The state of Pennsylvania was actively promoting use of this power source, and those seeking to do reactor-related business in the Commonwealth received red-carpet treatment from the governor and state lawmakers. Many of the business people had their eyes on the Susquehanna, which had been introduced to things radioactive two decades previously.

In 1947, a New Jersey–based company moved into a small plant along the north side of the river upstream from Bloomsburg, where the Susquehanna flows through a wide, terraced floodplain after the tight squeeze of the Wyoming Valley. The prior occupant of the factory had manufactured wooden toys, but the new owner was in a more sophisticated field: the production of self-illuminating watch and instrument dials. The firm's name left no doubt about its glow-in-the-dark products. The U.S. Radium Corporation was just one of many companies founded in the 1920s and 1930s to use the radioactive element in consumer products. Radium salves for the treatment of acne, ringworm, and baldness were widely available; prominent Americans touted the virtues of drinking radium water; radium belts, intended to cure all sorts of ills, were guaranteed to last "several thousand years." (No similar guarantee was offered for the wearer!) Tuberculosis sufferers received radium injections for years until doctors noticed that their patents were developing bone cancer.

U.S. Radium had a questionable track record by the time it arrived on the Susquehanna. Twenty-nine employees at its dial-painting plant in Orange, New Jersey, had died, many of bizarre illnesses induced by the common practice of licking the radium-coated brushes to produce a fine point.[1] The company was not particularly careful what it did with its wastes, either. The Orange plant was razed in 1932; sixty years later, the site remains so heavily contaminated with radium that it has been included as a federal Superfund project. About 274,000 cubic yards of soil must be removed at a cost of $200 million to reduce the hazard.

Dial painting was no longer done by hand in 1947, but the company still used radium and generated dangerous wastes, and the ten-acre property on the Susquehanna provided plenty of convenient places to put it. A section of the old North Branch Canal ran through the site, offering a ready-made burial trench for chemicals and radium, which loses only half its radioactivity after 1,600 years. The company injected other radioactive wastes into a dry well on the site. Wastes also were poured into "silos"— common steel culvert pipes sunk vertically into the riverbank and covered over when full. And there was always the most convenient means of getting rid of the waste: the Susquehanna itself. Over the years the river received undetermined amounts of radioactive discharges from the facility, located about ten miles upstream from the borough of Danville, which draws its drinking water from the river. (Federal authorities, who generally paid little attention to the plant, did draw the line at one disposal plan put forth by U.S. Radium. When the company proposed putting its wastes in abandoned coal mines, U.S. officials said no.)

The Atomic Energy Commission finally inspected the plant in 1957, a decade after operations began, and uncovered a host of problems, not the least of which were the radioactive discharges into the Susquehanna. Three years later, during another visit, AEC inspectors warned U.S. Radium again about such discharges and ordered the company to at least start

---

1. In 1927, when the jawbones of several deceased dial-painters were placed in a darkroom, the bones burned images on photographic plates. The company denied any connection between the deaths and the paint, and was vigorously defended by the public health community. Ultimately, U.S. Radium's death toll would rise to forty-four, forty-three of whom were women. Radium became one of the first substances to provide compelling evidence of the link between radiation and cancer.

keeping records. They offered a bit of advice: if radiation levels in the waste seemed high, simply dilute the material with water before discharging it in the river. Whether the company followed that suggestion is unknown; U.S. Radium apparently ignored the order on recordkeeping.

It was Pres. Dwight Eisenhower who opened the doors of the atomic age to private citizens. In a speech before the United Nations on December 8, 1953, he proclaimed that the power of the atom, once the exclusive province of the military, was to be turned over to anyone who would use it wisely, "for the benefit of all mankind." The following year, Congress fleshed out Eisenhower's Atoms for Peace plan with legislation promoting commercial applications for nuclear technology. Everyone began scrambling for a piece of the pie. Imaginations ran wild; there seemed no limit on uses for the atom.

The Curtiss-Wright Corporation, an airplane manufacturing firm with numerous defense contracts, believed its future lay in nuclear-powered aircraft engines. The company began searching for a suitably remote location to test the engines, to conduct experiments using a small nuclear reactor it planned to build, and to perform other research. Soon Curtiss-Wright found an area that seemed ideal: the vast wilderness between the West Branch of the Susquehanna and its big tributary to the north, the Bennett Branch of the Sinnemahoning. There are few areas of the state more isolated. Pennsylvania officials enthusiastically embraced the project, proclaiming that it would create 7,000 jobs in an area hard-hit by layoffs in the coal and lumber industries. To reward the company for locating in Pennsylvania, the state agreed to spend $1.6 million to build access roads. By June of 1955, the deal was signed; Curtiss-Wright purchased almost 8,600 acres and leased 42,596 more from the state for ninety-nine years. Company officials even coined a new name for their reservation—Quehanna—in honor of the river that drained the entire region.

Curtiss-Wright people spoke of creating one of the world's largest private atomic research facilities amid the forests, creeks, and wetlands of the Appalachian Plateau. The company built the town of Pine Glen to accommodate the physicists, engineers, and technicians it said would work hand in hand with the Air Force to perfect the nuclear engines. The experts would have other projects, too, such as the production of beryllium-oxide ceramic components for use in high-temperature radioactive environments.

Pennsylvania obligingly acceded to Curtiss-Wright's long list of requests. To ensure the necessary security for the secret engine project, scores of people who leased cabins on what was regarded as some of the best hunting land in the state were evicted. The Sanitary Water Board granted Curtiss-Wright a permit to discharge radioactive waste into a tributary of Mosquito Creek, which flows into the West Branch of the Susquehanna. Soon after, the Atomic Energy Commission issued Curtiss-Wright a twenty-year license to operate a four-megawatt nuclear reactor.

Even as work at Quehanna progressed, however, the Air Force became enamored of rocketry. Nuclear aircraft went the same way as two other popular ideas of the day: atomic automobiles and uranium-powered home heating systems. And in 1960, after spending $30 million on the Quehanna facilities, Curtiss-Wright announced that it was leaving north-central Pennsylvania. The company donated its reactor to the Pennsylvania State University. Hoping to recoup some of its investment, Curtiss-Wright leased a small piece of Quehanna to the Martin Company, a Baltimore firm that at the time was looking to capitalize on its own slice of the nuclear dream—manufacturing small atomic power plants for satellites and navigational devices. To Martin officers, as to executives at Curtiss-Wright, the remote wilds of the Susquehanna region seemed perfect for nuclear operations—plus they would have access to the Penn State reactor.

Before the lease was consummated, however, Curtiss-Wright officials sent an unusual letter to Penn State, warning the university that the radiation involved in Martin's operations would be "extremely high" and of a type that posed a particular risk to human health. The letter urged Penn State officials to clarify legal obligations for eventual cleanup of the Quehanna site before allowing Martin to use the reactor. (In fact, liability for the site was tangled. Penn State signed a two-year lease with Martin in 1960 allowing the company use of the reactor and adjacent facilities. The reactor was on state-owned land leased to Curtiss-Wright; Curtiss-Wright in turn had sublet some of that land to Martin.)

Curtiss-Wright's environmental concern seems odd in light of the conditions it left behind in 1960. When Martin moved in, its workers discovered liquid and solid radioactive wastes as well as extremely toxic beryllium-oxide contamination throughout the facility. Because Penn State, which held the reactor license, was legally responsible for the nuclear materials, it proposed a cleanup and disposal plan to the Atomic Energy Commission. The solids would be buried on the property. "It is anticipated that 90 percent of the low level [radioactive] liquids can be released under controlled conditions, directly to the environment," the university noted. Waste deemed too radioactive to be buried or released on the site would be shipped to disposal grounds out of state.

The Atomic Energy Commission okayed the plan. Furniture and equipment coated with the beryllium-oxide dust were covered in plastic and buried out in the woods, along with a variety of other contaminated materials. Maintenance workers would later discover that a bear and some deer, apparently attracted by the scents, had opened the trenches and rummaged through the items there.

The Martin firm, soon to become Martin Marietta, had its own grand dream for the Quehanna facilities. It planned to load strontium-90 fuel elements into tiny reactors it was building for sale. The project, known as SNAP 7 (Systems for Nuclear Auxiliary Power), required considerable safety precautions because of the danger posed by strontium-90, which is easily absorbed into human bones and tissues. Martin Marietta ultimately would be licensed in 1964 to possess 6 million curies worth of strontium-90, enough fuel for 150 of its small nuclear generators. The company used the Penn State reactor to process the fuel into a usable form, and then placed it into the generators by remote handling devices.

Among those interested in the SNAP 7 reactors was the U.S. Coast Guard. A Quehanna-made reactor was installed in the Baltimore Light, on the Chesapeake Bay just north of the Bay Bridge, and operated between May 1964 and April 1966. Another was installed in a marker buoy on the bay opposite the mouth of the Potomac River. A Coast Guard publication of the time touted "the world's first atomic-powered navigation" and described the rigorous safety precautions taken by Martin Marietta and the Atomic Energy Commission for the SNAP 7 project. "Fuel cores for some generators, for instance, have been slammed into granite by bazookas and burned in simulated missile fires and explosions at heats above 6000 degrees Fahrenheit and have remained intact."

But the world apparently wasn't ready for atomic lighthouses any more than nuclear cars. The Coast Guard, despite its initial enthusiasm, soon abandoned the new technology "due to cost and environmental considerations," and in 1966 Martin Marietta announced it would not renew its lease for the reactor at Quehanna.

With Martin Marietta preparing to leave, the future of the atomic reservation in the wilderness seemed bleak. Pennsylvania bought back the 8,600 acres, paying $992,500 for land it had sold to Curtiss-Wright for $181,250 just twelve years before. Unbeknownst to the state, it also was acquiring a number of radioactive and chemical waste-disposal sites. Curtiss-Wright's lease on the adjacent 42,596 acres was canceled and the land declared a wilderness area, which it remains today.

A search was launched for new tenants at Quehanna, and every pro-posal was considered, from a food-processing firm to a nuclear-waste dis-posal site. The latter idea was rejected after geologic and hydrologic sur-veys indicated that anything buried might leak and contaminate the streams that ultimately flowed into the Susquehanna. (No one apparently had thought it necessary to do similar surveys before authorizing burial of Curtiss-Wright's radioactive waste on-site.)

Curtiss-Wright's earlier warnings to Penn State were on the mark. Martin Marietta did not prove to be the neatest of tenants. During its four-year stay, the company released an undetermined amount of strontium-90 dust into the atmosphere. Contamination levels at Quehanna were found to be ten times higher than normal. (Experts speculated that some of the contamination may have come from atmospheric testing of nuclear weap-ons, which produced strontium-90 in the fallout.)

Just as it seemed that Quehanna would remain empty, a western Penn-sylvania company called Nuclear Materials and Equipment Corporation (NUMEC) inquired in 1966 about its availability. NUMEC, a subsidiary of Atlantic-Richfield Company, was among the few firms in the nation li-censed by the federal government to produce plutonium and enriched uranium for defense purposes.

Like U.S. Radium, NUMEC had a rather checkered operating record. Sometime in the middle 1960s, nearly 400 pounds of enriched uranium disappeared from the company's plant in Apollo, near Pittsburgh. The loss was kept secret for years and the circumstances surrounding it remain so. CIA analysts would later speculate publicly that the uranium was smug-gled to Israel where it was converted into that nation's first nuclear weap-ons. Nonetheless, NUMEC seemed a likely occupant for Quehanna, par-ticularly after state health officials determined in the spring of 1967 that the facilities there were so contaminated with radiation that they could never be completely cleaned up. Thus, the officials reasoned, a company that had some experience with nuclear materials would be preferable to, say, a food-handling concern.

NUMEC's nuclear projects at Quehanna were diverse. It experimented with irradiating food and sterilizing medical equipment. A group of NUMEC employees discovered that they could produce extremely durable hardwood floors by exposing plastic-impregnated wood to cobalt-60. That operation was spun off into a separate company, PermaGrain, which still processes wood for high-traffic areas, such as basketball courts. In 1971, NUMEC, but not PermaGrain, was acquired by a firm that also would earn a certain notoriety among nuclear cognoscenti. It was Babcock and Wilcox, which at the time was busy building two reactors destined for an island in the Susquehanna south of Harrisburg.

In keeping with the theme of President Eisenhower's Atoms for Peace speech, the Atomic Energy Commission looked to the Bible for help in naming one of its civilian nuclear programs. Project Plowshare came to the Susquehanna in 1967. It involved using nuclear bombs instead of dynamite for major excavation projects.[2]

When a nuclear bomb explodes underground, the tremendous energy it releases spreads outward from the center, and the surrounding rock and soil are melted or fractured. The result: a massive cavern beneath the earth's surface. This appealed to the petroleum industry, for the bombs not only would release oil or natural gas trapped in the rock strata, but would also carve out giant underground wells to contain it. Thus it was that an advance party from the AEC and Columbia Gas System, Inc., arrived in Harrisburg in early 1967 to sell state officials on Project Ketch, part of the Plowshare program. They proposed exploding a twenty-four-kiloton bomb in a thick shale formation 3,300 feet beneath the rugged and scenic Sproul State Forest, which straddles the West Branch of the Susquehanna, west of Lock Haven. Pennsylvania was chosen, backers said, because the state—home to the nation's first nuclear plant, in Shippingport—was regarded as friendly toward nuclear power. They envisioned the Sproul Forest detonation as the first of up to 1,000 underground explosions in the northeastern United States.

Although state officials were initially amenable to the plan, it provoked enormous opposition from those living near the blast site. Among them was Fred Iobst, who had been a forester at Sproul and lived in Renovo, which is surrounded by the forest. He and others listened skeptically to

2. Plowshare first surfaced after the Suez Canal crisis of 1956 closed off that vital shipping route, and a second canal across the Sinai Peninsula seemed imperative. What better way to quickly carve a new canal, planners reasoned, than by detonating a string of nuclear devices? Resolution of the Suez crisis shelved the plans, but the technology was kept alive by the nuclear hierarchy in Washington.

Among the most ambitious projects to evolve was the Panatomic Canal, to parallel the existing Panama Canal. Instead of building the costly and time-consuming locks necessary to lift vessels over the Continental Divide, backers of the Panatomic Canal proposed just blasting a new channel down to sea level. Not everyone was happy with the project, particularly some in Panama. It would have necessitated detonating 250 bombs with a total yield of 120 megatons (nearly 100 times more than was dropped on Hiroshima) and required the long-term evacuation of about 22,000 people.

assurances of the project's safety. (After all, they had heard the same things about Quehanna, just a short distance away, where at that very moment state officials were attempting to measure the extent of radioactive contamination.) Site preparation alone, the critics argued, would devastate huge sections of woodlands and streams, only then recovering from the depredation of lumbering and coal mining.

When Iobst and others questioned whether natural gas stored in a nuclear-built cavern might not become radioactive too, the project sponsors quickly replied that the gas would meet existing regulations. (In fact, there were no regulations.) Soon, groups as diverse as labor unions and women's clubs lined up to oppose the project; 25,000 people signed protest petitions. Among the opponents was U.S. Rep. John P. Saylor of Johnstown, who made the following offer to the project's sponsor, Columbia Gas: "If the company . . . is willing to put its assets on the line to protect the innocent public, then, perhaps, citizens of the Commonwealth will have a measure of safety assurance that is otherwise absent." Columbia Gas withdrew its proposal. Although at least twenty-four Plowshare blasts took place around the United States, none occurred in Pennsylvania.

As residents along the West Branch were battling to prevent a nuclear bomb from being detonated beneath them, and citizens at the lower end of the Susquehanna were hearing about the wonders of nuclear power plants, some unusual plans were being hatched for a pastoral stretch of the North Branch, where it curves amid the Endless Mountains in a slow meander toward the Wyoming Valley. The neat farms and small towns there reflect their prosperous Connecticut Yankee heritage, and the inhabitants retain their ancestors' strong-willed resourcefulness.

It was here, on 1,300 acres near the tiny riverside community of Meshoppen in Wyoming County, that plans for a $500-million liquid-metal fast-breeder reactor were unveiled in 1967. The Atomic Energy Commission had joined with North American Rockwell and a subsidiary of General Public Utilities, Inc., to build this new type of reactor. The AEC hoped that breeder technology would supersede the standard light-water reactor design, by then just ten years old and still full of kinks and surprises.

The breeder reactor has always had a siren's lure for some in the nuclear community, who consider it the key to true energy independence for America. The breeder theoretically could achieve this because it generates more fuel than it consumes. Its big drawback is that it converts uranium, the fuel in light-water reactors, into plutonium. Not only is plutonium the deadliest substance known to humans—one-millionth of a gram inhaled will produce lung cancer—but breeder reactors carry a far greater risk of explosions than light-water reactors. And the track record of the breeder, despite its loyal following in the nuclear community, was not all that reassuring. The Detroit Edison Company had constructed a small breeder reactor, and in October of 1966 its cooling system failed, the reactor core began to melt, and, in the words of a plant engineer, "we almost lost Detroit." The same thing had happened ten years before in a government-owned breeder reactor.

Upon learning that their quiet stretch of the river could become home to a half-billion-dollar plutonium-producing reactor that no one had yet figured out how to operate safely, a small group of residents banded together to fight the plan. "We cannot condone the logic which advocates siting a reactor of any type in a low-population area at a time when it is considered far too great a risk if sited in a highly populated area," the Citizens' Committee for Environmental Concern argued. Its members weren't the only people beginning to challenge the nuclear "experts."

By 1970, at least fifteen atomic power plants were operating, under construction, or in the planning stages in Pennsylvania—more than in any other state. Ten of them were to be located along the Susquehanna. It seemed an appropriate time to ask some questions about the advisability of such a commitment. Although the state had no authority over licensing of reactors—that is vested solely in the federal government—a special committee of the Pennsylvania Senate convened an extraordinary series of hearings to ask a simple question: how safe is nuclear technology?

Though simple, it was a question rarely raised in impartial public forums at the time. For years, Americans had been barraged by rosy reports from federal nuclear authorities in concert with the industry, and most people—particularly those in the heartland of Pennsylvania—still tended to trust the experts. Now those experts were being asked to substantiate their claims.

The nuclear community viewed itself as the hope of the nation, soon to guarantee America's economic prosperity with cheap, abundant energy supplies. Many reactor boosters truly believed that nuclear plants could not fail—that they were so meticulously designed, carefully built, and intelligently staffed that no problem could overwhelm them. Safety concerns, when they did surface, were routinely dismissed as the uninformed prattling of no-growth proponents. As debate grew, however, the nuclear authorities had to make public the true basis for some of their decisions, and a new phrase crept into the American language: risk versus benefit. Pennsylvanians, of course, were already familiar with the concept, if not the phrase. It hearkened back to the thinking behind the *Sanderson* coal ruling that gave coal companies freedom to pollute: "The trifling inconvenience of particular persons must sometimes give way to the necessities of a great community." In the case of reactors, though, the "inconvenience" could turn out to be a nuclear disaster.

When the Pennsylvania Senate convened its hearings in August 1970, many of the nation's leading atomic experts traveled to Harrisburg to wage the nuclear debate in public. Unfortunately, their views hardly cleared the air. Among the experts was Dr. Lauriston Taylor, a member of the quasi-governmental National Council on Radiation Protection and Measurement, who told the senators that radiation was

> probably the most studied, best understood, most wisely used agent found essential to our health and well-being, but its improper use or conceivably any use may also carry some element of risk to man.
>
> There is the cliché that the insidious part of radiation is the fact that you can't feel it or see it or taste it, but radiation can be detected and measured easily and instantly and at levels far below those occurring in the natural environment, and this can't be said for many of the other environmental pollutants which are of common concern today.

Other witnesses were more emphatic. "Opposition to nuclear plants, on the ground that they present a radiation hazard, is simply unfounded," declared Herman Dieckamp, president of the company that hoped to build the breeder at Meshoppen. He dismissed as "remote" the possibility that a loss of cooling water to a reactor's core could cause the uranium fuel to melt.

Joining the chorus of nuclear advocates was J. L. Everett, executive vice-president of the Philadelphia Electric Company, who had committed his utility to a heavy investment in reactors, including three at Peach Bottom on the lower Susquehanna.[3] Everett testified,

> We know from experience that nuclear power is safe, economical, and creates a minimal effect on the environment and, therefore, on balance, it is the best choice in many cases for the people of Pennsylvania. I know of no other industry which, from its inception, has evidenced a greater degree of concern for both workers and public safety.

3. Everett, who would eventually become chairman and chief executive officer of Philadelphia Electric, also was responsible for the utility's plans to build two more reactors across the Susquehanna in Fulton Township and another pair on the Schuylkill River not far from the Philadelphia suburbs. The Fulton project was officially scrapped in 1979 after the accident at TMI.

While concerns about the plants' impact on humans were far more prevalent, some discussion focused on what the reactors might do to the Susquehanna itself. Would fishing—at long last possible again thanks to improving water quality—be destroyed by heated discharges from the plants? Would the plants consume large amounts of water, rendering the river unusable? Even worse, would radioactivity make the Susquehanna unsafe?

Some of the fears about nuclear power reflected a fundamental naiveté. The president of the Pennsylvania Environmental Council, a statewide ecology group, worried about the steam rising from the cooling towers. "It could cause frightful ice storms in winter when the plume comes down, when you have a down-draft," Curtin Winsor told the senators. "It could cause frightful humidity and change the immediate area into a real tropical climate in the summer."

Of all the witnesses, the most qualified to dispute the nuclear proponents on the safety issue was a quiet-spoken, bearded scientist from California who already had become a troublesome thorn in their sides. The witness, John W. Gofman, had a stunning resumé: M.D., Ph.D. in nuclear chemistry, codiscoverer of uranium-233 while a graduate student, associate director at the government's Lawrence Radiation Laboratory, head of a prestigious research group formed to study the effects of radiation on human health. Gofman testified,

> Categorically, I can state—and I do state—that no amount of radiation is known to be safe. All the scientific evidence indicates proportional harm all the way to the lowest dosages, including those dosages from natural resources. The idea of a safe amount of radiation is referred to as the "threshold" concept. This is nothing more than a convenient, mythical hope of atomic energy promoters, unsupported by any evidence.
>
> In a "relative" sense, safety could be suggested if it could be demonstrated that the benefits to be received by those being irradiated exceed the damage to their health and life from radiation.
>
> Citizens of Pennsylvania will be a bit puzzled by the benefit versus risk calculations, where the benefits are expressed in corporate profits and the risks expressed in cancer, leukemia, and genetic diseases to themselves and their children.

Gofman urged the Senate to enact a moratorium on the construction of reactors, at least those built above ground, "until after we learn something about the hazards of major disasters." At the conclusion of his testimony, the senator from Franklin County, noting Gofman's informal dress (the eminent scientist was partial to sandals) and his open challenge to the pronuclear stance of the federal government, observed, "I think I learned a little more about campus unrest than I did about atomic energy."

Nuclear plant construction continued unabated along the Susquehanna and elsewhere around Pennsylvania. One project that did not proceed, however, was the liquid-metal fast breeder proposed for the North Branch. None other than Congressman Daniel J. Flood, who rarely if ever turned down a federally funded project for his region, did so on this occasion. In characteristic language, he accused the Atomic Energy Commission of a "monstrous abuse of the public trust" for attempting to foist on his constituents "history's 'dirtiest' and most effective radiological warfare weapon" which, he took pains to note, would be located "thirty-five miles north of my office in Wilkes-Barre."

The fast-breeder project eventually landed on another river, the Clinch, in Tennessee. After more than $1 billion in federal funds were invested, Congress refused in 1985 to spend the additional $2.5 billion necessary to complete it.

Although the breeder went elsewhere, new power plants—using uranium as well as conventional fuels—rose along the banks of the Susquehanna. Today there are thirty-three of them. They range in size from small oil-fired generators for use during periods of peak demand to four 1,065-megawatt reactors at the Peach Bottom and Susquehanna generating stations, two of which could produce enough electricity for the city of Philadelphia. Each day, the Susquehanna provides more than 4.1 billion gallons of cooling water for the plants. Those who despaired of putting the river to work had simply asked it to do the wrong job.

In the beginning, though, it was not water but the abundance of cheap coal that lured the first modern electric generating plant to the Susquehanna. Thomas Edison, who had developed the incandescent electric light in 1879 and had built a small generating station on Pearl Street in New York City in 1882, arrived in Sunbury the following year intent on perfecting his invention to make it commercially successful. On the night of July 4, 1883, when the electric lights flickered on at Sunbury's City Hotel (later renamed the Edison Hotel), modern history was forever changed. Today, electrical transmission lines dominate miles of the skyline along the Susquehanna, especially on the sixty-five miles of river between Harrisburg and Havre de Grace. Half of all the electricity produced along the river comes from here, and the spidery towers carrying current to much of the mid-Atlantic region loom over the rural landscape.

By the early 1970s, there were plenty of signals that the nuclear plants rising along the lower Susquehanna weren't going to live up to the grand promises their owners had made for them. As of May 1974 construction was years behind schedule and costs had more than tripled. The cost of the Peach Bottom reactors, initially estimated at $250 million each, had risen to $900 million a piece. Peach Bottom Unit 2 was four years behind its building schedule and Unit 3 was seventeen months behind. Three Mile Island units 1 and 2 had similar problems. The original $110 million price tag for Unit 1 had grown to $410 million, in part due to construction delays totaling forty-one months. Unit 2 was in worse shape. It was sixty-two months behind schedule, and its cost had risen from $190 million to $510 million (and would reach $700 million by the time it was completed in late 1978).

Some of the delays on Unit 2 had been caused by a last-minute decision to change the plant site from Oyster Creek, New Jersey, to Three Mile Island, where the Unit 1 reactor was already being built. General Public Utilities (GPU), the owner, decided on the move to avoid labor problems in the Garden State. As a result, management responsibility for the reactor wound up with GPU's central Pennsylvania subsidiary, a small company with no nuclear experience called Metropolitan Edison. Almost all the electricity to be generated by the TMI reactors was destined for somewhere else—eastern and western Pennsylvania and New Jersey—to supply the customers of Metropolitan Edison and its co-investors in the plant, Pennsylvania Electric Company and Jersey Central Power and Light Company. Met Ed, as it is known locally, was forced to borrow to the limit to finance its share of the reactors, and construction often was halted until more money could be obtained.

The financial drain on Met Ed and Philadelphia Electric wasn't the only trouble caused by the reactors' trouble-plagued construction. Both projects were encountering a significant number of technical problems—problems that should have concerned everyone involved.

Almost every nuclear power plant in the United States is unique, in essence built from scratch, subject to design modifications (often ordered midway through the construction) to satisfy the idiosyncrasies of the utility owners who will operate it and the regulators who oversee its performance.[4] Even side-by-side reactors, such as TMI units 1 and 2, aren't

4. One of the common misperceptions among utilities building reactors was the idea that except for the type of fuel used to heat the water, a nuclear reactor was no different from a coal-fired plant, simple in technology and forgiving of mistakes. This attitude prevailed from

carbon copies. Sorting through the engineering specifications to determine even *how,* let alone *how well,* a plant is built is akin to deciphering hieroglyphics. There may be 50 miles or more of pipes and 900 miles of wiring, for example.

As events would demonstrate, those charged with ensuring public safety at a plant often were far more interested in getting the thing running, or keeping the utility owners happy, or advancing the cause of nuclear energy, than they were in ascertaining whether the welds were solid, the piping properly sealed, or the monitors easy to read. Occasionally, early warnings were ignored. Nowhere was this more apparent than in Three Mile Island Unit 2.

In July 1969, when the plans for the Unit 2 reactor crossed the desk of Dr. Stephen H. Hanauer, a veteran safety expert at the Atomic Energy Commission, he warned his superiors of problems in the design. Equipment that was "vital to [protecting] the public health and safety," he wrote, could be rendered inoperable by a series of extremely simple events. He urged that corrections be made during construction. His warnings were not heeded.

During the start-up of Unit 2 in 1977, an equipment malfunction prevented vital cooling water from reaching the fuel inside the reactor. The gauge measuring pressure in the system gave an incorrect reading, failing to alert technicians to the worst possible accident that can occur in a reactor—loss of coolant to the radioactive core. This situation was discovered before major problems developed then, but no changes were made, and, apparently, no reactor operators were ever alerted to the potential for misinformation from the gauge.

Later that same year, at the Davis-Besse nuclear plant on the shores of Lake Erie, an accident took place that no one thought possible. A pressure-relief valve stuck open and cooling water poured out, diverted from the fuel core. Operators misjudged the nature of the problem and turned off supplemental cooling water, causing the liquid still circulating around the core to boil. Within twenty-one minutes, however, they had identified and corrected the problem and replenished the coolant.

The Davis-Besse accident was investigated by the AEC's successor agency, the Nuclear Regulatory Commission, by the Toledo Edison Company, which owned the plant, and by Babcock and Wilcox, the company

---

the executive offices on down to the control room, breeding a dangerously casual attitude toward the deadly fuel core.

that manufactured the reactor. They decided that the problem was unique to this single reactor. The owners of other Babcock and Wilcox reactors—including the two at Three Mile Island—were not notified.

Altogether, Three Mile Island Unit 2 carried a great many red flags prior to March 1979. So many, in fact, that one writer, Daniel J. Ford, former executive director of the Union of Concerned Scientists, observed only partly in jest that "there is some question whether the event at Three Mile Island should, in a strict sense, be called an 'accident.' "

Shortly before 4 A.M. on Wednesday, March 28, 1979—a year to the day and hour since the fission process had commenced in Unit 2—a few citizens of Goldsboro, directly across the Susquehanna from the plant, were awakened by a thunderous burst of steam. Most returned to sleep, by now familiar with the odd noises from their new neighbor, whose bright nighttime lighting made it resemble an amusement park on the water.

The same noise lured a Metropolitan Edison employee out of a warehouse and into the predawn darkness. He saw a spurt of steam erupt from a safety valve atop Unit 2. Inside the plant, the Unit 2 shift foreman, who was in the basement checking on some repair work, heard what sounded "like a couple of freight trains" rumbling past on the nearby Conrail tracks, he later recalled.

A maintenance crew had inadvertently cut off the main source of water to the Unit 2 reactor and turbine, which was then operating at 96 percent of its 900-megawatt capacity. (Unit 1 was out of service at the time.) The equipment next did precisely what it was designed to do: it shut down, in a shuddering spasm. Emergency pumps to move cooling water around the intensely hot reactor core switched on automatically. As the water temperature soared, pressure built up rapidly in the fifty-six-foot-tall steel containment vessel housing the fuel rods, and a six-inch electromagnetic relief valve popped open. So far, all was happening as the plant's designers had intended.

But then something went wrong. Instead of closing as it should when the pressure was relieved, the valve stuck open—just as its counterpart had done in the Davis-Besse plant. Cooling water, rendered radioactive by its contact with the fuel, poured out of the valve at a rate of 220 gallons per minute, flooding the floor of the containment building that surrounds the reactor. The supply of coolant to the core fell dangerously low. Even so, the backup safety systems that nuclear engineers so proudly boasted of should have compensated for such a malfunction. Unfortunately, however, during a test two days previously, a pair of valves that would have delivered the supplemental water where and when it was needed had been closed and not reopened.

A simple chain of events was about to grow into the nation's worst accident in a commercial reactor.[5] As Stephen Hanauer had so accurately predicted nine years before, TMI's safety systems were rendered useless by a series of simple mistakes. For more than two hours, no one realized it.

Right along, TMI Unit 2 had had a problem with its valves. They leaked. So extensive and pervasive were the leaks that the reactor operators often had to falsify data on water losses to meet the terms of their operating license.[6] During the first few hours of the accident, some control-room personnel attributed the bizarre readings they were receiving on their equipment to leaking valves, and as a result they failed to consider other possible causes.

The valve problem had been uncovered even before Unit 2 started operating, as part of an auditors' report ordered by the Pennsylvania Public Utility Commission. The PUC was considering a rate increase sought by Met Ed, the plant's owner, to help pay for construction costs. At a subsequent hearing, the president of GPU, the parent company, was asked about reports that Unit 2's valves had not been adequately tested. None other than Herman Dieckamp, who had given up on the breeder at Meshoppen and moved on to head the New Jersey–based utility, stoutly defended his company's use of valves that had not been tested under actual operating conditions. If the nuclear industry was required to test every piece of equipment before installation, Dieckamp asserted, "we would be still building carbon copies of Mr. Edison's Pearl Street Station." The utility was awarded a $49-million rate increase on March 29—the day after Unit 2 had begun to self-destruct. All told, Three Mile Island Unit 2 would gener-

---

5. The nation's *worst* nuclear reactor accident occurred January 3, 1961, at the Stationary Low Power Reactor No. 1 (also known as SL-1), belonging to the Atomic Energy Commission and located at the government's reactor-testing facility outside Idaho Falls. Three technicians were performing maintenance on the small reactor when one worker pulled a control rod out of the fuel core, starting a chain reaction. The reactor exploded. The body of one worker was impaled to the ceiling by a control rod; two others were found on the floor. All died of massive radiation exposure. The reactor, contained in a cylindrical building with quarter-inch steel walls and normal doors, was destroyed; despite the force of the explosion, no radiation apparently leaked from the building.

6. In 1984, Metropolitan Edison pleaded guilty and paid a $45,000 fine for falsifying safety records, including leak data. The plea came after a federal jury indicted the company for routinely underreporting the amount of water leaking from the plant's cooling system.

ate electricity only for ninety-one days, each day of which would ultimately cost nearly $21 million—hardly the cheap electricity promised by the plant's builders.[7]

Inside the Unit 2 control room, the operators knew little of what was occurring around them and understood even less. Nearly a quarter of a million gallons of radioactive water and steam was hemorrhaging from the relief valve, flooding the reactor containment building and rupturing a storage tank. From there, the water was flowing into an unsealed auxiliary building. The control room's banks of gauges, dials, and monitors—which filled several large desks, hung overhead, and occupied all available wallspace—confused rather than enlightened. The operators interpreted the complex signals to mean the reactor had too much water. (Nowhere in the control room was there a simple gauge that actually showed the reactor water level.) Four minutes into the accident, the operators turned off the emergency feedwater pumps—the only remaining source of water. It was a terrible error. Had they not done this, the reactor might have recovered on its own. But as it was, the much-debated, much-feared fuel core meltdown now began. It would be nine years before researchers determined that more than a third of the 100-ton reactor core had melted, flowing, as one company official said "like hot olive oil." Even later, they would discover a three-inch-deep crack in the five-inch-thick steel shell surrounding the reactor core. Only the remaining thin layer of metal contained the hundreds of millions of curies of deadly radiation emanating from the sizzling core.

A cacophony of buzzers and alarms echoed off the walls of the control room and a computer—unprepared for the data it was receiving—succumbed, its printer typing line after line of question marks. It was 7 A.M.—three hours into the accident—before a frightening fact became apparent. For the first time in U.S. history, radiation from a commercial nuclear power plant was escaping into the atmosphere, carried off over the Susquehanna in a four-mile-an-hour breeze.

Control-room personnel knew they had to alert the outside world. A call was placed to the duty officer of the Pennsylvania Emergency Management Agency in Harrisburg, who was told, "We have an emergency." The state's civil-defense machinery moved into action. Word of problems at

---

7. In addition to the reactor's $700-million price tag, the cleanup costs reached almost $1 billion, and the cost to decommission the reactor will be $195.6 million. Ratepayers bore the financial burden of construction and will pay for decommissioning. The cost of cleanup was shared by stockholders in GPU, the U.S. nuclear industry, the federal government, and the Japanese nuclear industry, which contributed $18 million in exchange for access to information on the accident and cleanup technology.

TMI was transmitted over the region's emergency radio bands, and the local news media received their first hint of a story that would dominate world headlines for days.

Still, reassuring answers abounded that Wednesday morning. A Metropolitan Edison spokesman declared, "There is absolutely no danger of a meltdown." The utility's vice-president for power generation said, "Right now—as I've indicated—the plant is in a safe condition. It's nothing we can't take care of." Lieutenant Governor William Scranton, citing information he had been given by the utility, told reporters that "everything is under control." (He later discovered that even as he was speaking radiation was being vented from the reactor. Visibly angry, he told reporters that evening, "The situation is more complex than the company first led us to believe. Metropolitan Edison has given you—and us—conflicting information.") The next day in Washington, NRC chairman Joseph M. Hendrie assured members of Congress that the problem was not serious. Reactor experts cautioned reporters that in nuclear parlance this was an "event," not an "accident." Accidents, they said, were much more serious. The experts still did not believe that an "accident" could happen.

It was not until two days later—Friday, March 30—that the real danger of the situation became apparent. By then all evidence pointed to severe damage to the reactor's core. At 8:45 A.M., a burst of radioactive steam erupted from Unit 2 and was measured at 1.2 rems per hour.[8] Upon learning that more unplanned releases were likely, Pennsylvania governor Dick Thornburgh lost patience with the lack of answers and action from the NRC and the plant's owners. He decided someone must act and assumed the duty himself. In an announcement that caused both relief and fear, the governor ordered pregnant women and young children to leave the area and closed schools within a five-mile radius of TMI. Soon, tens of thousands of Pennsylvanians were fleeing their homes in the nation's first radiation-induced mass evacuation. At least 75,000 people, perhaps as many as 200,000, would race for safety.

As Pennsylvanians abandoned their homes, the experts in Washington, in Harrisburg, and on Three Mile Island itself began to speak the most feared word in reactor parlance: *meltdown*. In the absence of sufficient cooling water, the nuclear fuel could get hot enough to burn its way through the protective steel vessel and through the concrete floor of the containment building. Such a meltdown would release 400 million curies

---

8. A rem is a measure of the biological effects of radiation. Current federal radiation standards set five rems per year as the maximum allowable exposure. By comparison, a dental x-ray contains less than .05 rems.

of radiation into the air and water—2,000 times that which was dropped on Hiroshima. The Susquehanna would become a river of death.

Bud Wilbern was out of town on business during the TMI accident. So was Rusty Beckey, but Rusty decided to return from West Virginia, telling his dispatcher at the trucking company that he wanted a load to haul back to the Susquehanna. "I just wanted to see what was going on here," he says.

Harry Myers, the airport fireman, recalls the extra shifts he put in at Harrisburg International, suddenly a very busy place. "There were C5As [cargo planes] coming in one after another around the clock. They were carrying twenty-pound lead bricks for the Unit 2 control room, tons and tons of them." The reactor operators struggling with the crisis had to be protected from radiation. In addition, seventy tons of bricks were used to reduce radiation escaping from the unshielded auxiliary building. Yet when Harry Myers came home at the end of a shift, there on his television screen were utility officials telling him—and others—not to worry, that there was no danger.

Inside the plant, conditions continued to deteriorate Friday.[9] The control room could not gain control of the reactor. In terms of touching off public panic, however, nothing would rival the "discovery" that day of a hydrogen bubble inside the reactor. NRC experts theorized that intense heat had caused the cooling water to break down into its components, hydrogen and oxygen. The hydrogen then had collected at the top of the reactor vessel, preventing new cooling water from circulating. And what did that mean? "It means that there is a possibility of an internal explosion and a break in the containment [building]," the governor's staff was told. The news drew a gasp of horror from the state's top radiation official. On Friday night, veteran newscaster Walter Cronkite intoned to millions of television viewers, "The world has never known a day quite like today."

For those who remained in the TMI area, the weekend of March 31 and April 1 was agonizingly long and frightening. Whole riverfront communities became ghost towns. Many who stayed were TMI employees and their families, demonstrating their belief that the reactor was in good

9. Into the chaos came the NRC's operations chief, Harold Denton, an unflappable Southerner with a bachelor's degree in science who was immediately accorded a Ph.D. by the harried news media until somebody realized that the reason "Dr. Denton" sounded familiar had nothing to do with his resumé. Among Denton's duties was presiding over the daily news briefings, which were teeming, screaming matches with hundreds of reporters from around the world.

hands. Others were farmers who could not abandon their livestock. (Dairy farmers were warned to keep their herds indoors and to prevent them from grazing on grass that might have received radioactive fallout.)

These God-fearing, conservative Pennsylvanians had had their trust in government shaken to its roots. Sunday morning saw many of them filling the pews of the countless churches that dot this region, seeking answers, or at least reassurance, there. The area's Roman Catholic archbishop authorized his priests to grant absolution to parishioners, and at a fundamentalist church in Middletown, the pastor proclaimed, "I believe we are living in the last days."[10] Sunday also brought Pres. Jimmy Carter and his wife, Rosalynn, who, in the company of Governor and Mrs. Thornburgh, toured the Unit 2 reactor, wearing yellow protective boots. The visit was an effort to calm the people of the lower Susquehanna—and America.

And at TMI, finally, there was some comparatively good news: the bubble was shrinking. No one knew why, or how, *or* if it might reappear. An embarrassed NRC would later concede that the prospects of the bubble exploding had been grossly exaggerated by the agency's own experts. Somebody had goofed. And panicked a region.

Teams of nuclear experts were arriving hourly at the TMI plant and, for the first time, it seemed as if a cataclysm had been averted. But questions that had been deferred in the frantic, round-the-clock battle to control the reactor now were being asked in some quarters. Exactly how much radiation had escaped from the plant? What were the health consequences of those releases—immediate and long-term? What threat did the plant pose to the people who were returning to their homes? And what risks would it pose in the future to the Susquehanna, south-central Pennsylvania, and all who lived and worked near the reactor filled with deadly radiation and contaminated water?[11] The answers to these questions were just as scarce as had been answers about the condition of the core.

It was late April before federal authorities announced that the reactor had been "stabilized," meaning that the experts again understood what it was doing. Met Ed officials began to talk of having the Unit 2 reactor back

10. Back in 1844, a group of central Pennsylvanians, members of an evangelical sect known as the Millerites, assembled on Hill Island, just upstream from Three Mile Island. Clad only in white sheets, the men and women gathered there to await the arrival of chariots from heaven and the end of the world. "They were disappointed," observed a local historian. The island now contains a number of summer homes.

11. Former U.S. senator Charles McC. Mathias of Maryland later observed that the accident at TMI did more to awaken Chesapeake Bay residents to the interrelationship between the bay and its main tributary, the Susquehanna, than any previous public-awareness campaign.

in service within a few months. On both sides of the Susquehanna, "For Sale" signs sprouted on homes and farms along with the bright flowers and lush grass of spring.[12]

In the following months, the events at TMI were subjected to microscopic review by a special presidential commission, various congressional committees, industry panels, federal and state regulators, courts of law, and courts of public opinion. One protracted legal battle involved restarting TMI Unit 1, which had been shut down for repairs in March 1979 and was unaffected by the accident. Opponents argued that the same people who had been responsible for the Unit 2 accident would be involved in operating and managing Unit 1. They cited evidence of the leak-rate falsification at the plant as indicative of the dishonesty that pervaded TMI. Among those lined up against restart were Governor Thornburgh, Pennsylvania's two U.S. senators, Arlen Specter and John Heinz, and scores of citizens.[13] Federal authorities stirred the debate with an announcement in early 1980 that the reactor had come within thirty to sixty minutes of a meltdown. For many, the TMI accident was the nuclear nightmare come true, the smoking gun that proved this technology was not safe and could never be made so. For others, the fact that humans and machines wrestled disaster to the ground—that no lives were lost at TMI, as bumper stickers declared—was a vindication of nuclear engineering. One thing was certain: along the Susquehanna, few people were ambivalent about nuclear technology.

It would be years before the inventory of damage was completed. In 1986, GPU officials reluctantly declared that Unit 2 would never be returned to service. Just cleaning it up cost almost $1 billion, nearly a third more than the cost of construction, and required development of entirely new procedures and equipment—including robots named Rover 1 and Rover 3 and a little yellow submarine.

Inside the reactor, nearly 150 tons of uranium fuel and other debris

12. Several studies of the economic impact on real estate values in the vicinity of TMI suggest that there has been no long-term effect. The strong demand for agricultural land throughout the region ensured buyers for farms, and home sales, which remained slow for several years after the accident, picked up by the early 1980s, also driven by market forces.

13. After five years of hearings and 30,000 pages of testimony, the NRC approved startup on May 29, 1985. A challenge was filed in the U.S. Third Circuit Court of Appeals, which upheld the NRC's legal authority to make such a decision. In a dissent, Judge Arlin Adams urged additional hearings. "The reactor's neighbors must bear the immediate physical and psychological burden of the March 1979 accident. But communities across the nation are looking to the [Nuclear Regulatory] Commission for assurance that they will not be victims of the next accident."

had crumbled or melted and resolidified into an intensively radioactive mass on the reactor floor. Cleanup crews could not enter the reactor vessel, of course; they could stand around its top, but for only a few minutes at a time due to the high radiation levels. After the crew members had pains-takingly guided the robots and other machines in cutting up the deadly fuel and vacuuming sediments, the materials were packaged and shipped by rail to the Idaho National Engineering Laboratory for disposal, a process not completed until the spring of 1990.

Cleanup crews also had to deal with more than 2 million gallons of contaminated water, which was stored in tanks on the island. Most of the water was only slightly radioactive, and GPU initially hoped to discharge it directly into the Susquehanna. But the public clamor—especially from the city of Lancaster, which draws some of its drinking water from the river below TMI—forced the utility to change its plans. GPU then installed equipment to filter and evaporate the water, which would remove most of its radioactive contaminants. (Radioactive tritium, which chemically bonds to the hydrogen and oxygen atoms, cannot be extracted in this way. Federal officials, however, concluded that the level of tritium in the TMI water posed no health hazard.) The water was then recondensed and dis-charged into the Susquehanna. The evaporate residue was sent to a low-level radioactive waste burial ground.

Even after all these steps, radiation levels inside TMI Unit 2 remained extremely high, isolated from the environment only by structures and equipment that had undergone severe stress, heat, and damage caused by the barrage of radioactive particles. The future of the idled reactor re-mained very much up in the air—and a subject of intense disagreement between those who wanted it removed entirely and those who maintained that the safest course was to let the radiation subside naturally over the next several decades.

Finally, in 1988, the NRC concluded what many residents along the Susquehanna feared most: that the best plan was to leave Unit 2 sitting right where it was. There was no better alternative, federal officials con-cluded. The decision outraged some local citizens. Among them was Eric Epstein, head of the organization TMI Alert, who accused the NRC of being "willing to accept a high-level waste site on an island in the middle of the Susquehanna indefinitely."[14] Statements from the NRC that there were no safer solutions failed to assuage concerns.

14. TMI Alert, formed two years before the accident in response to local concerns about safety at the plant, included some atypical members from the outset, according to Epstein. When he and eleven others were arrested in a demonstration at TMI's gates in 1983, he notes,

Indeed, the plant still poses a risk of radiation releases into the air or into the Susquehanna, either of which carries dangers for nearby residents as well as those along the Chesapeake Bay. About 2,000 pounds of highly radioactive debris remain in the basement of the reactor building. Plans call for it to remain there until 2014, at which time both TMI units 1 and 2 are scheduled to be dismantled.

No lives *were* lost in the accident. Whether it will have long-term consequences for the health of area residents remains a subject of considerable local debate. No one knows with any certainty just how much radiation was released from the reactor; estimates are based on extrapolations from very sketchy monitoring data. It is generally believed that 14 curies of radiation escaped from TMI. By contrast, 50 million curies spewed from the Soviet Union's Chernobyl reactor in 1986.

Although the state of Pennsylvania had no monitoring equipment at nuclear plants in March 1979—the legislature had refused to provide funding for the equipment—there is plenty now. In addition to measuring devices maintained by the state and the utility, a citizens' monitoring network was established around TMI, using equipment purchased with funds provided by the Grateful Dead rock band. Thirteen years after the accident, TMI's owners agreed to supply $1 million worth of radiation-testing devices to nearby residents and to make public detailed information about conditions in the Unit 2 reactor. The agreement settles a lawsuit brought by TMI Alert shortly after the accident. As part of the settlement, GPU also reaffirmed that Unit 2 will never reopen and that the company will never use the island to store radioactive waste from reactors owned by other utilities—something some residents feared would occur.

A panel of independent researchers conducted a four-year study of the effect of the TMI accident on residents' health. (The study was paid for from a court-supervised fund established by GPU to settle lawsuits after the accident.) In 1990, the panel issued its long-awaited report: there was no "convincing evidence" that the emissions had produced additional cancers. But the scientists cautioned that their data were by no means conclusive and that not enough time had elapsed for certain cancers to develop.

Two of the more noteworthy investigations of the accident produced damning assessments of nuclear technology and the competence of those

---

"the first line [of protesters] consisted of Republican Party committee women." They were fined $10—the same amount once levied against Henry David Thoreau for an act of civil disobedience.

who oversee it. A commission appointed by President Carter told the American people that the primary cause of the TMI accident was the "mindset" of the nuclear industry and its regulators that accidents would not happen. "The fundamental problems are people-related problems," and they exist among reactor operators, utility managers, and the NRC itself, the commission concluded.

The second panel, appointed by the NRC, came to an equally scathing assessment of the state of reactor safety in America. It said that "an attitude of complacency" enveloped everyone in the nuclear community, fostered in large part by the NRC's "business as usual approach," even in the wake of TMI.

If those who lived along the Susquehanna's nuclear corridor thought the accident at Three Mile Island—and such stinging condemnations— had scared the atomic power industry into cleaning up its act, they were in for a rude awakening. TMI's downstream neighbor was about to seize the spotlight.

Long after other American utilities had begun to back away from the atom for economic and efficiency reasons, as well as public opposition, the Philadelphia Electric Company remained fiercely loyal to nuclear power. Over two-thirds of the utility's generating capacity is nuclear, thanks large- ly to the stubborn determination of J. L. Everett, who headed the company until 1988. Everett, the man who had told a state Senate committee in 1970 of the nuclear industry's unparalleled "concern for both workers and the public safety," was bent on building two reactors along the Schuylkill thirty-five miles from downtown Philadelphia. He faced down both wide- spread opposition from area residents and displeasure from Wall Street. The $6.6-billion Limerick reactor project represented a staggering finan- cial burden for the company. Once construction began, corporate atten- tion and funding were channeled to Limerick with increasing frequency. The company's two older reactors at Peach Bottom were largely ignored, their best personnel transferred to the new plant, and their maintenance needs deferred to save money.

In March 1987, the Nuclear Regulatory Commission stunned the utility by ordering the Peach Bottom plant shut down. NRC inspectors had found that the plant's control-room operators routinely slept on the job. And not only had Philadelphia Electric officials been aware of the problem, the NRC said, but they had done nothing about it. Upon closer examina- tion, it appeared that dozing employees were just part of Peach Bottom's problem. The whole plant was in deplorable condition. One-third of the interior was contaminated with low levels of radiation, the result of sloppy maintenance. (Utility officials quickly pointed out that this posed no risk for the general public, but acknowledged that it *was* hazardous for their own workers.) The list went on: Pipes leaked radioactive water. No one was certain whether spare parts installed in the plant met safety specifications. In the midst of this, eight employees were arrested on drug charges.

A panel of industry experts reviewed Peach Bottom's operations and the management of Philadelphia Electric and then employed language never heard before in the nuclear power fraternity: Peach Bottom was "an embarrassment to the industry and to the nation." Heads rolled at Philadelphia Electric. Everett announced an early retirement. New management promised a wholesale housecleaning.

The Peach Bottom reactors remained shut down nearly two years, costing the utility $735 million, of which $235 million went toward improvements. One improvement of these consisted of buying less-comfortable chairs for control-room operators so they couldn't sleep.[15] When a chastened Philadelphia Electric went back to the NRC seeking permission to turn the reactors back on, the NRC chairman took the occasion to offer a warning, "Needless to say, I hope it is a lesson learned not only by your utility but by all the utilities in our country," said Lando W. Zech, Jr.

Compared to Peach Bottom and TMI, the Susquehanna's other nuclear plant, at Berwick on the North Branch, has produced relatively few headlines. But that's not to say the plant, owned by Pennsylvania Power and Light Company and completed in 1985, has not had its share of problems.

In July 1984, just after one of the two reactors had received a license to ascend to full power, an accident took place. It was another of those the experts believed could not happen. All electrical power to the reactor was lost, including emergency diesel generators, rendering every piece of safety equipment inoperative. Fortunately, power was soon restored. This "abnormal occurrence," as the NRC termed it, was investigated, and the causes found were officially listed as operator error, inadequate operator training, poorly designed control-room panels, and imprecise procedures.

---

15. Drowsiness would appear to be an occupational hazard at nuclear plants. In 1987, the NRC fined GPU $50,000 after determining that a shift supervisor at TMI Unit 2 had slept on the job in 1987. Although the reactor was shut down, fuel was being removed at the time and technicians were maintaining twenty-four-hour supervision to ensure no problems developed. The supervisor was fired by the company. The same year, a shift supervisor at the Susquehanna Steam Electric Station was reassigned after dozing off while on duty.

To those familiar with the accident at TMI, it was an alarmingly familiar litany of problems.

Not far downriver from the Susquehanna Steam Generation Station at Berwick is the ten-acre site once occupied by U.S. Radium. The current occupant is a company called Safety Light Corporation, a spinoff of U.S. Radium that manufactures emergency exit signs and similar illuminated equipment, using tritium rather than radium. The NRC has identified wastes containing tritium, cesium, radium, and strontium scattered around the property.

NRC officials estimate that the cost of ridding the plant site of its radiation and chemical contamination will be $1 million. Safety Light reports net income of approximately $200,000 a year. Just who will pay the cleanup costs remains uncertain. In the meantime, traces of the radioactive wastes are seeping into nearby groundwater supplies. From there, the Susquehanna is a short distance away. "Clearly there are risks associated with the site," an NRC official said in early 1992.

The legacy of the nuclear experiment on the West Branch continues as well. Today, only hints of the once-grand plans for Quehanna remain. Reactor Road leads off the Quehanna Highway, a rough ribbon of blacktop through the scenic Moshannon State Forest. For years, rumors about what was buried in the woods circulated among the hunters, hikers, and fishermen who frequented the Quehanna Wilderness Area. Fantastic tales of glow-in-the-dark deer would surface on occasion, and backpackers occasionally reported finding partially exposed barrels amid the wildflowers and bogs.

In response, state and federal officials surveyed the area in the 1970s and '80s and found no evidence of problems. Critics charged that those assessments were inadequate. In 1986, a state House conservation committee summoned ex-employees and contractors who had worked for Curtiss-Wright and Martin Marietta to testify at a hearing. They described placing barrels of radioactive waste, beryllium oxide, and other dangerous chemicals in trenches at a number of sites, some of which were marked, some of which were not. A state forester testified that after he discovered people had been using a spring flowing from an area believed to have been used as a dumpsite, he simply removed the outfall pipe to prevent access to the water.

While the hearing failed to provide evidence of a serious environmental hazard, monitoring wells have been installed around the site to detect hazardous waste in creeks or ground water. Due to the high cost of any other course of action, almost certainly the final "solution" to Quehanna will be to leave everything right where it is and hope it stays there.

It is the accident barely avoided that haunts the imagination. The would-be victim is left to wonder just how bad things might have been. The people who live along the lower Susquehanna occasionally speculate on just that question. The emergency brochures they receive annually, or the special section of their telephone books that provides the same information, or the occasional test of sirens, or simply the looming presence of these reactors along the tranquil banks of the river serve as constant reminders.

The Susquehanna has survived every assault human beings have inflicted to date, but they still hold in their hands the capacity to render a whole region uninhabitable. All that is required are a few careless mistakes, and humans have clearly demonstrated themselves quite capable of that. Perhaps in response to this brush with disaster, there has developed among many who live along the Susquehanna a heightened sense of protectiveness and concern for the river, as well as for the living things coexisting there.

Bud says he and Joe Millward will knock off early this afternoon from the clubhouse project and head over to his island to do some reconnoitering. It is Joe's idea, but Bud is happy to go along. Joe, Bud explains, likes to catch the rabbits that appear in the early morning at the landing and turn them loose on Bud's island. "He put six babies over there a while ago," confides Bud, "and he's only seen one. Now he's worried about what happened to the rest, so I guess we'll go over and check on them."

Chapter Seven

Farming

"Stewards of this garden"

From the hill that gives Harlan Keener's farm its name, he can see the past, present, and future of agriculture in Lancaster County, Pennsylvania. In the valley to the east, an Amish farmer guides a team of four mules, preparing the fields for spring planting, just as his father, grandfather, and great-grandfather did in this fertile country. Beyond the Amish farm, across a busy road, sit new, high-priced houses amid landscaped lawns, their picture windows carefully positioned to capture the pastoral scenes. Straight ahead, three miles to the north, the office towers of the city of Lancaster stand silhouetted against the sky. On a rise to Keener's left, a new retirement community sprawls over fields that until recently nodded with ripening grain. In between nestle a few farmhouses and barns, pastures with grazing Holstein and Guernsey cows, and a bubbling brook that flows to the Susquehanna River, which forms the forty-one-mile-long western boundary of the county.

Immediately behind him, inside a huge, windowless, climate-controlled building, are Harlan Keener's 11,000 hogs. There, too, is his pride and joy: the throbbing machinery that at this very moment is processing some of the 4.5 million pounds of manure generated each year at the Rocky Knoll Swine Farm.

In 1959, when Harlan Keener followed his father and grandfather into farming here in West Lampeter Township, he started with 24 cows, 1,000 chickens, and tobacco. "You could hardly pay your taxes with that now," he says. In the late 1970s, as his sons prepared to become the fourth generation of Keener farmers, he made an economic decision: he would change the way he farmed, all but eliminating cultivated crops and vastly increasing livestock production. Today, in addition to the family's hog operation—the largest in Lancaster County—the Keeners raise seventy-five dairy cattle.

Hundreds of other Lancaster County farmers have made the same choice. And as a result, some of the nation's best cropland now is used for raising livestock. While that has succeeded in keeping farmers on the land,

and in protecting the county's rich agricultural heritage, it has taken a high toll at home and on a neighbor most Susquehanna farmers rarely gave a thought to: the Chesapeake Bay.

The new livestock produces enormous quantities of manure, more than the farmers who still cultivate the land can use. Few farmers in the county have been as conscientious as Harlan Keener in finding ways to process the waste. As a result, thousands of tons of it wash into the Susquehanna and then into the bay, in effect "fertilizing" the Chesapeake and upsetting the delicate balance of aquatic life there.

If the bay is to survive, its nutrient levels must be drastically reduced. That, in turn, has spawned a scramble to solve the manure problem in Lancaster County. One thing is certain: before the next generation takes up this time-honored vocation, the face of farming in the place that calls itself the Garden Spot of America will have to change once again.

Lancaster County has 5,100 farms, most of them family-owned and -operated. They average eighty-five acres, just one-fifth the typical size elsewhere in the United States. But despite the smallness, their crop productivity is unsurpassed, thanks to the soils—a deep, fluffy loam, well watered and underlain by limestone or, to the south, a mineral-rich earth weathered from metamorphic rocks. Excluding areas where crop yields are boosted by irrigation—such as in the San Joaquin and Imperial valleys in California—there is no farmland in America more productive. Even competing against such places, Lancaster holds its own, ranking eleventh in the nation in the value of agricultural products sold. Each year, Lancaster County produces more food than thirteen states, including the Garden State, New Jersey.

Despite this amazing record, most of the farming in the county today has nothing to do with soil quality. Animals by the hundreds or thousands are raised inside metal buildings, never setting foot outside, or—in the case of cattle—leaving the barns only for muddy feed lots.

Once Pennsylvania was predominately a grain-producing state, but competition in the mid-nineteenth century from large western farms gradually caused the state's farmers to turn to livestock raising. A century later, livestock and related products accounted for about three-quarters of the state's agricultural revenues.

Lancaster County farmers were leaders in this trend. Today four-fifths of the nearly $750 million in farm revenue generated annually in the county comes from beef and dairy cattle, hogs, and poultry. (The rest is from grain—chiefly corn—and other food crops.) The county boasts the second largest hog and poultry industries in the United States, with more than 350,000 hogs and nearly 13 million chickens. On any given day, more than 17 million animals are being raised on county farms. Many farmers, like Harlan Keener, say intensive livestock raising is their only means of economic survival. When land costs $5,000, $10,000, or more an acre, devoting fifteen or twenty acres to a herd of dairy cows is a luxury few farmers can afford.

Despite its strong agricultural tradition, Lancaster County has the fastest population growth rate in the Susquehanna watershed. Each year, the county loses nearly 7,000 acres of its farmland to development, up from an average of 2,500 acres during the quarter-century ending in 1985. About two-thirds of the county's 602,240 acres remain agricultural, with 330,000 acres of that still cultivated.[1] But planners believe that as much as half the county ultimately will be converted to nonfarm uses—homes, retirement communities, shopping centers, office parks, recreational facilities, and schools.

In a survey taken in the late 1980s, half of the county's 410,000 residents said they had arrived since 1975. At the time of the survey the population was increasing by 5,000 people annually. Discussions about growth routinely appear on public meeting agendas and generate arguments about new sewer lines, traffic congestion, minimum lot sizes, scarce parkland, tax increases to pay for expanded municipal services, and all the other issues that accompany a burgeoning—and changing—population.

Yet amid all the debate, two truths emerge. The first is simple: whatever changes come, Lancaster County *is* farming. Agriculture is the only way of life for many of its residents. Like their ancestors, they cannot think of anything else they would rather do—or anywhere else they would rather be. And even those who do not farm find their lives touched by agriculture: its values, its politics, and its problems.

In recent years, however, another truth has emerged, one that is far more complex and far-reaching: decisions that once concerned only the individual landowner, or the local zoning officer, or even the township commissioners, now must be made with an eye toward their impact on people and places far away. Nowhere along the Susquehanna today is there a better example of the conflicts that arise from being a citizen of an *ecosystem.*

1. The remainder is forest, pasture, or feed lots.

Americans have always loved farms—or at least the idea of farming, and the simple, natural lifestyle they think it represents. Lancaster County *looks* like this ideal of farming, with its tidy stone farmhouses, silos, and barns beside sparkling creeks, its rolling fields green with wheat or corn, its tiny crossroads graced by eighteenth-century buildings and flowerbeds. That 20 percent of the farms are owned by Old Order Amish or Mennonites who still use horses and mules to tend their fields and to pull their buggies doesn't hurt the picture. Unabashedly, the county promotes this rural image to the hilt. In response, 3 to 4 million visitors a year flock to Lancaster County to crane out of car and bus windows at the Plain Sect people in their dark clothes and black buggies and to visit the related attractions—Dutch Wonderland Family Fun Park, the Amish Barn Gift Shop and Restaurant, with its Golden Tee miniature golf course, the Dutch Apple Dinner Theater, and many more. Before the visitors depart, they spend about $450 million each year, making tourism the county's third largest industry after farming and manufacturing.

A growing number of those tourists like what they see so much that they return to live in the county, buying Cape Cods and condominiums on what had been cornfields a few months before. (The retirement community visible from Harlan Keener's farm is a good example. Of its 1,134 residents, 75 percent were new to Lancaster County.)

In Pennsylvania, zoning and development decisions are a function of local government, and Lancaster County has sixty of those. They range in size from the city of Lancaster, which in 1990 had a population of 55,500, to Adamstown borough, population 1,107. While county planners offer advice, the local officials are free to act as they choose, and that doesn't encourage long-range thinking—or politically difficult decisions. So it's not surprising that development has occurred haphazardly. A common sight in the county are clusters of homes on tiny lots incongruously surrounded by farmland, as if they had been dropped there out of the sky.

This commingling of land use creates a variety of problems for all concerned. The occupants of those new homes presumably moved to the country to be a part of it, but farming isn't necessarily a pleasant neighbor. The smell of manure, the clank of equipment operating early in the morning or late at night, the traffic problems caused by slow-moving farm machinery on busy commuter roads are things the real estate agent neglects to mention when marketing a home in Country View Estates or Greenfield Commons. But the random development also raises an issue more fundamental than these: the philosophical question of the best use of the land.

Should the nation's premier farmland be converted to other uses? "The soil here is too good to hide under a basement," a farmer once explained to a visitor.

Perhaps the best way to understand the extent of agriculture in the county, and to see where its future is most vulnerable, is to examine the map that hangs in the offices of county planners. Like a finely pieced old quilt, it is covered with tiny squares of green representing the farms that take up much of the county's 941 square miles. But the green disappears in some areas where farms logically still should be. It is replaced by a rainbow of colors depicting other kinds of development, primarily housing tracts and shopping centers. This transformation is irreversible; once lost, the land will never be returned to farming.

In an attempt to protect the green areas still on its map, Lancaster in 1980 became the first county in Pennsylvania to preserve farms. The county created what are known as agricultural security areas, where farming is granted special concessions and protections. Townships in these areas agree not to enact ordinances interfering with a farmer's normal activities—such as regulating the hours he or she may operate machinery or apply manure. Although similar programs have been tried elsewhere in the nation, the idea was a radical departure for Pennsylvania, with its long tradition of local land-use decisionmaking.

To participate, owners of at least 500 contiguous acres currently used for agriculture may petition their local government (or governments, for the land need not be entirely in a single township) for designation as a security area. If the township agrees, the request is sent on to the county for review and action by the Agricultural Preserve Board, which has final say. Once a security area has been formally established, the second phase of the plan takes effect. Landowners may sign a deed covenant committing their property in perpetuity to agriculture. In return, the county gives them a cash payment reflecting the difference between the land's value as a farm and what a real estate developer might pay. At the outset, those payments averaged about $1,300 per acre. Prime farmland and farmland under the greatest development pressure get higher priority from the county than other parcels. Some farmland is deemed ineligible because program officials believe development in the area is inevitable. "We don't intend to spend our money just to preserve a pretty view," explained Thomas L. Daniels, director of the county's program. "We intend to preserve agriculture as an industry."

Initially, the program was greeted with great skepticism, for many farmers believed it would drive down the value of their only asset: their farmland. That view persists today. By the late 1980s, however, backers of the program proudly noted that farms under "permanent conservation easements," as the deed covenants are known, were selling for almost as much as those without restrictions on their future use. (A number of the purchasers are not farmers but well-to-do newcomers who don't want next-door neighbors.) As of 1992, about 111,000 acres in the county were in agricultural security areas and 12,000 of those acres had been placed under deed covenants.

Lancaster County's program became a model for a statewide farmland preservation effort, overwhelmingly approved in 1987 by Pennsylvania voters, who also authorized $100 million to underwrite it. (The measure won its greatest support not in traditional farming counties, but in suburban and urban areas.) The state has allocated about $1.5 million annually for Lancaster County, which supplements the approximately $750,000 budgeted by county commissioners for purchase of easements.

Activists criticize the county for not doing more, noting that the Lancaster County Chamber of Commerce and Industry and the Pennsylvania Dutch Tourist Bureau and Convention Center spend in excess of $1 million a year to lure new business, development, and tourism to the county—all of which seriously threaten the future of farming. Even so, in 1991, Lancaster County preserved more farmland than any county in the United States, according to Tom Daniels.

The county's program to save agricultural land is complicated somewhat by the number of Plain Sect farmers who for religious reasons won't accept money from the government. That spurred formation in 1988 of a second, private agricultural preservation effort, the Lancaster Farmland Trust. The trust accepts contributions from individuals, corporations, and foundations and uses the money to buy conservation easements from landowners. Because no government funds are involved, the farmland trust has been able to obtain easements from Amish and Mennonite farmers.

That there are still farmers who oppose the agricultural preservation program confounds people like Alan R. Musselman, head of the Farmland Trust and former director of the county's Agricultural Preserve Board. Musselman, who led a similar program in Maryland before coming to Lancaster County in 1983, says it is a classic case of farmers wanting to have their cake and eat it, too. They complain bitterly about encroaching development, but also want to retain their right to sell their land at the highest price—which means to developers—if they choose.

Harlan Keener falls neatly into that category. He wants no part of the agricultural security area program because, he says, it restricts a farmer's freedom to do what he wants with his most valuable possession, his land. Keener and his wife have a small retirement account; they sit atop the rest of their net worth. "I am in love with this land," he said as he toured his farm in his brown Chevy pickup. And while he has no plans to sell any of it, he fiercely guards that option. "It's there if you must," he says.

The debate over farmland preservation has led to considerable discussion of just what is best overall for the county and its residents—and with increasing frequency that leads in turn to the seemingly incongruous subject of manure management. Closely linked they are. "Although people talk about the prevailing view of stewardship of the land that exists here, there's also the feeling among farmers that 'The land is mine, I can do with it what I want,' " explained David R. Brubaker, executive vice-president of PennAg Industries, an association of 515 large and small agribusinesses in Lancaster County. "That may have been true in the 1800s, but in the 1990s what you do on your land ends up in my well. That complicates matters considerably, and people in the county are only beginning to recognize it."

Lancaster is the most intensively farmed county along the Susquehanna. From the county's southern tip, it is a mere twelve miles to the beginning of the Chesapeake Bay. Each minute, the Susquehanna delivers an average of 17 million gallons of water to the 2,200-square-mile estuary. And with that water comes the runoff from the land the river drains. Half of Pennsylvania's cropland and two-thirds of its livestock are located within the Susquehanna drainage basin.

The runoff from this agricultural land contains a potent mix of nitrogen and phosphorous, the basic ingredients of commercial fertilizer and manure.[2] An average of 151 million pounds of nitrogen and nearly 9 million pounds of phosphorus flow into the Chesapeake from the Susquehanna annually, with Pennsylvania accounting for 80 percent of that total and New York the remainder. Of the amount coming from Pennsylvania, the bulk enters along the lower portion of the river, in the form of agricultural runoff and eroded soil.[3] Lancaster County alone delivers millions of pounds of nutrients to the river and the bay each year. These nutrients represent the largest source of pollution on the main stem of the river.

Unlike the delicate Chesapeake, the Susquehanna has not suffered the

2. These chemicals also are contained in industrial and municipal sewage treatment plant discharges.

3. Phosphorous has a low level of solubility and a strong ability to bind to sediments, so much of the phosphorous arrives attached to eroded soils. Nitrogen, on the other hand, is highly soluble and can leach into ground water in addition to combining with surface runoff.

ill effects of agricultural abuse. It is a clean river, a fact attributable to its volume. But once the water hits the shallow headwaters of the bay, the nutrients settle out to do their dirty work. The nitrogen and phosphorus fuel *eutrophication,* a term that translates as "nourishing well." In this instance, however, it produces an undesirable effect: the rapid growth of algae that prevent light from reaching underwater vegetation. When the algae die, they sink to the bay floor and decay, consuming the oxygen needed by all living organisms. At times the bay is so depleted of oxygen that bottom-dwelling species, like clams and oysters, cannot survive.

The nation's agricultural activities came late to environmentalists' attention, avoiding much of the public scrutiny and regulatory oversight directed toward other industries since the 1960s. It was easy to see or smell the emissions from smokestacks, sewage lines, and industrial outfall pipes, so-called point-source pollution. Runoff from farmland is different. Like chemicals washing off urban streets or falling in the form of acid rain, this nonpoint-source pollution was largely overlooked in initial regulatory strategies.

Nor was there popular support for tackling agricultural pollution, in large part because farmers warned that regulation of their activities would raise the price of food or, even worse, drive them off the land. No politician wanted to be blamed for increasing the price of Wonder Bread.

The ratio of expenditures targeted toward the readily identifiable polluters in the Susquehanna watershed mirrored national trends. About $3.3 billion was spent in the two decades after 1972 on point-source pollution projects—primarily new sewage-treatment plants—in the Chesapeake and Susquehanna basins. (Many millions more were spent by private industries to reduce their discharges.) By contrast, only $150 million to $200 million was spent on controlling nonpoint sources of pollution, including the primary polluter, farmland.

While the massive point-source investments produced some reduction in the flow of nutrients to the bay, they did not come close to achieving what scientists regarded as improvements critical to the bay's restoration.[4] So the experts turned their attention to the role of nonpoint-source pollution, especially that coming from the bay's tributaries. And when it comes to delivering water to the Chesapeake, the Susquehanna has no rival.

"Unless the Susquehanna is cleaned up, it doesn't matter what we do in all the rest of the tributaries of the Chesapeake," says Alvin R. Morris,

4. One notable success was achieved by bans on the sale of phosphate detergents in Maryland, Virginia, the District of Columbia, and Pennsylvania. By 1992, the amount of phosphorous in the bay had declined by 39 percent from 1985 levels.

director of the water management division of the Environmental Protection Agency's regional office, who spent more than a decade overseeing the bay cleanup effort. "If the Susquehanna remains untended, we aren't going to make it."

As the 1980s began, there slowly evolved a new view of the river and bay—a single ecosystem, inextricably linked, for better or for worse. Nowhere would this union have a greater impact than Lancaster County.

There is much in common between the watermen of the Chesapeake Bay and the farmers of Lancaster County. For centuries both have depended on the goodness of nature to provide, and the bay and the land have been extremely generous. Yet rarely have the two glimpsed each other's worlds.

On a cold February day, the opportunity to do so arose for a group of watermen and two members of Lancaster County's Amish community. The Amishmen were historian and farmer Gideon L. Fisher and Stephen Stoltzfus, who farms fifty-two acres near Bird-in-Hand. For them, the decision to travel to Tilghman Island on Maryland's Eastern Shore was a difficult one. Their religion discourages acts that draw attention to oneself, and both men would be called upon to make brief speeches to those in attendance. Stoltzfus said later that he chose to participate because he believed the information he could share might be useful to others. He already knew something of the bay's history and problems, having read James Michener's *Chesapeake* several years before. But he also studied a variety of reports on the bay and the cleanup before journeying south.

Even so, as he stood talking with the watermen—his black suit and long beard in stark contrast to their flannel shirts and baseball caps advertising beer or shotgun shells—Stoltzfus discovered their common interests. "The water is to them like the soil is to us," he said after the meeting. "Their oyster crop determines what kind of Christmas they have and, for us, it is the soil and the weather." Enchanted by what he saw, he said that the next time he visited the Chesapeake he wanted to tour it aboard a skipjack.

In the early 1960s, the men who drew their harvests from the bay began to witness a troubling decline in their catches. Originally dismissed as one of the bay's periodic "natural cycles," the decline slowly revealed itself to be something quite different. Underwater grasses, a reliable barometer of the health of the bay, had all but disappeared in many areas of the Chesapeake. And that was before the devastation wrought by the tons of sediments washed down the Susquehanna in 1972 by Tropical Storm Agnes.

At the time, management of the Chesapeake was primarily a state matter, and Maryland and Virginia rarely saw eye to eye on their responsibilities. As they bickered, the bay's condition worsened. Oxygen levels in places were extremely low, and the catches of pollution-sensitive species such as oysters and rockfish dwindled. While the bay still seemed bountiful to the casual observer, the changes were alarming. "Maybe society doesn't care whether it catches bluefish or rockfish," said a Maryland environmental official who worked on bay problems. "But what that means is eventually they won't be able to catch *any* fish."

Finally, in 1975, members of Congress—many of whom spent their weekends on the bay, or savored its crabs, rockfish, and oysters—declared the Chesapeake a national resource and authorized a $27-million study to determine the state of its health. The huge amount of data collected during the seven-year project painted a picture that, although obvious now, had eluded officials for decades: the health of the bay is determined by events that occur even in the farthest reaches of its drainage area. What happens in one part of this system can affect things elsewhere.

Pennsylvania has no shoreline on the Chesapeake, and it initially was an unwilling partner in both the Chesapeake Bay study and early planning for a basin-wide recovery program. Several participants recall that the Pennsylvania representative often fell asleep at meetings in the early 1980s and finally stopped attending altogether.

Stymied by the lack of interest in Harrisburg, and alarmed by the continued decline of the bay, a small group of Maryland citizens, led by Frances Flanigan of Baltimore, headed north in 1982 to present their plea to what they hoped would be a receptive audience: the farmers of Pennsylvania. Flanigan, a veteran of bay issues, carefully chose her most effective weapon: statistics on the amount of topsoil and fertilizer carried from Pennsylvania farms into the bay. "She said it was our *money* washing down those creeks," said George Wolff, a respected and successful Lebanon County farmer, who became one of Flanigan's most valuable allies. Wolff is well connected in both the agricultural community and in Harrisburg; more important, his devotion to the land and the environment is unswerving, almost religious—a fact he traces back to his Pennsylvania Dutch heritage.

Flanigan's message about wealth washing away was not lost on the conservative farmers of central Pennsylvania. With Wolff's assistance, she buttonholed every agricultural group she could find on the lower Susquehanna and repeated it. As more and more members of the farming community got involved, lawmakers in Harrisburg began to pay attention.

Other bay advocates were active elsewhere, and finally their cumulative efforts paid off. In 1983, in a historic ceremony, the governors of Maryland, Pennsylvania, and Virginia, as well as the administrator of the U.S. Environmental Protection Agency and the mayor of Washington, D.C., signed the first of what would become several agreements to address the problems of the bay with watershed-wide programs. Attention soon focused on the Susquehanna and—very quickly—on manure. Lancaster County's efforts to solve its agricultural problems were about to be shifted to a larger forum.

Seated in the kitchen of his farmhouse, where pigs are the dominant decorative motif, Harlan Keener concedes, "Farmers are the source of the problem and the answer to the problem." His own farm generates as much waste as some of the small villages in the county, and he could not come close to disposing all of it on the 245 acres he and his sons still cultivate. That, of course, is the serious side-effect of the growth of intensive agriculture in Lancaster County and the concurrent loss of tillable acreage.

Each year the livestock of Lancaster County produce 4.9 million tons of manure. If all that manure was applied to the available cropland in the county, it would mean as much as 17.7 tons per acre, an amount far in excess of the land's ability to absorb it. By comparison, farmland elsewhere in the Susquehanna Valley receives an average of 1.47 tons of manure per acre. A farmer with a large livestock herd and a small number of acres under cultivation faces a supply-and-demand imbalance of enormous proportions. While there are farmers in the county in need of manure, they are outnumbered by those with huge excesses. (Even so, a few farmers import sewage sludge from Philadelphia to apply to their fields, and many add commercial fertilizers in addition to manure.)

As herd sizes grow and tilled acreage shrinks, the surplus is not likely to disappear. "There's just one sure way to get less manure," Amish historian Gideon Fisher is fond of saying. "Shoot the cow."

Until recently, manure management was left to the discretion of the farmer. Few were as enlightened as Harlan Keener. Before expanding his livestock herd, he read everything he could find on the subject of animal waste. He sought assistance from federal and state agricultural experts, but they had little useful advice. The Europeans and Chinese had tackled the problem, notes Keener; Americans had not accorded it a high priority. The only advice offered by state environmental officials, he says, was this: "If anything goes wrong, we told you so."

Keener spent $225,000 to install waste-digesting equipment, which heats the liquid manure and extracts methane gas. The gas provides more than enough power to run his massive hog barns; he sells the excess to the local utility company. With the methane removed, the odor of the manure is reduced and it can be stored in open-air ponds. One large pond sits near his son's home.

In the spring, Keener invites farmers who need manure to pump it from his ponds and spray it on their land. Demand for the fertilizer is so high that he cannot fill all the requests. That gave him an idea. He plans to establish a manure brokerage, linking farmers who have excess animal wastes with those who need it. "They have them in Europe," he says. "Why not here?" The only reason no one else has done something so logical, he explains with a little smile forming, is that "farmers are a lot like married couples— they don't communicate with each other."

"We don't have too much manure in Lancaster County," he adds. "It's just not in the right places."

Many people would argue that there *is* too much. To make their case, they'd have to go no farther than the 188-square-mile Conestoga Creek watershed, which contains the bulk of Lancaster County's best farmland. Nowhere does the level of nutrient runoff surpass that from the Conestoga. Farmers there apply twice as much manure to their land as those along any other tributary of the Susquehanna. And they often add commercial fertilizers in addition to livestock wastes. This practice has taken its toll, not only in the Chesapeake Bay but also in the farmers' backyards. When rain falls on their fields, the resulting pungent brew washes into creeks and streams, or trickles down through the limestone rocks to the ground water below.[5]

Today, nearly half the private water supplies in Lancaster County, serving 35,000 homes and businesses, carry traces of fertilizers or pesticides. Conestoga Creek, which supplies public drinking water to Lancaster City, Ephrata, and several other communities, routinely exceeds federal health limits on nitrates, which, like herbicides, remain in the water even after treatment. Some residents of the county are advised not to drink their tapwater because of the amount of nitrates.[6]

5. Almost all of the manure is in liquid form because the easiest way to clean the sprawling livestock sheds is by hosing them out with water. The liquid manure runs off into creeks or drainage ditches. It also often overflows holding tanks and poorly constructed retention basins.
6. Fecal coliform bacteria from human waste also have been detected in many drinking water supplies, leaking into wells from thousands of improperly sited septic systems, many connected to new homes in crowded subdivisions.

Of all drainage basins in Pennsylvania, the Conestoga watershed was deemed to be the hardest hit by such agricultural pollution. In 1981, the Conestoga was chosen as one of twenty streams for study and corrective action under the federal Rural Clean Water Program, and one of only two nationally where both surface and groundwater problems were studied. At the time, few of the 1,000 farms squeezed in along the upper Conestoga used so-called best-management practices, such as manure storage and contour plowing, which minimize nutrient runoff and erosion problems. Manure applications occurred year-round.

Researchers recall one instance when manure was applied to frozen ground just before a rainstorm; the resultant runoff constituted 80 percent of the full year's recommended nitrogen discharge from that farm. On another field, hydrologist Patricia Lietman of the U.S. Geological Survey measured 400 pounds per acre of nitrogen within the top four feet of soil, the root zone for corn. This was in the fall after the year's corn crop had been harvested, and amounted to enough nitrogen to grow at least two more corn crops without requiring an ounce more fertilizer. Experts believe that even if no additional applications of nitrogen were made to the soil here, it would take two or three decades for the chemical to work its way out of the aquifer.

Although many farmers along the Conestoga have been slow to accept the need to alter their farming methods, the worsening water quality has helped change their minds. "If the cows won't drink out of the creek anymore, the farmers get concerned," said Lietman. In the decade she and others worked on the Conestoga, subtle improvements were detected in water quality, but none so significant as to produce a rush of farmers eager to sign up for best-management practices. "We'd like to be able to show the farmer fish in his creek," she says, but knows that won't happen soon. It will take years to clean up the Conestoga, and funding for the Rural Clean Water Program there has run out.

It was the water-quality issue that stirred many Lancaster County farmers to action, including Stephen Stoltzfus, who raises several dozen Holsteins and 12,000 laying hens in Leacock Township on land acquired by his family in 1823. Nearly 95 percent of the water in the township contains high levels of nitrates—often exceeding federal health standards by three or four times.[7] Farmers there—most of whom, like Stoltzfus, are Amish—have noticed a decline in dairy-herd production and livestock reproduction and many blame it on the pollution.

7. Nitrogen combines with oxygen to produce nitrate.

While not harmful to human adults, nitrates are considered a health risk for infants and possibly for young livestock. Once ingested by human or animal, nitrate metabolizes into nitrite, which in turn is absorbed into the hemoglobin, rendering the bloodstream incapable of carrying oxygen. In humans this can cause the "blue baby" syndrome, and farmers fear a similar effect on their animals. So far there is nothing but anecdotal evidence that they are right.

The contaminated water troubles farmers not just for practical reasons, but for deeply moral ones. Not only do they depend on the land for their livelihoods, but many—as Stoltzfus explains—also believe that "God made us temporary stewards of this garden," and as such they are obligated to improve it, just as their ancestors did. "We looked into the future and saw a need to change," continues Stoltzfus, who has five sons farming in the county.

As the result of an encounter his son Samuel had, "a lightbulb went on in my head," Stoltzfus says, and that started him working to perfect his own solution to the nutrient problem. Samuel Stoltzfus and his wife, Ada, operate a small greenhouse on their farm in southern Lancaster County near the Maryland line. One day, a customer asked to buy some manure from their compost pile to use as fertilizer for the plants she had just purchased. Ada Stoltzfus sent the woman home with as much free compost as she wanted; soon other customers were making similar requests and Ada was cheerfully filling them.

Composting involves mixing manure and household or garden wastes with other biodegradable materials, such as straw, fodder, or even shredded newspaper, which is now increasingly used as animal bedding. The dry materials absorb the liquids, bind up chemicals such as nitrogen, and create a stable fertilizer easy to store and apply when it can do the most good. Compost has been used to improve soils for centuries. It holds a special appeal for Stephen Stoltzfus because it can lessen the manure-management problems plaguing his Amish community without relying on technology.

The "lightbulb" he refers to is a compost bay, forty-eight feet long and four feet wide, with twelve-foot-high sides topped by rails, which he and several others designed and built. A chisel plow was mounted on wheels and suspended from the rails into the compost bay to turn the materials and speed decomposition. Stoltzfus is confident it will be enthusiastically accepted by other farmers, who have heard about the project through the Amish community's highly efficient grapevine. "We already have a fifteen-person waiting list" of farmers who want to buy the composters, Stoltzfus said with a smile.

One reason for such interest is that people in the Old Order Amish and Mennonite communities know that nutrient management will soon be a legal requirement. The Plain Sect farmers, with an aversion to government involvement in their daily lives, hope to be ready with their own acceptable responses to whatever Harrisburg or Washington may require. They also have come to recognize that, unchecked, the waste problem will threaten their ability to live on and farm this bountiful land.

The future of farming in Lancaster County may depend on such simple, sensible solutions. They captivate the imagination of such people as Alan Musselman of the Lancaster Farmland Trust; Don Robinson, who heads the adult farmer program for the Eastern Lancaster County School District; and young Amish farmers such as Samuel and Ada Stoltzfus.

It is a measure of the importance accorded agriculture in Lancaster County that school districts employ teachers whose full-time job is to educate farmers, long since departed from classrooms. Don Robinson, who began teaching a quarter-century ago, spends his days visiting the farms around New Holland in the Conestoga Valley, answering questions and offering technical advice. Here the farms are smaller than elsewhere in the county, just fifty to sixty acres, and many are owned by Old Order Amish and Mennonites.

Here, too, is where development and farming constantly nip at each other's heels. Stephen Stoltzfus's farm is a few miles from New Holland along busy Route 340, which is traveled each year by millions of tourists to Lancaster County, intent on getting to the must-see towns of Intercourse, Bird-in-Hand, and Paradise. Patrons at the red-sided Amish Barn Restaurant eat their pancakes or shoo-fly pie and stare out at the real thing across the road, which happens to belong to Stoltzfus. While there are occasional complaints about the daily activities of farming offending the sensitivities of the hordes of tourists, Stoltzfus tries to be understanding. "The restaurant owners want us to continue to farm," he says. "It helps their business."

To the west of the restaurant sits the Amish Country Motel; the Plain and Fancy Restaurant, with its parking lots for buses, is located to the east. Scattered amid the tourist establishments are working Amish farms and the support network that sustains them: a blacksmith, a horse-blanket laundry, a buggy repair shop, and a farm-implement store. Preservation of such enterprises is as necessary to the future of farming as protecting the farms themselves. In 1984, the county began a survey of the businesses and industries that serve its farm community and halted when the number topped 1,000. There may be no other place in America with such a densely concentrated agricultural service base, and that gives farmers an incentive to remain in Lancaster County. Accessibility is especially important because Plain Sect farmers cannot hop into a pickup truck and drive thirty miles for a spare part.

There is no wasted land in the Conestoga Valley, or much of Lancaster County, for that matter. Farmers plow right to the boundary, and the density of livestock in feed lots, hog barns, or poultry sheds can be quite high. The shortage of available farmland has forced residents to make choices: to leave and farm elsewhere; to open small businesses, such as machine repair, carpentry, or metalworking, on the farms themselves; or to find other forms of work. A growing number of the 16,000 Amish and Mennonites in Lancaster County now have nonfarm jobs, some at the new woodworking plants or poultry-packing houses that have sprung up along the back roads, others in jobs at great distances from their families. Many have moved up the Susquehanna, to Snyder, Union and Centre counties. Church leaders worry about the consequences of cultural integration, and the necessity for one or more members to "work away," as it is known, is stressful for the close-knit Old Order communities.

In seeking answers to the many problems confronting the farmers of the Conestoga Valley, Don Robinson looked in the past and found what he thinks is a sure-fire solution: fruits and vegetables. Inviting a visitor to accompany him, Robinson climbs into his Toyota for a farm tour and sales talk that at times takes on a missionary fervor.

Once the Conestoga Valley was the market basket for Philadelphia, supplying the city with premium dairy products, vegetables, and fruits, delivered from the backs of the high-sided Conestoga wagons built by the German farmers to ferry their goods over rugged roads. The soil and climate of Lancaster County were ideally suited for growing a host of food crops, and the tradition of large families guaranteed the necessary labor to plant, tend, and harvest what they raised. With the exception of the mode of getting the goods to market, none of that has changed over the years.

Today, produce farming as Robinson envisions it offers two appealing advantages. It can be as profitable as intensive livestock farming, and instead of generating manure ensures a use for it. And it can be as low-tech as the individual grower wants it to be, which is a prerequisite for Plain Sect farmers. Greenhouses can range from flimsy wooden frames covered with plastic sheeting to sophisticated glass-enclosed structures. On this sunny

March morning, Robinson stops at an Amish farm and heads into the greenhouse he had encouraged the owner to build. There two young boys are tending tiny tomato and pepper plants. Seedling trays of impatiens, lettuce, geraniums, and petunias fill adjacent tables.

If there was any doubt about the economic prospects for this type of farming, it has been erased with the success of the Leola Produce Auction, which a dozen local farmers established as a cooperative business venture in 1985. Six days a week between May and Thanksgiving, farmers arrive with fruits, vegetables, and flowers from their own gardens for sale to wholesale dealers, or to each other to supply the hundreds of front-yard produce stands that line the busy roads in this part of the county. (Robinson jokingly calls one stretch of U.S. Route 322 north of Leola "Cantaloupe Alley.")

In the first year of operation, the auction grossed $500,000. Within five years, its annual receipts topped $5 million. Behind the large, open-sided auction shed, with its hitching posts and buggy parking area, Robinson dug a three-quarter-acre demonstration plot where he experiments with a variety of seeds, compost mixtures, and mulches. "I'm kind of learning, too," he says. But the test garden is vitally important to him, for it helps persuade farmers that they do not need large quantities of commercial fertilizers to grow abundant, top-quality crops.

Robinson admits that he was once a believer in the propaganda that for decades urged farmers to use chemical fertilizers heavily, often in addition to manure. "That's what the university research and [fertilizer] manufacturers said we should do." But the county's water-quality problems prompted Robinson and others to question the conventional wisdom. In recent years, commercial fertilizer consumption in this part of the county has sharply declined.

Robinson's enthusiasm for produce has struck a responsive chord among farmers in this area. "People used to grow tobacco here to pay the mortgage," he explains as he drives along a narrow road bordering Conestoga Creek. "It was a good cash crop that involved the whole family." While tobacco once earned the farmer $2,000 to $2,500 per acre, farmers who have planted tomatoes report gross revenues of $20,000 an acre. "You can't earn that kind of money unless you depend on your family to help you with the harvest," Robinson acknowledges. "But that's one thing in abundance here: families who work hard."

The growers haven't limited themselves to traditional crops. One area farmer whose tobacco field was destroyed by a spring hailstorm was approached by a wholesale produce buyer who asked if the farmer would be interested in growing bok choy for Chinese restaurants in New York City. The seeds were planted, the crop thrived, and that was the last of tobacco.

Ada and Samuel Stoltzfus also have recognized the booming market for specialty produce. While they jokingly claim to own "Old Mac-Donald's Farm," with horses, chickens, several dozen hogs, and assorted other animals, their real interest is in plants. Since they moved to their southern Lancaster County farm in 1985, they've been busy learning everything they can about horticulture. One wing of their small greenhouse is filled with dozens of varieties of culinary herbs—basil, sage, tarragon, thyme, chervil, bay, parsley, and rosemary. In the greenhouse work area one day, Ada sat thinning seedlings as a yellow-orange canary sang cheerfully from its cage overhead. Samuel showed a visitor the tables of herbs while at the same time trying unsuccessfully to keep a black-and-white kitten from reaching the trays of catnip. They dream of someday expanding their production of herbs and flowers, and possibly growing organic vegetables. For now, the young Stoltzfuses concentrate on raising tomatoes and bell peppers, which they plant and harvest themselves or sell to other farmers for planting.

To better market the fruits and vegetables, Samuel Stoltzfus and others formed the Dutch Country Growers Cooperative in 1986. The organization soon grew to twenty-five members. "We've made some mistakes," he says, but notes that these have been balanced out by major successes. The quality of the cooperative's produce has earned it an excellent reputation with buyers. "I know some of our peppers have gone to Florida and Boston and Pittsburgh," Stoltzfus tells his visitor. "And to Cincinnati," calls out Ada from her end of the greenhouse.

William Penn authored the first farm report for Pennsylvania in 1685, noting that the four-year-old colony already was producing wheat, rye, oats, hemp, flax, tobacco, peas, beans, cabbage, peaches, melons, grapes, and other foodstuffs. The next year, he wrote that it had developed a thriving export trade in grain, tobacco, skins, and furs, and that the colony's farmers had begun to raise cattle, hogs, horses, chickens, ducks, and turkeys. Penn's reports served more than one purpose. In them, he urged his colonists to make Pennsylvania self-sufficient in its food production and to avoid dependency on a single crop, such as the tobacco that dominated the colonies to the south. And Penn engaged in some shrewd marketing: as his glowing descriptions of the colony's fertile soils spread throughout Europe, immigrants flocked to Pennsylvania, seeking the opportunity to own and cultivate this rich land.

Some of them had been among the best farmers of the Old World, those whose ancestors had tended the rich limestone soils of the Upper Rhine Valley for centuries. The first German settlers came a mere two years after Penn established his colony; others followed in a steady stream. It was said of these farmers that they could judge the composition of the soil merely by looking at the trees on the land. Stands of oak, maple, hickory, beech, and particularly black walnut signaled the same productive soils they had known in Europe. From Philadelphia, they followed the broad limestone valleys that arc across Pennsylvania from the Delaware River to the Susquehanna and beyond. And they found no better land than that drained by the Conestoga and Pequea Creeks.

It was the Conestoga that proved most alluring to the early settlers. Unlike the Susquehanna, it could be made navigable—and was, by five or more dams along its eighty-mile length. Those dams also powered mills that ground the colonists' grain. Today, similar dams provide electrical power to adjacent farms. Also in contrast to the big river, the Conestoga was accessible, meandering invitingly through gently rolling countryside. Steep bluffs and rocky outcroppings rendered the Susquehanna of little use to the newcomers here.

The first farms were deeded along the Pequea in 1710 and ranged in size from 265 acres to more than 1,000. Within a decade, there was very little land to be had along either creek. Twelve hundred Swiss, Germans, and Palatines had settled in the vicinity by 1724.[8]

Five years later, when the new county of Lancaster was carved from the western portion of Chester County at the behest of John Wright and his fellow Quakers in Wright's Ferry, 130,400 acres already were under cultivation and farmers were producing surpluses. Into their wagons they loaded grain, produce, or dairy products and set out on the sixty-mile trip to Philadelphia for market days. (The city dwellers grumbled that the Lancaster Countians arrived so well equipped that they had no need to spend a penny during their visits. Their commodious covered wagons even provided a comfortable place to sleep.) The settlers on the rich limestone soils along the west side of the Susquehanna made similar trips south to Baltimore, strengthening the economic ties between Maryland and York, Cumberland, and Adams counties.

8. Their prosperity caused some in the provincial government to fear that Philadelphia's dominance of the affairs of the colony would soon be usurped. Indeed, Lancaster City *would* temporarily replace Philadelphia as the state capital when the government fled advancing British troops in 1777. Later, it would vie to become the permanent seat of state government, ultimately losing out to Harrisburg in 1810.

In 1742, when King George II granted a charter creating the City of Lancaster, he also decreed that a market be operated by the city "forever." Two and a half centuries later, Lancaster's Central Market remains a showcase for the county's abundance. On market days in late summer, stalls in the vaulted brick market in the heart of the city overflow with celery, apples, peaches, beans, plums, tomatoes, squash; other stands purvey hams, sausages, cuts of beef, plump chickens and ducks, as well as the handiwork of those who live on the farms—flowers, pretzels, apple butter, cider, herbs, pies, bread, cakes, ice cream, and jam.

The early Germans brought more than farming skills to their new land. Unlike others who came to America, they chose their land intending to remain. This was not a temporary stop on the way to some new frontier; they meant their farms to be the homestead for present and future generations. That explains why many Lancaster County farmers can trace the title to their land in an uninterrupted chain to the first family member who plowed it. For such people, farming was not an occupation but a way of life. It still is.

The Germans soon were joined by members of the Anabaptist religious sects—Mennonites, Amish, and Brethren—whose unconventional beliefs in adult baptism and nonresistance made them outcasts in Europe. Over the years, they had been evicted from their prosperous farms in Switzerland and Germany and forced to resettle on poor, inhospitable ground. There they learned the importance of enhancing the soils with animal wastes, of irrigation, and of careful stewardship of the ground they tended. Believing that the soil was a gift of the Lord, they also believed that to steal its fertility was to steal from God.

Early travelers through the colonies wrote frequently of the industrious Germans and Swiss, taking careful note of the differences between their farms and those of immigrants from the British Isles. The Germans, they observed, carefully cleared their fields of trees; the English merely girdled the trees and allowed them to die, or left stumps in the ground—a practice that made cultivation difficult. The Germans practiced crop rotation; the English did not. George Washington, an enlightened farmer in his own right, wrote extensively about the husbandry practiced on these German farms.

The Germans also devoted great care to their livestock, building massive stone barns and fences for the animals, while most other farmers allowed theirs to range free year-round. The German priorities weren't lost on cartographer and natural historian Lewis Evans, who toured the countryside of Pennsylvania in 1753. "It is pretty to behold our back Settlements where the barns are large as pallaces, while the owners live in log hutts; a sign tho of thriving farmers . . . How much we are indebted to the Germans for the Oeconomy that they have introduced and how serviceable they are in an infant colony."

Because his animals were confined, the German farmer had access to the manure they produced. With this he mixed straw, corn husks, and other refuse and each spring plowed it into the soil, an annual practice continued well into the twentieth century—until the volume of waste necessitated more frequent applications. "Everything about his farm shows order and good management in all that concerns the care of the land," wrote Johann David Schoepf, a German surgeon and natural scientist who spent seven years in America after the Revolution.

Manure often was scarce, and farmers soon began applying limestone, which provided longer benefits and was readily available.[9] A visitor to the farms of the Pequea Valley in 1754 found "on every farm a lime kiln and the land adapted for the best of wheat."

Such careful management was not common everywhere, and by 1840 many Pennsylvania farmers were producing just half of what they had once grown. "Apparently they looked upon the soil as a bank on which drafts could be drawn indefinitely without diminishing the capital," wrote Pennsylvania agricultural historian Stevenson W. Fletcher.

The desire to increase production spurred interest in soil supplements— particularly exotic ones.[10] But these additives were not always what they

9. Even the large dairy farms around Philadelphia in the late 1700s could not generate enough waste to replenish their cropland, and as the soils were depleted, some farmers began to search for substitute fertilizers. Richard Peters, a Philadelphia judge considered by George Washington to be the most astute farmer in Pennsylvania, seized upon the gypsum blocks that were disposable ballast in the ships that docked in the city. These he crushed and applied to his land. Thousands of tons of gypsum quarried from deposits in western New York were floated down the Susquehanna on rafts and arks, with 6,000 tons reported in 1812 alone. While this so-called land plaster enriched the soil, its effects were short-lived.

10. For several decades, American agriculture was seized by the guano craze. The popularity of guano, dried and pulverized droppings of South American sea birds, swept farming communities after the first shipment arrived in this country in 1842 and its benefits were widely, and wildly, promoted. Although it was expensive, guano's virtues were so highly touted that farmers couldn't get enough and prices rose accordingly. A ton of guano sold for $40 in 1850, peaking at $75 during the Civil War, with the customary rate of application being 300 to 400 pounds per acre. Guano dealers, many of whom operated out of Baltimore, soon discovered that they could enhance their own yields by mixing the bird droppings with ash or dirt, without fear of detection. So rampant did the sale of adulterated guano become that in 1855 the Pennsylvania Agricultural Society asked the legislature to create the position of State Inspector of Guano. The lawmakers ignored the request, and the need for such a

were reputed to be, nor did farmers understand the specifics of their application. Out of frustration they sought the advice of a new kind of entrepreneur, the soil chemist, who, for a fee, promised to analyze soil needs and recommend the proper fertilizers. More often than not the product happened to be one in which the self-styled chemist held a financial interest. That prompted the farming community to seek protection from phony experts pushing worthless products. In 1879 Pennsylvania began to license fertilizer manufacturers and to require certification of the contents of their products. Until then, farmers had been forced to rely on their noses to make that determination; usually the rankest smelling was deemed to be the most effective. Reassured about what they were buying, Pennsylvania farmers began their love affair with commercial fertilizers.

The proper use of fertilizer has always been a hard question for farmers, for it is a low-cost insurance policy of sorts. Given the choice of using too much or too little, many understandably opt for the former. The prices of fertilizers, as well as those for pesticides and herbicides, remained low for decades, and it could seem foolhardy not to apply extra amounts just for good measure. That was the view promoted by available experts, some of whom also happened to be the manufacturers and dealers who marketed the products. State and federal agricultural agents also espoused the increased use of chemicals to keep America's farm yields high.

This captivation with agricultural chemistry was challenged in 1962 by Rachel Carson, who wrote in her classic *Silent Spring:*

> The chemicals to which life is asked to make its adjustment are no longer merely the calcium and silica and copper and all the rest of the minerals washed out of the rocks and carried in rivers to the sea; they are the synthetic creations of man's inventive mind, brewed in his laboratories, and having no counterparts in nature.

Indiscriminate use of chemicals was upsetting the balance of nature, Carson warned.

Even without chemicals, farming changes the environment. Soil erosion has longed plagued farmers, and Pennsylvania's were no exception. The problem is especially acute in some areas of southern Lancaster Coun-

---

public servant passed as the market for guano collapsed, a victim of its own corruption.

Farmers then turned to superphosphate, a fertilizer made of bones treated with sulphuric acid. To supply the demand, buffalo bones were shipped in from the West, and in 1860 a shipment of human bones, from the victims of the 349-day siege of Sevastopol during the Crimean War, arrived in the United States for processing into fertilizer.

ty, where erosion losses in excess of seventeen tons per acre have been measured.

The county has the state's worst record on soil loss. So serious is the sedimentation rate along the lower Susquehanna that two of the three reservoirs on the lower Susquehanna are filled to capacity with nutrient-laden sediments and the third is nearly full. Authorities worry that a major storm could release even more sediments than the 22 million tons that were flushed from behind the dams and into the bay during Tropical Storm Agnes. Such a release would also carry with it millions of pounds of nitrogen and phosphorous.

One often-cited reason for Lancaster County's soil loss problem is the refusal of members of the Old Order communities to participate in government-funded soil conservation programs. Another reason is their sense of aesthetics. A third is the failure among agricultural agents to accord conservation a high priority. "The Plain People think the ground must look like a garden before you begin cropping," explains Robert Gregory, head of the county soil conservation district. As a result, many don't plant winter ground covers that could hold the soils in place, and they refuse to allow stubble from the fall crops to remain because it gives a field what Gregory calls a "woolly" appearance. "We often say in Lancaster County that conservation is not pretty," he says. Today, farmers are encouraged to use contour strips, terraces, and grassy buffers in fields. To persuade Plain Sect members to follow suit, teachers like Don Robinson often are utilized. "I'm not government, I'm an educator," Robinson says.

Contour farming—in which fields are planted in strips across the slope of the land to minimize runoff—had its start in Pennsylvania, according to historian Stevenson W. Fletcher. As early as 1865, farmers in rugged Lycoming County realized that the only way they could preserve the soil was to alter the manner in which they plowed their fields and planted their crops. It was not until the 1930s, however, that the federal government began to encourage farmers to adopt soil-conservation methods, including strip farming. And it was not until 1985, with passage of the Food Security Act, that use of such methods became a prerequisite for receiving federal farm aid.[11]

---

11. At that time, about 3 billion tons of topsoil were washing or blowing off American farms each year. While one ton of topsoil, spread over one acre, is the thickness of a sheet of paper, erosion involves more than just the loss of productive earth. Prior to enactment of the 1985 farm bill, one conservation group estimated that eroding sediments from farmland caused an estimated $6 billion annually in indirect costs, such as dredging of rivers and lakes and additional water treatment expenditures.

The Food Security Act also included two other important changes in agricultural policy: a commitment to reduce reliance on agricultural chemicals and a shift away from the traditional view that high yields were the ultimate measure of a good farmer. While targeted primarily at the mega-farms of the Midwest and West, all three provisions had an impact on the small farms of Lancaster County.

In 1978, when Michael W. Brubaker graduated from college with a degree in agronomy, he took a look at the future of his family's business—fertilizer sales—and decided "things looked pretty bleak." On the other hand, he recalls, "Growers were starving for more on-farm, independent consultation." So Brubaker, a Lancaster County native, decided to provide it.

Drawing from his father's customer lists, he offers farmers sophisticated soil and manure analysis, crop rotation advice, insect and disease control plans—all on computerized data sheets. Starting with just three fields, his consulting firm now has more than 500 clients who farm nearly 200,000 acres.

What Brubaker believes separates him from the traditional agronomist is his independence. "I'm not pushing any product or practice," he says. In fact, like the soil chemists of a century ago, many consultants advising farmers are in the employ of chemical companies. Only recently have university-affiliated agricultural agents begun to eschew the traditional view that "more is better" when it comes to the use of pesticides and fertilizers.

For Brubaker, the "more is better" view has no currency. "We're no longer just stressing increased yields, but how to increase the profitability on a farm, how to assess the environmental risks of our present farming practices and how to lessen the environmental risks of farming," he explained.

In the evenings, when he is not in his office, Mike Brubaker grapples with farming from behind a different desk. He serves as an elected supervisor for Warwick Township, home to 200 farms in northeastern Lancaster County. In 1988 the township enacted the county's first manure-management ordinance. It requires farmers who want to expand their livestock by 10 percent or more to submit a plan to township officials demonstrating an environmentally sound way to manage the additional manure. Not surprisingly, the measure drew opposition when it was first proposed, and again after some requests were denied. Brubaker said he and others argued that the ordinance would protect the township's farms by ensuring that they remained good neighbors.

Persuading farmers to change their ways is not an easy task. "It's amazing how many times you'll ask someone why he is doing something and he'll look you right in the face and say, 'Because that's the way my father and my grandfather did it, and it worked,'" said Don Robinson. Mike Brubaker learned that lesson the hard way. "The first few times I went to a client's farm I had a list all drawn up of proposed changes without having first talked to the farmer himself. Now, we make changes as quickly as the farmer is comfortable."

The days when farming practices were pretty much up to the farmer alone are ending, a result not only of the Chesapeake Bay cleanup effort but also of concern about drinking water. This trend toward more regulation worries some, including Mike Brubaker, who notes that "the people who write laws don't own a pair of workboots." Even so, he is among the first to acknowledge that many farmers are open to criticism for the way they conduct their business.

Harlan Keener says his greatest fear is that "some wide-eyed kid just out of college is going to tell me how I can farm." Yet he and Mike Brubaker, who not so long ago fit Keener's description exactly, have a solid working relationship on a number of enterprises, including the new manure brokerage. They share a belief that farmers must assume most of the burden of correcting the problems they have created. They chafe, however, at the emphasis currently placed on agriculture while other polluters are overlooked. Keener points to East Hempfield Township, northwest of Lancaster City, as an example. Much of its farmland has been replaced by suburban sprawl, but the amount of nutrients emanating from the township remains high—the runoff from heavily fertilized lawns and gardens in the new subdivisions. "Farmers aren't as guilty as they've been portrayed," he says.

In the years since the 1983 Chesapeake Bay cleanup agreement was signed, vast amounts of data about the watershed and its problems have been compiled. That information led in 1987 to a second, far-reaching agreement that called for a 40 percent reduction in the flow of nutrients entering the bay and set the year 2000 as the deadline. Pennsylvania believed it could come close to that goal simply through strict nutrient-management programs on farms along the Susquehanna, and that is where it has concentrated its efforts.

In 1990, with the support of the state's farm community, a nutrient-management bill was introduced in the Pennsylvania legislature that would require all farms larger than ten acres to institute best-management practices within five years. That would encompass 90 percent of the state's

53,000 farms, and would substantially reduce runoff and erosion state-wide. Pennsylvania is the only jurisdiction in the Chesapeake watershed proposing to make nutrient controls mandatory.[12] Maryland and Virginia hope to meet their 40 percent reduction through voluntary programs, something many observers believe is unrealistic.

While agriculture remains the prime target in the bay cleanup, other sources of pollution have been identified in recent years. Among them is air pollution, which delivers substantial amounts of nitrogen to the watershed.[13] Airborne pollutants from automobiles and power plants may be reduced under federal regulations adopted in 1990, but it will take years to see results. Researchers also have determined that runoff from forest land, especially along the West Branch of the Susquehanna, is contributing sizable quantities of nutrients in the watershed. Finally, rapid population growth around the bay has significantly added to pollution levels.

Indeed, as Harlan Keener observes, responsibility for the problem isn't as clear-cut as once believed. Nevertheless, in the summer of 1992, when signers of the Chesapeake Bay agreement gathered in Annapolis to assess their progress and reevaluate strategies toward meeting the year-2000 goals, the reduction of agricultural runoff remained their number one priority. And they asserted that the bulk of that reduction would have to come from the Chesapeake's tributaries, particularly the Susquehanna. "Nutrient management, of course, is the key," Pennsylvania governor Robert Casey told the group.

Standing atop the hill overlooking his farm, Harlan Keener delights in what he sees. He tells the story of a young couple who moved from Pittsburgh, rented an attractive Victorian farmhouse on his property, and leased some land from him on which they keep two horses. "My son said he came upon them as they were out riding and he heard them singing at the top of their lungs 'This land is your land, this land is my land,'" recounts Keener with a smile. "I love this land, too." Before climbing back into his pickup, he pauses and offers one more thought: "I have one grandson, and I hope he farms here, too. It won't be easy. I told his father he'd better make sure the boy gets the best college education he can. Because by that time, he'll need it."

12. Although the bill was enacted by the state House in 1991, it stalled in the Senate.
13. Ironically, many of the large manure storage vats and storage lagoons constructed with federal Chesapeake Bay funds in Pennsylvania may be contributing to the problem. Nitrogen in the liquid manure volatilizes in the atmosphere and returns to earth in rain or snow.

Chapter Eight

Shad Restoration

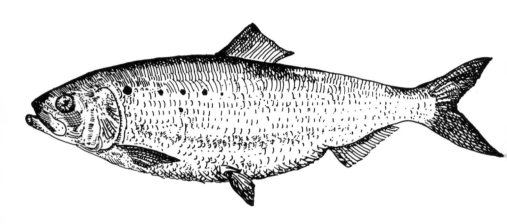

"You can't be half-hearted"

$\mathbf{D}$usk descends slowly on the Delaware River in late May, and this night six men wait impatiently for the darkness. Beside them at a boat-launching ramp on the rocky beach are two beat-up aluminum fishing boats into which the men are quietly loading their gear: galvanized tubs filled with orange gill nets, anchors, large gray rectangular plastic tubs, high-powered spotlights, and pole nets. Here on the riverside above the Pennsylvania village of Shawnee, a makeshift camp has been set up: two tripods holding Coleman lanterns, a rickety folding table and an odd assortment of kitchen utensils—colanders, bowls, and dishpans.

Out on the Delaware, fishermen wring what they can from the remaining daylight. In the shallows, two flycasters try one last time, unsuccessfully, and then gather their equipment and head up the hill toward their cars. One by one, the boaters reluctantly depart the river, leaving the cluster of men on the beach alone. Now their work is about to begin, for with the approaching darkness the river comes to life.

Among the group are Richard St. Pierre, a biologist with the U.S. Fish and Wildlife Service, and Dan Bourke and Bob Moase of the Pennsylvania Fish Commission.[1] This is Bourke's stretch of the Delaware; he has worked it for nearly two decades as a biologist. Moase, a fisheries manager on the Susquehanna River west of Wilkes-Barre, has come out of curiosity. With them are Andrew Gurzynski, a biologist for a private consulting firm, and two of Gurzynski's young helpers. Over the past two weeks, Gurzynski and his crew have been here almost every night.

The mood is upbeat. The water temperature is ideal and conditions on the river are deemed to be perfect. The men are here to collect eggs from the American shad *(Alosa sapidissima)*, which arrive each spring to spawn. Their task is one small component of a million-dollar-a-year program whose goal is to return this prized species to the Susquehanna River, once regarded by some as the greatest fish highway in the United States. In years

1. In 1991 the agency changed its name to the Pennsylvania Fish and Boat Commission.

gone by, shad sustained commercial fishing industries as far north as New York State. Annual catches in the millions of pounds were commonplace. These days, Dick St. Pierre has little doubt that the restoration project will succeed. The fish have begun to return in increasing numbers each year, more than have been on the Susquehanna in three generations. But others remain skeptical, convinced that the annual increases are inconsequential compared to what it would take to make the species self-sustaining once again on the Susquehanna.

The campaign to return shad to the river began in Pennsylvania as the Civil War was ending. In recent years it has inspired costly lawsuits and creative biology, political brinkmanship and hardnosed bargaining, all driven by a simple belief: humans broke the natural cycle that once brought the fish to the Susquehanna. Now humans must smooth the way for their return.

It is no easy task, for shad are among the most finicky of species. The effort entails raising them in a hatchery on a scale never attempted before. It also involves enhancing the shad's prospects in the wild, both by learning more of their habits and by improving their habitat, which will benefit other species as well. On both fronts, the challenges have been enormous, and success slow to materialize. "One thing about shad," says Dick St. Pierre, "you learn to be patient."

The American shad is an anadromous fish—one that spawns in fresh water, swims to sea where it grows to adulthood, then returns to the stream in which it was born to beget another generation.[2] It takes a shad three to five years out at sea to reach its full growth of about twenty inches and four to six pounds. But even after all that time, so strong is the homing instinct

2. All Atlantic Coast shad, including adults that survive spawning and newly hatched juveniles, migrate to the Gulf of Maine and the Bay of Fundy, arriving between July and September to feed and regain their strength—"pumping up for the winter," as Dick St. Pierre describes it. In the autumn, the adults ready to spawn head south to one of two major staging areas. One is located in the Hudson Canyon near Nantucket and the other is off Cape Hatteras and north Florida. It is this southern group that migrates to rivers as far north as the Susquehanna each spring. As water temperatures increase, the fish instinctively return to their spawning grounds, arriving at the St. Johns River in Florida as early as December. The rivers of the Carolinas have shad by February and March, and the fish reach the Chesapeake and Delaware bays by April or May. The northern group arrives later, filling the rivers of New York and New England. Post-spawning mortality among fish returning to the rivers of the far South is almost 100 percent, and biologists speculate it may be the result of the long distances the fish swim between the northern feeding grounds and the southern spawning rivers. Shad that travel the shorter distance to northern rivers may spawn as many as seven or eight times.

of these fish that they have been known to flail themselves to death against an obstacle blocking their path.

Shad once flourished in all Atlantic Coast rivers as far south as Florida, and in the 1800s shad was the most lucrative commercial catch taken by fishermen. In 1897 the total catch of shad on the Atlantic Coast amounted to 29.6 million pounds, with nearly 7.9 million pounds caught in the Chesapeake Bay alone. But the species has been declining for more than a century, in large part because of overfishing. By 1940, the total Atlantic Coast catch amounted to less than 10 million pounds, with the Chesapeake accounting for a third of that. And then even the rich fisheries of the Chesapeake experienced a severe drop in shad. In 1946, just a half-million pounds were caught on the bay, and by 1980—when a ban on shad fishing finally was imposed by the state of Maryland—biologists estimated that only about 20,000 *fish* had returned the prior spring.

Shad still migrate to the Chesapeake and the rivers of Maryland and Virginia. Many still head north seeking out the Susquehanna. But ten miles above the river's mouth, they encounter the nine-and-a-half-story concrete face of the Conowingo Dam and can proceed no further without human help.[3] The extent of that assistance—or even the obligation to provide it—has been a point of bitter contention for years, and it took a lengthy struggle to clear the way. In 1987, a federal agency declared that the shad must be given access to the river of their origin. For those who believe that these and all other native species of fish belong on the Susquehanna, it was a moment of sweet triumph.

With the last of the fishermen gone from the Delaware, the crew on the beach stirs into action. Eleven gill nets, each 200 feet long and six feet deep, will be set parallel to the shore, anchored against the strong current by grappling hooks. The nets intended for females have a 6½-inch mesh; those for the males (which are smaller), 5½ inches. The gill nets are so efficient in entangling fish that their use by sportsmen is illegal in Pennsylvania.

At 9:15, in the now-full darkness, Dick St. Pierre gleefully announces, "It's spawning time! The ritual has begun!" Indeed, almost in the blink of an eye, the surface of the Delaware appears to be simmering. A low swishing noise, known among oldtimers as "washing," can be heard. Thousands

3. The Delaware River, on the other hand, contains no dams for most of its 390-mile length. Thus it still witnesses the rites of the spring migrations of shad, river herring, and the American eel.

of shad—some of which have been waiting here as long as two months for this moment—have begun to rise toward the surface to mate. Each adult female releases into the water some of the 200,000 to 300,000 eggs she carries. The males in turn release milt, which fertilizes any eggs it encounters in the current. They do this several evenings in a row, and while the process is haphazard, the female "only has to replace herself and one male for the species to survive," says St. Pierre. A quiet, dark-haired fisheries biologist, he has been coordinator of the Susquehanna River Anadromous Fish Restoration Project since 1977, and still has an endless fascination and respect for the habits of the *Alosa sapidissima.*

"I didn't know shad from shinola twenty years ago," he had admitted earlier in the evening. But as a graduate student at the Virginia Institute of Marine Science, St. Pierre became involved in a shad-restoration project there. In 1975 he joined the U.S. Fish and Wildlife Service, and two years later this project fell into his lap. Now as a one-man field station for his agency, he oversees the work of the Susquehanna River Anadromous Fish Restoration Committee—a group of representatives of highly disparate interests who are supposed to work together on behalf of shad. St. Pierre's job, he says, "is to keep an eye on what is a shared resource and must be managed as such." Interstate squabbles—and there have been plenty—are his to resolve.

The committee consists of representatives from the U.S. Fish and Wildlife Service, the Maryland Department of Natural Resources, the Pennsylvania Fish Commission, the New York Division of Fish and Wildlife, the Susquehanna River Basin Commission, and the four utilities that have dams on the lower Susquehanna—Pennsylvania Power and Light Company (Holtwood Dam), Philadelphia Electric Company (Conowingo Dam), York Haven Power Company, a subsidiary of Metropolitan Edison Company (York Haven Dam), and Safe Harbor Water Power Corporation, co-owned by Baltimore Gas and Electric Company and Pennsylvania Power and Light (Safe Harbor Dam). Simply keeping them all at the negotiating table has been a herculean task for St. Pierre, who observes with a modest grin, "We haven't come to blows yet."

Although the primary focus of the restoration effort is shad, other migratory species will also benefit from its work. One day, St. Pierre believes, striped bass, American eels, blueback herring, and alewives will again pass in great numbers up and downstream, along with the several varieties of shad that once swam in the Susquehanna. White perch will become more prevalent above Conowingo, he predicts, and the range of other species now on the river—walleye, bass, and bluegills—will increase.

In other words, says St. Pierre, the river will return to its natural state.

After the shad eggs are fertilized in the river, they sink to the bottom and, if conditions are favorable, hatch within three to eight days. The tiny shad, barely larger than pencil points, swim from the sandy flats and shallows to the middle of the stream, seeking plankton to eat and safety from predator fish. Here they grow at a rate of about an inch a month and await the drop in water temperature that signals the arrival of fall, when they will begin the long trip downstream to the ocean. It is a phenomenon that occurs in every river inhabited by shad.

By 9:35—just twenty minutes after spawning began—Andy Gurzynski is deftly maneuvering one of the aluminum boats between the narrow rows of nets with one hand while shining a high-powered spotlight onto the rapidly flowing water with the other. His helpers stand in the boat watching for shad. Once a fish is spotted, it is freed from the net and placed in a gray tub filled with river water. Soon it will die—but its genes may survive in dozens of offspring, many more than nature alone likely could provide.

The first fish of the night is an unusually small male, or buck, about three pounds. Then there is another male, followed by a female, whose fat belly shows she has yet to release her eggs. The same is true of the fourth, fifth, and sixth females pulled from the nets. Females that have already spawned are declared to be "hard," their sides now nearly concave. After spawning, many shad die of exhaustion, for they haven't eaten since leaving the ocean and the act of reproduction is stressful. The spotlight occasionally catches the pearly white belly or opalescent sides of a carcass as it drifts by on the current. Even in death the fish are beautiful. "Iridescent with a chrome sheen," says St. Pierre. "The taxidermist just can't catch it." Even if the shad has survived spawning, the encounter with the gill net will kill it, for the fish are so delicate that the loss of a single scale usually is fatal.

As Gurzynski returns his boat to shore, St. Pierre grabs a fat female shad from the tub, turns it sideways and gently pinches just behind the head, moving his fingers down the belly toward the tail. Eggs, the color and consistency of canned applesauce, flow from the fish into one of the waiting plastic dishpans. Milky white sperm from the males is obtained the same way, and floats atop the growing quantity of eggs in the pan until St. Pierre mixes it in with his forefinger. Once stripped of their eggs or sperm, the dazed shad are thrown into garbage cans that later will be hauled to a landfill. In the course of an evening, dozens of fish are discarded. St. Pierre acknowledges, "We do meet with some resistance from sportsmen because they know we're killing fish." But his project soon will be returning many more to the river.

Cell division starts within minutes of fertilization. In the meantime, the eggs are rinsed in river water to remove scales, blood, slime, and fecal material that can contaminate them. They are then placed in large buckets full of river water. Within an hour, the eggs have solidified into tiny crystal beads that glisten in the light of the Coleman lanterns. For the first twenty-four hours, these eggs are extremely hardy and can withstand most rigors; after that, even the slightest disturbance causes death.

In the wild, an estimated 96 percent of shad eggs die during their first twenty days, victims of spawn-eating fish, bad weather, or changes in water quality. But the eggs being taken from the fish this night had much better odds. Half or more would survive the trip to the hatchery, but once in the carefully controlled conditions there, 90 percent would make it through their first twenty days of life, when they are released.

Until recently, biologists had no idea about one other important statistic: the ratio of eggs required to ensure one returning adult. St. Pierre now calculates the number at 100,000 to 1. "That explains why they carry so many eggs," he says. "If they were chickens, they could get away with just laying one egg a day."

According to folk wisdom, the shad run begins as the first dogwood blooms, and ever since human beings have occupied the banks of the Susquehanna they have greeted the arrival jubilantly. Often it erased the threat of starvation. Early Native Americans carved stylized fish into the rocks along the lower end of the river, signifying the importance they accorded the many species, including shad, that found their way there. At the opposite end of the Susquehanna, Oneida Indians demonstrated their fishing techniques for Richard Smith as he traveled south from Otsego Lake in the spring of 1769: "They tye Bushes together so as to reach over the River, sink them with Stones and hawl them around by Canoes; all persons present including strangers, such is their laudable Hospitality have an equal Division of the Fish."

Word of the abundance of shad on the Susquehanna persuaded many Connecticut settlers to move to the Wyoming Valley in the 1760s and 1770s. In the years of vicious fighting over the land, Pennsylvanians routinely burned the Yankees' farms and destroyed their livestock, forcing the new arrivals to rely on the shad they netted from the river. Failing to drive out the Connecticut immigrants, marauding Pennsylvanians then destroyed the seines themselves. The Yankees replaced the nets and remained.

The carnage of the Yankee-Pennamite Wars—and the Revolutionary War—produced so many widows and orphans around what is now Wilkes-Barre that the first Sunday of the spring shad run became known as the "widow's haul." All of that day's catch was set aside for the misfortunates. One widow's haul, at a fishery located between Wilkes-Barre and Plymouth, produced 10,000 fish. In the stretch of the North Branch between Northumberland and Towanda there were at least forty permanent fisheries, narrow places where it was easy to lay a seine. The rights to those sites were bought, sold, and handed down among families like real estate. At Bloomsburg, the river surface actually bulged in springtime when the schools of shad made their way upstream. The only limit to the amount of shad a family could put away for the year was the persistent shortage of salt. One hundred shad usually could be traded for a bushel of salt if any was available.

Once, the size of the annual shad catches on the Susquehanna was staggering. In an 1881 issue of the *Bulletin of the United States Fish Commission*, a writer recalled one record catch of shad, herring, and rockfish (striped bass) fifty-four years earlier:

In the spring of 1827, Thomas Stump owned and operated the largest shad fishery in the United States, immediately below the [present] railroad bridge on the opposite side from Havre de Grace. At the mouth of the river his seine was laid across the river and down for miles along the shore below the village of Havre de Grace. A violent wind commenced, which put a stop for four days and nights to any further action with the seine, the wind blowing constantly down the river, and no shad could get past the seine. The wind at one o'clock on the fourth night changed and blew directly up the river, and by daylight the outer end of the seine had reached the windlass, one and a half miles from the railroad bridge. At eight o'clock one hundred wagons and carts that had congregated from Lancaster and Chester Counties were loading shad at $4.00 per hundred. Herring, rock, and other fish were thrown in without charge. Mr. Stump sent word for miles around Cecil County to farmers to get herring to manure their lands. It took three and one-half days to get the seine in shore; hundreds of wagon and cart loads of fish were put on lands as fertilizers from that one haul. Shad are not caught at this shore at the present. If my memory serves me right, Mr. Stump, computing the wagon and cart-loads, made the amount, in round numbers, 15,000,000 caught at that one haul.[4]

4. The abundance of shad in season was not celebrated universally. A history prepared to accompany Pennsylvania's fish exhibit at the 1893 World's Columbian Exposition in Chicago

It wasn't long, however, before such recordbreaking catches came to an end, for humans had begun to extract an additional toll on the river. Wastes from sawmills and coal mines commingled with discharges from tanneries and other industries to render the once-pristine streams black and stinking. But the single event blamed for ending the annual migrations occurred in 1840, when a ten-foot-high dam was built on the Susquehanna at Columbia to create a pond connecting the canals on either side of the river. The free-flowing Susquehanna was free no more.

As additional dams were erected, the numbers of fish returning to spawn dropped precipitously. That, in turn, set off a frenzy of fishing that all but eradicated shad and other species on the Susquehanna. In both Pennsylvania and Maryland, the river was lined with fish baskets and weirs that trapped anything and everything passing up or downstream. Drift nets clogged the lower portion of the river, and no one heeded the twelve-hour "close time" each Sunday when fishing supposedly was banned. When Pennsylvania sought support for limits on fishing hours and devices, Maryland demurred.

In 1866, the Pennsylvania legislature created the post of Commissioner for the Restoration of Inland Fisheries and assigned him just one mission: to restore migratory fish to the Susquehanna River. That meant shad. "A competent person" was to be chosen, according to the legislation. (He wouldn't be paid much, but was entitled to "fish at any time or any place with any device.") The "competent person" was Col. James Worrall, a former engineer on the state canal system. He wasted no time fulfilling his mandate. Worrall ordered the construction of fish passageways at the low canal feeder-dam at Columbia.

Worrall's annual reports to the state legislature proclaimed that the fish utilized these rudimentary passageways, but he appears to have been counting shad that weren't there. No one had yet designed a ladder the species could ascend. But Worrall and the three-member Pennsylvania Fish Commission, created in 1873, persevered. In 1883, the commission learned of a successful fishway used in Nova Scotia and contracted with the designer to build two at Columbia. So successful was the design that even while the ladder was being built, two black bass and a sunfish tried to ascend it.

In addition to enacting stringent regulations banning devices such as

---

reported that earlier in the century the master mechanics in Philadelphia and Pittsburgh fed their apprentices so much shad and other fish that some employees finally revolted. Ultimately, the apprentices gained a clause in their indentures limiting fish to two meals a week.

traps and weirs, the commissioners began a program of artificial propaga-
tion, setting up hatchery boxes directly in the Juniata River at Newport in
Perry County. The U.S. Fish Commissioner dispatched one of his employees to Pennsylvania to assist, and although the first year's effort was
plagued by extremes of weather, more than 3 million young shad were
released in the Susquehanna basin that year. The state Fish Commission
even acquired its own railroad car to ferry fish eggs around Pennsylvania.

It soon became clear, however, that no restoration effort could succeed
until limits on catches were imposed on the lower Susquehanna and in the
Chesapeake Bay. But politicians were unwilling to take that step, for commercial shad fishing still represented an important part of local economies
there.

Toward the end of the nineteenth century, shad season on the Susquehanna Flats—where the river flows into the Chesapeake Bay—still saw
frenzied activities on dozens of enormous rafts. Crews would spend weeks
each spring aboard the 300-foot-long floating factories, hauling in tons of
fish headed north. Records of the National Marine Fisheries Service for the
year 1889 report that more than 7 million pounds of American shad were
taken by commercial fishermen in Maryland alone. Millions more were
captured in the waters of Pennsylvania and New York. But those days
were numbered.

The turn of the century brought a host of changes in the lives of most
Americans. The age of the lightbulb and widespread use of electrical power
produced a scramble to build generating plants. The Susquehanna caught
many an entrepreneur's eye. Its final fifty-five miles, where it picks up speed
and drops over the fall line, tantalized engineers. Not only was the river
ripe for harnessing, but markets for the hydroelectric power were nearby.
In the face of such opportunities, the fate of a few fish seemed inconsequential.

In 1884, the Maryland legislature authorized the Susquehanna Water
Power and Paper Company of Harford County to acquire land for a dam at
the village of Conowingo, which in the language of the Susquehannock
Indians means "at the rapids." A small "wing" dam was constructed, only
partially obstructing the river. The project was sold to another corporation, the Susquehanna Power Company, which in 1905 began planning a
much larger dam on the site. Some 27,000 square miles of watershed
spread out above Conowingo, and the potential for electrical generation
from those waters appeared limitless and enticing.

But Susquehanna Power ran into financing problems, which ultimately delayed the project for over two decades. In the meantime, two other companies were generating electricity from the river. In 1904, the York Haven Water and Power Company completed a dam at the Conewago Falls, south of Harrisburg. Twenty-six feet high, it lit the small town of York Haven and a local paper company. In 1910, Pennsylvania Power and Light Company completed the Holtwood Dam. With a fifty-one-foot spillway and a distribution system capable of sending power to Lancaster and Baltimore, Holtwood was the largest dam in Pennsylvania at the time.

With financing finally in place, ground was broken at Conowingo in the spring of 1926 for a mile-wide concrete dam whose ninety-five-foot-high spillway would tower above the rocky shoals at its base.[5] Cost: $59 million. The Conowingo Dam was an engineering marvel of its day, second only to the hydroelectric development at Niagara Falls. When completed, its seven waterwheels could generate a total of 252,000 kilowatts of electricity—the largest capacity ever installed in a power plant at that time. Four more generating units would be added later, and all told, the hydro plant could generate electricity to supply 250,000 homes.

For more than two years, 3,800 men labored to impound the Susquehanna, living at the river's edge in segregated bunk houses and dining halls. In sheer size, Conowingo's generating units were the largest in the world, thirty-seven feet high, each weighing 250 tons. Each unit required 6,000 cubic feet, or 47,000 gallons, of water per second to develop full power.

Yet as the builders of the canal system and loggers on the West Branch had discovered a century earlier, that was the one thing the Susquehanna could not guarantee: a dependable supply of water. Spring brought floods; summers and autumns drought. Even the fifteen-mile-long reservoir behind the dam could not smooth out the radical fluctuations in water supply. Thus Conowingo was utilized by its owner, the Philadelphia Electric Company, parent company of Susquehanna Power, largely to supplement other generating stations within its system. During periods of high water, Conowingo was the prime source of electricity for utility customers in one region of its service area. In times of low flow, water was impounded for a day or so at a time and then released to coincide with hours of peak usage.

5. The dam was also designed to carry U.S. Route 1, a major north-south highway, across the Susquehanna, replacing an old bridge. In November 1927, the relocated highway was officially completed, and Philadelphia Electric officials staged a ceremony to mark the occasion, culminating in detonation of the bridge. An army of news photographers gathered to capture the event. Unfortunately, before they focused their cameras on the bridge, an over-eager company employee pushed the plunger and destroyed half of it.

In short, engineers in the control room of the dam had the ability to stop the Susquehanna at will, and they did. The result was havoc downstream.

The utility's fifty-year operating license, granted by the Federal Power Commission in 1926, said nothing about maintaining minimum flows of water through the turbines. Long-time residents recall that days would sometimes elapse before the intake gates were opened. William W. Jeanes lived on a promontory on the Upper Chesapeake at Elk River for fifty years until his death in 1987. He documented the long-term effects of the dam on this portion of the bay and the nearby Susquehanna. Most vivid in his mind was an extremely dry period shortly after World War II when the turbines were shut off at Conowingo for an extended time. He later wrote of the incident:

> Millions of fish seeking fresh water to spawn were trapped [in the shoals below the dam]. There was no inflow of water to replenish the oxygen or keep the temperatures down. It was a fish kill to top all fish kills. For miles the shores down here were laden with rotting fish. For a full month afterward, the stench was unbearable.

Jeanes was one of the founders of the Upper Chesapeake Watershed Association in 1952 and was an active supporter of efforts to make the river accessible to migratory fish once again.

Despite the growing frustration of people like Jeanes who felt that the use and enjoyment of the Susquehanna had been wrongly diminished by Philadelphia Electric, their occasional protests were ignored. The utility countered criticism by noting that it had been assigned control of the river by the federal government. And the government accorded the generation of electricity a higher value than any other. For two decades, resentment smoldered among those along the river and upper bay.

In 1971, the Susquehanna's flow was again cut off at Conowingo, killing 1.2 million river herring. Responding to the resultant outrage of anglers and local politicians, Philadelphia Electric agreed to maintain a minimum flow of 5,000 cubic feet (or 37,400 gallons) per second through the dam, to be augmented at its discretion with additional releases.

That was only about 13 percent of average normal flow, and critics were unappeased. Jeanes wrote in 1980:

> Now the dam is often operated in a way which closely resembles the flow of a leaky but still effective flush toilet—minimum flows for a number of hours and then great surges to carry peak loads when needed. How a fish copes with such sudden changes when it is attempting to spawn has not been explained.

The "great surges" continue today. When the intake gates at Conowingo, twenty-two by forty-three feet, are about to open to allow the Susquehanna to flow through the aging water wheels and feed the power needs sixty-five miles away in Philadelphia, alarms sound up and down the broad valley. A river's worth of water is about to race out of the generating bay, across the low-lying islands. Fishermen and others along the banks proceed to higher ground.

As early as 1910, rudimentary efforts were made by the Pennsylvania Fish Commission to help migrating fish around what were then the only obstacles on the lower river, the Holtwood and York Haven dams. Fish were netted, placed in containers, and transported to the open waters above Harrisburg. But the project moved only small numbers of fish, many of which didn't survive the journey. With the construction of the big dam at Conowingo, the effort was abandoned as futile. In 1932, owners of the three dams—plus officials of Pennsylvania Water and Power Company, which had just completed the fifty-six-foot-high Safe Harbor Dam twenty-one miles north of Conowingo—agreed to make annual payments of $4,000 each to Pennsylvania or Maryland "in lieu of fish passage."[6]

Shad, river herring, and striped bass, once plentiful along the entire 448-mile length of the Susquehanna, were, in the space of a quarter-century, pushed back to the southernmost ten miles of the river. It would be almost half a century before that high-handed act was challenged.

The tenaciousness of the anadromous fish in seeking to return to its birthplace has always fascinated scientists. For years after the completion of the dams, the fish would collect below Conowingo, thwarted in their quest to reach the shallow waters of the Juniata, Towanda, Chemung, Catawissa, or scores of other creeks and rivers spreading hundreds of miles across the watershed. A few of the fish, captured and transferred upstream, made it to their spawning grounds, but then their offspring faced a treacherous passage back to the sea. Mortality was high as they were swept through the dams' turbine blades; the rapid change in pressure as the water surged through the generating units often caused the eyeballs of the fish to explode.

6. The Safe Harbor Dam became economically feasible as a result of an agreement reached with the Pennsylvania Railroad by Pennsylvania Water and Power Company. The utility devised a regional transmission system, interconnected with Consolidated Gas Electric Light and Power Company in Baltimore, and together they provided all the electrical needs of the railroad from the Susquehanna River to the trainyards outside Washington in Virginia.

The Susquehanna was not the only American river where dams blocked fish migration. On the Merrimack, the Columbia, the Connecticut, and elsewhere during the 1930s and 1940s, scientists and engineers were experimenting with ladders and lifts to carry several species of fish around the tall obstructions. In 1938, biologists reported that even shad were utilizing the fish ladder built for salmon at the Bonneville Dam on the Columbia River. The findings buoyed hopes along the Susquehanna, but little else. No construction program was undertaken.

In 1962, another study concluded that passageways could be constructed to move fish up the Susquehanna. The researchers neglected to address the question of who would pay the estimated $5 million to build them. Nor did they answer another question: even if the fish used the passageways, could the river once again sustain large populations of shad? Or was it too altered and polluted by humans?

Two years later, the four utilities with dams agreed to fund a project that might provide some answers. They paid to import and stock 16 million shad eggs from the Columbia. (The adults that produced these eggs had used the ladders at Bonneville Dam, so the eggs might contain genes to make them similarly inclined, the theory went.) An additional 3.5 million eggs were collected from the Chesapeake, which still had ample stocks of shad.

Researchers concluded in 1968 that three-quarters of the Susquehanna River and its major tributaries by now were clean enough to support shad. (The missing one-quarter was the acidic West Branch—which never contained many shad anyway.) More than 100 years after James Worrall first took up the cause, it finally seemed that the Susquehanna was about to be filled with its premier species once more.

With the encouraging news about water quality, the restoration effort gained momentum. In October 1970, Pennsylvania governor Raymond P. Shafer announced that the Philadelphia Electric Company had agreed to install $500,000 worth of fish-collection equipment at Conowingo, and that the three other utilities had pledged another $250,000 over the next five years to collect and distribute 50 million fertilized shad eggs in the upper reaches of the Susquehanna. "We all hope," said Shafer, "that this decision will result in a series of fish ladders on which the fish will swim to their historic spawning grounds." His optimistic prediction was premature.

The next spring, eggs collected from five rivers—the Pamunkey, James, and Mattaponi in Virginia, the Delaware, and the Columbia in Oregon—

were released directly into the Susquehanna. The results were disappointing; few eggs survived, and biologists began to consider other techniques to replenish the stocks.

By the springtime of 1972, Philadelphia Electric's fish lift was ready on the west side of Conowingo, and it has remained in use ever since. The lift consists of a square, open-topped hopper, which is lowered into the river below the dam. Fish, attracted by a flow of water, swim into the hopper, which has a 5,000-fish capacity. The device then is hoisted up about forty feet on a gantry and travels overhead on rails to a sorting tank on shore. There, workers in chest-high waders move among the fish, extracting desirable species such as shad, river herring, and striped bass. The rest—about 90 percent of the haul, consisting of so-called junk fish, such as catfish, perch, and gizzard shad—are returned to the river via a chute. The anadromous species are placed in a round tank full of circulating water and taken by truck to various points above Conowingo, where they are released.

During the first nine years of operation, 1972 to 1980, an average of just 105 shad were collected in the hopper each spring, and Philadelphia Electric repeatedly claimed that the low yields did not warrant the $300,000 a year it was paying to operate the lift. "There are no shad," a company official said in the late 1970s, "and those who believe there are, or ever will be again, are hopelessly naive." Such statements infuriated supporters of the shad-restoration program. Chief among them was Ralph Abele, who in 1972 took over as executive director of the Pennsylvania Fish Commission. To Abele, the state legislature's 1866 mandate to restore migratory fish to the river became a mission. Philadelphia Electric was about to meet a tireless challenger, whose vocabulary did not contain the word *retreat*.

In some respects, Abele, who delighted in telling new acquaintances that his name was pronounced "Ah-bull," was an unlikely choice to head the commission. Raised in Pittsburgh and educated as a petroleum engineer, with a background as a Boy Scout leader, Abele had gone to Harrisburg in 1969 to help the General Assembly draft comprehensive new environmental laws, many of which were aimed at cleaning up Pennsylvania's polluted waterways. It was he who helped author Pennsylvania's eloquent constitutional amendment ensuring environmental rights for all citizens. The legislative initiative well underway, a restless Ralph Abele was searching for a new outlet for his energies, and the Fish Commission came calling. No one seemed to mind that he didn't like to fish.

"I don't bet you he wet his line in a stream for more than an hour when

I was with him," says one close friend. Explains another acquaintance, "Ralph was an intensely impatient person. I guess he just found fishing dull." Fishing, perhaps, but not the job of Fish Commission director. One in every eleven Pennsylvanians holds a fishing license, and the state boasts some of the best fishing streams on the East Coast, many of them in the Susquehanna watershed. Presidents have sneaked out of the White House to cast for the native brook trout that swim in a few prized creeks.[7] Pennsylvania's sportsmen have always formed an influential and readily mobilized constituency—as they demonstrated in battling polluted streams from the 1930s onward—and Abele never failed to wield that leverage in dealing with the state legislature, the governor, or any other person he believed was sullying the environment of his beloved state.

Before anyone realized it, Abele had transformed his little agency from one that managed the fisherman to one that managed a natural resource: the 45,000 miles of streams in Pennsylvania, everything that lived in them, and any nearby activities that impacted upon them. (His aggressive stance on water-quality enforcement often put him at odds with the state's Department of Environmental Resources, which occasionally succumbed to political pressures to go easy on polluters.)

At one of his first meetings with Fish Commission employees, Abele explained his vision, drawn from a conservation ethic espoused by naturalist Aldo Leopold and others. The fish and the water they live in are but one part of the ecosystem, he told a somewhat skeptical staff. To manage and preserve that part is to significantly improve the whole.

He drew his authority from the 1970 amendment to the state Constitution that guaranteed every Pennsylvanian the right to clean air and water. Now, he persuaded his agency's biologists, waterways patrolmen (as the fish wardens are known), the hatcheries workers, and administrative personnel that the decades of environmental abuse to Pennsylvania's vast natural resources were about to end. "Our work isn't only for the sportsmen," he once explained. "The fish is an indicator animal. If the fish can't survive in the water, then there are serious problems for man."

For Abele, the shad-restoration project assumed the importance of a religious crusade. "Dammit, we were mandated in 1866 to do it," he explained in his gravelly voice when asked why he was devoting so much time and energy to the effort. "We're just a little slow getting around to it."

---

7. In the 1870s, Pres. Ulysses S. Grant discovered that he had been fishing out of season on a trout stream in Elk County. He surrendered to a local justice of the peace. The startled justice imposed a lenient sentence, only to have the president lecture him on the values of strict law enforcement. Grant insisted on paying the full fine.

The pace quickened markedly after 1972. In one of his first decisions as executive director, Abele told his staff to dramatically increase the number of eggs and ready-to-spawn adults acquired from other states.

He recalled that moment several years later with unabashed joy. "I said, 'What are we waiting for, let's order the bastards!' " Between 1971 and 1986, more than 463 million shad eggs were collected from the Columbia, the Delaware, and the three Virginia rivers and trucked or flown to Pennsylvania; about half of them survived the trip. They were released directly into the Susquehanna, or delivered to hatcheries.[8]

On this May evening on the Delaware River, the shad eggs squeezed from the spawning females have a three-hour truck ride ahead of them, and the crew on the beach prepares them for the trip. Well-worn styrofoam ice chests are lined with clear plastic bags and filled with river water. Five liters of eggs, measured in a glass beaker, are added to an equivalent amount of water. The air in the plastic bags, which might contain impurities, is squeezed out; oxygen is pumped in from a portable tank; then the bags are sealed, the lids of the coolers put in place, and the containers loaded onto the back of a waiting truck.

Well past midnight, the nets are hauled up and the equipment stowed away until the next evening's return to the Delaware, which will be the last of the season. Fifty liters of eggs—more than 2 million—have been collected this night, a new record. The prevailing mood is gleeful. Exclaims St. Pierre, "Oh, Hendricks is going to be happy tomorrow!"

Indeed, Mike Hendricks is an excited, if worried, man. The manager of the world's only American-shad research and production facility at the moment has a full house; more shad eggs are coming in the afternoon from the Columbia River, and he has no place to put them. "It's been crazy this year," he says with a grin. The week before, 14 million shad eggs had arrived at the hatchery, which is located near Thompsontown on the Ju-

8. For a portion of the eggs, it was something of a round trip. The Columbia River shad are the progeny of fish eggs collected more than a century ago from eastern rivers, including the Susquehanna. Beginning in 1872, four years before Gen. George Custer met his demise at Little Big Horn, shad eggs were placed in milk cans and shipped by train and wagon cross-country to the Sacramento River. Despite the grueling journey, some of the eggs hatched and the American shad was introduced to California. The species thrived and spread up the Pacific coast. Now, the delicate descendants of these hardy travelers make the reverse trip, this time by airplane from Portland, Oregon, to Harrisburg. "How well those eggs do depends on how good the airline connections are," quips Dick St. Pierre.

niata River, twenty miles upstream from its confluence with the Susquehanna.

Mike Hendricks has run the Van Dyke Fish Hatchery for the Pennsylvania Fish Commission since 1985. A one-story wooden building with a tin roof, the hatchery sits alongside a busy rail line and occasionally a train rumbles by, shaking the ground. Inside, the sound of running water pervades every room, emanating from a Rube Goldberg–style maze of pipes and valves. With good reason, Hendricks is never far from a wrench. "My job is more plumbing than biology," he jokes.

Here the shad eggs hatch, and after eighteen to twenty days the young fish are released into the Juniata or into the Susquehanna below Conowingo Dam. About 15 million shad are raised each year by Mike Hendricks and the four seasonal workers who assist him.

On a rainy, overcast day, Hendricks offers a quick tour of what he cheerfully refers to as "our state-of-the-art shad culture facility," rebuilt after the first one—a wooden frame covered by plastic—blew down in a storm. In one room, newly arrived eggs sit in clear plastic containers, filled with circulating spring water heated to a temperature of 60 to 62 degrees. Normally, the eggs remain here for seven days, but a recent spate of cool weather has taxed the hatchery's ancient heater and the cooler water has slowed the eggs' development—creating the potential backup that worries Mike Hendricks today. "We just don't have much flexibility in our schedule because we don't have any extra capacity," he explains.

As the eggs near the point of hatching, they grow clearer and darker. The tiny creatures inside emerge from their yolk sacs and become visible through the clear egg wall. They are yellow to gray in color with eyes smaller than specks of fine black pepper. The eggs are then carefully transferred to 1,200-liter blue fiberglass tanks, each capable of holding 400,000 shad. Above each tank dangles an automatic feeding apparatus, and for five seconds every five minutes a dusting of orange-colored food is dropped onto the circulating water. There the eggs hatch.

By five days of age, the shad are about half an inch in length, each with a barely perceptible head and a transparent body through which a hair-thin digestive tract can be seen. "That's how we know they're eating," says Hendricks. "We finally can see them." By the time they are ready to be released into open water, they have grown to about two-thirds of an inch and swim in giant undulating schools that darken the water in the big tanks.

Maintaining accurate data on the fish produced by the hatchery—and

Residents of the fertile farmland in Lancaster and York counties had grown accustomed to having the cooling towers of the Three Mile Island nuclear plant in their midst *(left)*. On March 28, 19 pictures of those towers were flashed around the world as terrifying events unfolded inside the Unit 2 reactor. (*Philadelphia Inquirer*/Charles Isaacs, with permission)

Journalists flocked to Three Mile Island to record the dramatic events *(below)*. It was left to Harold Denton (center) of the Nuclear Regulatory Commission to conduct the daily news briefings, which frequently erupted into jostling, shouting matches. (*Philadelphia Inquirer*/Michael Viola, with permission)

The future of farming in Lancaster County may lie in places like the Leola Produce Auction, where local growers buy and sell fruits and vegetables. Encouraging farmers to abandon high-density livestock production and other practices that have contaminated water supplies and hastened erosion may preserve the centuries' old agricultural tradition in the county. (© Barbara Johnston; reproduced with permission)

Shad season on the lower Susquehanna once saw frenzied activities aboard
floating "factories," whose crews would haul in tons of fish headed north to
spawn *(above)*. In 1889, more than seven million pounds of American shad were
caught by commercial fishermen in Maryland alone, with millions more taken
from the waters of Pennsylvania and New York. This scene is at Port Deposit,
between 1880 and 1910. (From the collection of William W. Jeanes)

In 1928, the Philadelphia Electric Company completed construction of the
Conowingo Dam, a mile wide and 95 feet high *(opposite, top)*. Second only to
the hydroelectric development at Niagra Falls, Conowingo could provide
enough electricity for 250,000 homes. However, the dam destroyed what some
have called the greatest fish highway in the nation. (The Philadelphia Electric
Company)

After years of bitter and costly litigation brought by those seeking to return
migratory fish to the Susquehanna, Philadelphia Electric Company agreed to
build a fish lift on the east side of Conowingo Dam *(overleaf)*. The $12-million
facility allows shad and other species to ascend the face of the dam and swim
into the impounded waters upstream. Upon completion of fish passageways at
the three upstream dams, shad will again have free range of the Susquehanna.
(The Philadelphia Electric Company)

Until the upstream fish passageways are completed in 1999, shad still must be captured and transported to open water so they can resume their upstream migration. Workers at Conowingo collect shad, herring, and other species, load them onto large tank trucks, and release them near Harrisburg *(right)*. (The Philadelphia Electric Company)

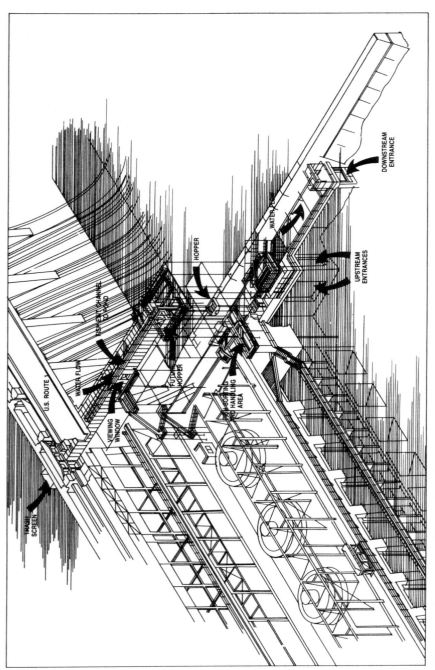

Fish lift on the east side of Conowingo Dam

what happens to them after they have left—is a time-consuming process, but it is vital to measuring the success of the restoration effort. And in recent years it has begun to yield the ultimate dividend: proof that shad eggs introduced on the Susquehanna will return there to spawn, provided they can get around the manmade obstacles.

It is this information that Mike Hendricks, Dick St. Pierre, and others struggled so long to obtain. They know that no hatchery can take the place of nature in replenishing the river with fish. Nor would that be desirable. "If all we're doing is putting young fish in and getting adults back that never reproduce, all we have is a put-and-take fishery," explains Dick St. Pierre. "The hatchery is not a forever thing; it's a starter, a quick fix to get us moving, and it's doing very well. But once these fish [populations] take off on their own, the hatchery component should be almost invisible."

To keep tabs on the fish raised at Van Dyke, and to distinguish them from the "wild" progeny of hatchery-raised adults who return, Mike Hendricks has managed to equip the fish with their life histories: at various stages of their young existence, the Van Dyke shad are immersed in a bath of the chemical oxytetracycline, which is added to the water in their holding tanks. The chemical bonds to calcium ions, and thus attaches itself to bones. The only true bone present in these young fish is the otolith, which helps them maintain hearing and balance; their other future bones are still just cartilage. The otolith grows like rings on a tree, and in the shad a new ring forms each day. Days in which the fish encounters oxytetracycline produce different-colored rings. Thus, a shad bathed in the chemical on the fifth and tenth days of its life, for example, can forever be distinguished from another bathed in the chemical at ages seven and twelve days merely by counting the rings. In addition, the structure of the rings differs between hatchery-raised and wild shad, clearly establishing their origins.

To obtain the vital statistics of the shad, it is killed, its otolith is removed, a thin cross-section is cut, and the slice is examined in ultraviolet light under a microscope, where the coloration is discernible. Because of Mike Hendricks's meticulous recordkeeping, it is possible to determine such things as the exact age of the fish, the river from which the eggs were taken, where the juvenile was stocked and when.

Although oxytetracycline tagging is not a new technique, no one has done it on the scale that takes place each spring at Van Dyke. Since Hendricks's program was begun in 1985, millions of shad, each bearing a permanent identification record in its inner ear, have reached the Atlantic Ocean. Now, increasing numbers have begun to return each spring through the Chesapeake, bound for home—the Susquehanna and its many tributaries.

In 1989, for the first time, tagged shad appeared at Conowingo. They were accompanied by "wild" shad, the offspring of adults transported to the river who then spawned there, instilling in their young an instinctive urge to return to the Susquehanna. The much-celebrated return resolved a question that had troubled Dick St. Pierre and Mike Hendricks: precisely when in a shad's life cycle is it imprinted with its river of origin? Did imprinting occur within a day or two of spawning? If so, the fact that the eggs at Van Dyke were being raised in water from a nearby spring, rather than from the Juniata or Susquehanna, would doom the project. "We were afraid we'd do all that stocking, the fish would go to sea, and when they came back they'd spend all their energies looking for some spring near Thompsontown," St. Pierre explains. Although the two biologists now theorize that imprinting occurs gradually in young fish, the matter no longer dominates their discussions. "It's a moot question for us now," says St. Pierre. It is clearly the Susquehanna that draws the shad.

Lunchtime at the world's only American-shad hatchery is a modest affair. Mike Hendricks and his three college-age assistants perch on chairs in the office that doubles as their laboratory and library. In the corner sits a large gray cooler with "Blood Bank" emblazoned across the top. "I heard it was available for free from Scranton State Hospital," says Hendricks, his voice echoing from its interior as he rummages around for his brown-bag lunch amid containers of fish food. "So we went over, picked it up and hauled it back here. That saved us $200."

The Van Dyke Hatchery operates on an annual budget of $100,000, which is provided by the three utilities with dams above Conowingo. That amount includes Hendricks's salary and the cost of running the hatchery for four months in the spring while the shad are being raised and released. Then the facility is closed, its tanks drained, and Hendricks returns to the Fish Commission's large Benner Springs hatchery, sixty miles away, to write reports, examine otoliths, and order supplies for the next year. Each March he returns to Van Dyke and prepares for the new crop of shad eggs.

Before he joined the Fish Commission, Hendricks worked for the private firm that conducts shad research at Conowingo Dam for the Phila- delphia Electric Company. He left that job because of what he saw as a fundamental difference in philosophies. His superiors had stated often and publicly "that shad restoration can't work and won't work," he explains with a touch of bitterness in his voice. "So if they made it succeed they would prove themselves wrong. I put up with that for a few years, working for them, and I just couldn't take it anymore. I can tell you from being around shad, you can't be half-hearted and make it work."

During the spring, the hatchery is active twenty-four hours a day. Because eggs may arrive at any time (those from the Delaware came at about 3:30 A.M.), a small pop-top camper sits in the parking lot outside. There Hendricks, or one of the assistants, can grab a few hours' sleep at night.

Those who believe the shad-restoration program *will* succeed drew reassurance from a 1988 decision by the U.S. Fish and Wildlife Service to expand its involvement in the project. "It shows that it's not just the states who are interested in restoration; the federal government is willing to spend taxpayers' money," Hendricks says.

Scientists at the federal agency's National Fishery Research and Development Laboratory in Wellsboro, Pennsylvania, are assigned to shad studies. One of them, biologist Robert M. Ross, arrives while the Van Dyke staff is lunching. He brings two plastic bags of fish eggs—produced by the first three females that spawned after being injected with a human hormone, chorionic gonadotropin. The biologists at Wellsboro are seeking to trigger spawning artificially, in hopes of producing eggs under optimum conditions. Unlike the crystal-clear eggs collected from the Delaware, the eggs in Ross's bags are opaque. "They look terrible," observes Hendricks. "There's no point in doing anything. They won't hatch."

"This is a learning process this year," Ross acknowledges. "Eventually, we'll get there."[9]

The federal researchers also want to study the behavior of shad—"their fixed action and social patterns," as Ross describes it. The studies interest Hendricks because he sees so much distinctive behavior at the hatchery. Extremely young shad and adults, for instance, are attracted to light colors but swim away from dark ones. Juvenile shad, however, are repelled by light—a phenomenon that is proving useful in directing the fish away from the whirring blades of turbines blocking their migration to the Atlantic.

Ross departs with buckets containing 10,000 Hudson River shad, scooped from the Van Dyke tanks for his behavioral studies, and Hendricks readies another 450,000 shad for release into the Juniata later that afternoon. Two days before, he had released 1.4 million shad just below the Conowingo Dam, the only other stocking point in the river

---

9. Additional work has produced some encouraging results, but the project still has not succeeded as Ross had hoped.

basin. It was the single largest release in the history of the program to date.

To obtain this day's batch of emigrants, water from one of the blue tanks is gradually drained. When only a quarter remains, Hendricks begins removing the tiny shad, who swim right into the white scoop he is using. The fish—exceedingly delicate at this stage in their lives—are carefully placed into fourteen buckets lined with plastic bags. Oxygen is added, the bags are sealed, and the shad are ready for their first taste of freedom.

As dark storm clouds build above the Juniata, Mike Hendricks loads the buckets into a pickup truck and heads for a boat-launching ramp four miles downstream. Because the river is warmer than the spring water the fry have grown accustomed to, the buckets are set into the Juniata to temper. Using a dark scoop this time to keep the fish away, Hendricks slowly adds river water to the buckets, gradually raising the temperature.

An intense storm hits just as the last bucket of fish is emptied into the river. Unbeknownst to Mike Hendricks this would be one of many storms to sweep the Susquehanna Valley this spring, and much of his painstaking work will be for naught. High waters will wash the tiny shad downstream long before they have any hope of survival in the open waters of the bay or ocean. An entire class of shad, as the researchers describe it, will be lost.

The unusual springtime weather was also playing havoc with the shad collection and transfer efforts far to the south, at Conowingo. High water had shut down operation of the fish lift for fifteen days—about half the duration of the typical spring migration. Even so, 4,000 adult shad had been moved upstream before the interruption, and 1,400 had been captured just the day before—an all-time record for a single day. Not so long ago, trapping even 1,400 shad during a full season at Conowingo would have set off a celebration among conservationists. In 1980, when the state of Maryland banned shad fishing in the Chesapeake Bay, biologists believed that no more than 4,000 shad remained in the upper bay; 139 made it to Conowingo that spring.

The recent higher numbers have heartened many in the restoration effort, but Dilip Mathur, the fisheries project manager at Conowingo, is not as optimistic. Says Mathur, a New Delhi–born biologist who's been involved in shad restoration for more than two decades:

> The goal right now is to restore a run of 3 million shad. What's 1,400 of 3 million? And you have only thirty days to catch them. If you catch 1,400 every day, you get 42,000. That's not very much. You have to think in terms of very, very large numbers.

What is exciting, though, is that compared to the early '70s when we were catching 40, 50 fish a season, 1,400 looks super. But in terms of the ultimate goal, it's zilch. I don't think I'm going to see 3 million shad unless some miraculous event occurs.

Mathur begins any discussion of the restoration effort with a bit of history, for he firmly believes that dams such as Conowingo had little to do with the decline in Susquehanna shad populations. The number of fish began to shrink during the colonial era and, with certain fluctuations, has continued downward ever since. "The dam is the most visible structure, so you can blame the dam for everything," Mathur says. "There are rivers right now that don't have dams, and don't have shad, either." That's the case in the Potomac River, which once had abundant shad runs. Mathur and Dick St. Pierre blame the absence of shad there to overfishing in the Atlantic and poor water quality.

Of one thing Mathur is certain, however: building fish passageways on the Susquehanna will not guarantee that the species will return in the numbers envisioned by supporters of the restoration program—or by the dozens of fishermen who each day take up positions along the catwalk on the downstream side of Conowingo and cast their lines into the rushing water below, biding their time with herring, perch, carp, and catfish until the premier species of the Susquehanna returns in healthy numbers.

As senior fisheries scientist for RMC Environmental Services, the contractor employed by Philadelphia Electric Company at Conowingo and the other power plants nearby on the Susquehanna, Mathur has, like Dick St. Pierre and Mike Hendricks, made shad his life's work. Much of his time, he volunteers, is spent figuring out "how to trick the fish into doing things we want them to do."

In 1976, the same year that the Van Dyke hatchery opened, the fifty-year operating license granted by the federal government to Conowingo expired. Fisheries officials in Pennsylvania, Maryland, New York, and Washington, D.C., as well as conservation and sportsmen's groups, realized that this could represent the last opportunity to return migratory fish to the Susquehanna. In the license, the federal government held the only leverage that might force Philadelphia Electric to do more to accommodate the fish migrations. Shad-restoration advocates were convinced that the utility cared little about making a success of its fish lift or about improving water flow.

"Conowingo holds the key to shad restoration in the Susquehanna,"

Dick St. Pierre said at the time. "Upstream and downstream passage at this facility must be solved in order for our restoration efforts to be successful." Brent Hare, an attorney with Maryland's Department of Natural Resources, described it more succinctly: "Conowingo is the cork in the bottle."

As part of their strategy, the restoration advocates persuaded federal regulators to review the operating licenses of the three upstream dams when they considered Conowingo. The three upstream dams also block the migration; indeed, fish that got past Conowingo could only proceed another fifteen miles before encountering the fifty-one-foot-high Holtwood Dam. But the owners of those dams had historically been far more receptive to the restoration project than Philadelphia Electric. The three utilities that operate the York Haven, Safe Harbor, and Holtwood dams let it be known that they would provide access for the fish as soon as Conowingo was ordered to do so.

All four utilities, however, argued that they should not be required to build new ladders or lifts, estimated to cost in the tens of millions of dollars, until enough shad were present below Conowingo to justify the investment. On August 14, 1980, the Federal Energy Regulatory Commission gave them all operating licenses, but ordered that the question of fish passageways be decided at a separate administrative hearing. The utilities argued that passageways would be justified when 35,000 shad were counted during the spring migration in the Susquehanna at Conowingo. Conservationists protested that this number was unattainable in the foreseeable future.

With a long fight looming, the state and federal partners in the shad-restoration effort took several important steps, determined not to let the opportunity pass them by. The hatchery program was moved into high gear to provide enough juveniles to survive the downstream trip over the dams, years out at sea, and the long trek home. That same year, 1980, the state of Maryland banned fishing for shad in the Chesapeake. (A similar ban on another important anadromous fish—the striped bass, or rockfish—went into effect in 1985, and fishing for both species on the Susquehanna also has been banned.)

The hearing ordered by the Federal Energy Regulatory Commission began in Washington on October 6, 1981, and lasted until March 30, 1982. The transcript was 5,227 pages long. Philadelphia Electric, which retained a prestigious Manhattan law firm, mounted a full-scale defense of its operations at Conowingo, offering volumes of scientific data to show that shad could never be restored to the river. The opposition could not muster similar firepower. Dick St. Pierre remembers sharing low-cost motel rooms and eating countless fast-food meals.

The shad-restoration forces had two major goals: first, to make Philadelphia Electric dramatically improve the numbers of fish passing over Conowingo; and second, to require the utility to increase its minimum flows of water through the dam. The state of Maryland led the battle on the second point, arguing that there was often insufficient fresh water below the dam to sustain aquatic life.

And to make that point, Maryland could have found no better witness than Earl Ashenfelter, who had spent 59 of his 74 years fishing below Conowingo and was regarded as the best fishing guide on the lower Susquehanna. A diminutive, outgoing man who lives in Aberdeen, Maryland, Ashenfelter suggested to the state's lawyers that aerial photos be taken of the river after Conowingo's engineers had shut off the Susquehanna's flow. The photos—depicting areas of dry riverbed dotted by stagnating pools of water—were introduced as evidence during Ashenfelter's testimony. "That's what scrubbed 'em," he later boasted.

In addition to casting doubts about the likelihood of adequate numbers of shad returning to Conowingo, Philadelphia Electric also argued that the increased flow requirements would cost the utility money, and ratepayers should not be forced to pay higher electric bills to accommodate just a few fish.

In early December 1984, before the hearing judge had issued a decision, the utilities that owned the three upstream dams signed an agreement committing them to spend $3.7 million over a decade toward the restoration effort. The money would go to place 10 to 15 million young shad—the output of the Van Dyke hatchery—in the Susquehanna annually. If the shad's mortality rate proved to be high as they passed downstream through the three dams, the utilities pledged to devise means to move the fish safely. They also agreed to help transport adult shad upstream once these fish made it to Holtwood. In return, the challenge to their operating licenses by fisheries agencies and sportsmen's groups was dropped.

Philadelphia Electric, however, did not sign the agreement and continued to negotiate its own settlement with the other side while awaiting the ruling from the Federal Energy Regulatory Commission's administrative law judge, David I. Harfeld, who had presided at the contentious and protracted hearing.

On March 19, 1986, Harfeld issued his initial finding. It was a stunning defeat for Philadelphia Electric. The reason the utility was not trapping many fish "is not attributable to the absence of shad," Harfeld wrote.

It was because the utility's fish lift was in the wrong place. Anyone who had ever fished at Conowingo knew that, Harfeld said. Anglers on the dam drop their lines 800 feet to the east, near the outfall of the giant turbines, where the current is strong, the water is full of oxygen, and the sport fish congregate. If an accurate count of shad was to be obtained, Philadelphia Electric must construct a second trap near the outfall, the order noted. "It follows that the more efficient the collection facilities at Conowingo, the greater the chances of implementing a successful restoration program." Dismissing the utility's argument about cost, Harfeld cited an earlier commission decision, writing, "Fish passage measures are a cost of doing business on a river containing anadromous fish populations."

In early January 1987, the five-member Federal Energy Regulatory Commission upheld Harfeld's findings. It ordered Philadelphia Electric to continue with the restoration effort at least through 1995 and to make sure enough water got through the dam to sustain aquatic life in the river below. According to the ruling, Philadelphia Electric would be compelled to install a new fish passageway at Conowingo when migrating shad "return in large enough numbers to become self-sustaining." It did not specify how many fish that would be.

Philadelphia Electric was not ready to concede yet. On the last day remaining to appeal the commission ruling, the utility did so, claiming that the continuous-flow requirement would cost it millions of dollars. Dick St. Pierre and the others involved in the restoration program braced themselves for another round.

But then a totally unexpected chain of events brought a swift conclusion to the 11½-year battle. In March 1987, the Nuclear Regulatory Commission ordered Philadelphia Electric's nuclear plant at Peach Bottom, within sight of Conowingo, shut down as "an immediate threat to the public health and safety." The regulatory rebuke and ensuing public outcry prompted a wholesale change in the company's top management, and as new faces appeared in its executive suites, Philadelphia Electric announced a policy shift. Not only would it build a second fish passageway—on the eastern side of the dam, where the fish gather—but it would also guarantee to release enough water for shad to survive, 10,000 cubic feet per second during the critical spring season. "It's almost too good to be true," declared Torrey C. Brown, Maryland's secretary of natural resources. Said a newly hired Philadelphia Electric spokesman, "If we're going to use the Susquehanna for our purposes, we have to put something back into the river."

In the spring of 1991, Philadelphia Electric completed construction of a $12.5-million fish passageway on the east side of Conowingo. Capable of moving 750,000 shad and 5 million river herring, the new lift, in conjunction with the older one, can carry a total of 3 million shad and 20 million herring over Conowingo during the season. Unlike the older lift, which operates just like an elevator, carrying trapped fish up to a tank on land, the new passageway will enable any fish to swim in stages up the face of the dam and exit at the top through a channel directly into Conowingo Reservoir.[10]

The fish that have been released above Conowingo have shown every inclination to head directly for the Holtwood Dam. "If those fish didn't go to Holtwood, we'd be in trouble," explains Dick St. Pierre. "Thankfully, the fish did the right thing."

During the upstream migration in the spring and the downstream trip each fall, biologists carefully monitor the shad's whereabouts using sophisticated equipment scattered along the Susquehanna. At Conowingo, biologist Paul Heisey has become expert at installing tiny radio transmitters in adult shad. An antenna consisting of twelve inches of thin, flexible wire protrudes from the fish's mouth. The transmitter allows researchers to track the movement of the fish. In addition to providing valuable data, the radio-tagging program has generated some good stories.

Heisey's favorite involves locating a hybrid striped bass that was carrying a transmitter. A fisherman who had caught and cleaned the bass discovered the two-inch radio inside it but failed to report his discovery to officials, apparently fearful he had taken an illegal fish. He stuffed it, transmitter and all, into a freezer. "We tracked it right to the freezer," recalls Heisey. "He was surprised, to say the least." The transmitters also have been found along the banks of the river amid piles of fish bones, the remnants of a meal for a raccoon, osprey, or one of the many bald eagles that today inhabit the lower Susquehanna.[11]

The young shad began to move downriver sooner than Dick St. Pierre and others had anticipated. By mid-September, the first juveniles, now about four inches long, had shown up on the hydro-acoustic monitors at the York

10. Until fish passageways are constructed in the three upstream dams, the trap-and-transfer program must be continued. Shad are captured in the fish passageway at Conowingo, transported, and released in the Susquehanna above York Haven.

11. So abundant are bird predators, such as great blue herons, that local fish hatcheries have been forced to install protective covers over their facilities. Young trout are especially vulnerable, and predator losses at some hatcheries amount to more than half a million dollars annually.

Haven dam, the first obstacle the fish would encounter on their migration to the sea. That prompted a flurry of activity at the massive old brick power plant on the west bank of the Susquehanna. Now, as the setting sun bathed the river in golden light, all was in readiness.

Built in 1904, York Haven resembles a fort perched along the river, with only the jumble of transmission lines and towers and the constant hum of turbines giving away its true function. A long dam extends for more than a mile upriver, ending at Three Mile Island near the opposite shore. The plant itself is U-shaped, with its arms pointed upstream to draw the Susquehanna's flow into the center of the U, or forebay. There the current turns eastward at nearly a right angle and takes a twenty-one-foot plunge through the row of turbines that line the river side of the structure. In the southeastern corner of the base of the U is a large iron sluice gate that can be raised to release water not directed through the turbines.

Floating in twenty feet of water near the turbines is a long platform. On it sits a small metal storage shed. Submerged beneath the platform is an assortment of sophisticated equipment: banks of underwater strobe lights, two scanning sonar units, and a large net with two orange ball-shaped floats attached. A two-inch-thick electrical cable snakes out from the plant to provide power. The shed houses control units for the sonar devices. The units are hooked up to a pair of Sony color monitors, now displaying the activities of thousands of young shad that are swimming in confused schools beneath the platform. But with the growing darkness, you don't need the monitors in the shed to know the whereabouts of the shad.

"It's called dimpling," says Dick St. Pierre, watching the surface of the water. "It's a term I've heard applied only to shad." The young fish grow increasingly active with the onset of early autumn darkness. They feel the ageless call to head out to sea. Soon, the water in the forebay looks as if it is being pelted with large raindrops, dimples in the surface made by the schooling fish. It is a sight St. Pierre will never tire of.

If the fish are busy as nightfall nears, so, too, are Paul Martin, a young, bearded fisheries biologist, and his two-member crew this evening, Michael Klozik and J. H. Rumpp. All three work for Stone and Webster, a Boston-based engineering firm that has been retained by the Susquehanna River Anadromous Fish Restoration Committee, the Electric Power Research Institute, and Metropolitan Edison Company, which owns York Haven. The organizations are paying $40,000 apiece to sponsor studies of the shad's downstream migration—along with an experiment that begins this evening and will continue seven days a week until the last of this season's crop of shad has departed the Susquehanna.

Each participant in the project has a special interest in the outcome. For those hoping to restore shad to the Susquehanna, reducing the mortality rates of the young fish as they pass through four hydroelectric dams is critical. For Metropolitan Edison, the experiment may provide a relatively inexpensive way of diverting the shad from the turbines at York Haven. And the data collected here may prove valuable to other members of the utility-funded electric research institute; they, too, are coming under increasing pressure from the U.S. Fish and Wildlife Service, state fisheries agencies, and sportsmen's groups to reduce losses of sport fish at the nation's hydroelectric plants.

Relying on what Martin calls the shad's "startle response" to bright light, biologists believe they can scare the fish away from the turbines by placing the strobes in front of the giant metal blades. In the shad's haste to escape the light, they may head directly for the open sluice gate and safety. When the lights are first turned on, the "startle response" of the young shad is clearly visible on the sonar monitors. They dart away.

The results of this experiment won't necessarily be applicable to other species, for some types of fish do not respond similarly to light sources. Nor will the information gathered solve the problems that exist in moving shad downstream past the other dams on the Susquehanna, including Conowingo, which Stone and Webster engineers constructed in the 1920s.

"There's nothing you can do at Conowingo," says St. Pierre. "It's a mile-wide dam with no forebay. There's no way to concentrate the fish." It is unclear what the utility will have to do to keep the juveniles away from the turbines there. That it will have to do something, however, is not in dispute, at least not in St. Pierre's mind.

Klozik and Rumpp busy themselves making last-minute adjustments to the strobe lights. Paul Martin, in his second year in this project, tinkers with the $12,000 worth of electronics in place to monitor the fish. Although everything had been ready at York Haven the previous year, the experiment was "blown out," he says, by the same high water that plagued Mike Hendricks's stocking efforts. "We went from 9,000 cubic feet per second to 90,000 almost overnight," Martin explains, and the young fish were simply swept downstream with the surge. This night, about 15,000 cubic feet per second of water is coursing through the turbines—a good flow—and the water temperature is nearing the ideal of 60 degrees.

Mike Hendricks is due to make his first visit to York Haven the following week. "He'll love this," says St. Pierre, leaning on the platform railing in the fading light. "It's a shame Ralph Abele can't see this, too."

By 8:00 darkness has fallen and it is time to begin. The television monitors show dense schools of shad circulating nervously through the forebay, confused by the obstacle impeding their flight to the sea. This year, 5.8 million shad had been stocked in the Susquehanna, and St. Pierre estimates that about 10 percent of that number have survived to make the downstream migration, which may last eight weeks. The numbers in the forebay this evening excite Dick St. Pierre. "You look out here and say, What have we got here? This disproves those who doubt the fish will survive in the wild."

Everything is ready now. With a blinding flash, the lights are turned on and begin blinking 300 times per minute, 5 times per second. The dark waters of the forebay turn seafoam green and the area above it resembles an open-air strobe-lit discotheque. To everyone's surprise, the startle response of the shad is slow. "What? Do they all of a sudden like the light?" asks St. Pierre, peering at the television screen. "We saw a much more definite clearing out last year," agrees Martin, watching with him and taking copious notes. "Maybe it's just too early in the season. They may not be juiced up yet."

The lights remain on for thirty minutes, creating a dark corner in the forebay near the sluice door. Then, the sluice gate is opened for five minutes to allow the current to carry out those fish that have fled to the darkness there. Only a few can be seen in the flood of water cascading down the side of the plant, however. The others have moved to a dark patch along the west wall of the forebay. Throughout the night, variations of the test will be conducted to measure how the fish respond. Paul Martin and his crew will finish just before daybreak, return to their motel rooms to catch a few hours' sleep, and then return to the dam to begin again.

Dick St. Pierre says he will judge the shad restoration project a success if "we can offer the fisherman something for this long wait. It may be [the ability to catch] just one fish a day, or certainly a limited fishery. Everyone recognizes that the restoration program is going to go on for decades on its own after we've gotten it started. But to be able to offer the first open season on shad on the Susquehanna—that's going to be a major sign that we've succeeded."

And when might that be? "It will be the very first spring after we have fish passage at all dams," he says with confidence.

For the first time, he knows when that will be: the spring of 1999.

At a meeting in October 1992, the three upstream utilities caught St. Pierre completely by surprise and dropped their resistance to building the passageways. "I had almost decided to cancel the meeting," says St. Pierre, who was leaving the next day on a government-sponsored research trip to

China. "When we met, I kept trying to raise the usual areas of disagreement. Everybody kept saying, 'Dick, why can't you just accept the fact that
we're here to resolve the problems?' It's unbelievable! What a nice send-off
present."

The utilities' decision was based in part on the evidence collected by
the Stone and Webster crew at York Haven and at Conowingo which
proves that shad will thrive in the Susquehanna and, given a chance, migrate up- and downstream just as their ancestors did. Each spring brings
sizable populations of shad to Conowingo: 15,964 in 1990; 27,227 in
1991; 25,721 in 1992. Eventually, the shad trap-and-transfer program at
Conowingo will be phased out, as will operations at the hatchery on the
Juniata. The shad will be on their own then and Dick St. Pierre is confident
they will thrive. "People should be thinking of opening bait and tackle
shops at Sunbury and Clarks Ferry," says St. Pierre.

A half-moon has risen in the sky, and Martin, Rumpp, and Klozik prepare
to begin again, the sonar showing large clusters of shad gathered in the
darkened forebay. Standing on the high walkway above the sluice gate, the
dimpling water alive behind him, St. Pierre stares down at the handful of
fishermen who have strung themselves out along the river below the power
plant. The anglers come almost every night, hoping for a few bass, or
whatever the river has to offer. He smiled the smile of a man with a wonderful secret. "They have no idea of what's inside here."

The River and the Bay

"A long-term investment"

Ron Saacke and Paul Willey had brought the *Lady D* up the Chesapeake from Annapolis the day before, and now they are scurrying about the old wooden workboat preparing for the morning's cargo: a class of seventh-graders, due to arrive any minute at the dock in Havre de Grace. This is new territory for the two young men, and as they tape a map of the Susquehanna watershed to a large piece of plywood, they joke that they will be learning along with the kids. The nineteen youngsters scheduled to arrive on this first day of October will be among the 35,000 people who participate each year in educational programs conducted by Ron and Paul's employer, the Chesapeake Bay Foundation.

Saacke and Willey were intrigued by the opportunity to spend time on the Susquehanna and the upper bay. Both had worked on the lower portions of the Chesapeake for several years, and had heard a lot about the river. Now they itch to explore its islands and hilly shoreline. Already they are planning an excursion upriver on their next day off.

As the yellow school bus pulls into view, Paul heads out to meet it. The youngsters from Edgewood Middle School and their science teacher, Tom Markowski, are about to receive a fast-paced introduction to the watershed that stretches more than 400 miles to the north and nearly 200 miles to the south. "You're here," Ron announces enthusiastically as the students crowd around him, "to learn and have fun."

With lunch bags stowed below, and everyone swaddled in bright orange life-jackets, Ron and Paul ease the *Lady D* from her slip into the hazy sunshine and breezy waters of the Susquehanna Flats, the shallow delta that marks the union of river and bay. For the rest of the day, the Susquehanna will be their stage, and its secrets their script. It is a show-and-tell extravaganza that has always captivated their audience.

Many of these youngsters had never given any thought to the mighty river that flows into the bay at their doorstep. That's not surprising; it is only in recent years that the Chesapeake Bay and the Susquehanna have been considered the way nature created them—as a single, diverse ecosystem that spreads over more than 64,000 square miles. Like the navigational chart Paul uses to find the channel, most maps of the Chesapeake include just a few miles of the Susquehanna. And most maps of the Susquehanna depict just a few miles of bay. Those are humans' boundaries, not nature's.

If there is a single place in this sprawling watershed best suited to deliver a message about the synergy of river and bay it is here, at what is both the mouth of the Susquehanna and the beginning of the Chesapeake. For starters, there is absolutely no way to distinguish between these two bodies of water, as the seventh-graders quickly discover.

With the broad expanse of sparkling water as a backdrop, and their young passengers intrigued by the prospects of adventure, Ron and Paul know they have a few hours to drive home a single message, one that many adults have difficulty grasping. The message: personal responsibility. One person—even a seventh-grader in a small Maryland town—can have an impact on this huge watershed.

On a normal day, 25 billion gallons of fresh water—more than enough for every U.S. household—flow past Havre de Grace and into the bay, an infusion that constitutes 90 percent of all the fresh water entering the Chesapeake as far south as the Patuxent River, ninety miles from here. So dominant is the river in the health of the bay that if the Susquehanna arrives depleted of life-sustaining oxygen, as has occurred in periods of low water, it can upset oxygen levels in tributaries as far away as the Rappahannock in Virginia.

But the bay also affects the river. Twice daily, the tidal force that is the Chesapeake's own heartbeat pulses north against the current, into the river's rock-walled corridor, and then back down again, stirring and blending the waters to create a unique elixir. Surviving in this heady environment are countless species, some permanent residents, others migratory, some awesome to a seventh-grader, others so subtle as to be practically undetectable, some nearly extinct.

Without the Chesapeake, the Susquehanna would remain a mighty river, albeit one devoid of many creatures that the bay helps sustain. Without the Susquehanna, however, the Chesapeake would see its extraordinary mix of plants and animals shrink to that contained in a large saltwater inlet. But the marriage of the two has more complex consequences than that. The Susquehanna's contribution toward making the Chesapeake North America's largest estuary, and one of the world's most productive, has been offset by the harm the river has done to the bay in recent decades. At the same time, the Chesapeake Bay cleanup effort has produced a windfall for the Susquehanna that has enhanced its natural value. And it has given birth to a new generation of dreamers for the Susquehanna—every bit as zealous as those gone before.

From the stern of a workboat drifting off Havre de Grace, the river and bay appear as a seamless entity. But the idea of managing them that way—of looking at the watershed as a unit, oblivious to manmade boundaries—has struck many in government as *unnatural* and practically unworkable. This bodes poorly for both the bay and the river. For that reason, Ron Saacke and Paul Willey see their mission this morning—and every morning for the foreseeable future—as helping to ensure that such a concept *will* be second nature to every student who visits the *Lady D*—the future state legislators, real estate developers, factory managers, poets, county planners, chemists, and newspaper editors who will share this watershed in coming years.

A popular game onboard the *Lady D* involves a cleverly disguised lesson to drive home this point. As the boat drifts up the Susquehanna on the tide, passing beneath a soaring osprey, Paul hands out numbered plastic-coated cards, each of which represents a piece of property. "Your Great-aunt Emma has died and left each one of you 2 million dollars and, even better, 100 acres along the river," he tells the students. "Now it's up to you to decide what you want to do with your land." Grease pencils in hand, the youngsters go to work on their cards.

"Okay," announces Paul a short time later, "now we're going to build our riverfront. Who's got number One? Tell us what you want to do with your property."

One at a time, the students come forward to place their cards on the floor of the *Lady D*'s cockpit, and the riverfront slowly begins to take shape. Paul offers a running commentary based on the students' artwork. "A house, cars behind it, a pool and, what's that, a mall? A mall on Card One." As the second youngster joins his card to the first, Paul continues: "A movie theater, two Rolls Royces, three BMWs, an eighteen-hole golf course, and a mall on Card Two. Three: a house, tennis court and a barn with lots of horses. A wharf with lots of boats, an arcade, a supermarket, a parking lot and a 'money bin' on Four. A *money bin?*" He laughs. "Five: a house, shoe store, swimming pool, trees and a boat. Six: a mansion, a barn, a hayfield, and—what's this tiny house?"

"That's where my brother will live," explains the artist.

Card Seven is densely covered with buildings. "I made a major metropolis," proclaims its owner proudly. "There's a mall, a town hall, post office, airport, train station. And a recycling center at the airport."

Card Eight depicts tennis courts, a car dealership, swimming pools, an island, a guest house, and a mall.

"There's a mall every block!" Ron protests.

Cards Nine, Ten, and Eleven also contain malls.

"Can we do this again?" begs the creator of Card Seven. What did he want to change? "I'd build a bigger development."

By the time the final card is laid in place, the winding riverfront has two more malls, three more movie theaters, several large houses, a submarine dock, a yacht basin, a helicopter pad, stables, dog kennels, and a few trees.

"Let's see if we can figure out what's going on," says Paul, as the students study their handiwork. "Actually, this is the Susquehanna River. What will the mall clear up here on Card One do to the headwaters as it starts to flow down? And what about the golf course and the horse farm and the major metropolis? What will the river be like when it gets down here to the end?"

"Fishless," replies the metropolis's developer.

"Yucky," adds the submarine owner.

Paul waits a moment before asking, "Do you see how what you do has a cumulative effect on everyone and everything else?" Heads bob around him.

The point is an easy one to make to seventh-graders drifting on a sun-spangled river. It hasn't been easy to embrace for those in the halls of government, however. Still, *some* people thought in large terms.

In the spring of 1949, the Wyoming Valley's personal emissary to Washington, Congressman Daniel J. Flood, proposed creation of a Susquehanna Valley Authority to oversee activities along the river from its origins in New York State to its mouth in Maryland. Flood, who was both a member of the U.S. House Appropriations Committee and president of the Wilkes-Barre Chamber of Commerce, wanted the Susquehanna to benefit from the federal government's heightened interest in river development. Seeing a means to finance the levees needed to protect the Wyoming Valley from devastating floods, he came up with a rationale for the authority that sounds familiar many decades later.

"Halt water run-off at the source and you have real flood prevention," he declared. "You also keep the soil where it belongs. Right now the fertile soil of the Susquehanna Valley is going to the bottom of the Chesapeake

Bay." An integral part of Flood's proposal was reforestation in the water-shed, including the brutally scarred lands of his own anthracite region.[1] In calling for a Susquehanna Valley Authority, Dan Flood was premature by a dozen years or so. He was not alone, however, in realizing that some major action was needed if the increasingly apparent problems along the river were to be corrected.

Far downstream, at the mouth of the Susquehanna, a group of "responsible Cecil County residents," as a 1953 newspaper article described them, organized the Upper Chesapeake Watershed Association. The group, comprised of "boatmen, commercial watermen, bathers, gunners, campers, property owners, merchants, conservationists and vacationers," included among its members William Jeanes, who would later record the massive fish kills on the Susquehanna.

The members set four goals: to protect the charm and beauty of the upper bay; to eliminate existing sources of pollution and forestall new ones; to increase fishing, crabbing, and wildlife resources; and to make sure that the upper bay would remain available for recreation. They chose this moment to organize, wrote the newspaper reporter, "while the warning light is just beginning to flicker."

Indeed, the light was flickering. The growing population along the shores of the river was contributing large volumes of raw sewage to the bay's shallow waters. Everyone relied on the Susquehanna to carry this waste away—downstream. In Havre de Grace, most homes and businesses simply disposed of their sewage through pipes extending down to the water line. This was true into the 1970s.

During periods of drought, the Susquehanna's restorative powers were held in check by the Conowingo Dam. With increasing frequency, parts of the river and upper bay were declared unsafe for swimming. Summertime fish kills caused by pollution, a lack of oxygen in the water, and even a lack of water itself alarmed those living downstream.

Although Dan Flood's 1949 proposal for a Susquehanna Valley Authority went nowhere, he doggedly continued to promote his idea. In Washington and elsewhere, others also came to consider the value of watershed management. In 1951, a presidentially appointed Water Resources Policy Committee recommended the creation of federal commissions to

1. Apparently concerned that a cleaner Chesapeake and flood-free Wilkes-Barre might be inadequate to produce the federal dollars he envisioned, Flood added a favorite sweetener for good measure. The Susquehanna Valley Authority, he declared, would contribute to national security, although he apparently was never asked to elaborate just how.

oversee all of the nation's major river basins.[2] The federal role in such commissions was to be purely advisory. But state officials were wary, fearful that a federal toe in the door would soon be followed by the whole foot. Yet these same officials found themselves in a ticklish position: Congress was offering them expensive and popular flood-control projects and other public works investments in exchange for a federal say in local development.

And it was not as if the states were being asked to surrender a dominant role in river management. By and large, the nation's waterways were laxly regulated. What occurred downstream was of little consequence—particularly if downstream happened to be in another state.[3]

Although there were a number of efforts to create federal-state management agencies for river basins, few ever materialized. The rivalries between states and jitters about federal involvement proved insurmountable. One proposal did overcome the hurdles, however. In 1961, a compact creating the Delaware River Basin Commission, an independent federal-state agency charged with regulating and administering activities within an entire watershed, became law. Dan Flood's moment seemingly had come.

The Susquehanna was considered by many to be the last major "underdeveloped" river in the Northeast and Middle Atlantic region. Flood and others warned that without an agency to look after it, growth when it did occur would be "fragmented, duplicative and unplanned" and the watershed would suffer. "There was still time for forward thinking, time in which to plan for both development and conservation," wrote William Voigt, Jr., who had headed the Pennsylvania Fish Commission and would serve as the executive director of the Interstate Advisory Committee on the Susquehanna River Basin.

2. This was, in reality, a variation on an idea proposed in 1878 by John Wesley Powell, who was exploring and surveying the American West. In his *Report on the Lands of the Arid Region,* Powell recommended that boundaries in the West be drawn not according to arbitrary lines that followed latitudes and longitudes. Rather, he urged that the boundaries be based on natural features, notably watersheds, to ensure that those residing within a single basin would recognize their dependence upon each other in sharing a common, scarce resource. Powell's idea, of course, was not heeded by Congress.

3. While declining water *quality* worried some, it was concern over water *quantity* that drove much of the early official interest. Surveys of future demand for water in the nation's river basins, conducted by the Army Corps of Engineers (never known to err on the side of conservatism), routinely warned of severe shortages unless costly dams and reservoirs were constructed—by the Corps of Engineers, of course. (At one point, more than 120 dams of varying sizes were proposed for the Susquehanna River alone.) The great economic development foreseen for America's rivers could not occur if there wasn't adequate water, and ensuring that supply seemed a legitimate role for Washington to assume.

Representatives from New York, Pennsylvania, and Maryland formed an Interstate Advisory Committee, which met throughout much of the 1960s to work out details of a Susquehanna compact. Elected as the group's chairman was Maurice K. "Doc" Goddard, Pennsylvania's venerable secretary of forests and waters, by then in his third decade of public service. (It was a wise choice for many reasons, not the least of which was that Goddard was so widely respected around Pennsylvania that he held onto his job regardless of who served as governor. As the advisory committee's task dragged on year after year, staying power became a useful commodity.)

From the outset, political realities collided with the group's well-reasoned objectives. Land-use planning, particularly along the floodplain, was an especially troublesome issue. "We believed it was better to keep man's door away from high water than to try to keep high water away from man's door," wrote Voigt in his history of the committee's deliberations. But regulation of land use, even when it was clearly in the public interest, was denounced by local officials, who saw it as a usurpation of their authority over zoning decisions. (Protests were vociferous in Pennsylvania, which has always vested such matters in the hands of its 2,600 local governments.) Concerned that this single issue might destroy the fragile negotiations, the advisory committee members settled on language that, in effect, preserved the status quo of local control.

Other high-minded goals also were reluctantly discarded, including one that would have placed preservation of the Susquehanna's natural beauty on an equal footing with development of the river. The proposed language stated that water projects must be compatible with "values inherent in the historic and the scenic and other natural amenities of the . . . basin for the enjoyment and enrichment of future generations." In the end, all that remained of this lofty proposal was a requirement that aesthetic values be "considered" by the commission before approval of a development plan. Although disappointed at the outcome, Voigt and others took solace in the fact that "we were planting the thought in law that in river basin management and conservation 'other public values' were not worthless."

As they haggled over the language of a Susquehanna compact, the participating states eyed each other warily, chary of relinquishing any power to a neighbor. Dan Flood, who labored behind the scenes to build support for the Susquehanna River Basin Commission, nevertheless made no attempt to hide his views of certain participants at the bargaining table.

"Anybody who's ever done business with Maryland knows you've got to hold on to your watch," he told one congressional luncheon group.[4]

As for the Maryland representatives drafting the Susquehanna compact, their greatest concern was a guaranteed flow of water to the Chesapeake. Maryland regarded itself "almost as a supplicant" in the negotiations, according to William S. James, who participated in the discussions in his role as president of the Maryland Senate and an avid conservationist. "We were mainly interested in controlling pollution and about diversions of water out of the bay," he recalled nearly three decades later, sitting in the historic old farmhouse on the Chesapeake in Havre de Grace where he's lived most of his life. "We wanted to prevent that." Maryland therefore asked that the comprehensive plan for the Susquehanna ultimately "take into consideration the effect . . . on the receiving waters of the Chesapeake Bay."

It was one of the few times that the river and bay had been regarded as a single resource. But the language was so vague that it failed to provide Maryland the assurances it sought. The guaranteed minimum flows would come only upon resolution of the shad-restoration battle some two decades later.

As it turned out, agreeing on the language of the compact was easy compared to what lay ahead. When Pennsylvanians realized that Maryland, New York, and the federal government would have equal status with the Commonwealth in decisions affecting the Susquehanna, a lot of them were angry. Voigt wrote in his history of the commission,

> Many Pennsylvanians simply could not see the situation in any way other than that the Susquehanna was mostly a Pennsylvania river and, by golly, Pennsylvania should have a dominant voice in commission deliberations and voting. They could not and would not see that water was not fixed in place, as are land and buildings, but is transient and that Pennsylvania people, broadly speaking, had no ownership in it. They declared that since Pennsylvania had three-fourths of the basin in her borders, she should have

4. In 1978, Dan Flood was indicted on federal charges of taking $65,000 in bribes in a hospital financing project. He resigned from Congress in 1980 after being stripped of all his committee assignments. His first trial on the charges ended in a hung jury. Rather than face a second trial, he pleaded guilty to a misdemeanor charge of conspiracy and spent a year on probation. He retired from public life in poor health. Even after the scandal broke, 89 percent of his constituents rated his performance as excellent or good. Seven years after his departure from Congress, a "Salute to Dan Flood" party in Wilkes-Barre drew 1,500 people. "If it were not for Dan Flood," said one public official who attended, "Wilkes-Barre would not be the city it is today."

three-fourths of the say-so about what should be done with [the] Susquehanna's water.

It fell to people like Doc Goddard to smooth the way for the compact, and he was indefatigable. Elsewhere, support for it seemed solid. Governor Nelson Rockefeller issued a strong endorsement and Maryland's governor, J. Millard Tawes, urged prompt enactment of legislation creating the commission. The most vocal critics in Pennsylvania were the farm organizations, including leaders of many soil conservation districts. While they publicly objected to Pennsylvania's lack of special status, their opposition was rooted in fears that their activities along the river might somehow be regulated by the new commission.

While Pennsylvanians argued, the New York legislature approved the compact in May 1967, and Governor Rockefeller signed the bill. In Maryland, Senate president Bill James sponsored the legislation, and it was signed by Gov. Spiro T. Agnew later that same year.

The stalemate in Pennsylvania continued, with opponents popping out of the woodwork. When the state League of Women Voters announced its support for the compact at a public meeting, an official of the association representing Pennsylvania's rural townships declared, "If they're for it I'm against it."

Some lawmakers raised the scariest specter they could think of—that the commission might force small towns on the river to build their first sewage-treatment plants. The Pennsylvania Chamber of Commerce worried that industries might be barred from discharging their wastes into the Susquehanna. Others objected to giving the commission what was described as "raw, naked power." Indeed, the compact language seemed to give the commission sweeping powers, granting it the authority to "plan, design, acquire, construct, reconstruct, complete, own, improve, extend, develop, operate, and maintain any and all projects, facilities, properties, activities and services which are determined . . . to be necessary, convenient, or useful" pertaining to water quantity *and* quality.

Finally, more than a year after Maryland and New York had agreed to form the Susquehanna River Basin Commission, Pennsylvania consented, too. On July 17, 1968, Gov. Raymond P. Shafer signed the compact legislation into law. The look of relief on the faces of Goddard and Voigt in the signing-ceremony photograph is palpable.

Federal approval was the final task, and that was by no means assured, for interest in watershed management had all but disappeared in Washington while the compact negotiations dragged on. For nearly two years the measure languished. Finally, on Christmas Eve, 1970, it was signed by Pres. Richard M. Nixon. More than twenty years after the idea was first proposed, the Susquehanna River was to be managed as a single entity. (No one at the time gave any thought to taking on the Chesapeake Bay for good measure.)

Conceived as a steward of the river, a guardian of the watershed, the Susquehanna River Basin Commission turned out to be a hollow promise. It studiously maintained such a low profile that for years the agency didn't even have a sign outside its headquarters building, situated north of downtown Harrisburg. It wasn't that the commission was oblivious to problems in the watershed—nutrient runoff and groundwater contamination in Lancaster County; acid mine discharges to the West Branch; the threat of flooding along many parts of the Susquehanna; the struggle to restore migratory fish to the river. The commission conducted studies and issued reports galore on these topics and others. But the reports ended up on dusty shelves, filed away and forgotten. And the various governmental agencies within the Susquehanna watershed, charged with overseeing bits and pieces of its well-being, continued to make important decisions in isolation. The one governmental body that could have monitored the cumulative impact of all those decisions—and challenged those not in the best interest of the entire watershed—remained mute.

After two decades, the consequences are glaringly obvious to someone like Doc Goddard. Sitting at lunch in a crowded suburban Harrisburg restaurant, a snowy-haired Goddard speaks with disappointment and anger about the agency he labored so mightily to create. Citing just one example, he asserts, "If the commission had done its job, there would have been no need for the Chesapeake Bay program here in Pennsylvania." The commission, he says, could have insisted years ago that farms in Lancaster County take steps to control erosion and nutrient runoff. It could have demonstrated the link between increased livestock production and fouled drinking water. And, at the very least, it could have built a constituency of people in three states who care about the Susquehanna. "Instead," he said, his gruff voice booming over the noontime conversations at nearby tables, "they just laid back and said nothing about anything."

Similar sentiments are shared by Bill James. The watchdog that he hoped would "protect the river and the river valleys" as well as his beautiful Chesapeake has been toothless. James still receives minutes of the commission meetings, and he says with a trace of irony, "I have difficulty figuring out *what* they do. They never seem to say 'no,' however."

Asked to respond to such criticisms, Paul O. Swartz, the executive director of the Susquehanna River Basin Commission thought for a moment and responded, "Yes, I'm afraid I agree."

Swartz took over as the commission's chief in February 1992, replacing Robert Bielo, who ran the agency for twenty years. Swartz has pledged to reinvigorate an organization few people on the river know. (When he arrived, its mailing list was down to 185 names.) "The Susquehanna River Basin Commission was a well-kept secret," he said. Swartz, who had been director of Pennsylvania's Bureau of Soil and Water Conservation until he took this job, was one of the earliest officials in the state active in the Chesapeake Bay program. Over the years in that job, he observed firsthand the direct connection between the Susquehanna and the big estuary to the south.

Although not everyone could see it, the impact of the piecemeal management throughout the watershed soon became hard to ignore in the Chesapeake. In more and more places, stocks of fish were dwindling and plants were disappearing. Alarmed by the deteriorating conditions and frustrated by the failure of Maryland and Virginia to address them, a small group of people formed the Chesapeake Bay Foundation in 1966 and set about studying its problems, defending it against further degradation, and lobbying for its rescue. Private studies, augmented by a growing body of state and federal research, identified the Susquehanna as the most visible culprit in the bay's decline. In truth, however, that was too simple a solution, for the real villain was something far more complex than a single polluting river—even one the size of the Susquehanna.

Nevertheless, it provided a starting point. And, in 1983, the states of Maryland, Pennsylvania, and Virginia, the District of Columbia, and the federal government pledged to manage the 64,000-square-mile river and bay drainage basin as a single entity. Absent such a comprehensive view, the intricate problems confronting the Chesapeake and its major tributary could not even be understood, let alone resolved.

The scope of the Chesapeake Bay program is intimidating but reflective of the forces at work in the watershed. It encompasses improving oyster harvests, upgrading sewage-treatment plants, reducing industrial toxins, protecting wetlands, minimizing the impact of development on water-quality and wildlife habitat, restoring species of migratory birds and fish, controlling erosion, managing manure, and a score of other programs, each of which raises its own set of complicated questions.

It has fallen to such people as Edward Stigall to find some of the answers. Stigall is an engineer with the Environmental Protection Agency's Chesapeake Bay program. Working in one of the many fashionable office complexes on the Annapolis waterfront, he and his colleagues may be fifty miles from the mouth of the Susquehanna, but the river is not often out of their thoughts. The maps that line the office walls start above Cooperstown and end at Virginia Beach, and stretch from Georgetown, Delaware, to Monroe County, West Virginia, and Carrolltown, Pennsylvania. Within this watershed, which is shaped like New Hampshire but is seven times larger, the Chesapeake occupies less than half of the lower right quadrant.

It takes six days for water to flow from the farthest corners of the watershed to Havre de Grace. Of that, Stigall is certain. Once the water passes Havre de Grace, however, all certainty is lost. Some of the scientists estimate that it takes half a year for the water to move from Havre de Grace to the Atlantic, but even that guess is qualified, for unlike the Susquehanna, the Chesapeake Bay doesn't *flow*. The bay is a shallow bathtub with a malfunctioning drain.

"We can't use a lot of the water-quality standards we used in the past for rivers and streams because the water in an estuary, rather than going past you, tends to stay in place and slosh back and forth with the tide," says Alvin R. Morris, director of water management for the EPA office that oversees the Chesapeake region. "Therefore, the effects can be much more long-term than you see in rivers and streams."[5]

If the bay program produced one indisputable fact, it was that an entirely new management scheme was needed, and along with it leaders who could see beyond their own jurisdictions.

Ron Saacke finishes helping the seventh-graders locate the *Lady D*'s position on the navigational chart and then asks, "Why would we come to the Susquehanna to talk about the Chesapeake?"

"That's where all the pollution comes from," volunteers Jason Spittler (who later confides that he plans on becoming a microbiologist when he grows up, "so I better pay attention to this").

"Well, that's where *some* of the pollution comes from. What about the Bush River?" The youngsters are familiar with that small bay tributary, which flows near their school. Canoe trips on the Bush are part of the

---

5. Scientists studying the bay increasingly have come to rely on sophisticated computer modeling to measure the impact of specific pollutants and to project remedies. A supercomputer allows researchers to ask "what if?" What if more emphasis was placed on nutrient reductions in streams flowing into the lower Chesapeake than the Susquehanna? What if nutrients were reduced by 60 percent rather than 40 percent? The reliance on computers worries some, for despite its sophistication the $3.5-million computer program is limited and thus may direct scientists' attention away from certain aspects of the bay's problems.

Edgewood Middle School's science curriculum. "But the Susquehanna is the biggest of all the rivers entering the Chesapeake," explains Ron. "Does anybody know how much water there is in the bay?"

Not even Jason comes close. "There are 18 trillion gallons of water in the Chesapeake. But the average depth is just twenty-two feet. And in that shallow water live all sorts of interesting things. So, . . . " Ron pauses, allowing anticipation to build, "let's go fishing!" He readies a large green trawl net.

"If we catch a shark, can we keep it?" asks Ralph Taylor, who has edged to the front of his classmates. The question evokes some nervous laughter among them, for no one is entirely sure just what might be swimming beneath the boat.

"There's an old story that the watermen tell," continues Ron, who stands on the stern holding a faded mallard decoy that is affixed to the end of the net. "To catch anything, the watermen believe it's very important to conjure up some good spirits for the net. To do that, you have to kiss the duck for luck. Who's going to volunteer?" Volunteers are in short supply, but Ron finally enlists two boys, who gamely kiss the decoy before it is tossed over with the net. "The other superstition is that all the watermen would get together and start thinking like fish. Get your gills going, get your mouths going," he exhorts the kids, flapping his arms. "Move those tails!" Although they'd never be mistaken for watermen, or fish, the cockpit of the *Lady D* suddenly is awash in gyrating bodies as Paul slowly pilots the boat back and forth across the water, the net dragging behind.

Soon, with plenty of willing hands, the catch is hauled aboard. "We got a huge fish!" screams someone at the front of the crowd. It isn't a shark, to everyone's relief, but a yellow-gold carp, more than a yard long and almost too large for the glass aquarium secured in the cockpit of the *Lady D*. "Who gave us the big kiss?" Ron teases. Far less exciting to the seventh-graders is one of the small fish hauled aboard, a young rockfish, representing a species whose numbers have only recently begun to increase after dropping precipitously in the bay. The net also yields a flat fish called a hogchoker and a shiny bay anchovy.

Now the students are divided into four groups to study each fish and answer a series of questions about food and habitat. "First," Ron tells them, "give your fish a name." The carp is dubbed "Slimer" after everyone has felt the filmy coating on its body. "This fish will eat anything and doesn't need much oxygen to live. If we found nothing but this carp out here, what would it tell us about the water quality?" Ron asks. "It wouldn't be very good," comes the response. Slimer chose that moment to propel himself out of the aquarium in a wave of water, requiring three pairs of hands and some squealing to wrestle him back into his temporary home.

The "Silver Strainer," a tiny, pearl-colored fish, doesn't survive its examination by lots of thirteen-year-old fingers. Stumped as to its identification, the students look to Ron for a hint. "It's a relative of the fish you eat on pizza." "Catfish?" comes a timid voice from the back.

The rockfish is named "Spike" because someone thought it had sharp teeth, and the hogchoker becomes "Henry Flatface." "Farmers used to feed these fish to their pigs," says Ron, holding Henry. "If the pig swallowed it headfirst, it went down easy, but look what would happen if it was swallowed tail-first. See the way its fins stick out, and feel how rough its skin is if you rub it backwards." Henry is stroked by the class. "This fish probably won't move out of this area its entire life. But Spike travels all over the bay and up in the river. Finding him is a good indicator about the health of the Chesapeake."

"Now, before you can eat your lunches, you have to write a poem or a skit about your fish," directs Ron, and the students bend over their papers as Paul turns the *Lady D* south, passing two fishermen in an outboard, who wave. The destination is Fishing Battery, a pretty island with an abandoned lighthouse in the center.

If Paul and Ron have any concern about whether the morning's nonstop lessons have been received, it is dispelled when Jason leads his group in reciting their poem:

> We're a bunch of anchovy fish
> We do not like pollution and stuff
> We like fresh water and can't get enough
> Don't throw in trash and litter
> Because it all tastes very bitter
> We eat plankton
> It tastes very good
> Plankton makes us happy
> And we're in a very good mood.

"It's amazing what they retain," says Tom Markowski of his students, who at that moment are tearing into their lunches. "They see things about the bay in pictures, films, and in what they read, but when they experience it first-hand, it's so much more meaningful. They go home and tell their parents and grandparents, who then tell the kids about fishing and crabbing when they were young."

Markowski, a tall, thin man with glasses and a mustache, has lived near the Chesapeake all his life and spent several summers working at the small hatchery that Maryland once maintained on this island. "I grew up fishing on the river, catching hickory shad and white shad up at Conowingo in the 1960s."

"We tend to take all this for granted," he notes. "A trip like this is good for us adults, too."

If kissing the duck had tested the seventh-graders' sense of adventure, Ron and Paul's next idea might have provoked a mutiny. The post-lunch lesson involves underwater grasses—submerged aquatic vegetation, as it is known—that once grew in abundance in the Chesapeake, especially here in the Susquehanna Flats. Show-and-tell on the *Lady D* is about to become show-and-tell-and-taste.

The Susquehanna's broad delta once attracted legendary flocks of migratory waterfowl, lured by the lush grasses that thrived in the sediment carried downstream each year by the river.[6] The wild celery alone sustained huge populations of canvasback ducks. John James Audubon came here to study and paint the birds. Wealthy New Yorkers and Philadelphians used to travel to Havre de Grace by train for the shooting season. J. Pierpont Morgan was a frequent visitor to the luxurious hunting lodge on Spesutie Island, which is now part of the Army's Aberdeen Proving Ground.

The duck hunting in the shallow water was done from sinkboxes, described by one practitioner as "a tin coffin, sunk beneath the water, with the [boat's] wings just even with the surface." The occupants lay for hours flat on their backs, drifting through the shallows. Bagging a hundred or more ducks a day was not uncommon. Today's hunters prefer what is known as a "body boot," an oversized pair of waders.

It was the sharp decline in underwater grasses that showed most alarmingly that the ecological balance of the Chesapeake had been upset. Because of their extreme sensitivity to such properties as nutrient levels and water clarity, the grasses magnify the stresses endured by other species of plants and animals in the estuary. They had been in decline for years before 1972. That year, the Susquehanna, which normally delivers more than a million tons of sediments annually to the bay, dumped years' worth of soil during the week-long fury that was Tropical Storm Agnes. The grasses were either buried or starved of light, and they died. The loss to the Chesapeake was enormous, for the grasses serve three vital functions: They act as

6. Between the years 1846 and 1938, 85 million cubic yards of sediment were deposited at the head of the bay. According to one study, water levels rose 2½ feet over an area of 32 square miles, and 787 acres of land surface was added to the state of Maryland.

filters, straining out nitrogen and phosphorus and recharging the water with oxygen. They act as safety valves, absorbing the heavy loads of pollutants washed down in the spring rains and gradually releasing them during the summer and fall. Finally, the grasses provide ideal shelter for hundreds of aquatic species.

The trawl net that produced Henry Flatface, Slimer, the Silver Strainer, and Spike also carried up two nonnative grasses, hydrilla and Eurasian watermilfoil. These are now floating around in the aquarium with Slimer. Grabbing a handful, Ron launches into a discussion of the importance of submerged aquatic vegetation. Attention is wandering a bit, so he stuffs some of the watermilfoil into his mouth. "Oooh, good. Want some submerged aquatic vegetation?" he says, offering pieces to the students, who stare. "Try some." Soon, everyone is chomping away, as if Ron had handed out potato chips instead of something that tastes faintly like soggy iceberg lettuce with pepper on it.

While these so-called exotic, or introduced, species of grasses are flourishing, the water quality in many parts of the bay is still too poor for more fragile plants to thrive. Wild celery is one, and Ron explains to the students just what its return to these waters would symbolize for the river and bay.

Unbeknownst to him, just a few hundred feet west of the *Lady D* during the trawling run, in the shallow water near an old green farmhouse on a bluff, is quite a nice sample of wild celery. That's Bill James's house, and it seems appropriate that the best stand of Susquehanna Flats wild celery in recent memory is growing near the man who has spent a lifetime protecting its waters.

There are plenty of other encouraging signs throughout the basin. Cindy Adams Dunn doesn't need a trawl net to learn what is living on the river bottom in her part of the watershed. One of her favorite pastimes is floating face-down on the Susquehanna with a snorkle and mask, watching the panorama of biota passing beneath her. "I discovered the hard way it's better to do it feet-first," she says, grinning. "Otherwise you keep hitting your head on the rocks."

Says Dunn of her float trips, "It's amazing how many different things you can see." But this afternoon she's walking, not floating, down the middle of the Susquehanna, dragging her seventeen-foot Grumman aluminum canoe over the rocks that form bony ribs across the warm water. A severe autumn drought has lowered the Susquehanna to less than three feet in depth. "As they say, the dryer the weather, the cleaner the river," she observes, leaning over to pluck a tiny mussel shell from the riverbottom.

Dunn, who grew up along Fishing Creek north of Harrisburg, recalls that her father forbade his children even to wade in the Susquehanna because of the pollution. That contributed to her decision to become a biologist and an environmental activist.

Dunn began her career with the Chesapeake Bay Foundation, teaching kids, just as Ron Saacke and Paul Willey do today, and went on to a brief stint as an air-quality enforcement officer with the Pennsylvania Department of Environmental Resources (DER). Since 1986 she has headed the Pennsylvania office of the Alliance for the Chesapeake Bay, a citizen-awareness program funded by the U.S. Environmental Protection Agency.

Dunn's job has its difficult moments. Her task is to tell Pennsylvanians that what they've done so far to help save the Chesapeake isn't nearly enough. But a secondary aspect of her mission—one she particularly enjoys—is to introduce Pennsylvanians to the grandeur of the river that drains almost half their state.

The commonwealth has been, and continues to be, the reluctant partner in the bay cleanup effort. Initially, its cool response had a certain legitimacy that had nothing to do with geography. Pennsylvania, well in advance of many other states, including its neighbors to the south, had made an impressive effort at cleaning up the Susquehanna and other rivers. Thanks in large part to Doc Goddard, who headed DER, and to the backing of supportive governors, Pennsylvania's water-treatment record improved markedly during the 1970s.

While acid mine drainage and nutrients still flow into the Susquehanna, the days when it was a stinking sewer of human and industrial wastes had long since ended. At precisely the time the Chesapeake was diagnosed as terminally ill, the river was again becoming a source of pride and pleasure to those living along its banks. Then came the finger-pointing. "Pennsylvania was never included before as part of the bay, even on the maps—not until the bay people decided *it* was a polluter," Dunn says.

Pennsylvania's position as an environmental leader in water quality slipped considerably in the 1980s. Still, the Susquehanna routinely meets or exceeds most federal water-quality regulations. If it flowed directly into the Atlantic, it might be regarded as a model among East Coast rivers. But it flows into the Chesapeake and the rules are different. Decisions on such testy matters as land use, sewage treatment, farming methods, and lumbering practices—once largely the province of local governments and private citizens—now must all be made with one thing in mind: the fragile environment that begins 12 miles below the Pennsylvania boundary and extends 195 miles to the south.

"It's a hard pill for Pennsylvanians to swallow," says Dunn. And the fact that the Susquehanna appears so revitalized to those who use it compounds the problem. Dunn, a tall, athletic woman with shoulder-length blonde hair, finds the canoeing, fishing, and birdwatching on the river unsurpassed. It is the arrival of fall's first migratory birds that lures her to the Susquehanna one September morning. A strong cold front had swept across Pennsylvania overnight, clearing the skies to a dazzling blue. She launches her canoe at Fort Hunter north of Harrisburg, planning to paddle past the deserted heron rookery on Wade Island, which lies in sight of the state capitol to the east and, on the western bank, Conrail's sprawling Enola Yard, where the screaming of train wheels on steel tracks routinely pierces the air.

"When the herons are here they make such a deafening racket, you can't even hear Enola," she says. Most of the herons have moved on by now, but during the Pennsylvania Game Commission's annual nesting count on the island the previous spring, Dunn and other volunteers tallied 350 nests. The island is home to black-crowned night herons, American egrets, great blue herons, and some yellow-crowned night herons (although, Dunn says, the yellow-crowned night herons tend to favor the island just off the Governor's Mansion).[7]

A short distance downstream, the manmade noises along the Susquehanna's shores are silenced by a cluster of small islands covered with golden water willow. Dunn navigates the canoe through a fast-water channel. "The last time I was out here a beaver swam right up and under my canoe. I guess he was just curious." Beaching the canoe near her favorite summertime swimming hole and turning it over to use as a picnic table, Dunn says that public attitudes about the river basin are slowly changing. She is a good barometer; she spends many nights each month meeting with anyone who will listen about the Chesapeake and her beloved Susquehanna.

"People here used to think about the bay as so terribly far away," she says. "There wasn't that much willingness to do things to help the bay.

---

7. If the city of Harrisburg succeeds with plans to build the controversial Dock Street Dam, the rookery will be a casualty. Water behind the dam will flood the islands, killing the trees where the birds make their nests. Despite opposition from most federal and state regulatory agencies and conservation groups, city officials still favor construction of the low hydroelectric dam.

Now, it's an accepted reality. I think that's the result of the news coverage its problems have received. Even so, it's very hard when you have to ask people to do things differently, especially the farmers."

Dunn has found allies in farmers, but they insisted on approaching the problem in their own way. "When they first organized, they called themselves 'the committee that didn't exist' because they were so afraid of getting bogged down in bureaucracy," she recalls, laughing. "And the word 'regulation' was never, *ever* mentioned, it's such a reviled concept among farmers. Now at least you can mention 'regulation' at their committee meetings." Dunn's conversation is interrupted by a loud splash as a smallmouth bass leaps out of the water for its own lunch. "Wow, that was a big one!"

As she rights the canoe and eases it back into the water, she continues: "We are making a difference. Where the program has failed so far is in convincing more Pennsylvanians that these are things we should be doing anyway—for the Susquehanna and for the people who live along it."

That is something the farmers have already come to understand, she says. Others, notably the state's many sportsmen, have been slow to grasp the idea. "Reestablishing a viable shad fishery in Pennsylvania will do a lot more for the program than me going around with a slide show about the Chesapeake."

Occasionally, the connection between bay and river gets a bit tenuous, but Dunn even sees a positive side to that. "People way up the river now cite the Chesapeake Bay at the drop of a hat. They may be fighting a landfill or some development," she says, "but in their minds what they do to protect the river will also help the bay and vice versa. That's the kind of thinking we want to institutionalize, because Pennsylvania will only end up with a better resource. And it's already pretty nice."

After nearly six decades of watching environmental policy take shape, Doc Goddard knows that people are what drives government. That was true of Pennsylvania's efforts to rid the Susquehanna of sewage and coal wastes and to restore forests to the river's rugged hillsides. It is also true today of the state's participation in the Chesapeake Bay cleanup program.

But even with public support for change, those inside government must share in the conviction before it can occur. As the problems of the Susquehanna and Chesapeake Bay become more clearly defined, some new faces have been added to the ranks of decisionmakers, bringing with them fresh ideas and open minds. Among them in Harrisburg is Caren Glotfelty, a small, energetic woman with sandy-red hair, glasses, and a hearty laugh.

She raises sheep on a historic Lancaster County farm when not at work as deputy secretary for water-quality programs within Pennsylvania's Department of Environmental Resources.

Glotfelty says her job would be very much different if her responsibilities ended where the Susquehanna crosses into Maryland. "If that were the case, I don't suppose we'd be paying a lot of attention to the river," she says. "The water quality of the Susquehanna is quite good." But Pennsylvania's inclusion in the Chesapeake Bay cleanup program has forced officials in Harrisburg to give the river a high priority it would not otherwise receive. And Glotfelty, who was educated as a land-use planner and has worked in both Pennsylvania and Maryland state governments and in the private sector, sees the benefits of this new way of thinking every day.

"Focusing attention on a watershed is a great way to integrate programs, and we don't do that in state government very often," she explains. "The Chesapeake Bay has been very good at forcing us to do this. If it weren't for the bay program, we wouldn't be taking a global view." That "global view" has turned traditional decisionmaking on its head, Glotfelty notes with a certain glee. One notable change was a reorganization within DER that finally put all water programs under a single person; for twenty years they had been scattered through several offices, making communication difficult and wise resource management nearly impossible.

Such victories aside, the Chesapeake Bay represents the antithesis of a traditional environmental problem, and offers a view of environmental challenges that will arise in other venues into the next century. There is no single polluting industry that can be fined or shut down, no single resource, like water, that can be targeted for regulatory action. Nor will the problem be solved by a massive infusion of government dollars.

The solution to such problems rests in "getting more people to claim ownership," to assume a stake in the solution, says Glotfelty, sounding a lot like Cindy Dunn. "We need to get away from the idea that environmental protection comes down from Washington or Harrisburg. We've got to get people to understand that it's their personal choices that affect the environment—where they live, how they farm, how much fertilizer they put on their lawns, small things like that." In short, it is no longer someone else's responsibility. As a result, this will be the most difficult environmental struggle that has ever been waged along the Susquehanna.

It has been on the issue of land use that the toughest fights in this battle have occurred—and will be mounted in future years. That doesn't surprise Bill James one bit. James, a quiet-spoken, courtly Southern gentleman, with fine features and thinning white hair, has been called a lot of things during his lifetime in politics. He was branded a Communist years ago for declaring that "you can't preserve the bay unless you take control of the land." In 1970, he shepherded a bill through the Maryland Senate that barred development within 300 feet of the tideline. "To the extent you protect open space, you protect the bay," he said at the time. But the legislation went no further in Annapolis. It wasn't until 1984, with passage of Maryland's Critical Area Act, that the subject was tackled again. Once more, limitations on land use—real or imagined—aroused the greatest opposition, and the measure was substantially weakened to win final passage.[8]

"There was an old lawyer in Harford County who used to say that the most sensitive nerve in the human body is the pocketbook," says James, sitting in his den which, like the rest of his house, is paneled with white pine floated down the Susquehanna more than a century ago. "That was true when he said it, and it's true now."[9]

Depriving landowners of the right to do what they wish with their property is widely regarded as un-American, yet it is this right that most seriously imperils the watershed today. Slowing the wildfires of growth and development—and all the environmental problems accompanying them—will be a herculean and thankless task.

An additional 2.6 million people—equivalent to the population of metropolitan Atlanta, Georgia—are projected to move into the Maryland, Virginia, and Pennsylvania portions of the watershed by the year 2020. That would boost the population from 13.6 million to 16.2 million. But they won't spread out evenly when they come. Virginia's portion of the watershed will experience a 32 percent jump; Pennsylvania's, 8 percent. Already, the Baltimore-Washington-Annapolis megalopolis, with 5.8 million people, ranks fourth in the nation in population, behind New York, Los Angeles, and Chicago. Within Pennsylvania, the greatest population shifts are occurring in one of the areas least capable of absorbing any more people—the rich farmland of Lancaster County.

This rise in population is like a wave that threatens to wash away the scattered successes that have occurred in the watershed so far. While agricultural pollution seems to have peaked (except in areas with dense con-

8. The law designates a thousand-foot strip around the Chesapeake and its tidal tributaries as a so-called critical area. Within that zone, additional development will be strictly limited. In areas where no development exists, stringent limits on all growth will be imposed.

9. The sawmill built at Havre de Grace by West Branch lumberman John DuBois to process logs that broke through the Susquehanna boom and floated to the bay was located not far from the marina where the *Lady D* was currently berthed.

centrations of livestock, such as Lancaster County), the pollution produced by humans shows no sign of slowing its rapid rise. The neat subdivision of country tract houses, each with its own septic tank and perfect green sod, adds more nutrients to the soil than an overfertilized field of corn. And while there may never be enough malls to satisfy the average seventh-grader, many new ones will be built, along with parking lots and roads to get there, all contributing huge quantities of runoff.

Shortly after the Chesapeake Bay Agreement was signed in 1983, a special panel was created to study growth in the watershed through the year 2020, and to recommend ways to ameliorate its impact. In late 1988, the group issued its report, concluding that "procedures currently being used throughout the Bay region for managing and providing for growth and development are inadequate, and must quickly be changed if current trends are to be reversed." This was hardly a revelation, but it was a revolutionary document.

The so-called 2020 Panel proposed shifting prime responsibility for land-use planning from local governments to the states. The recommendation prompted some debate in Maryland and Virginia; it elicited a howl of protest from Pennsylvania, where Gov. Robert P. Casey labeled the idea "draconian." And then, everybody conveniently forgot about it.

When the governors gathered in August 1992 to assess the progress of the Chesapeake Bay cleanup, and to set the agenda for the next few years, they renewed their commitment to cut the level of nutrients flowing from the Susquehanna. They spoke of the need to reduce airborne pollution that contributes nitrogen to the bay and river. They talked of pressuring outlying states to do more to help the bay. And, amid much hoopla, they launched a cute publicity campaign whose theme, "The Bay Starts Here," decorated caps and buttons. As part of the effort, meeting-goers were given shower-head nozzles to reduce water consumption, and tiny rulers to encourage homeowners to let their lawns grow three inches high before mowing to retain soil moisture.

The subject of controlling population growth—key to solving the bay's problems—was never mentioned.

It's a rule that no one can leave the *Lady D* at the end of a cruise without describing what impressed him or her most about the adventure on the water. Ron Saacke and Paul Willey, showing no signs of their day's frenzied pace, take up positions along the side of the old workboat and prepare to say their farewells to the seventh-graders from Edgewood Middle School. One by one, the kids step up and offer their impressions.

"Learning how many different things live in the water."

"How many?" asks Ron.

"Uh—2,800."

"Right on!" shouts Ron.

"Catching the carp—twice."

"You've got to wet your hand before you pick up a fish."

"That's it?" Paul asks in mock dismay. "That's all you learned this whole day?"

"Well," comes the reply, "some fish are very delicate. I learned that, too."

"Okay, you can go," says Ron. "That will certainly get you through life. Who's next?"

"Touching the hogchoker."

"Seaweed is really good to eat."

"Here, take some to take with you," offers Ron, grabbing the last little piece from the aquarium.

"The thing I liked most was getting out of school. Can I come back tomorrow?"

"Goodbye!" exclaims Paul.

"I liked designing the river."

"And what did you learn from that?" asks Ron, not willing to pass up this last opportunity. The youngster thinks a minute before answering.

"We ought to think of how what we do affects our neighbor . . . "

As the yellow school bus pulls away, Ron and Paul begin cleaning up the *Lady D*. "This is an investment in the future," says Ron. "A long-term investment."

Epilogue

The Susquehanna seizes your soul as quickly as it grabs the prow of a canoe on a bright June morning. That the river could exercise such power should have come as no surprise. I had read its history, traveled its length, and talked with those who know it well. I had listened and thought I understood its lure and its ability to inspire grand dreams. But now, pushing off into the fast-moving water, a new voice is heard. The river itself is speaking to me. And I hear it with my heart.

A seven-day canoe trip on the West Branch of the Susquehanna, from the town of North Bend ninety-three miles to Northumberland, grew from a modest idea that a flotilla might stir interest in this part of the river and provide an opportunity to talk about events elsewhere in the watershed. (It would also be fun.) Word of the trip filtered out, and it drew an eclectic group, some of whom came for a purpose, others purely out of curiosity. A handful canoed the entire distance; most joined for a day or two, intrigued by this river odyssey.

The group included Pennsylvania's environmental secretary and two laid-off machinists; a young social worker and a veteran county planner; several experts on the Chesapeake Bay who had never ventured to the West Branch, and several West Branch natives who had never seen the Chesapeake. There were a forest biologist, a retired Navy captain and his wife, the owner of a carpet-cleaning firm, some parents with kids, a couple happy to be away from their kids, and a writer about to spend a week on a river she had come to love in the abstract.

For each, it was a voyage of discovery.

Along the way, the river showed off its triumphs. Miles of dense forest on endless green hills. Solitude at times so enveloping that even the sound of water dripping from the canoe paddle seemed annoying. Geese, heron, and osprey. An icy trout stream or two, arriving with a noisy fanfare. Places so pristine it seemed as if humans had never visited.

And it bared its grievous wounds. Farm fields plowed to the waterline. Streambeds stained orange. Water so poisonously clear, so devoid of any

303

living thing, that deep in a channel we could see cast-off golf balls lying incongruously on the rocky bottom.

The river defiantly proclaims itself a survivor. That it *has* survived says more about the power of nature than the intelligence of humans.

Caught in the current that originates somewhere near Carrolltown and continues on to the Chesapeake, it is impossible not to feel the strength of the Susquehanna and to understand that no one can lay claim to just a piece of it. There are no boundary lines on the water; such an idea is the vain notion of human beings. Gliding downstream, the river is seamless; the geographic reference points on land lose their relevance. It is the river that sets the itinerary.

Today's stewards of the Susquehanna—like their predecessors—are a determined lot. Their dream for the river is grander than any yet conceived. They speak not of a river, but of a watershed, one that encompasses their homes and their neighbors as well as land and people hundreds of miles distant, places they may never see but have come to care about.

The language used in the conversations on the water and around the nighttime campfires on this trip is revealing. Elsewhere along the Susquehanna, some still speak in the past tense when referring to the river. But the verbs of choice among these travelers are in the present and future. And when someone mentions *ownership* of the river, it is a term of inclusion—not exclusion, as was the case during the eras of logging, mining, or development. The river, they believe, belongs not to one person but to *everyone*.

The work of those who labored over the years to build a constituency for the Susquehanna has taken root and is flourishing as never before. But the magnitude of the task ahead is daunting. The obvious problems have been identified—but only in some cases are they resolved.

There is no better way to gauge the broad, and often conflicting, interests that still must be balanced along the Susquehanna than to paddle a distance with some of this journey's participants or to strike up a conversation along the shore.

Jerry Walls confronts these competing interests every day as executive director of the Lycoming County Planning Commission. An articulate, bright, independent man, Walls has guided his county in devising a rarity in Pennsylvania: a strong zoning plan, one that decidedly looks to the future. Growth is directed to areas where it can be accommodated; it is restricted from floodplains, farmland, and scenic areas. Industry is welcomed where infrastructure exists to serve its needs; even residential development must meet certain aesthetic requirements.

As he maneuvers his green canoe through a stretch of the Susquehanna that is being considered for National Wild and Scenic River status, Walls explains that backers of the county plan had expected resistance from local governments—each of which was expected to adopt its own zoning code, modeled on the county's. But to everyone's surprise, opposition to the 1992 plan was minimal. Walls attributes the response to the growing public recognition that decisionmaking must take a long-term view of the county's needs versus a short-term, politically expedient one.

"The results of poor planning are easy to see," he explained. "What's more difficult to see are the results of good planning." Two of the county's largest industries are located along the West Branch. Thanks to a little foresight, however, they are so unobtrusive that Walls had to point out their presence.

Two likely critics of Lycoming County's reins on development might have been Paul Calvert and Larry Patchen, laid off from their jobs at a Williamsport airplane-engine firm. Much heavy industry has departed from this portion of the Susquehanna, and it is unlikely that the two men will find comparable work. But they see the county zoning plan as a means of protecting the abundant hunting, fishing, and open spaces that they both love.

With time on their hands, Calvert and Patchen joined the canoe trip, eager to learn more about the river that they had always taken for granted. Patchen was astounded at the impact of acid mine drainage on the West Branch above Lock Haven. Calvert was interested in the Chesapeake Bay, and sought out veteran bay writer Tom Horton, who was making his first visit to the West Branch. "Is it pesticides that are hurting the bay?" Calvert asked Horton. "It's nutrients," Horton replied. "If the whole Susquehanna looked like this country, we'd have a lot fewer problems in the Chesapeake."

The mayor of Lock Haven, Bob Edmondston, was en route to a business appointment when he caught up with the group at a campsite early one morning, as the mist lifted from the water. He ended up paddling a short distance in a leaky, homemade kayak. He spoke of the impact that a flood-control project was having on his pretty, old town. Despite local opposition, the Army Corps of Engineers was erecting eighteen-foot-high levees along the river. "We love this river just as it is," he said. "These 'improvements' are destroying it."

Not far downstream, Don Hufnagle had his own ideas about improvements on the Susquehanna. "The government ought to spend some money on this river," said Hufnagle, who owns a riverside campground. What he had in mind was a channel, dredged as far south as Harrisburg, that would allow powerboat traffic access to the Susquehanna. He'd also like a dam or two along the way to supplement water levels. "Now *that* would make this a real useful river."

While visions for the future of the Susquehanna may not always be in harmony, the fact that so many people are thinking of the river is a good sign. At each stop along the route, residents dropped by to talk and listen. Members of the Lycoming County Soil Conservation District arrived one evening with soft drinks and pretzels and vivid memories of the way the Susquehanna used to be. "Now the river is beautiful," said Gordon Hiller, "and for that we have to thank the people I call the 'wise men.'" He cited John Youngman and Doc Goddard. "The challenge now is ours. As soon as we drop our guard, something will happen to the river."

On a cold, rainy evening in Montgomery, with soggy gear dangling from the rafters of a picnic pavilion, Mayor George Smith and some townspeople talked about the absurdity of letting hundreds of local jurisdictions govern the river. "We've got to break down those barriers, and think instead of what's best for the river," Smith said. No one summarized the task ahead any better.

The history of the Susquehanna is in many respects the history of resource management in this country—of private gain superseding public interest, of exploitation encouraged and the common good ignored. Here too stands a disheartening example of national environmental policy—of belatedly repairing damage already done, a challenge far more complex and costly than preventing it from happening in the first place.

This is a lesson to be learned and not repeated.

But the future course is far less clear.

What *is* best for the Susquehanna? Society's views of what is valuable change over time. Certainly, past decisions affecting the river seem unconscionable now. Yet, we must wonder, will the actions taken today appear any more responsible to future generations?

What of decisions on land use and development that consider only the here and now? What of the concentration of nuclear power plants, any one of which, in a moment, could render the Susquehanna lifeless for centuries? And what of the reluctance to view the Susquehanna as nature created it—an inseparable piece of a large and fragile ecosystem? These are issues never envisioned a generation or two ago.

When our stewardship of the Susquehanna is judged, what accomplishments can we cite? The river is cleaner than it has been in decades, once more a source of pleasure to many people. Soon, shad and other migratory fish will have returned to the river in abundance, free to roam the massive watershed again. But what of our record on management of the river basin's diverse resources—its fertile soils, abundant coal, and valuable timber? Will we finally be able to claim that they are being utilized wisely, sensitive to the needs of others—and to the Susquehanna?

If there is reason to be optimistic about the future of the Susquehanna—and I believe there is—it springs from the fierce loyalty the river has engendered in the people described in the pages of this book. They love the Susquehanna and revel in its remarkable comeback. But they also understand their obligations toward ensuring that the progress continues.

Every day along the river, the ranks of those with great hopes for the Susquehanna are growing. And the dreams they dream for this majestic river are no longer selfish ones.

Recommended Reading

Several books have been written about the Susquehanna River prior to this one. My favorite is Richmond E. Myers's *The Long Crooked River* (Boston: Christopher Publishing House, 1949). Myers, a geologist and geographer, weaves much natural history into his extremely readable account. Another general history of the river is *The Susquehanna* by Carl Carmer (New York: Rinehart and Co., 1955), published as the forty-eighth volume of the Rivers of America Series. Carmer fills his book with as much folklore as history. A third book, which unlike the others contains photographs, is *Pennsylvania's Susquehanna* by Elsie Singmaster (Harrisburg: J. Horace McFarland Co., 1950).

A fascinating book that includes some extraordinary watercolors and sketches of the lower Susquehanna by Benjamin Latrobe, as well as details of his survey of the river, is *Latrobe's View of America, 1795-1820*. Edited by Edward C. Carter II, John C. Van Horne, and Charles E. Brownell, the book was published for the Maryland Historical Society by Yale University Press in 1985.

Some additional readings, arranged by chapters, are listed below.

Chapter One. Geology

There is no single work describing the geologic features of the river. A useful book that includes information on specific places along the Susquehanna is *Roadside Geology of Pennsylvania* by Bradford B. Van Diver (Missoula, Mont.: Mountain Press Publishing, 1990). Using diagrams, photographs, and text, Van Diver offers the reader interesting explanations of what is visible from the roadways along the river. If you are even remotely interested in the state's geology, this would be a good book to keep in your car.

A more technical, but still readable, book is George Ashley's *The Scenery of Pennsylvania,* published by the Pennsylvania Department of Internal Affairs in 1933. A skilled geologist, Ashley also excels as a writer, creating vivid word images of the rock formations and geologic activities he is describing.

Chapter Two. Economic Development

Susquehanna's Indians by Barry C. Kent (Harrisburg: Pennsylvania Historical and Museum Commission, 1989) is a thorough study of the native Americans who inhabited the river. While some of the text is technical, it offers a rare and accurate look at this aspect of the Susquehanna's history.

Another publication of the Pennsylvania Historical and Museum Commission is a comprehensive and well-footnoted account of the race to control the river's resources. *The Philadelphia-Baltimore Trade Rivalry, 1780-1860* by James Weston Livingood (1947) is an examination of the political and economic forces at work in the two cities and elsewhere. *The Pennsylvania Main Line Canal* by Robert McCullough and Walter Leuba (Martinsburg, Pa.: Morrisons Cove Herald, 1962) is a detailed account of the canal era.

Two booklets published by the American Canal and Transportation Center in York provide additional information on this aspect of the Susquehanna's history. *The Amazing Pennsylvania Canals* by William H. Shank (1973) includes photographs and a nicely organized text describing specific canals around the state. *Journey Through Pennsylvania—1835* is a reprint of the 1836 pamphlet by that master of alliteration, Philip Houlbrouke Nicklin, who authored *A Pleasant Peregrination through the Prettiest Parts of Pennsylvania, Performed by Peregrine Prolix.*

Chapter Three. Logging

In the early 1970s, a series of eight pamphlets was compiled, entitled *Logging Railroad Era of Lumbering in Pennsylvania.* Authored by Thomas T. Taber III or Benjamin F. G. Kline, Jr., and printed by the Lycoming Printing Co. of Williamsport, the series contains descriptions of the many logging operations that flourished along the Susquehanna and elsewhere in the state in the late nineteenth and early twentieth centuries. The series includes many photographs detailing life in the logging camps.

An interesting book is *The Last Raft* by Joseph Dudley Tonkin, published by the author in 1940. Tonkin provides a history of the white pine lumber industry along the West Branch, and includes his account of the ill-fated Last Raft trip. In 1958 Tonkin also authored a book entitled *My Partner, the River; The White Pine Story on the Susquehanna* (University of Pittsburgh Press), which provides more information.

Chapter Four. Floods

Two quite different books provide a nice contrast on the subject of flooding. *Appointment with Disaster. The Swelling of the Flood: Wilkes-Barre, Pennsylvania, before and after the Agnes Flood of June 23, 1972* by Anthony J. Mussari (Wilkes-Barre, Pa.: Northeast Publishers, 1974) is a dramatic firsthand account of the 1972 Agnes disaster in the Wyoming Valley. And if you're left wondering just why so many people occupied a flood-prone stretch of the Susquehanna, a scholarly work will answer your questions. *The Army Corps of Engineers and the Evolution of Federal Flood Plain Management Policy* by Jamie W. Moore and Dorothy P. Moore (Program on Environment and Behavior, Special Publication No. 20, Institute of Behavioral Science, University of Colorado, 1989), explains the evolution of the federal policy that has encouraged development in flood-prone areas.

Chapter Five. Pollution

There is no environmental history of Pennsylvania, and very little written to document the severity of its pollution problems. Nor, sadly, has anyone tackled a history of the men, and a few women, who labored to end the widespread degradation.

Chapter Six. Nuclear Development

Much has been written about the Three Mile Island accident. An excellent account, detailed but very understandable, is *Three Mile Island: Thirty Minutes to Meltdown* by Daniel F. Ford (New York: Penguin Books, 1981). Another book, prepared by the Union of Concerned Scientists where Ford once served as executive director, is *Safety Second: The NRC and America's Nuclear Power Plants* (Bloomington: Indiana University Press, 1987). And a U.S. Senate committee report of the TMI accident is a complete and skillfully written document, replete with footnotes and excellent technical explanations. *Nuclear Accident and Recovery at Three Mile Island*, prepared by the Subcommittee on Nuclear Regulation for the Committee on Environment and Public Works (June, 1980, Serial No. 96-14) reads like great nonfiction.

Chapter Seven. Farming

In the 1950s, Stevenson W. Fletcher, former dean of the Pennsylvania State University's College of Agriculture, compiled a two-volume *Pennsylvania Agriculture and Country Life*. Volume 1 covers the years 1640 to 1840 and volume 2 documents the next hundred years. Both were projects of the Pennsylvania Historical and Museum Commission and are excellent resource books on this important aspect of Pennsylvania's history and economy.

Chapter Eight. Shad Restoration

With the exception of the annual reports published by the Susquehanna River Anadromous Fish Restoration Committee, and some scientific journal articles, little has been written on this subject.

Chapter Nine. The River and the Bay

Turning the Tide: Saving the Chesapeake Bay, by Tom Horton and William M. Eichbaum (Washington, D.C.: Island Press, 1991), reports on the health of the bay and the Susquehanna's role in its restoration. *Bay Country* (Baltimore: Johns Hopkins University Press, 1987) is a collection of Horton's essays on the bay and is must reading for anyone interested in this great estuary. *The Susquehanna Compact, Guardian of the River's Future* by William Voigt, Jr. (New Brunswick, N.J.: Rutgers University Press, 1972) recounts the formation of the Susquehanna River Basin Commission. Voigt's language at times is eloquent.

A final word has to do with Susquehanna reading matter lost, not found. A fertile source of material for this book was supplied by the journals published by county historical societies along the river. These journals recorded bits and pieces of local history that otherwise would have been forgotten. Although the scholarship and writing in the articles occasionally left a bit to be desired, the worth of this material in fleshing out life on the Susquehanna is incalculable.

Unfortunately, many of the journals are no longer published, or appear erratically, the victim of economics as well as a dearth of contributors. The research that is being done at the historical societies and libraries today is primarily genealogical, and it rarely appeals to a wider audience.

A notable example of this phenomenon is the *Proceedings and Collections of the Wyoming Valley Historical and Geological Society,* which began publication in 1885, reprinting papers delivered at society meetings. A century later, publication ceased and the editor of the *Proceedings,* Monica Reynolds, said a few years later that she doubted if it would be resumed in the foreseeable future. "Important material is being lost," she said. "We just don't give history much of a priority anymore."

Index

Abele, Ralph W., 173n, 256–58, 275
Aberdeen, Md., 271
Adams County, Pa., 233
Adamstown, Pa., 218
Agnew, Spiro T., 287
Agriculture: farmland preservation, 219–
21; fertilizer, 221, 225, 226–28, 231,
235–36, 238; Food Security Act (1985),
237–38; guano, 235–36n; livestock,
215–17, 221, 230, 234–35, 238; ma-
nure, 216, 221, 225–29, 235, 238, 239;
nutrients, 221–22, 226–28, 239–40,
299–300, 305; produce, 230–34; soil
erosion, 236–37
Albany, N.Y., 52
Alexander, Bob, 174–75, 176
Allegheny River, 58, 105, 107
Alliance for the Chesapeake Bay, 295
Alwine, Diane, 175
American Association for the Advancement
of Science, 29n
Amish, 218, 223, 227, 229–31, 234
Androscoggin River, 86
Annapolis, Md., 279, 290
Antes, Amelia, 161
Antes, John Henry, 161
Antes Creek, 26, 120–21, 161–63
Apollo, Pa., 191
Ashenfelter, Earl, 271
Ashley, George A., 12
Athens, Pa., 16, 67n, 71
Atlantic-Richfield Company, 191
Audubon, John James, 293
Austin, Pa., 107

Babcock and Wilcox Company, 192, 199–
200
Bald Eagle Creek, 25, 154
Baltimore, Md., 44, 45, 49, 50n, 51, 52n,
54, 56, 61, 64–65, 80, 100, 150n, 235n,
252
Baltimore Gas and Electric Company, 246
Barber, Robert, 44, 45, 50

Barnes and Tucker Coal Company. *See*
Coal
Barnum, P. T., 61
Bartram, John, 79
Bascom, Florence, 33n
Beckey, Rusty, 145, 147–48, 183, 204
Benezette, Pa., 97
Bennett Branch, 75, 97, 154, 188
Bermingham, James C., 100, 102
Berwick, Pa., 16, 18, 210
Bethlehem Steel Corporation, 145, 146,
149
Bielo, Robert, 289
Binghamton, N.Y., 16, 53, 150n
Bird-in-Hand, Pa., 223, 229
Blake, Thomas H., 100
Bliss, Eleanora, 34n
Bloomsburg, Pa., 18, 186, 249
Blunston, Samuel, 44, 45
Boude, Thomas, 65–66
Bourke, Dan, 243
Bridges, 133, 134; Brooklyn, 60n;
Columbia-Wrightsville, 55, 55n, 66n;
Havre de Grace, 87n; Market Street Per-
manent Bridge (Philadelphia), 53;
Muncy-Montgomery, 113; Pennsylvania
Turnpike, 145, 185
Brockway, Chauncey, 82–83, 96
Brown, Torrey C., 272
Brubaker, David R., 221
Brubaker, Michael W., 238–39
Bryn Mawr College, 33
Buck, Frank, 8
Bucknell University, 11
Buffalo, N.Y., 52
*Bulletin of the United States Fish Commis-
sion*, 249
Burnside, Pa., 84, 112
Bush River, 290

Cadzow, Donald A., 41n
Cairo, Richard, 9
Calvert, Paul, 305
Calvert family, 43–44

313

Thorowgood, Cyprian, 42
Three Mile Island. *See* Islands
Three Mile Island Alert, 207, 207n, 208
Three Mile Island Nuclear Station: acci-
dent at, 183, 195n, 200–209, 211;
cleanup, 202n, 206–8; construction,
198–200. *See also* Nuclear power
Tioga County, Pa., 15, 176
Tioga Point, 42n
Tioga River, 154
Toledo Edison Company, 199–200
Tonkin, R. Dudley, 111–12. *See also* Log-
ging, "Last Raft"
Towanda Creek, 254
Towanda, Pa., 16, 67n, 249
Townend, Frank, 129, 130–32, 134
Transportation: arks, 50n, 54, 55, 56, 80–
81, 126, 151, 235n; Conestoga wagons,
230; rafts, 48, 49, 54, 55, 235n (*see also*
Logging); steamboats, 52–53 (*see also*
Coal, river coal fleet)
Tropical Storm Agnes. *See* Floods, 1972
Twain, Mark (Samuel Clemens), 95
Tydings, Millard E., 127n

Underground Railroad, 66. *See also* Columbia, Pa.
Union County, Pa., 230
Union of Concerned Scientists, 200
United States: Army, Aberdeen Proving
Ground, 293; Army Corps of Engineers,
8, 8n, 71, 122, 123–24, 125–27, 133,
143, 153, 170, 284n, 305; Atomic Energy Commission, 186, 187, 189, 190,
192, 193, 197, 199, 201n (*see also*
United States, Nuclear Regulatory Commission); Central Intelligence Agency,
191; Coast Guard, 118, 190; Congress,
48–49, 52n, 71, 72, 108–9, 122–24,
127, 136–37, 141, 188, 197, 224, 284;
Department of Agriculture, Division of
Forestry (Forest Service), 109, 109n; Environmental Protection Agency, 175,
223, 225, 289–90, 295; Federal Energy
Regulatory Commission (formerly Federal Power Commission), 253, 270–72;
Federal Insurance Administration, 141;
Fish and Wildlife Service, 243, 246, 267,
275; Geological Survey, 8, 9, 34n, 108,
151, 227; House of Representatives, 48;
National Marine Fisheries Service, 251;
National Weather Service, 129; Nuclear
Regulatory Commission, 199, 203,
206n, 207, 209–10, 210n, 211, 272 (*see
also* United States, Atomic Energy Commission); Office of Emergency Prepared-

ness, 129; Postal Service, 131; Rivers
and Harbors Act (1890), 71; Small Business Administration, 137–38; Water Resources Policy Committee, 283
U.S. Radium Corporation, 186–88, 191,
211; Safety Light Corporation, 211. *See
also* Radium
University of Pennsylvania, 29, 109
Upland, Pa., 44
Upper Chesapeake Watershed Association,
253, 283

Van Buskirk, Samuel, 101
Van Dyke Fish Hatchery. *See* Pennsylvania
Virginia Beach, Va., 290
Virginia Institute of Marine Science, 246
Voigt, William, Jr., 284, 285, 286, 287

Walker, Guy B., 164
Wallace, Paul A. W., 97
Walls, Jerry S., 304–5
Warwick Township, Pa., 238
Washington, George, 234, 235n
Washington, D.C., 54, 104
Washington Borough, Pa., 41, 45
Waterfowl, 145, 184–85, 293; canvasback
ducks, 293; herons, 273, 296
Water pollution, 146–47, 149–50, 154–
55, 164–66, 168–76, 222, 250, 255,
283, 295; acid rain, 176, 178, 178n;
Federal Clean Water Act (1972), 149;
Federal Water Pollution Control Act
(1972), 174; fish kills, 146, 154, 169,
172; nutrients, 174, 222, 226–28, 231,
293–94, 295, 300; Pennsylvania Clean
Streams Act (1937), 163; Pennsylvania
Clean Streams Law (1965), 171; Purity
of Waters Act (1905), 155; radiation,
174 (*see also* Nuclear contamination and
waste); Rural Clean Water Program,
227; sewage treatment, 166, 174, 222,
287; toxics, 174, 176
Waverly, N.Y., 16
Weightman, William, 104n
West Lampeter Township, Pa., 215
Westmoreland County, Pa., 170
Whitten, A. J., 100, 101
Wilbern, David "Bud," 145–48, 180,
183–84, 185, 204, 212
Wilkes-Barre, Pa., 49, 118, 119, 124, 126,
127, 128, 130, 131, 134, 136–37, 138,
140, 141, 143, 164, 166, 169, 174, 249,
283n, 286n
Wilkes College, 134
Willey, Paul, 279–80, 281–82, 292, 293,
295, 300–301

Susquehanna River

Sinnemahoning Creek

Bennett Branch

Clearfield

WEST BRANCH

Bald Eagle

Clearfield Creek

Carrolltown

Hollidaysburg

Frankstown Branch

Raystown Branch